THE COMPLETE TAJ MAHAL

and the Riverfront Gardens of Agra

Thames & Hudson

EBBA KOCH

THE COMPLETE TAJ MAHAL

and the Riverfront Gardens of Agra

with drawings by Richard André Barraud

To Benedikt, Sophie, Caroline, Maia and Lukas

A dome of high foundation and a building of great magnificence was created.
The eye of the Age has seen nothing like it under the nine vaults of the enamel blue sky,
and the ear of Time has heard of nothing like it in any past age . . . it will be a
masterpiece for ages to come, increasing the amazement of all humanity.

Muhammad Amin Qazwini, *Padshahnama*, early 1630s

Frontispiece
The Taj Mahal seen from the Yamuna river. Rising above the riverfront terrace are
the white marble mausoleum, flanked by the Mihman Khana (assembly house)
on the left and the mosque on the right.

First published in 2006 in hardcover in the United States of America by
Thames & Hudson Inc., 500 Fifth Avenue, New York, New York 10110

thamesandhudsonusa.com

Library of Congress Catalog Card Number 2005910936

ISBN-13: 978-0-500-34209-1
ISBN-10: 0-500-34209-1

Printed and bound in Singapore by C. S. Graphics

Contents

Preface

The Taj Mahal is the best-known monument of India, and the most magnificent in a series of mausoleums built by the emperors of the Mughal dynasty. No other culture of the medieval or early modern period produced mausoleums in such numbers and of such vast proportions: even the tombs of the Mamluks in Egypt, and of the Mongols and Timurids in Iran and Central Asia, are not on such a monumental scale.

What is even more remarkable is that the Emperor Shah Jahan raised this grandest of all Mughal mausoleums for a woman: his favourite wife, Mumtaz Mahal, 'the Chosen One of the Palace'. This romantic aspect – which defies all general ideas about the position of women in a Muslim society – has long appealed to visitors, beginning with British travellers in the late 18th and early 19th centuries who came to India in the wake of colonial conquest and in search of the picturesque. They carried the fame of the Taj Mahal to the West, and the tomb became known as a monument of conjugal love, its perfect aesthetics reflecting the pure sentiment to which it owed its existence. In today's popular culture the Taj Mahal is a symbol of excellence; it is used as such proverbially, and no other building has lent its image so frequently to advertising.

But there is more to the Taj Mahal than this. The mausoleum is Shah Jahan's great contribution to world architecture, and, as the contemporary sources reveal, it was conceived as such from the very beginning. In the words of Shah Jahan's historian Qazwini, which feature as the motto of this book (p. 4), the building would be 'a masterpiece for ages to come', increasing 'the amazement of all humanity'.[1] It was to be a magnificent burial place for Mumtaz Mahal, an image here on earth of the heavenly mansion prepared for her in Paradise; but also, 'until the Day of Resurrection', it was to testify to the power and glory of Shah Jahan and Mughal rule.[2] The Taj Mahal was built with posterity in mind: we, the viewers, are part of its concept.

The mausoleum and its garden were originally part of an even vaster complex, in which funerary architecture was linked formally and functionally with utilitarian buildings, bazaars and caravanserais. The ambitions of the builders to combine paradisiacal symbolism with political propaganda were, as will be seen, realized by means of perfect planning and minute attention to every architectural detail. The mausoleum expresses in canonical form the architectural principles of the period: the Mughals had no written architectural theory, but it is set out physically in the Taj Mahal. The seductive aesthetics of the architecture and its successful appeal to the senses make the message of the building all the more persuasive.

Today the complex of the Taj Mahal stands almost by itself on the bank of the river Jamna or Yamuna. Originally, however, it formed part of the urban landscape of Mughal Agra, the core of which consisted of bands of gardens lining the river on both sides [26]. At the time of Shah Jahan Agra was a riverfront city, described by the poets as 'a sweet-smelling garden with new blossoms'. Many of those gardens can be studied, and a few survive, at least in part. The Taj Mahal is a monumentalized, ideally planned, version of a typical Agra garden. The interaction between monument and city is essential for its understanding, and crucial for its future.

Despite its importance and fame, the Taj Mahal has been very little studied. This is the first scientific and documentary monograph dedicated to the building, to the entire complex, and to its urban context. It has evolved from almost three decades of study of Mughal architecture. Since 1976, I have directed the project of a survey of Shahjahani palaces and gardens, focusing since the mid-1990s on the Taj Mahal and the gardens of Agra. With the Indian architect Richard A. Barraud, I have spent months in the Taj Mahal complex, measuring the buildings, as the first Western scholar since India's independence to have been given this generous permission by the Archaeological Survey of India. We used metal and plastic tapes and a laser measuring instrument made by Leica called Disto. Based on our survey, Richard Barraud did the scale drawings by hand. With a few exceptions, the photographs were taken by me with a Nikon FS Photomic.

The field studies brought me into the remotest corners of the Taj Mahal, and the close encounter with the architecture revealed the contribution of the anonymous workmen who inscribed their masons' marks on the stones.

In my investigation I have tried to take a holistic approach. The basis is to document precise stylistic changes within the Mughal architectural repertoire and to combine formal analysis with contextual studies based on Persian, Urdu, Sanskrit and Western sources. The aim is to arrive at an understanding of the ethos of the Mughal court in the 17th century – its evolution within Timurid dynastic forms of legitimation, the sensitivity of the Mughals to Islamic Persianate cultural norms, their larger than South Asian presence, and their ability to appropriate ideas from a world that crossed their imperial threshold.

1 Looking from the centre of the garden towards the mausoleum and flanking minarets. The domes of the mosque and Mihman Khana or assembly hall appear above the trees at left and right.

Introduction:
The Mughal dynasty, Shah Jahan and Mumtaz Mahal

The Mughal dynasty

The Mughals in India were the most glamorous of the three Muslim superpowers of the early modern period, the two others being the Safavids in Iran and the Ottomans in the Near and Middle East and the Balkans. At the time of its greatest extent, in the early 18th century, the 'Empire of the Great Mogul', as it was known in the West, reached from Kabul in present-day Afghanistan to Aurangabad north-east of Bombay (Mumbai), and from the Arabian Sea to the Gulf of Bengal [map, p. 255]. In the Indian subcontinent the Mughals were the most important politically, the most influential culturally, and the last in a series of Muslim dynasties which established themselves from the 12th century onwards. Their universalist approach and integrative power brought large parts of South Asia together under a single government. The British presented themselves as successors to the Mughals, to legitimate their colonial rule in India, and from 1877 Queen Victoria was styled 'Kaisar-i Hind', Empress of India. Even today the president of republican India addresses the nation from the Red Fort of the Mughal emperors at Delhi.

2 *opposite* Shah Jahan receives his three eldest sons and Asaf Khan during his accession ceremonies in 1628, painted by Bichitr, Mughal, *c.* 1630, from the *Padshahnama* – the oldest known illustrated manuscript of Lahauri's history of Shah Jahan's reign. The *darbar* image is a visual manifest of the ordered court society under Mughal rule. On the imperial axis in the centre, lions flanking a lamb, the chain of justice, and shaikhs symbolize the emperor's worldly justice and spiritual authority. He tops the pyramid of governance formed by his nobles, who are arranged in two symmetrical groups, according to the principle of *qarina*, which governed all imperial art (pp. 104–5). Of the princes and nobles present, fourteen were distinguished with a riverfront garden or *haveli* at Agra.

Key: 1 Shah Jahan; 2 Dara Shikoh; 3 Shah Shuja͏ᶜ; 4 Aurangzeb; 5 Murad Bakhsh; 6 Asaf Khan (Mumtaz Mahal's father; see p. 74); 7 Wazir Khan (see pp. 45, 76); 8 Jai Singh Khachhwaha (see pp. 28, 97); 9 Mahabat Khan (see p. 64); 10 Khan-i ͏ᶜAlam (see p. 61); 11 Khan-i Dauran (see p. 58); 12 Asalat Khan (see p. 64); 13 Musawi Khan (see p. 54); 14 Ja͏ᶜfar Khan (husband of Mumtaz's sister; see p. 77); 15 A͏ᶜzam Khan (see p. 65); 16 Shayista Khan (Mumtaz's brother; see p. 75); 17 Afzal Khan (see p. 43); 18 Islam Khan Mashhadi (see pp. 65–66); 19 Shah Nawaz Khan (see p. 37)

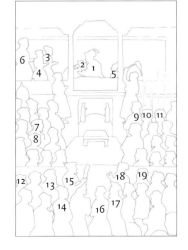

Babur (r. in Hindustan 1526–30)

The founder of the Mughal dynasty was the young Central Asian prince Babur [4, 20]. In 1526, he moved with his followers from Samarqand (in what is now Uzbekistan) via Kabul into India, carrying with him the *Zafarnama*, in which the conquests of his famous ancestor Timur [4], who had taken Delhi in 1398, were described and extolled by the historian Sharaf-ud-Din ͏ᶜAli Yazdi (the work was completed in 1424/25). Timur, or Tamerlane as he was known in the West, had brought a vast area, from Samarqand to Asia Minor, under his sway in a neo-Mongolian drive of conquest. Living up to his Latin epithet *Orientis terror* – the terror of the East – at Ankara in 1402 he defeated Sultan Yildirim Bayazid so devastatingly that the Ottomans were kept from taking Constantinople for another fifty years. This put him in the good books of Europe; and the Mughals always felt superior to the Ottomans because of the humiliation of Bayazid, whom Timur, so the rumour goes, carried along in a cage on his way back to Samarqand, using him as a stepping stool to mount his horse.[1]

The Mughals were at all times more closely engaged with the Safavids, the third Muslim superpower. The descendants of the Sufi shaikh Safi-ud-Din (b. 1252/53) had established the Safavid state under Shah Isma͏ᶜil I (r. 1501–24) and were the immediate neighbours and rivals of the Mughals. As shahs of Iran, the Safavids were the heirs of the ancient Persian kings, the Achaemenids and Sasanians, long admired in Islam as model rulers. Persian was the language of the Muslim courts of Asia, and Persianate culture formed the life of the elite at the courts and in the cities.[2]

As the latest of the three superpowers to emerge, and as a minority ruling over a vast territory of peoples of different creeds and cultures, the Mughals were particularly driven to legitimate themselves, relying above all on their impeccable Turko-Mongolian lineage. In 1508 Babur claimed supreme rulership over the Timurids, Chaghatai Turks, and Mongols by adopting the title *padishah* (*padshah*, in India *badshah*). This – usually translated as 'emperor' – became the official designation of the Mughal rulers. Babur's assertion was boosted by the fact that he was descended not only from Timur but also, on his mother's side, from the even greater pan-Asian force, Genghis Khan, who had inspired Timur. The attitude of the Mughals towards Genghis was ambivalent: on the one hand they were proud of his lineage; but on the other they preferred to be associated with the more recent and more refined Timurids. For the people of India, however, they remained 'the Mongols' (*Muggula, Mugala*).[3] The Portuguese, Dutch, British and Germans followed suit and gave them the dynastic title 'Grão Mogor', 'Groote Mogul', 'Great Mogul', or 'Großmogul'.

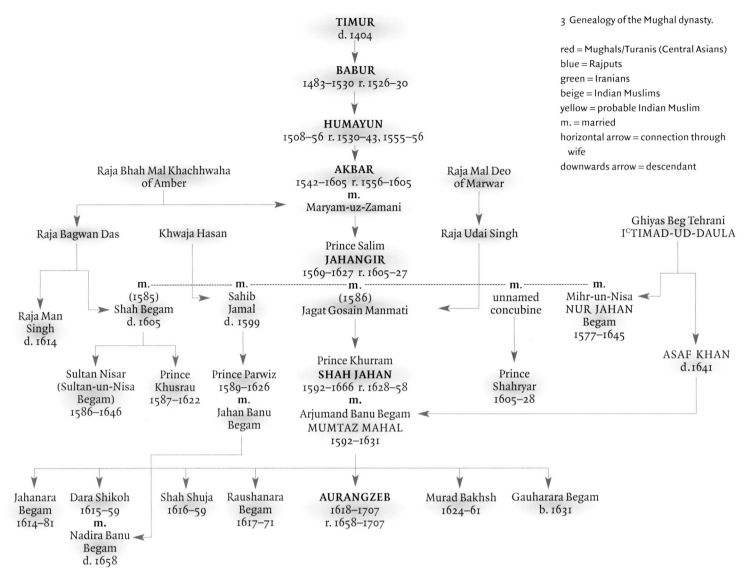

3 Genealogy of the Mughal dynasty.

red = Mughals/Turanis (Central Asians)
blue = Rajputs
green = Iranians
beige = Indian Muslims
yellow = probable Indian Muslim
m. = married
horizontal arrow = connection through wife
downwards arrow = descendant

TIMUR
d. 1404

BABUR
1483–1530 r. 1526–30

HUMAYUN
1508–56 r. 1530–43, 1555–56

Raja Bhah Mal Khachhwaha of Amber

AKBAR
1542–1605 r. 1556–1605
m.
Maryam-uz-Zamani

Raja Mal Deo of Marwar

Raja Bagwan Das   Khwaja Hasan

Raja Udai Singh

Ghiyas Beg Tehrani
IᶜTIMAD-UD-DAULA

Prince Salim
JAHANGIR
1569–1627 r. 1605–27

m. (1585)
Shah Begam
d. 1605

m.
Sahib
Jamal
d. 1599

m. (1586)
Jagat Gosain Manmati

m.
unnamed
concubine

m.
Mihr-un-Nisa
NUR JAHAN
Begam
1577–1645

Raja Man
Singh
d. 1614

ASAF KHAN
d.1641

Sultan Nisar
(Sultan-un-Nisa
Begam)
1586–1646

Prince
Khusrau
1587–1622

Prince Parwiz
1589–1626
m.
Jahan Banu
Begam

Prince Khurram
SHAH JAHAN
1592–1666 r. 1628–58
m.
Arjumand Banu Begam
MUMTAZ MAHAL
1592–1631

Prince
Shahryar
1605–28

Jahanara
Begam
1614–81

Dara Shikoh
1615–59
m.
Nadira Banu
Begam
d. 1658

Shah Shuja
1616–59

Raushanara
Begam
1617–71

AURANGZEB
1618–1707
r. 1658–1707

Murad Bakhsh
1624–61

Gauharara Begam
b. 1631

Timur's sons and successors had established a splendid courtly culture of Persianate orientation in their first centre at Samarqand, and then, towards the end of the 15th century, at Herat, in present-day Afghanistan; it was reflected in smaller Timurid principalities like that of Farghana, where Babur came from. Still, this background does not explain Babur's astonishing career as an adventurer and ruler, and how he came to write his memoirs, the *Baburnama* [20], an autobiography that would be outstanding at any time, but is particularly remarkable for a Central Asian prince of the 16th century. He comments with candid self-observation and in almost Proustian detail on subjects varying from his youthful infatuation with a boy in his encampment to his peregrinations and campaigns in Central Asia and India, and notes the flora and fauna of the newly conquered Hindustan, as the Mughals called North India.[4] He also set down, presumably with his descendants in mind, the ideal qualities of a ruler that he expected from himself and from others, namely virtue, education, truthfulness, humanity and dignity. The *Baburnama* did indeed become the foundation book of the Mughal dynasty, something like a 'mirror of princes'. Shah Jahan had it read out to him every night.[5] Babur's matter-of-factness, rational approach and love of nature remained generally characteristic of the Mughal dynasty, at least until Aurangzeb.

In Hindustan Babur overthrew the Lodi dynasty, the last rulers of the once powerful Delhi sultanate, which during the 15th century had increasingly shrunk while regional sultans had asserted themselves.[6]

Humayun (r. 1530–43, 1555–56)

Babur was succeeded by his son Humayun, 'the August' [4] After more than a decade on the throne, Humayun was ousted by his local rival, the Afghan Sher Shah Sur, and had to take refuge in Iran with Shah Tahmasp for some twelve years before he could reconquer Hindustan from Kabul in 1555. This sojourn intensified the Mughal contact with Persian culture and further inspired the eccentric Humayun to enrich the Mughal myth of kingship, which he had begun to develop in India, with borrowings from ancient Persian concepts.

The historian Badauni tells us that when Humayun was in Bengal he adopted the practice of casting a veil over his crown: he would then remove it, and people were to exclaim, 'Light has shone forth.'[7] Humayun thus associated himself with the Indian and Iranian practices of sun rulership and with the old Persian concept of the divine effulgence of the king, ideas that were not forgotten in Islamic times. The learned theologian, poet and moralist Dawani, for instance, who visited Persepolis in 1476, claims that the mythical Persian king Jamshid, after having constructed Persepolis, 'caused

4 Dynastic group portrait of the Mughals, attributed to Bhawani Das, Mughal, c. 1707–12. Timur occupies the centre. To the left is his son Miran Shah, then Abu Saʿid, ruler of Samarqand, and the Mughal emperors Babur, Akbar and Shah Jahan. To the right are Timur's grandson Muhammad Sultan, Timur's son ʿUmar Shaikh, and the Mughal emperors Humayun, Jahangir and Aurangzeb.

a golden throne studded with shining jewels to be placed on the columns . . . and sat on it in state. At sunrise he ordered the throne to be turned towards the Sun, and the eyes of the onlookers were dazzled by the brilliancy. Saying that they beheld two suns, one in the sky and the other on earth, they knelt down . . . thenceforth he was surnamed Jamshid, his name being Jam and *shid* meaning "Sun."'[8] The concept was to become a leading idea in the Mughal myth of rulership (p. 69). Back in India, Humayun must have thought of the legendary carpets and throne of the Sasanian kings when he conceived a large cosmological carpet with concentric rings on which his court had to sit according to origin and rank, with the emperor 'like the Sun' in the centre.[9] Besides eccentric court settings, Humayun also designed highly original buildings: a wooden boat palace consisting of four floating four-arched pavilions, joined to form a central pool between them,[10] inspired the form of his own tomb, built by his son Akbar [24, 104, 335].

Humayun's stay in Iran also had a decisive impact on Mughal painting. By the time he left, his host Shah Tahmasp had lost his early interest in painting, so Humayun could bring to India some of the outstanding masters who had worked on the shah's great illustrated manuscript, the *Shahnama-i Shahi*, completed in the late 1530s.[11] The painters Mir Sayyid ʿAli and ʿAbdus Samad joined Humayun in 1549 in Kabul, where he resided before his return to Hindustan, and then later, under his successor Akbar, they became the leading masters of the new court atelier in which a large number of artists created a specific Mughal style, bringing together Persian, Central Asian, Indian and also European painting traditions.

Akbar (r. 1556–1605)

Akbar ('the Great'), the son of Humayun, succeeded to the throne at the age of fourteen and became the most outstanding ruler of the Mughal dynasty [4]. With the support of highly capable nobles, in particular his friend the liberal thinker and historian Abu'l Fazl

ʿAllami, Akbar expanded the empire over the greater part of India and secured the north-west frontier by recapturing Kabul and Qandahar. He provided India with an efficient administration based on a militarily structured elite, composed of Central Asian Turks, Afghans, Iranians, and among Indians both Muslims and Hindu Rajputs, the indigenous ruling class of India. Nobility was not inherited but had to be acquired through military rank (*mansab*). All were *mansabdars* ('rankholders'); the higher rank were called *amir*. The nobles were granted titles which usually contained the Turkish-Mongol component *khan*. The title replaced the personal name; the same title was never assigned to two nobles at the same time. Limits on the rights of the Muslim nobility to own property and bequeath it restricted their architectural patronage (p. 28).

Akbar himself was a great builder: he covered India with fortresses and residences, and also erected mosques and tombs. Akbari architecture synthesized Central Asian and regional Indian building traditions into a new universal Mughal imperial style, expressed in red sandstone and highlighted with white marble, on a scale not emulated until the reign of his grandson, Shah Jahan.[12]

Akbar was a true humanist and strove for a reconciliation of his Muslim and Hindu subjects, in particular in the intellectual and religious spheres. He had outstanding works of Sanskrit literature translated into Persian, which he established as the sole administrative language, and propagated an enlightened religion based on reason. His deep intellectual curiosity about religions in general led him in 1580 to invite Jesuit missionaries to the Mughal court. But even in their most liberal and tolerant hour the Mughals remained pragmatists. Akbar felt that his tolerant stance towards different religions and cultures gave him the right to rule them all: 'as it has been our disposition from the beginning of our attaining discretion to this day not to pay attention to differences of religion and variety of manners and to regard the tribes of mankind as the servants of God, we have endeavoured to regulate mankind in general'.[13]

Akbar implied that he was superior to other rulers, such as Shah ʿAbbas of Iran, whom he addressed on this matter: they accepted only one religion and acted merely within one culture, whereas his tolerance gave him the moral authority to take care of all mankind and thus be a true universal king. To confirm his position as a ruler, and his lineage, the emperor also sponsored historiography on a large scale, culminating in the *Akbarnama*, the history of his own reign, written by Abu'l Fazl at the end of the 16th century [101]. In order to establish his status internationally, the emperor had contacts with the Safavids, Uzbegs and Ottomans, planned to send an envoy to the pope, and wrote to King Philip II of Spain (from 1580 also king of Portugal).

The consolidation under Akbar provided the base for the flourishing of the Mughal empire during the rule of Akbar's son Jahangir and his grandson Shah Jahan.

Jahangir (r. 1605–27)

Jahangir ('Worldholder') [4, 5, 50] was the first Mughal emperor known not under his given name – Salim – but under his regnal title. From then onwards the Mughals followed the common practice of Muslim dynasties of adopting regnal and honorific titles on their accession.

Jahangir continued politically more or less on the lines of Akbar. He widened the contacts with Europe: in addition to the Jesuits, from 1615 to 1619 he had resident at his court Sir Thomas Roe, sent by James I to negotiate trade privileges for the English.[14] Art was the key to the Mughal court. In the 1620s the Dutch East India Company, who had come to know about Jahangir's interest in European art, placed the painter Hendrick Arendsz. Vapoer as their representative at Agra. As a first-hand source of Netherlandish techniques of illusionism, he was indeed well received by the emperor and his nobles – while at the same time providing his employers with the desired inside information.[15] From 1621 to 1627 the Company's senior factor was Francisco Pelsaert, who has left an invaluable account of his impressions.

Jahangir's outstanding achievements were in literature, the arts and science. He wrote his memoirs like Babur, like Akbar sponsored painting and architecture, though the latter on a lesser scale, and was a naturalist of rank. Jahangir's observations on the breeding habits of the sarus crane (*Grus antigone*), for instance, are acknowledged as an original contribution to ornithology.[16] The emperor's interest in the natural world combined with his personal involvement in the arts led to an intensified realism in Mughal painting: portraiture, nature studies and landscape were the themes in which his painters excelled, and for which they studied European art to improve their techniques of illusionism. European sources also inspired allegories, as a new genre in which to glorify the Mughal emperor. Jahangir's love of nature led him to turn to Kashmir as the ideal landscape; it reminded the Mughals of their ancestral lands, and they introduced new fruits there from the northern regions. Srinagar became the favourite summer residence of the court, and there the emperor, his family and his nobles laid out numerous gardens. In architecture the reign of Jahangir was a time of refinement and new experiments, with emphasis on decoration in varying techniques. The tomb emerged as the most prominent building type, beginning with Jahangir's own highly

original project for his father's mausoleum at Sikandra, Agra [107]. His office-holders established a whole range of mausoleum types, engaging with regional traditions.[17]

In the last phase of Jahangir's reign real power lay in the hands of his Iranian wife, Nur Jahan ('Light of the World') [5], and her family – her father Ghiyas Beg Tehrani, given the title Iʿtimad-ud-Daula ('Pillar of the Empire': see p. 48) [54], who was the highest

5 Jahangir and Prince Khurram (given the title Shah Jahan in 1617) feasted by Nur Jahan in a garden; Mughal, 1620s. The pavilion is patterned on one of those in the Nur Afshan garden or Ram Bagh at Agra [36].

official of the empire, and her brother Abu'l Hasan (given the title Asaf Khan [2:6]: see p. 74). Her niece, Arjumand Banu Begam, was married to Jahangir's third son, Prince Khurram, later Shah Jahan, and, as Mumtaz Mahal, became famous as the person for whom the Taj Mahal was built.

Shah Jahan (r. 1628–58)

Under Shah Jahan ('King of the World') [2:1, 6, 18] the Mughal empire experienced its period of greatest prosperity and stability. Already in the 18th century the historian Khafi Khan looked back on it as a golden age.[18] Shah Jahan brought the centralization of the administration to its peak and systematized court life and the arts for his self-representation. Pomp and show, architecture and the arts were emphasized as indispensable instruments of rulership. Highly aestheticized form was used consistently as an expression of his specific state ideology, where central power and hierarchic order were seen to bring about balance and harmony (pp. 83–84).

Under Shah Jahan's patronage poetry in Persian came into its own in the *sabq-i Hindi*, 'the Indian style', developed by Iranian poets who flocked to the Mughal court in search of more generous and supportive patronage than that of the Safavids.[19] One of the main exponents of the genre was Shah Jahan's poet laureate, Abu Talib Kalim from Kashan in Iran (d. 1651). He composed for the emperor a versified history, the *Padshahnama*, on the model of Firdausi's great *Shahnama* (c. 1000); but whereas that told of the mythical and historical kings of Iran, the *Padshahnama* extolled the life and deeds of a single, living, ruler.

In his foreign politics Shah Jahan was not so successful as within his realm. His ambition to extend Mughal power north to Balkh and Badakhshan ended in 1646 in failure, and his later reign was overshadowed by the first signs of decline. When the emperor fell ill in 1657, his son Aurangzeb waged a savage war for the succession. The struggle culminated in the public execution on an accusation of heresy of Dara Shikoh ('the Glory of Darius'), the emperor's favourite son and designated successor [2:2, 90], and Shah Jahan was imprisoned in the Agra fort until his death in 1666 (p. 101).

Aurangzeb (r. 1658–1707) and his successors

Aurangzeb ('Throne Ornament') [2:2, 4, 65] on becoming emperor assumed the title ʿAlamgir ('Worldholder'), but remained known under his given name.[20] He subjugated the Deccan and brought about the greatest expansion of the Mughal empire; but he was a strictly orthodox Muslim and broke with the liberal attitude towards the Hindu majority among his subjects. This stance, together with a loosening grip on the administration, whose officials became increasingly powerful and independent, was not conducive to the unity of the heterogeneous empire.

Under Aurangzeb's weak successors the Mughal empire disintegrated. During the greater part of the 18th century northern India was in the hands of various indigenous and foreign powers. The British extended their influence from Bengal westwards through Oudh until they occupied Agra and Delhi in 1803 (p. 237). The last two Mughal emperors, Akbar Shah II and Bahadur Shah II, were allowed to rule at least nominally until 1858, when the British took the great Indian uprising, the so-called Mutiny, as an occasion to depose and exile the last Mughal ruler.

6 Shah Jahan standing on a globe, painted by Hashim, Mughal, 1629. This formal full-length portrait became the official image of the emperor [cf. 18]. It is an allegory of his rule. He stands on the globe of world rulership, holding a sword and a jewel. He wears a necklace of pearls and rubies, a prerogative of the imperial family. The flowers on his *pay-jama* (trousers) symbolize the flowering brought about by his good government (see pp. 222–24). His spiritual authority and the blessings of heaven are expressed by elements borrowed from Christian imagery: the halo, and the angels who rush through clouds with imperial symbols – sword, crown, and in the centre a pearl-fringed parasol on which Shah Jahan's genealogy is traced back to Timur. Inside the globe, Muslim shaikhs holding explanatory inscriptions support the emperor's rule, and the scales, and the lion lying down with the lamb, testify to his justice [cf. 2]. (Below them appears the dated signature of the artist, evidence of the privileged position of Mughal painters, in contrast to that of architects who had to remain anonymous.)

The legacy of the Mughal emperors

From Babur to Aurangzeb the Mughal dynasty produced, in uninterrupted succession, six generations of outstanding rulers [3, 4]. For the world-travelling German philosopher Count Hermann Keyserling, an enthusiastic interculturalist who was in India in 1911–12 (p. 246), the first six emperors were 'the grandest rulers brought forth by mankind' because they combined in their personalities so many diverse talents: they were men of action, refined diplomats, experienced judges of the human psyche, and at the same time aesthetes and dreamers. He felt that such a 'superior human synthesis' had not shown itself in any European king.[21] Even scholars critical of the notion of 'personalized charismatic power' are ready to concede 'clear traces of charisma . . . surrounding a figure such as Akbar'.[22] Their brilliant abilities qualified the first six Mughals particularly well to stand as sovereigns at the head of an increasingly centralized state, and to give credibility to their complex ideal of kingship, which drew on Muslim caliphal, Qur'anic prophetic, Sufi, Achaemenian and Sasanian Persian, Perso-Islamic, Turko-Mongolian, Indian, Christian-Messianic and recent European concepts of universal monarchy. On this eclectic mixture each emperor set his own stamp.

The descendants of Timur – at least Akbar, Jahangir and Shah Jahan – saw themselves as representatives of God on earth who united both spiritual and political authority. They also prided themselves on being second Solomons, the prophet-king of Qur'anic sanction. From Humayun to Shah Jahan, the Mughals surrounded themselves with the aura of the mythical and ancient historical kings of Iran and India and claimed that their divinely illuminated kingship and their wise and just rule would bring

8 *right* A fantastic scene of the court of Shah Jahan, by Willem Schellinks, third quarter of the 17th century. The emperor and his daughter Jahanara watch a parade of his sons on composite animals, which are a popular subject of Mughal painting; in the clouds above are Akbar (right) and Jahangir, their grouping also based on a Mughal model.

7 Shah Jahan and one of his sons: a drawing by Rembrandt after a Mughal painting [cf. 14], *c.* 1656–61.

to the world a golden age of peace. The Mughals tried earnestly to live up to this image, and architecture, art, historiography, poetry, and court life were all called upon to manifest the imperial ideal.

In 17th- and 18th-century Europe the 'Great Mogul' became a synonym for oriental despotism, of which absolute rulers were secretly dreaming. Rembrandt (1606–69) and his school copied portraits of Mughal emperors [7], and Willem Schellinks (1627–78) used Mughal miniatures as models to compose proto-Orientalist fantasies of Shah Jahan's court [8]. In 1708 the goldsmith Johann Melchior Dinglinger created for Augustus the Strong, Prince Elector of Saxony and King of Poland, a precious miniature scene known as 'The Birthday of Aurangzeb' or 'At the Court of the Great Mogul', which catered to his patron's oriental ambitions [9]. In the 1760s the Habsburg empress Maria Theresa had one of her audience chambers in the Schönbrunn Palace at Vienna decorated with miniatures from the Mughal empire in which Shah Jahan features at least twenty-eight times [10]. And Akbar even appeared in opera, lending his name to a tyrant king in *Zemira*, composed by Pasquale Anfossi to a libretto by Gaetano Sertor and staged in Venice in 1782.

The legacy of the Mughals as synonyms for power, wealth and oriental splendour reaches into our own times. Successful American movie or business tycoons are known as 'moguls', and a Mughalizing style, derived in the last analysis from Shahjahani architecture, is used for mosques in the Arab world, in Bollywood settings, and in the creation of eccentric buildings such as Donald Trump's 'Taj Mahal' casino at Atlantic City, New Jersey.

9 *above* Detail of 'The Birthday of Aurangzeb', by Johann Melchior Dinglinger, 1708. The emperor is imagined as seated on a raised throne, flanked by attendants and ceremonial umbrellas. The tableau is of made of gold, silver, enamel, and precious stones, including a large diamond on the platform of the throne.

10 *below* Shah Jahan on horseback, cut out from a Mughal miniature painting and glued into cartouche 60 of the Millionenzimmer in the palace of Schönbrunn, Vienna, 1760s. (Photograph taken in 1979 during conservation)

Shah Jahan and Mumtaz Mahal

Shah Jahan was born at Lahore on 30 Rabi^c al-Awwal 1000 of the
Islamic calendar, which begins in 622, the year of the Hijra, the
flight of the prophet Muhammad from Mecca to Medina; the date
corresponds to 15 January 1592. He was the third son of Akbar's son
Salim, who was to rule as Jahangir. His elder brothers were Khusrau
(d. 1622) and Parwiz (d. 1626). Akbar took a keen interest in his new
grandson, giving him the name Khurram ('Joyous') and ordering
that he should be taken from his mother, Jagat Gosain, a Rajput
princess from the house of Jodhpur, Marwar [12], to be brought up
by one of Akbar's own wives, Ruqaiya Sultan Begam, who had no
children of her own.[23] Despite being put in the care of the *begam*,
a niece of Humayun and thus a pure Timurid, Shah Jahan was to
be the first Mughal emperor who was not very proficient in Turki,
the ancestral idiom of the Mughals. He spoke Persian, the official
language of the Mughal empire, and Hindavi, the language of North
India.[24] He had also inherited his mother's features, and looked
more like an Indian Rajput than a Central Asian Turk.

'Baba Khurram', as he was affectionately called by Jahangir, had
a very careful education which began, according to custom, after his
circumcision, when he was a little over four years old. Distinguished
scholars were selected as his teachers; poets and Sufi mystics, and
the eminent scholar and physician Hakim ^cAli Gilani, formed part of
the circle. The prince was not only educated by 'the masters of the
pen', to use the Mughal expression, but also by the 'masters of the
sword', and seems to have been more inclined to the latter.[25] He
became a proficient swordsman, passionate hunter and excellent
shot, who, when emperor, even named his guns, his favourite being
'Khassban' ('the Royal Keeper').[26] His bravery became the subject
of history in 1610 when, as an eighteen-year-old, during one of

11 *above* Prince Khurram attacking a lion, to rescue a Rajput noble who had
sought to protect the Emperor Jahangir (far right – depicted, like Khurram, with
a halo). The future Shah Jahan shows himself a worthy successor to the Mughal
throne. Painting by Balchand, Mughal, *c.* 1640, from the *Padshahnama*.

12 *left* Shah Jahan's maternal grandfather, the Rajput ruler Mota Raja Udai Singh
of Jodhpur, painted by Payag after an earlier image, Mughal, *c.* 1640–50.

13 *opposite* Jahangir has Prince Khurram weighed in the Urta Bagh at Kabul,
ascribed to Manohar, Mughal, *c.* 1610–15, from the *Jahangirnama*. The main
participants are identified by name or title; the emperor is assisted by the
eminent noble ^cAbd-ur-Rahim Khan-i Khanan (see p. 18). In the year this event
took place, 1607, the prince was betrothed to the future Mumtaz Mahal.

Jahangir's hunts, he attacked a lion with a sword to save a Rajput
noble who in turn had come to the aid of the emperor [11].[27]

Khurram was not only Akbar's favourite grandson but also
Jahangir's favourite son. In 1607, when only fifteen, he got his first
military rank, together with the insignia of banners and drums.
He was allowed to use a red tent, an imperial privilege generally
accorded only to the eldest prince,[28] and was given the special
honour of a ceremonial weighing on his lunar birthday [13].[29] The
weighing of the emperor, a great court festival, was one of many
Indian customs adopted by the Mughals. It corresponds to the
charity entertainments of our times, for he was weighed against
various goods which were then distributed to deserving and poor

persons.[30] The princes were also weighed, but usually only on their solar birthday. In the same year 1607, in March after the celebration of Nauruz, the Persian New Year, Khurram was betrothed to Arjumand Banu Begam ('Excellent Lady'), later known as Mumtaz Mahal. She was the granddaughter of a distinguished noble from Iran, later to be given the title Iᶜtimad-ud-Daula, who had entered Mughal court service under Akbar (p. 48) [54], and the daughter of his son Abu'l Hasan, later known under the title Asaf Khan (p. 74) [2:6]. Arjumand Banu Begam was even younger than Khurram, only a little over fourteen. The engagement ceremony took place in the fort of Lahore where the court resided at the time. The young *begam* was brought to the women's quarters of the palace (in India called *zanana*), where she was received by Jahangir, and, Shah Jahan's historian Muhammad Amin Qazwini records, 'in the manner of the glorious emperors (*padshahs*), having performed the ceremony of betrothal, he adorned with the ring of luck the fortunate finger of that excellent lady'.[31] The wedding was, however, for unknown reasons, delayed for another five years, and Khurram was married instead, in 1610, to the daughter of Mirza Muzaffar Husain, a descendant of Shah Ismaᶜil, the founder of the Safavid dynasty of Iran.[32]

In the meantime the imperial ties with the family of Iᶜtimad-ud-Daula were strengthened by Jahangir's own marriage in 1611 to the aunt of Mumtaz Mahal, Mihr-un-Nisa, with whom Jahangir, despite her age of thirty-four, had fallen deeply in love [5]. She was not only an extraordinarily attractive and talented woman but also highly capable and politically much more ambitious than the emperor himself (p. 48). He gave her the title Nur Jahan ('Light of the World') and she became a central figure in the Mughal empire; he left the government to her and elevated her father and brother to the highest ranks. Together with other well-placed relatives they formed the 'Iranian clan', which was the dominant power group at court. The new status of the family of Iᶜtimad-ud-Daula is reflected in the celebrations of Khurram's wedding to Arjumand Banu Begam when that finally took place in 1612. First, the emperor honoured the house of Asaf Khan, the father of the bride, with a visit, and on 10 May, after he had fastened on the prince with his own hands a *sihra* of pearls (a fringed veil covering the face of the bridegroom at Indian weddings), he proceeded with him in a festive cortege to t he house of Iᶜtimad-ud-Daula where the actual marriage ceremony (*nikah*) took place.[33] Khurram was so delighted with his new wife that, Qazwini explains, 'finding her in appearance and character elect (*mumtaz*) among all the women of the time, he gave her the title Mumtaz Mahal Begam [Chosen One of the Palace], on the one hand so that it might be a source of pride for that Chosen One of the Age, and on the other, so that her original renowned name of good reputation in this world and the next, which was exactly like her nature, might not occur on the tongues [of the common people]'.[34]

A few years later, in 1617, Khurram – given the title Shah Jahan by Jahangir – was married again, for political reasons, to the daughter of Mirza Iraj, with the title Shah Nawaz Khan Bahadur, the son of Mirza ᶜAbd-ur-Rahim Khan-i Khanan [13], the great general, statesman and scholar who at the end of the 16th century had translated the *Baburnama* into Persian.

Shah Jahan was apparently not very interested in his polygamous rights as a Muslim husband, though he dutifully fathered a child with each of his other two wives. After that, according to Qazwini,

> they had nothing more than the status of marriage. The intimacy, deep affection, attention and favour which His Majesty had for the Cradle of Excellence [another title of Mumtaz] exceeded by a thousand times what he felt for any other. And always that Lady of the Age was the companion, close confidante, associate and intimate friend of that successful ruler, in hardship and comfort, joy and grief, when travelling or in residence . . . The mutual affection and harmony between the two had reached a degree never seen between a husband and wife among the classes of rulers (*sultans*), or among the other people. And this was not merely out of sexual passion (*hawa-yi nafs*): the excellent qualities, pleasing habits, outward and inward virtues, and physical and spiritual compatibility on both sides caused great love and affection, and extreme affinity and familiarity.[35]

Such open words about erotic attraction between royal spouses are unheard of in the 17th century – especially in a Muslim context, where privacy in marital matters is so important. Even in Europe such sentiments became a subject for literature only in the 18th century.

Throughout their married life, for nineteen years, Mumtaz had no rival in the affection of Shah Jahan. She bore him fourteen children, of which only seven survived: four sons, Dara Shikoh

14 Shah Jahan and one of his sons, probably Shah Shujaᶜ, attended by a nurse, Mughal, *c.* 1620. This very unusual intimate portrait was probably inspired by a European *Madonna and Child*, and was in turn freely copied by Rembrandt [7]. The flower vase as a status symbol appears again in the Taj Mahal.

(b. 1615 at Ajmer) [2:2, 90], Shah Shuja^c (b. 1616 at Ajmer) [2:3, 14], Aurangzeb (b. 1618 at Dhod in Malwa) [2:4, 4, 65], and Murad Bakhsh (b. 1624 at Rohtas fort in Bihar) [2:5, 90]; and three daughters, Jahanara (b. 1614 at Ajmer), Raushanara (b. 1617 at Burhanpur), and Gauharara (b. 1631 at Burhanpur).³⁶

Jahangir entrusted Khurram with all his major campaigns and the prince took Mumtaz with him, despite her frequent pregnancies. Khurram's rise as a prince culminated in 1617 with his victory against the Muslim sultanates in the Deccan, for which Jahangir showered him with presents and awarded him the title Shah Jahan, 'King of the World' – an extraordinary distinction which 'no king during his own lifetime had ever bestowed on a son'.³⁷ He was to keep this honorific title after his accession, to claim universal rule.

Succession to the Mughal throne was not regulated by primogeniture: it depended largely on the position which the sons of the emperor could carve out for themselves during their careers as princes and at the crucial moment of the death of their father. This uncertain situation led princes to rebel; so Jahangir, at the end of Akbar's reign, had set up a counter court at Allahabad, styling himself Shah Salim. In consequence Akbar favoured Khusrau, Jahangir's eldest son, who, thus encouraged, rebelled when his father came to the throne. Khusrau was defeated and kept in custody at court; his younger brother Parwiz showed himself less capable; and as a result Shah Jahan – who had distinguished himself by his military achievements – became Jahangir's designated successor. But he did not remain the favourite, for tensions arose between him and Nur Jahan: in 1622 he reacted with open rebellion, and became 'Bi-daulat' ('Without Authority') in the eyes of Jahangir; his rebellion was suppressed, and he spent the rest of Jahangir's reign in exile in the Deccan, his three eldest sons being kept as hostages at court. Shah Jahan's interests were however maintained by his father-in-law, Asaf Khan, who by then had become one of the most powerful men in the empire.³⁸ With his support, and against the resistance of Nur Jahan, Shah Jahan succeeded in gaining the throne: other pretenders were, for the first time, eliminated through murder (the Mughals had lost the moral standards of their early years). The deed was excused by Shah Jahan's historian Kanbo as a rightful means to secure the succession and to save the country from turmoil.³⁹

The accession ceremony took place on 14 February 1628 in the Hall of Public Audience, the Diwan-i ᶜAmm, of the Agra fort [2, 83, 84]. After Shah Jahan had been dressed with a jewelled turban, a royal robe, and an ornamented sword, he 'came to the throne of the empire of Akbar with the fortune of Timur and the success of Babur, and sat with royal ease . . . under a golden parasol', whereupon his court broke out in loud congratulations. An orator praised the new padshah and his ancestors, poets read congratulatory verses, and the court orchestra played. New coins were issued which carried his regnal titles – Father of Victory, Star of Religion, Second Lord of the Auspicious Conjunction of Jupiter and Venus (the first Sahib-i Qiran had been Timur), King of the World, Emperor, Warrior of the Faith. After that the new emperor went to the zanana, where Mumtaz Mahal awaited him with all the ladies and was the first one to congratulate him by scattering gens and rubies over his head and presenting him with precious objects from Arabia and India.⁴⁰

The reign of Shah Jahan began. According to the rhetoric of the accession, the new emperor would end a period of chaos and religious decline, meaning the reign of Jahangir when imperial power had been in the hands of a woman, Nur Jahan.⁴¹ A new era had begun under the second Timur, who had been born at the beginning of a new millennium and thus could claim to be a mujaddid, a religious renewer, a mahdi, who would bring a new golden age to mankind and a new spring to Hindustan (p. 224). Shah Jahan was the new Solomon and Mumtaz the Bilqis – the Queen of Sheba – of the Age.⁴²

Mumtaz Mahal was to survive as Shah Jahan's queen for only three years. Their relationship was as intense as that of the previous imperial couple, Jahangir and Nur Jahan, with the difference that Mumtaz Mahal has come down in history as the model wife, the support of her husband, who bore him one child after another, and did not try to arrogate political power. She only sought to alleviate suffering, when seeking pardon for those condemned to death or imprisonment, and in her daily afternoon audiences with Shah Jahan she put deserving cases for charity before him, brought to her notice by her chief lady-in-waiting, Satti-un-Nisa Khanum. Mumtaz also continued the Mughal tradition of female architectural patronage, and built a garden at Agra (p. 41). Her possible political influence comes out posthumously, when Shah Jahan attacked and vanquished the Portuguese at Hughli in Bengal, one of their offences having been to have captured two of her maidservants.⁴³ It does not seem to be a coincidence that the Hughli attack was started on 20 June 1632, two days before Shah Jahan began the commemoration at Agra of the first anniversary of the death of Mumtaz Mahal. The Mughal forces were under the command of the governor of Bengal, Qasim Khan Juwaini, nicknamed 'Manija', who was married to Manija, the aunt of Mumtaz. The move appears like an offering for the departed queen.⁴⁴

We see Mumtaz Mahal through the eyes of Shah Jahan because it was he who constructed the history of his reign. He did not possess the searching mind, the humanism, or the pronounced idiosyncrasies of his predecessors. He was reserved and self-controlled (he even refused to drink wine, until Jahangir forced him to do so when he was twenty-four).⁴⁵ His main agenda was the formulation of perfect rulership, and one of his most important tools was historiography. Shah Jahan was highly concerned to find a historian who would come up to his expectations, and during the first ten years of his reign he entrusted several people with the task of writing his official history, the Padshahnama. After trying out Indian historians he employed two Iranians, first Jalal-ud-Din Tabataba'i (d. 1636) from Isfahan, and then Mirza Muhammad Amin Qazwini (d. 1646/47). Finally, in the twelfth year of his reign, he decided on the elderly scholar ᶜAbd-ul-Hamid Lahauri, then living in Patna, but originally from Lahore, as his name indicates. When Lahauri died in 1654, having completed two volumes (each covering ten regnal years) and written the greater part of the third, his pupil Muhammad Waris (d. 1680) took over and carried on the history up to 1657. In addition, Shah Jahan's poet laureate Abu Talib Kalim was commissioned to write a Padshahnama in verse, in which he covered the first ten years of Shah Jahan's reign. A self-appointed historian was Muhammad Salih Kanbo (d. 1674/75), also from Lahore, who wrote the ᶜAmal-i Salih or Shah Jahannama: the main part of this was completed in 1659–60, but Kanbo added an epilogue when the emperor died on 31 January 1666.⁴⁶ Shah Jahan had daily editing sessions with his historians, to make sure posterity would see him as he wished to be seen: as a perfect impersonal ruler who dedicated every minute of his life to the just administration of his empire, an empire where – because of his justice – the lamb could fearlessly lie down with the lion [2, 6]. It stands in stark contrast to this construct that he allowed his historians to document his passionate love for his wife and his utter devastation when Mumtaz Mahal died in 1631.

Shah Jahan had moved to Burhanpur to quell the rebellion of one of his nobles, Khan Jahan Lodi, who had joined forces with the Deccani sultans. The court stayed in the palaces of the fort which Shah Jahan had built during his Deccan campaigns of 1617 and 1621, when he was still a prince [15]. In the night of 16–17 June, Mumtaz gave birth to her fourteenth child, Gauharara Begam, but after the delivery her condition suddenly deteriorated, and she sent her eldest daughter, the seventeen-year-old Jahanara, for the emperor, wishing to bid him farewell. The deeply shocked Shah Jahan arrived in greatest distress at her bedside. Mumtaz recommended her children and her family to him, and then 'responded to the call of "Return to thy Lord"' and died, at the age of only thirty-eight. (The often reported story that the dying Mumtaz asked Shah Jahan not to marry again, and to build her a tomb without equal, is not reported by the historical sources.[47]) Shah Jahan broke down completely, wept uncontrollably, and put on a white garment, the Indian colour of mourning. His whole court was made to don mourning clothes. The emperor did not appear for a whole week in audience, which was unheard of in the history of the Mughal emperors, and against everything Shah Jahan stood for: he himself had turned his appearances to his court and subjects into a strictly regulated, daily repeated ceremonial (p. 69). He even considered abdicating, dividing the empire between his sons, and living as a religious recluse.[48] Shah Jahan, the supreme emperor, had become Majnun, the ultimate lover of Muslim lore, who flees into the desert to pine for his unattainable Laila [16].

For two years the emperor gave up listening to music, wearing jewelry and rich and colourful clothes, and using perfumes, and altogether presented a heartbroken appearance. His eyes got so bad from constant weeping that he needed spectacles, and his beard which up to then 'had not more than ten or twelve grey hairs, which he used to pluck out' turned grey, and eventually white.[49] During the great court celebrations, like ʿId, when the ladies arranged festive gatherings, he broke down in tears because he did not see Mumtaz among them; he also postponed for two years the weddings of his sons Dara Shikoh and Shah Shujaʿ, which he had planned with the queen.[50] Mumtaz had died on a Wednesday, so on Wednesdays he forbade all entertainments, in particular the spectacular elephant fights;[51] she had died in the month of Zi'l-Qaʿda, and for several years he and the court wore white and abstained from all entertainments throughout the whole month. Shah Jahan's condition was regarded with great concern by the imperial family. Qasim Khan 'Manija', who as the husband of an aunt of Mumtaz had something like the status of an uncle of Shah Jahan, wrote to the emperor from Bengal that if he continued to abandon himself to his mourning, Mumtaz might think of giving up the joys of Paradise to come back to earth, this place of misery – and he should also consider the children she had left to his care.[52]

Shah Jahan's main support was their eldest daughter, Jahanara, who had not only inherited half of the estate of Mumtaz Mahal – the other half went to her other children – but now, with the title Begam Sahib ('Lady Lordship'), also took over the duties of Mumtaz as the first lady at court, for which Shah Jahan raised her yearly income to 100,000 rupees.

After her death in the palace of Burhanpur Mumtaz Mahal was buried temporarily in the garden of Zainabad, on the opposite bank of the river Tapti. A week later Shah Jahan visited her grave for the first time and recited the *Fatiha*, the first and briefest *sura* of the Qur'an, which is the customary prayer on such occasions (p. 229). Throughout his stay at Burhanpur he visited the grave every Friday, the holy day of the Muslim week.[53]

In the days following the burial the planning of her mausoleum as a monumental funerary garden palace began, inspired by a verse of Bibadal Khan, 'May the abode of Mumtaz Mahal be Paradise.' Negotiations for a suitable site on the bank of the river at Agra were carried out (p. 97). In disregard of Muslim strictures against delays in burial and the transportation of corpses over long distances,[54] Mumtaz's body was taken out of its temporary grave in early December 1631 and brought to Agra, escorted by Prince Shah Shujaʿ, Mumtaz's lady-in-waiting Satti-un-Nisa Khanum, and the distinguished courtier Hakim ʿAlim-ud-Din Wazir Khan [47] (p. 45). Shah Jahan left Burhanpur in March 1632 and arrived at Agra the following June, for the first ʿurs, or anniversary, of the death of Mumtaz Mahal, which was celebrated on the construction site (p. 98).

15 *opposite* Burhanpur fort, seen across the river Tapti. (Photograph taken in 1984)

16 *right* The death of Majnun on Laila's grave, painted by Sur Gujarati, Mughal, from a *Khamsa* of Nizami, dated 1595. The unhappy lover Majnun was a figure with whom the bereaved Shah Jahan could well identify.

1 Mughal Agra, a riverfront garden city

What a city! A perfumed garden, newly in flower –
Its buildings have grown tall like cypress trees.

Abu Talib Kalim, poem in praise of Akbarabad (Agra),
from his Diwan, 1630s[1]

The Taj Mahal complex seems unique today; but when it was created, it was integrated into the scheme of Mughal Agra as one of its constituent elements [17, 26, 27]. The prevailing garden type of the city, the riverfront garden, was enlarged on an unparalleled scale and arranged in a perfectly symmetrical composition. The typical was used to create the outstanding.

Agra was first conquered by Muslim invaders in the 1070s or 1080s, when Mahmud of Ghazni captured it from its Hindu ruler, Jaipal; Sikander Lodi made it his capital in 1505.[2] In 1526, when the Mughals established themselves in Hindustan, Agra became their capital, and began to acquire its distinctive character as a riverfront garden city. The Mughals, coming from Central Asia via Kabul, were used to formally planned gardens. Babur, founder of the dynasty, and his followers began to lay out gardens 'on the model of Khorasani constructions' along the wide river Yamuna, known to the Mughals as Jaun,[3] and the formal garden was creatively adapted to a riverfront situation. The Yamuna – one of the great holy rivers of India[4] – was to form the artery that bound all the gardens together, a broad water avenue, as the poet Kalim saw it (pp. 32–33), on which one could move by boat from one residence or tomb to the other.

By the time Shah Jahan came to the throne in 1628, Agra was, as Abdul Aziz put it, 'a wonder of the age – as much a centre of the arteries of trade both by land and water as a meeting-place of saints, sages and scholars from all Asia . . . a veritable lodestar for artistic workmanship, literary talent and spiritual worth'.[5] The German traveller Johann Albrecht von Mandelslo in 1638 judged it 'at least twice as big as *Ispahan*';[6] others thought that it was one of the biggest cities in the world, with a population of perhaps 700,000 people.[7] The nucleus was formed of gardens lining the river on both sides; the rest of the city encircled the waterfront to the west.[8] The gardens contained the residences of the imperial family and the highest-ranking nobles; some had been transformed as settings for tombs. The centre of Agra thus had a suburban character. The riverfront garden was the microscopic module of this urban landscape. The city reflected the concept of the garden as primordial residence of the Mughal dynasty and, in a wider ideological sense, served as a symbol of the flowering of Hindustan under the just rule of Shah Jahan.

17 *opposite* Map of Agra made for the Maharaja of Jaipur, 1720s, showing the layout of the city along the Yamuna river. The Taj Mahal appears at the bottom right, the largest of all the riverfront garden complexes (for a key, see pp. 30–31).

18 *right* Shah Jahan as lord of the riverfront city, by Chitarman, Mughal, dated 1627/28. The image was painted on the emperor's accession. Later it was mounted into an album, apparently after the death of Mumtaz: verses pasted around it express grief and despair, such as 'How can my distressed heart open in the flower garden? In my sad eyes the rose and the thorn are all one!'[9]

The Mughal garden, its buildings and its ownership

GARDEN TYPES

The garden was the first architectural expression of the Mughals in the Indian subcontinent; it reflects their love of nature as well as their nomadic life in tents or open pavilions. Typical of the Mughal garden is its strictly planned form with the use of uniform architectural elements. From the beginning it fulfilled diverse functions with strong symbolic connotations. The garden served initially as a territorial marker to demonstrate the new Mughal presence in Hindustan.[10] It served as residence, as module in the planning of cities, later also as module in the planning of palaces; as a paradise-evoking site for tombs; and finally, under Shah Jahan, as political metaphor for a golden age.[11]

The history of the Mughal garden begins with Babur (pp. 9–10), who informs us in his autobiography about his attempts to introduce the Persian Timurid garden tradition of his native Central Asia into Hindustan [20].[12] Babur refers to his first garden at Agra, laid out in 1526, as a *chahar bagh*, like some of his earlier gardens in what is now Afghanistan. In its strictest interpretation, the much-discussed term *chahar bagh*, or its abbreviated form *charbagh*, designates a cross-axial four-part garden, *chahar* in Persian meaning 'four' and *bagh* 'garden'. Babur, however, uses the term in its widest sense, for large architecturally planned gardens with intersecting raised paved walkways, platforms and pools.

David Stronach traces the cross-axial *chahar bagh* concept back to the 6th century BC, to the palace of Cyrus the Great at Pasargadae in Iran, the first monumental capital of the Achaemenid empire.[13] The four-part garden was adopted by Islamic patrons. It appeared in the 8th century in the Umayyad palaces at Rusafa in Syria and was brought from there to Spain;[14] and it was realized in the 9th century on a grand scale by the ᶜAbbasid caliphs at Samarra. The cross-axial garden appeared in South Asia long before the Mughals: the large royal gardens of Sigiriya in northern Sri Lanka, laid out in the 5th century AD, contain well defined cross-axial units.[15]

After Babur the Mughals did not use the term *chahar bagh* very much; in Shahjahani sources it is employed metaphorically, for the earth or the terrestrial, as in 'the *chahar bagh* of the world'.[16] A garden was usually just called *bagh*. Still, the Mughals built the grandest and most consistently planned *chahar baghs* in the entire history of garden architecture. We can identify three formal versions.

In its ideal form the Mughal *chahar bagh* consists of a square, divided by cross-axial paved walkways (*khiyaban*) into four equal parts. The centre, which is highly charged symbolically, may be occupied by a building – typically a garden pavilion (ᶜ*imarat*, *nashiman*), but also a tomb – or by a pool (*hauz*). The walkways may contain sunk channels (*nahr*), and, at the points where they meet the garden wall, there may be real or false gateways (*darwaza*). The quadrants may in turn be subdivided into further squares. The whole composition is enclosed by a wall with towers at its corners. This form becomes the Mughal garden par excellence: with a building in the centre, it finds its most monumental and perfectly planned expression as a funerary garden at the great imperial mausoleums of Humayun [19:a], Akbar [107] and Jahangir [108].

The second type is the terrace garden, which the Mughals had developed in Kabul and Kashmir by introducing the Central Asian concept of a garden laid out on a slope into the landscape of those regions. The main buildings are arrayed on ascending terraces along a central axis formed by a channel sunk in a paved walkway which collects water from a spring. The individual terraces may be given the canonical four-part form, as in the imperial gardens of Shalimar in Kashmir [19:b], which the future Shah Jahan founded on Jahangir's orders in 1620, and which as emperor he enlarged in 1634. They consist of two square *chahar bagh* units on different levels.

The third type is the waterfront garden [19:c].[17] The Taj Mahal expresses this in its grandest form [149]. It is a variant of the *chahar bagh* invented by the Mughals for the specific conditions of the Indo-Gangetic plain. Here the main water source was not lively springs on a mountain slope but a large slow-flowing river, from which the desired running water had to be raised into the garden. The Mughals conceived a garden type to take advantage of this situation: the main building was not placed in the centre as in the classic *chahar bagh*, but was set on an oblong terrace (*kursi*) running along the riverfront. Usually the terrace had rooms below the main building opening onto the river, and stairs leading down to a landing. Its two ends were accentuated by towers. The *chahar bagh* component lay on the landward side. In this way the garden was turned toward the river, and the main pavilions enjoyed its cooling effect. The scheme presented a carefully composed front to those who saw the garden from a boat or across the river; and from inside, the buildings provided a backdrop for the garden [88].

The riverfront scheme emerged as the favourite formula for the residential gardens of Agra. After having been idealized and monumentalized in the Taj Mahal, however, it became an imperial prerogative,[18] and at Shah Jahan's new city, Shahjahanabad, at Delhi (1639–48), it was almost exclusively used for the gardens and courtyards of the emperor's riverfront palace, the Red Fort, and the residences of the emperor's son Dara Shikoh and a few selected nobles.[19] The majority of the nobles, and even Princess Jahanara, had to build their gardens and houses inland.

While we are informed in detail about the architectural features of Mughal gardens, the sources tell us less about what was planted and where. Gardens were expected to be not only beautiful but also useful; they were planted with decorative and sweet-smelling trees, flowers and bushes, and also with fruit trees. The fruit harvest from the Taj Mahal garden continued from Mughal times into the British period (p. 101).

19 *opposite, left* The three types of Mughal *chahar bagh*:
a canonical cross-axial: the tomb of Humayun, Delhi, 1562–71
b terraced: Shalimar gardens, Kashmir, 1620, 1634
c waterfront: Lal Mahal, Bari, 1637

20 *opposite, right* Babur laying out the Garden of Fidelity near Kabul, painted by Bishndas with portraits by Nanha, Mughal, *c.* 1590, from a *Baburnama*. The strips of text point out that the pool surrounded by a clover meadow and orange and pomegranate trees was the best place in the garden. The channels sunk into cross-axial walkways show the characteristic *chahar bagh* design.

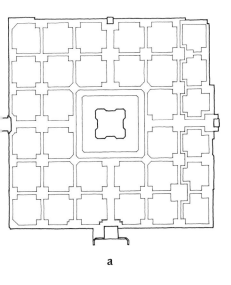

a

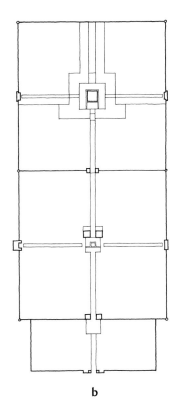

b

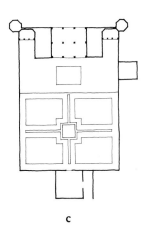

c

Architecturally, the gardens made use of two distinctive forms of building: centralized pavilions based on the *hasht bihisht* or 'eight Paradises' form, and tower pavilions.

The 'hasht bihisht' or 'eight Paradises' pavilion

In the 16th and early 17th century the favourite Mughal form for pavilions and also for mausoleums, which were seen as a funerary form of garden pavilion,[20] was a centrally planned building known in Persian as *hasht bihisht*, 'eight Paradises' [21–24]. Later in the 17th century, in the time of Jahangir and Shah Jahan, centralized plans were gradually given up for residential pavilions and replaced by structures consisting of large halls flanked by side rooms [36], but the *hasht bihisht* continued to be used for tombs. It appears most grandly in the Taj Mahal [220].

The *hasht bihisht* design consists typically of a square or rectangle, with corners sometimes marked by towers but also sometimes chamfered so as to form an irregular octagon, termed *musamman baghdadi* by the Mughals (the significance of this term, 'Baghdadi octagon', has not been established). The *hasht bihisht* is divided by four intersecting construction lines into nine parts, comprising a domed chamber in the centre, rectangular open forehalls in the middle of the four sides, and two-storeyed, often vaulted, rooms at the corners. These eight forehalls and rooms surrounding the hall in the centre are the eight Paradises – the *hasht bihisht*. The central chamber is connected to the forehalls in a cross-axial pattern (+) [22]. In the radially planned versions of this scheme a diagonal cross-axis (x) is introduced through additional passages linking the corner rooms to the main domed chamber [23].

In the Mughal *hasht bihisht* each element of the plan is reflected in the elevation [21, 22]. The axial forehalls are expressed by large vaulted niches or by pillared verandahs, called by the Mughals *iwan* – a distinctive use of the term, denoting a pillared construction of any dimension and plan, not, as usual in Islamic architecture, a monumental niche or a palace hall. The corner rooms are expressed by superimposed niches. The domed central chamber is signalled in tombs by an outer dome, and in garden pavilions and gate buildings by a flat roof, which may be topped by one or more *chhatris* (pillared and domed kiosks).

The *hasht bihisht* plan has many ancient relatives. It resembles the cross-in-square plan of Byzantine architecture and older Classical designs, which, it has been suggested, were themselves derived from Near Eastern and Asian antecedents.[21] The ninefold 'magic square' was employed throughout Chinese history for many different purposes, such as the 'well field system' by which the Zhou in the 4th century BC ordered agriculture: a square li covered nine squares of land, of which the central one was the 'public field', cultivated in common by eight families.[22] The Mongols and Turkoman tribes also valued the number nine as an ordering scheme.[23] In India ninefold schemes appear in mandalas, the cosmic maps of Hinduism and Buddhism.[24] The ninefold scheme can also be related to the magic square (*wafq*) of Muslim mathematicians, a harmonious arrangement of numbers corresponding to each other which became associated with magic.[25]

In Islamic architecture the ninefold plan made an early appearance in the Umayyad period, *c.* 700–750 AD, in the gate

21 The water palace of Shah Quli Khan at Narnaul, 1591. A *chhatri* rises over the central chamber; smaller *chhatris* mark the corners. (Photograph taken in 1979)

opposite
22 *left, above* The basic *hasht bihisht* design: plan of the pavilion of Shah Quli Khan at Narnaul [21].

23 *left, below* A radially planned *hasht bihisht* design: plan of Todar Mal's Baradari, Fatehpur Sikri, *c.* 1571–85.

24 *right* Plan of the tomb of Humayun, Delhi, 1562–71: four radially planned *hasht bihisht* elements are combined in an overall *hasht bihisht* plan.

pavilion (or reception hall?) of the palace in the citadel of Amman in Jordan, which may rest on Byzantine foundations,[26] and in the reception pavilion of the baths of Khirbat al-Mafjar in Palestine.[27] A well designed example is the garden pavilion of the northern palace of Lashkari Bazar in Afghanistan, datable between the 10th and 12th centuries.[28] The plan also appears in a group of nine-bay mosques, built between the first half of the 9th and the 12th century, in Egypt, Iraq, Tunisia, Spain and Central Asia. This type eventually reappears in Ottoman architecture.[29]

The use of the term *hasht bihisht* for a building on the ninefold plan is attested in the case of the palace of the Aq Qoyunlu Turkoman rulers at Tabriz, built by Uzun Hasan (1457–78) or his son Yakub (1478–91) in the middle of a large garden:[30] an anonymous Italian merchant traveller calls the structure 'Astibisti', and describes it as 'divided into eight parts, which are subdivided into four rooms and four anterooms, each room having the anteroom towards the entrance, and the rest of the palace [i.e., the central hall] is a fine circular dome'.[31]

In the Islamic tradition Paradise has at least seven levels, often eight, and heaven has nine vaults.[32] The celebrated Spanish mystic philosopher Ibn ᶜArabi, in his *al-Futuhat al-Makkiyya*, or 'Meccan Revelations' (finished *c.* 1231), described Paradise as consisting of three gardens of which the third is subdivided into eight gardens with eight doors.[33] Muslims viewed the number eight as a symbol of Paradise; eight-sided plans were favourites for funerary structures.[34]

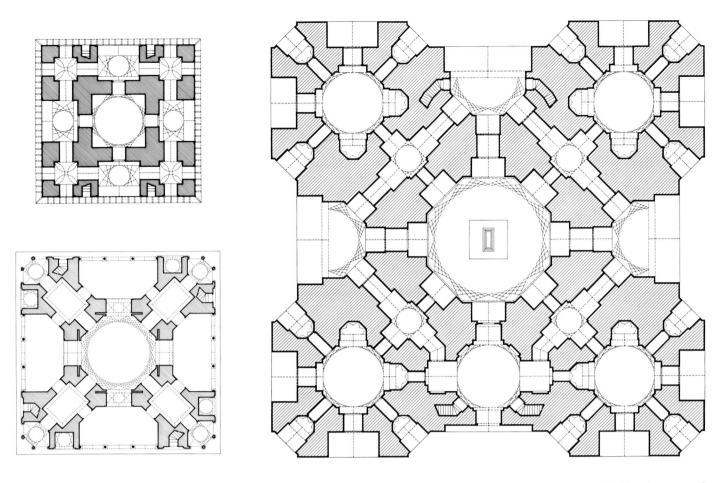

Accommodating as it did Islamic symbolism within an ancient plan which also connected to Turko-Mongolian and Indian cosmological ordering schemes, the *hasht bihisht* concept was attractive to peoples of those traditions. The design became popular in the later Timurid architecture of the 15th and early 16th century, where the Mughals came to know it.[35] Babur records in his autobiography that in 1506, when he was twenty-three years old, he was tempted by his Timurid cousins of Herat to drink wine for the first time, and he found the setting worth describing. It was a pavilion called Tarabkhana, set in a garden called Bagh-i Safid. The pavilion's upper level had a *hujra* (a rectangular or square enclosed room) at each corner, and between these, four *shah nishin* (rooms in the form of vaulted niches) opening into a central hall. It was clearly a *hasht bihisht* plan, though he does not use the term.[36]

The ninefold plan was the architectural scheme about which the Mughals thought most intensely, and their solutions rival those of the great 16th-century Italian architects Bramante, Michelangelo and Palladio, who were also interested in this design. In Mughal architecture the *hasht bihisht* made its most spectacular appearance in the tomb of Humayun (1562–71), where four radially planned *hasht bihisht* elements form the corners of the overall structure, which itself follows the ninefold plan [24, 104]. It was built by Sayyid Muhammad, son of Mirak-i Sayyid Ghiyas from Herat and Bukhara;[37] the composition was inspired by a wooden boat palace devised by Humayun himself: his historian, Khwandamir, reports that the floating structure was made of four two-storey pavilions (*chahar taq*) on boats, joined together so that between them four arched elements (*taq*) were produced. These eight *hasht bihisht* units enclosed an octagonal

pool, which in the tomb is replaced by the domed hall in the centre.[38] The idea of generating a larger form out of smaller versions of itself has more to do with Indian conceptions than with Persianate Timurid architectural ideas.[39] In their treatment of the ninefold plan the Mughals showed themselves to be the masters of syncretism, which was characteristic of their approach and which gave their creations a universal appeal. In this way they made an outstanding contribution to a design found widely in world architecture.[40]

Tower pavilions

Elaborate tower pavilions were and still are a characteristic feature of the riverfront of Agra [32, 41]. They have their origin in military architecture, and were adapted to function as garden pavilions by opening out their upper storeys with niches or pillared galleries surrounding an inner octagonal chamber, topped by a *chhatri*. In a characteristic Shahjahani riverfront arrangement the towers accented the beginning of the walls that enclosed a garden on its three landward sides, and framed the open riverfront terrace [55], in the centre of which stood the main garden pavilion. The tops of the towers also provided a beautiful view over the surrounding landscape.

THE GARDEN 'OWNERS' AND THEIR STATUS

Two Mughal customs are significant when we attempt to identify garden creators and owners, and to appreciate the relative status of the gardens. The first is the practice of awarding titles, by which a person became known: thus Ghiyas Beg Tehrani, Jahangir's chief minister and father of his powerful wife Nur Jahan, was given the title I\(^c\)timad-ud-Daula ('Pillar of the Empire'). The second is the

Mughal system's dependence not on aristocratic origin but on merit. The central expression of this meritocracy was the *mansab*, or numerical rank, which defined the status and income of its holder, known as the *mansabdar* ('rankholder').[41] Related to that arrangement was the fact that land property could generally not be inherited.

The *mansabdars* governed the empire and commanded its armies in the emperor's name. The system had been organized by Akbar, who with its help turned a loose military confederation of Muslim nobles into a multi-ethnic bureaucratic empire, integrating Muslims and Hindus. Every office-holder was given upon appointment a *mansab* which indicated in the form of a number his rank, payment, and military and other obligations: thus Akbar gave Muqim Khan (owner of garden no. 40: see the key p. 31) the rank of '700'. From 1595 a *mansab* could be expressed as a pair of ranks, *zat* and *sawar*. The double ranking was fully established under Shah Jahan: thus the emperor's finance minister, Afzal Khan (owner of garden no. 6), had a rank of '7,000 *zat* / 7,000 *sawar*'. The *zat* came to determine the personal pay of the holder, and his comparative status; while the *sawar* determined the size of the contingent of soldiers and horses he had to provide, and the amount of pay sanctioned to cover the cost of their maintenance. By the 17th century the *sawar* remuneration, or part of it, could be doubled by the further specification of *do aspa sih aspa* (two and three horses – abbreviated below as '2–3 horses'). Shah Nawaz Khan (see garden no. 1) had a final rank of 5,000 *zat* / 5,000 *sawar* (2–3 horses), meaning the entire *sawar* figure was doubled, making a total of 10,000; whereas Wazir Khan (see garden no. 7) had a rank of 5,000 *zat* / 5,000 *sawar* (1,000 x 2–3 horses), which means that out of his *sawar* rank of 5,000, 1,000 were doubled, making a total of 6,000. Ranks ranged from as low as 20 to a maximum of 7,000 *zat*. As it has been observed, 'rank inflation set in rapidly',[42] and princes might obtain *mansabs* in the tens of thousands, though they were not expected to field the equivalent number of men and horses. The emperor, or a high-ranking noble acting with his approval, raised or lowered a man's rank on the basis of perceived performance as well as favour at court. Those five or six hundred *mansabdars* who in the mid-17th century held a *zat* rank of at least 1,000 were called *amir*, and constituted the ruling elite.

Mansabdars held major offices at the centre, in the provinces, and in the army.[43] At the centre were the *wakil*, the highest minister at the imperial court but without any department under him, equal to a prime minister; the *diwan* (*diwan-i kul*) or *wazir* (*wazir-i kul*), a minister in charge of imperial finance, land (*jagir*) assignments, and revenue collections, with three principal subordinate *diwans* taking care of the respective departments; the *mir bakhshi*, the official in charge of awarding *mansabs* and checking *mansabdars*' contingents, and controller of intelligence; the *sadr*, an official entrusted with administering revenue and cash grants, and recommending the appointment of judges; and the *mir saman* or *khan saman*, the imperial steward. In the provinces there were the *subadar*, or governor of a province, and the *faujdar*, or officer commanding a military force stationed in one of the administrative divisions of a province, in charge of law and order. Finally, in the army there was the *khan-i khanan*, or commander in chief.

The income of a *mansabdar* was first, under Akbar, paid in cash; later it came from revenues of assigned land, which was ordinarily administered not by the holder but by another noble. *Mansabdars* were controlled by their dependence on salaries, by frequent transfers from one appointment to another, and by the diversion of revenue collection, giving them little opportunity to build up local connections or financial resources with which to raise private armies.

While the system did not depend on aristocratic birth, that made it easier to get into, and ethnic origin played a considerable role. Turanis (Central Asians) and Iranians held the highest ranks, Iranians being especially favoured by Jahangir because of his wife Nur Jahan and her clan. Then followed Afghans, and then Indian Muslims and Rajputs, the latter two forming roughly equal groups.

Mughal nobles were significantly limited in their right to own property and bequeath it to their heirs. They had no base in land and derived power mainly from their rank, determining their military strength, for which they depended entirely on the emperor. As a rule, they were allowed to own land only on a temporary basis: this applied even to members of the imperial family. Information on Mughal escheat law, by which a noble's garden or palace reverted to the crown on his death, has to be pieced together from a few *farmans* (imperial orders) and from those cases considered particularly noteworthy by Mughal historians.[44] Not surprisingly, the system had a certain dampening effect on non-imperial architectural patronage. The point intrigued European observers, who were familiar with a land-based hereditary nobility and saw in the Mughal emperor's claim on private property a sure sign of oriental despotism. Sir Thomas Roe, envoy of James I to the court of Jahangir from 1615 to 1619, remarked that the emperor's 'great men build not for want of inheritance'.[45]

After the death of its 'owner', a garden or a palace would usually be integrated into the imperial estate. If the emperor did not keep it for himself, it would be given to another member of the imperial family, or to another noble, who would then refashion the building and/or the garden. The garden or palace of a Mughal noble had the character of a temporary status symbol; it could thus go through a chain, a *silsila*, of owners. At Agra, the chain for the site of the Haveli of Aurangzeb, part of which is now known as 'Mubarak Manzil' (no. 35: p. 74), can be traced back to the middle of the 16th century.

A tomb seems to have been exempt from these regulations, and thus it became the favourite building type of powerful Muslims (in addition to structures for the common good, such as caravanserais, baths and mosques, with which a patron could make him- or herself a name and assure rewards in the next world). Francisco Pelsaert, senior factor of the Dutch East India Company at Agra from 1621 to 1627, did not fail to notice the peculiarities of the architectural patronage of the Mughal nobles, and informed his readers that 'Here the great lords far surpass ours in magnificence, for their gardens serve for their enjoyment while they are alive, and after death for their tombs, which during their lifetime they build with great magnificence in the middle of the garden.'[46]

In contrast, the Hindu Rajputs who participated in the administration were in a better position than the Muslim nobility: they could usually keep their ancestral lands and raise large palaces on them.[47] The site where Shah Jahan wanted to build the Taj Mahal had been in the possession of the Khachhwaha rajas of Amber – the first Rajput house to cooperate with the Mughals, under Akbar – since Man Singh (d. 1614). Shah Jahan made a point of acquiring the land legally from Man Singh's grandson, Mirza Raja Jai Singh, by giving him in exchange four other mansions from the crown estate at Agra (p. 97).

The riverfront garden city

When Babur took Agra in May 1526 he initiated a remodelling of its urban landscape. For him, as a Timurid, gardens were the preferred type of residence; and since none, or none to his taste, was available at Agra, his first enterprise was to create a garden in the city.[48] Babur deplored the lack of springs and streams which he considered indispensable for such a project, and found it difficult to reconcile himself to the idea of having to make do with a wide, slow-flowing river and its surrounding terrain. He tells us so in his own words:

> One of the great defects of Hindustan being its lack of running waters, it kept coming to my mind that waters should be made to flow by means of wheels [the 'Persian wheel' principle, where water is lifted in buckets attached to wheels that are turned by animals] erected wherever I might settle down, also that ground should be laid out in an orderly and symmetrical way. With this object in view, we crossed the Jun-water [Yamuna] to look at garden grounds a few days after entering Agra. Those grounds were so bad and unattractive that we traversed them with a hundred disgusts and repulsions. So ugly and displeasing were they, that the idea of making a Char-bagh in them passed from my mind, but needs must! As there was no other land near Agra, that same ground was taken in hand a few days later. . . . Khalifa also and Shaikh Zain, Yunas-i ᶜali [his close companions] and whoever got land on that other bank of the river laid out regular and orderly gardens with tanks, made running waters also by setting up wheels . . . The people of Hind who had never seen grounds planned so symmetrically and thus laid out, called the side of the Jun where [our] residences were, Kabul.[49]

Only traces remain of Babur's first garden, the Chahar Bagh or Bagh-i Hasht Bihisht (no. 16: p. 54), which was situated almost opposite the Taj Mahal [27:16]. Babur's choice of the riverfront site introduced a new type of urban planning in Hindustan, and it was also to have a decisive impact on the design of Mughal gardens of the Plains. It led to the creation of the riverfront garden as a module of the riverfront city, a *chahar bagh* with the main buildings on a terrace overlooking the river.[50]

The development of Agra as a riverfront city was taken up again by Akbar. Humayun had chosen Delhi as his residence and planned to built a new city there, a plan abandoned because of his exile in Iran. In 1558 Akbar moved the court back to Agra, and the city grew in size, wealth and power. His historian Abu'l Fazl tells us that 'abodes (*manazil*) were distributed to the grandees' and that 'on either side [of the river] the servants of fortune's threshold [i.e. the court] erected pleasant houses and made charming gardens'.[51] Under Jahangir the riverfront scheme was fully developed.[52] In the 1620s Pelsaert observed that 'The breadth of the city is by no means so great as the length, because everyone has tried to be close to the riverbank, and consequently the waterfront is occupied by the costly

25 A nobleman is entertained by musicians in an airy pavilion beside the river. Visible across the water, dotted with boats, is a sequence of riverfront gardens. Detail of a Mughal or Deccani painting, late 17th century.

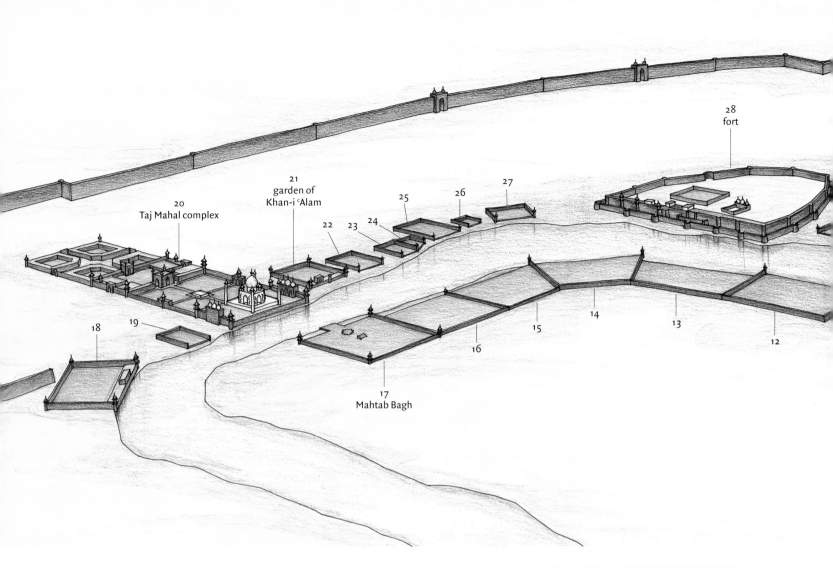

palaces of all the famous lords, which make it appear very gay and magnificent [17, 25–27].'[53] In his eyes, 'the luxuriance of the groves all round makes it resemble a royal park rather than a city'; he found it noteworthy that there were no building restrictions, 'and everyone acquired and purchased the plot of land which suited or pleased him best'. He lists thirty-three gardens with their names – about a third of them created or remodelled during Jahangir's reign.

The earliest surviving Mughal riverfront garden that can be securely identified and dated belongs to Jahangir's time. Now known as the Ram Bagh, it was built, or rebuilt, by the emperor's wife Nur Jahan as the Nur Afshan garden in 1621 (no. 3) [33–36]. The garden follows the waterfront design in an informal arrangement: instead of a single solid terrace extending along the entire riverfront, as in the later Shahjahani examples, there are terraced parts which contain subterranean rooms and support the main pavilions. The tomb garden of I^ctimad-ud-Daula (no. 9) also dates from this period. Here a classic *chahar bagh* layout was employed, with the *hasht bihisht* pavilion for the tomb in the centre [57, 59]. This was the plan of all Mughal funerary gardens in a riverfront context until the Taj Mahal.

That the centrally planned *chahar bagh* was still used, as well as the additive *chahar bagh* plus terrace, for residential gardens along the riverbank, at least up to Shah Jahan's time, can be gathered from Peter Mundy of the East India Company. A reliable eyewitness, who was at Agra in 1632–33, he writes that 'the better sort' of gardens had an enclosing wall with at the corners four towers with domes

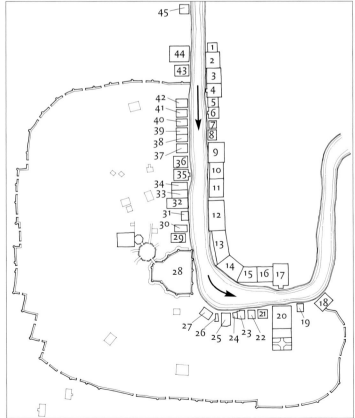

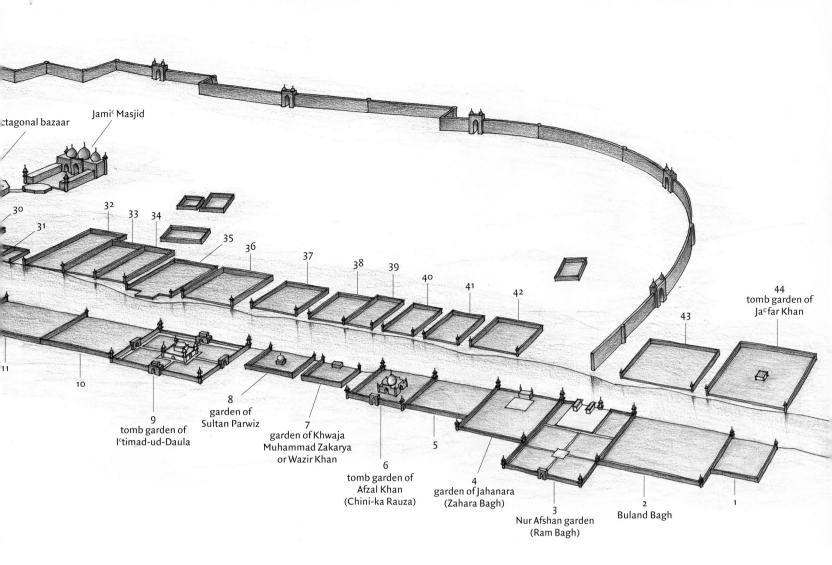

ctagonal bazaar   Jamiᶜ Masjid

30
31
32
33 34
35
36
37
38 39
40
41
42
43
44
tomb garden of
Jaᶜfar Khan

11
10
9
tomb garden of
Iᶜtimad-ud-Daula

8
garden of
Sultan Parwiz

7
garden of Khwaja
Muhammad Zakarya
or Wazir Khan

6
tomb garden of
Afzal Khan
(Chini-ka Rauza)

5

4
garden of Jahanara
(Zahara Bagh)

3
Nur Afshan garden
(Ram Bagh)

2
Buland Bagh

1

26 *above* Perspective reconstruction of the scheme of riverfront Agra, based on the Jaipur map [17, 27]: as there, the gardens north of the fort are shown slightly too far north, so that they get out of step with the gardens on the left bank. Named sites are preserved to a greater or lesser extent. The Jamiᶜ Masjid is shown as it appears today, without its east wing, which was taken down after the Uprising of 1858.

27 *opposite* The riverfront gardens as named on the Jaipur map (with corrected spelling).

ON THE LEFT BANK

1   Bagh-i Shah Nawaz Khan
2   Buland Bagh (High Garden)
3   Bagh-i Nur Afshan (now Ram Bagh)
4   Bagh-i Jahanara (now Zahara, Zehra, or Zahra Bagh)
5   Un-named garden
6   Rauza of Afzal Khan (tomb garden of Afzal Khan; now Chini-ka Rauza)
7   Bagh-i Khwaja [Muhammad] Zakarya (probably Bagh-i Wazir Khan)
8   Bagh-i Sultan Parwiz
9   Maqbara of Iᶜtimad-ud-Daula (tomb garden of Iᶜtimad-ud-Daula)
10 Bagh-i Musawi Khan Sadr
11 Bagh Padshahi (Imperial Garden)
12 Moti Bagh Padshahi (Imperial Pearl Garden)
13 [Bagh] Padshahi (Imperial Garden)
14 Lal Bagh Padshahi (Red Imperial Garden)
15 Second Chahar Bagh Padshahi (Imperial Chahar Bagh)
16 Chahar Bagh Padshahi (Imperial Chahar Bagh: Babur's first garden at Agra, in Mughal times called Chahar Bagh or Bagh-i Hasht Bihisht)
17 Bagh-i Mahtab Padshahi (Imperial Moonlight Garden; now Mahtab Bagh)

ON THE RIGHT BANK

18 Haveli of Khan-i Dauran
19 Haveli of Agah Khan
20 Rauza of Shah Jahan (tomb garden of Shah Jahan, i.e. TAJ MAHAL)
21 Bagh-i Khan-i ᶜAlam
22 Haveli of Asalat Khan
23 Haveli of Mahabat Khan
24 Haveli of Hoshdar Khan
25 Haveli of Aᶜzam Khan
26 Haveli of Mughal Khan
27 Haveli of Islam Khan
28 Padshahi Qilᶜa (Agra fort)
29 Haveli of Dara Shikoh
30 Haveli of Khan-i Jahan Lodi
31 Haveli of Hafiz Khidmatgar (two enclosures)
32 Haveli of Asaf Khan
33 Haveli of ᶜAlamgir
34 Haveli of ᶜAlamgir
35 Masjid Mubarak Manzil
36 Haveli of Sasat (Shayista) Khan
37 Haveli of Jaᶜfar Khan
38 Rauza of Sasat Khan (tomb garden of Shayista Khan)
39 Haveli of Wazir Khan
40 Haveli of Muqim Khan
41 Haveli of Khalil Khan
42 Bagh-i Rai Shiv Das
43 Bagh-i Hakim Kazim ᶜAli
44 Rauza of Jaᶜfar Khan (tomb garden of Jaᶜfar Khan)
[45 Chhatri (memorial pavilion) of Jaswant Singh – beyond the end of the map]

and galleries, between one and four gates, and long walks lined by cypresses leading 'commonly . . . towards the midle . . . where is the cheife howse of pleasure and Tancke . . . This square Garden is againe divided into other lesser squares, and that into other like bedds and plotts.'[54]

Shah Jahan, after his accession, changed the name of Agra 'which had no sense and meaning' to Akbarabad, 'the city of Akbar', in honour of his grandfather. His historians describe it as one of the great cities of the world, as the new Mughal seat of the caliphate, surpassing the old Baghdad of the ʿAbbasid caliphs in size, beautiful buildings, and cosmopolitan population. Every rarity of the world could be found in its bazaars, and it was a haven for nobles, learned men, artisans and craftsmen. The river with its pure water formed the main artery of the city, which had a circumference of about 40 km (c. 25 miles).[55] On the right (west) bank were the fort, the mansions (manzil) of the princes, and the residences (haveli) of the nobles. Inland were the houses of the majority of the population, which in contrast to those of the elite were several storeys high. On the left bank were the magnificent imperial gardens (bagh) with delightful buildings (ʿimarat) set among trees and flowers (bustan), and also a few non-imperial residences.[56]

In Shah Jahan's reign the garden with buildings on a riverfront terrace became the more widely used residential form. The artist of the earliest known map of Agra, made in the 1720s for the Maharaja of Jaipur [17], considered it so characteristic of the urban landscape of Mughal Agra that he even showed centrally planned chahar baghs in this way, such as the tomb garden of Iʿtimad-ud-Daula (no. 9) [30]. The impression that Agra made on contemporaries is put in flowery words by Shah Jahan's historian Muhammad Salih Kanbo:

> On either side of that sea full of pleasantness [the Yamuna], buildings and gardens (ʿimarat-ha wa bagh-ha) of paradisiacal space are placed together in such a handsome close way that from the charming entertainment of each of them the sight of the beholder gathers the flowers of bounty of the month of Urdi Bihisht [spring]. Because of the riverfront buildings and the flower gardens in front [on the landward side], it appears that garden is linked to garden and garden plot (chaman) to garden plot, [and thus] the desire to stroll in the garden of Paradise is completely erased from the page of memory . . . In particular, the spacious buildings (ʿimarat-i waziʿ) and wonderful pavilions (nashiman-ha-yi badiʿ) of the princes of exalted origin and other famous amirs . . . give a display of the garden of Rizwan [the gate-keeper of Paradise] and the palaces of the garden of Paradise.[57]

The garden character of Agra also impressed the French physician François Bernier, one of the best observers of the Mughal court, who was in the city in 1659: he found that though it did not have the uniform and wide streets of Shah Jahan's new city of Shahjahanabad at Delhi, it made up for that because of its 'luxuriant and green foliage . . . Such a landscape yields peculiar pleasure in a hot and parched country, where the eye seeks in verdure for refreshment and repose.'[58] Another Frenchman, Jean de Thévenot, who visited India in 1666–67, recorded his impression of the riverfront city:

> This Palace [Agra fort] is accompanied with five and twenty or thirty very large [palaces], all in a line, which belong to the

Princes and other great Lords of Court; and all together afford a most delightful prospect to those who are on the other side of the River, which would be a great deal more agreeable, were it not for the long Garden-walls, which contribute much to the rendering the Town so long as it is [cf. 17, 55]. There are upon the same line several less Palaces and other Buildings. All being desirous to enjoy the lovely prospect and convenience of the Water of the Gemna [Yamuna], endeavoured to purchase ground on that side, which is the cause that the Town is very long but narrow, and excepting some fair Streets that are in it, all the rest are very narrow, and without Symmetry.[59]

Comparable waterfront schemes were developed in the capitals of the other two great Muslim empires: in Ottoman Istanbul royal and non-royal suburban garden villas lined the Bosphorus, and in 17th-century Safavid Isfahan garden residences were built on the banks of the Zayanda river. However, the layout at Agra differs from these more informal arrangements in its tight, systematic, and uniform planning, in which we recognize a distinctive Mughal logic. The scheme of Agra remained unique, however: it was only realized to a limited extent at the other great Mughal capital, Lahore; and at Delhi the waterfront scheme was severely restricted (p. 24).

Mughal Agra is also different because the riverfront development was the nucleus of the city: the remaining urban fabric was tucked away inland to the west. This has not been recognized by previous writers, who regarded the right bank as part of the city, and the left bank as suburbia.[60] The riverfront had been the intended site for a Jamiʿ Masjid, or congregational mosque, and foundations had been laid; the new project for the Taj Mahal took precedence,[61] and eventually the mosque was built on a different site: perhaps it was felt that an isolated religious structure would not fit into the scheme of residential gardens, or perhaps the mosque which forms part of the riverfront group of the Taj Mahal was to remain without competition. Shah Jahan did undertake initiatives to develop Agra inland. The Jamiʿ Masjid was now to be built west of the fort, and in 1637 he ordered the construction of a bazaar in the form of a large irregular octagon, as an organizing link between fort and mosque [17, 26]. The piazza enclosed by the bazaar wings (all now lost) was to serve as a jilaukhana or assembly square for the court: at a time of greater concern for ceremony, the absence of such a space had been criticized as a shortcoming of the Agra palace, and eventually served as one of the official reasons for the establishment of the new city at Delhi.[62] To widen the streets leading to the mosque, finally built in 1643–48 by Shah Jahan's daughter Jahanara, a great number of houses were demolished.[63] But even after the project was completed, the emphasis of the city remained on the riverfront. Observers like Thévenot found nothing noteworthy to report beyond it.

Abu Talib Kalim, Shah Jahan's court poet (p. 13), composed two eulogies on Agra. One is integrated in his verse history of Shah Jahan, one of several Padshahnamas written for the emperor. The other is a long poem which forms part of his Diwan, or collected works. The poet focuses on the attractions of the topography of the waterfront city, singling out the emperor's great fortress palace (no. 28) and the garden of Jahanara (no. 4), but also taking extensive note of the charming traders in the bazaars (see p. 201).

In response to the garden character of the city, in his *Padshahnama* Kalim introduces his verses metaphorically as flowers.

The flower of the description of Agra of the gardens
has blossomed from the branches of my speech.

Don't call it Agra – it is a world of peace and safety;
in each of its corners is a Cairo and a Damascus.

A world has been placed in the city:
who sees Agra has seen the world.

Strangers are [here] freed from the memory of their countries,
and are happy and cheerful like flowers in a garden.

Its atmosphere is so clear and free from dust
that one can see the scent of the flowers.

To the princes of the dignity of the sky,
to the pillars [i.e. nobles] of this solidly based kingdom

Belong the high buildings facing the water,
and their excellence causes the water to form whirls [of envy].

The heart-attracting buildings lie on both sides [of the river]:
like the face and the mirror they are opposite each other.

The buildings are so lovely
that the river does not want to pass by.

On each house several *lakh* [100,000 rupees] have been spent.
All face the water and raise their heads to the sky.

If you travel at leisure by boat on the river
on each side you will be met by the spectacle of buildings.

Like choice verses of heavenly dignity,
they are all cypresses lining the avenue of the water (*khiyaban-i ab*).

They are adorned like a beloved one;
they have raised themselves to capture the heart of the sky.[64]

DECLINE

Agra began to decline when in 1648 Shah Jahan moved his court to Shahjahanabad at Delhi, which took over the title Dar al-Khilafa, 'Seat of the Caliphate': Agra was left as '[Settled] Abode of the Caliphate'.[65] The neglect of the city by the ruling elite increased when Shah Jahan was imprisoned in the fort here by his son Aurangzeb until he died in 1666 (p. 101). The garden residences were no longer repossessed by the crown after the death of their owners; or, if they went to the crown or to somebody else, they generally kept the name of their last Shahjahani owner, several of whom also served under Aurangzeb. A number of garden residences were converted into funerary sites, and this, together with the dominant mausoleum complex of the Taj Mahal, gave the riverfront a funerary character. Yet in the 1690s Sujan Rai, a Hindu *munshi* (secretary or writer), in his description of Hindustan still points out the riverfront buildings as the foremost attraction of Agra, besides its population from all parts of the world and its flourishing trade, especially in textiles embroidered with gold and silver.[66]

Gradually the riverfront city was taken over by the ordinary inhabitants of Agra. This led to the development of a remarkable swimming culture, in which people from all walks of life participated, young and old, rich and poor. The waters of the Yamuna were higher than now, and clean. The entertainment culminated in an annual swimming festival, the Triveni, held by both Muslims and and Hindus: the former celebrated Khwaja Khizr (a legendary Sufi saint connected with water, renewal of life and vegetation) and the latter Krishna.[67] Sil Chand in the early 19th century (see p. 34) gives an account of the 'Tirbaini Mela', which took place from July to September in the rainy season: every Thursday a great number of people gathered in and around the Rauza or tomb of Ja'far Khan (no. 44); at the climax of the festival the master swimmers and their disciples stayed there all night, swam, danced, ate, and gave food to the Brahmins. Swimmers put paper lions and other figures on the water, and also a figure of Khwaja Khizr. The Hindus made an image of Kanhaiya Lal Jiu, a form of Krishna, and filled it with gunpowder which they set afire. The spectacle was watched by huge crowds on both banks of the river, and people also came in boats to see it.[68] The festival features in a highly original poem by Nazir Akbarabadi, who had come to Agra from Delhi in 1758. Though a Muslim, he had strong leanings towards the Krishna cult. His poem is remarkable not only for its subject but also for its detailed realistic observation.[69]

. . . O friends, from the waterfall up to the basin of Sajja,
    from the Chhatri [?of Jaswant Singh, no. 45] to Burj-i-Khuni
    [89] and up to the Chontra (platform) of Dara [Shikoh [91]]
    they swim.
Mahtab Bagh [66], Sayyid Taili [no. 4?], the fort [82] and
    the mausoleum [74] [are the places] where merriment
    is at its height and the crowds throng noisily together.
They swim at each of these places, taking care.
O friend, in this Agra all sorts of people swim.

In the Bagh-i Hakim [no. 43] and the garden (*chaman*) of
    Shiv Das [no. 42] people gather in different places.
There they eat sweetmeats and thoroughly enjoy dancing.
Some like to swim, while others make merry.
They swim at each of these places, taking care.
O friend, in this Agra all sorts of people swim. . . .

What merriment is there not at Tirbaini (Triveni) when the
    swimming comes to its peak!
There the crowds throng to that place, swimmers in many rows.
There they swim, dip, jump, quarrel, and shout at each other.
    Many dive without splashing and enjoy the sport.
There numerous amusements are displayed in swimming.
O friend, in this Agra all sorts of people swim. . . .

After the British takeover in 1803 the people still celebrated Triveni, but the gardens continued to disintegrate. Eventually the British became, though with good intentions, instrumental in the destruction of large parts of the riverfront scheme (p. 60). In the 20th century the original urban landscape of Mughal Agra was largely forgotten, and absorbed by the ever-expanding city. The water level of the Yamuna was reduced by dams built upstream, to draw water for irrigation, and what remains is heavily polluted by untreated sewage and industrial wastes.[70] The river's edge, once the most privileged site, is used as a latrine, for garbage, and for the illicit entertainment of gambling.

RECONSTRUCTION OF THE RIVERFRONT SCHEME

Today only a few gardens of Mughal Agra remain. Most stand isolated from each other, and have lost their original urban context. Apart from a few exceptions they are largely ruined: depending on their situation, they are used for cultivation or built in and over by later structures of the encroaching city. With the help of Mughal and European records and a map in the Jaipur Palace Museum, however, it is possible to reconstruct the original scheme, to visualize the individual gardens, and to populate them with their owners.

The Jaipur map came about after Maharaja Sawai Jai Singh of Jaipur had been appointed governor of the Agra province in 1722 by the Mughal emperor Muhammad Shah; he in turn appointed as his deputy Rai Shivadasa (see no. 42).[71] The maharaja was then planning and building his own new city at Jaipur,[72] and, obviously for comparative study, he instructed Rai Shivadasa to prepare a map of the old capital of the Mughal empire and plans of prominent buildings.

The chief result, a large map on cloth, gives an image of Agra much as it had been under Shah Jahan [17, 27, 30].[73] The gardens and buildings are shown in schematic form. Their names are given in Devanagari script, often with corrupted spellings. The river enters Agra from the north. For the residential gardens on the left bank, opposite the modern city, the Persian word *bagh* is used; for those on the right bank, the term employed is the Arabic *haveli* (which came to replace the term *manzil*, used up to the time of Shah Jahan for these non-imperial residences). A *haveli* was a building type with one or more enclosed courtyards, and thus a more substantial construction than a *bagh*, where individual pavilions were set into a garden; but the riverfront *havelis* of Agra followed the general design in that the main structure overlooked the Yamuna. The Arabic words *rauza* (garden) and *maqbara* (tomb) are employed for tombs in a garden; in India the word *rauza* is used for tombs of persons of standing or of Sufi mystics.

Most of the gardens bear the names of members of the imperial family and of the highest ranking *amirs* of Jahangir and Shah Jahan. The left bank was occupied with a few exceptions by gardens of the emperor and the imperial women; a few *baghs* on the left bank and the *havelis* or *manzils* on the right bank served as residences of the princes and nobles when the court was in the city.

The only significant problem with using the Jaipur map to reconstruct the garden sites is that the right-bank gardens north of the fort are shown slightly too far north, so that they get out of step with the gardens on the left bank (see e.g. no. 39: p. 76).

In the early 19th century, a hundred years after the Jaipur map, many of the gardens were still known under the same designations. This is evident from accounts of the buildings of Agra written at the request of British administrators. An important source is Sil Chand's *Tafrih al-ʿimarat* (Delectation of buildings) or *ʿAhwal-i ʿimarat-i mustaqir al-khilafa* (Account of the buildings of the Abode of the Caliphate), composed in 1825–26 for James Stephen Lushington, Acting Collector and Magistrate at Agra.[74] It was copied again in 1836–37 for James Stephenson, Sessions Judge, Agra.[75] Both manuscripts were written in Persian, the administrative language of the Mughal empire, which continued to be used in the early British period. Sil Chand felt bound to produce traditional eulogistic descriptions, but at the same time he attempted to integrate into his flowery metaphors factual information which his patron sought about history, topography, horticulture and architecture. His listing of gardens follows the order of the Jaipur map quite closely.

Another account followed in mid-century, that of Raja Ram, a *tahsildar* (revenue collector) of Kirauli in the district of Agra, who wrote his *Tamirat-i Agra* (The monuments of Agra) 'a few years before the Mutiny' (1857–58) at the suggestion of John Russell Colvin, Lieutenant-Governor of the North-Western Provinces. It is composed in even more flowery idiom, and lists the gardens and *havelis* in a haphazard manner.[76]

A map of Agra prepared by the British administration in 1868–69 [28] shows the progressive disintegration of the riverfront scheme.[77] The outlines of most of the gardens are indicated, but only five are now designated as such. On the left bank are 'Chini's Raoza' (the tomb garden of Afzal Khan, or Chini-ka Rauza, no. 6), 'Jagannath's Bagh' (the garden of Khwaja Muhammad Zakarya or of Wazir Khan, no. 7), and 'Itmad Dowla Sarai' (the tomb garden of Iʿtimad-ud-Daula, no. 9). On the right bank are 'Jatni's Bagh' (unidentified)[78] and 'Hakimji's Bagh' (the garden of Hakim Kazim ʿAli, no. 43). In 1871–72 the Archaeological Survey of India report contained an account of Agra (minus the Taj Mahal) by the archaeologist A. C. L. Carlleyle. The first monograph on Agra was published by Sayyid Muhammad Latif in 1892; it also contains references to the riverfront gardens.

Contemporary comments on the gardens can also be found in the notes and reports of foreigners, some of whom we have already met. They include Sir Thomas Roe, James I's envoy at the Mughal court from 1615 to 1619; Francisco Pelsaert, with the Dutch East India Company at Agra from 1621 to 1627; the Flemish geographer Joannes De Laet, who was for some time a Director of the Dutch East India Company and published his compilation of accounts of Mughal India in 1631; and Peter Mundy, an agent of the English East India Company in Agra in 1632–33. A later account accompanied by images of some of the gardens is the *Notebook* of Florentia, Lady Sale (p. 240), who described the sights of Agra in 1832–33 and included drawings by Indian artists. The first photographic record is that of Dr John Murray in the early 1850s (p. 243).

I began surveying what is left of the riverfront gardens [29] in 1978. Their measurements were mostly taken in 2000–2003 (where known, these will be found in the Notes).

The gardens of the left bank

The left bank of the Yamuna, opposite the city, preserves the character of the original garden character of Mughal Agra to a greater extent than the right bank. This is where Babur and his followers founded their first gardens. The stretch between the gardens of Shah Nawaz Khan (no. 1) and of Iʿtimad-ud-Daula (no. 9) can still show some surviving Mughal gardens [31, 33, 55], as well as commercial nurseries. The following stretch, after the bend of the river, is occupied by agricultural fields, up to the Mahtab Bagh (no. 17) [66], opposite the Taj Mahal; at the edge of the river and within the planted areas remains of the old Mughal gardens can be traced. The Mughal chronicles only describe imperial gardens of note.

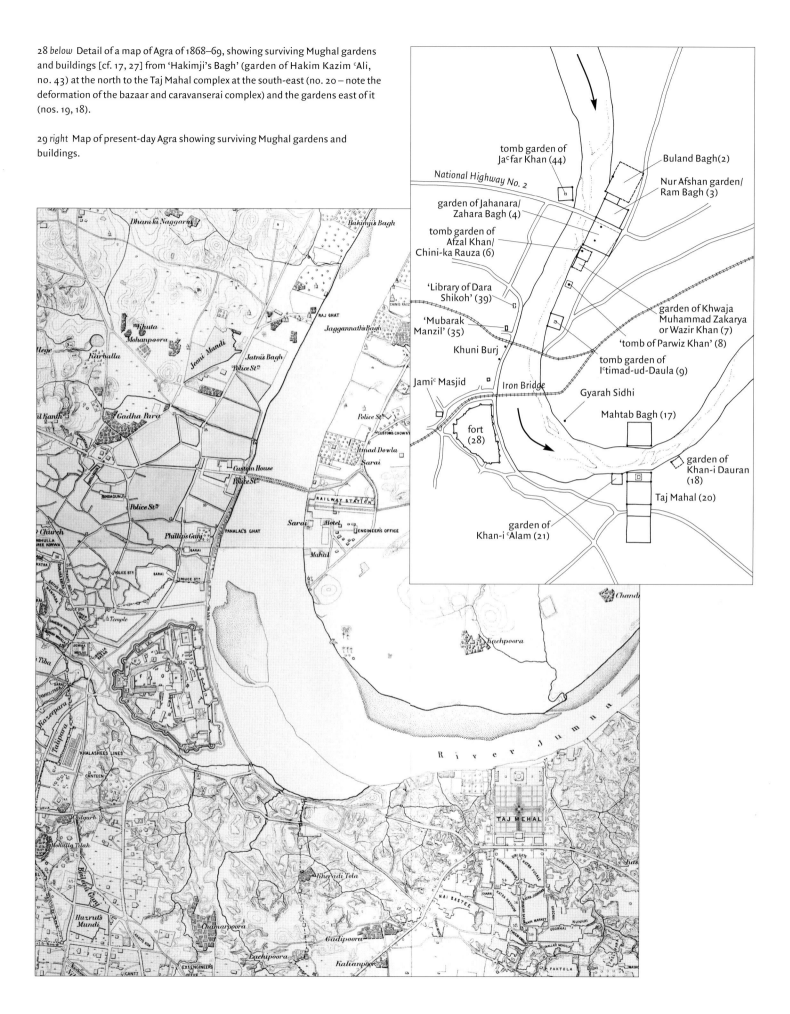

28 *below* Detail of a map of Agra of 1868–69, showing surviving Mughal gardens and buildings [cf. 17, 27] from 'Hakimji's Bagh' (garden of Hakim Kazim ʿAli, no. 43) at the north to the Taj Mahal complex at the south-east (no. 20 – note the deformation of the bazaar and caravanserai complex) and the gardens east of it (nos. 19, 18).

29 *right* Map of present-day Agra showing surviving Mughal gardens and buildings.

tomb garden of
Jaʿfar Khan (44)

National Highway No. 2

garden of Jahanara/
Zahara Bagh (4)

tomb garden of
Afzal Khan/
Chini-ka Rauza (6)

'Library of Dara
Shikoh' (39)

'Mubarak
Manzil' (35)

Khuni Burj

Jamiʿ Masjid

fort
(28)

garden of
Khan-i ʿAlam (21)

Buland Bagh (2)

Nur Afshan garden/
Ram Bagh (3)

garden of Khwaja
Muhammad Zakarya
or Wazir Khan (7)

'tomb of Parwiz Khan' (8)

tomb garden of
Iʿtimad-ud-Daula (9)

Iron Bridge

Gyarah Sidhi

Mahtab Bagh (17)

garden of
Khan-i Dauran
(18)

Taj Mahal (20)

30 *below* Detail of the Jaipur map of Agra, showing the twelve northernmost gardens on the left bank of the Yamuna. From left to right, they are the garden of Shah Nawaz Khan (no. 1), Buland Bagh (no. 2), Nur Afshan garden/Ram Bagh (no. 3), garden of Jahanara/Zahara Bagh (no. 4), an un-named garden (no. 5), tomb garden of Afzal Khan or Chini-ka Rauza (no.6), garden of Khwaja Muhammad Zakarya or of Wazir Khan (no. 7), garden of Sultan Parwiz (no. 8), tomb garden of Iᶜtimad-ud-Daula (no. 9), garden of Musawi Khan Sadr (no. 10), Bagh Padshahi or Imperial Garden (no. 11), and Moti Bagh Padshahi (no. 12).

31 *bottom* Part of the same stretch of the left bank of the Yamuna, seen obliquely from the south-west across the river. In the foreground are the two riverfront towers of the garden of Khwaja Muhammad Zakarya or Wazir Khan (no. 7), and between them the ruined pavilion. Behind the pavilion is an anonymous tomb known as the Kala Gunbad. Beyond that rises the large tomb of Afzal Khan or Chini-ka Rauza (no.6); its fragmentary northern riverfront tower appears farther to the left. Just to the left of that is the tall southern riverfront tower of the garden of Jahanara/Zahara Bagh [41]. (Photograph taken in 1986)

The gardens and mansions of the princes and the nobility are merely mentioned in passing, on the occasion of an imperial visit, a wedding, when a property changed hands, or when a new building had been completed. An exception is the garden of Shah Jahan's daughter Jahanara (no. 4), which is eulogistically described by Kalim.

1 Bagh-i Shah Nawaz Khan (garden of Shah Nawaz Khan)
not preserved

Mirza Badi^c-uz-Zaman, with the title Shah Nawaz Khan Safavi [2:19], was a high-ranking noble in Shah Jahan's service and a relative of the shahs of Iran. At the end of the emperor's reign he held the high *mansab* of 5,000 *zat* / 5,000 *sawar* (3,000 x 2–3 horses).[79] (As explained above, p. 28, these figures indicate the relative ranks of the garden owners.) He was closely connected to the imperial family: one of his daughters was married to Shah Jahan's son Aurangzeb in 1637, and fifteen years later another of his daughters was married to the emperor's youngest son, Murad Bakhsh. The wedding of Aurangzeb took place here, in Shah Nawaz Khan's garden palace; Shah Jahan came to the ceremony by boat from the fort (no. 28) across the river.[80] The site of the garden is now wasteland and no trace of the original remains.[81]

Florentia Sale includes in her *Notebook* (1832–33) two views of a building, one labelled 'Huwalee Shah Wuz Khan', the other 'Howalie Shah Woz Khan'. The name is a corruption of Shah Nawaz Khan; but is is not certain whether she means this garden, because a Mughal noble might have had a *haveli* in the city as well.

2 Buland Bagh (High Garden) *partly preserved*

The garden is attributed by tradition to Buland Khan, or Sarbuland Khan, an otherwise unknown *khwajasara* or eunuch of Jahangir. It serves today as a nursery and is largely ruined, but it retains a high tower known as Battis Khamba [32]. This is unusual in being set in the middle of the riverfront, where one would expect the main garden pavilion. A similar tower appears in a river view which probably shows Agra, in the background of a late 17th-century painting [25]. As the main garden building, the Battis Khamba was given a distinctive, elaborate four-storeyed form, of an experimental type characteristic of the architecture of Jahangir. The large pavilion tower was flanked by smaller towers at either end of the garden's river frontage, of which only the southern one remains.[82]

2a Utilitarian complex *preserved but ruinous* [83]

An oblong architectural complex is still discernible here, but is not designated on the Jaipur map. It consisted of an open street flanked on both sides by rows of squarish cells (*hujra*) preceded by an arcaded verandah. On the east and west sides are gates. This type of complex was used for bazaars, and in this function it must have served the adjoining gardens. In 1923 it was being used as a cattleyard.[84]

3 Bagh-i Nur Afshan (Light-Scattering Garden), now Ram Bagh, previously also Aram Bagh *preserved* [85]

This garden features as Bagh-i Nur Afshan on the Jaipur map [17] (in Hindi spelling, 'bag nur apasa') and in most of the 19th-century descriptions of Agra.[86] It is now known as Ram Bagh, but I am advocating the use of its original name.[87] The component 'Nur' (light) is typical of foundations of Jahangir and his queen; it alludes,

32 Battis Khamba tower in the Buland Bagh, first quarter of the 17th century. (Photograph taken in 2001)

as he tells us in his autobiography, to his honorific title Nur-ud-Din ('Light of Religion') and to the title he gave his wife, Nur Jahan ('Light of the World').[88] Jahangir says that the garden belonged to Nur Jahan and that it was used by the imperial family. He mentions several visits to it: it was where, in early March 1621, he awaited the auspicious hour designated by the astrologers for his victorious entry into the Agra fort after his conquest of the fort of Kangra, and where, later in the month, Nur Jahan arranged the celebrations of the Persian New Year (Nauruz).[89] The pavilions can be identified as the settings of two paintings of the 1620s [5].[90]

The architecture clearly dates from Jahangir's time and testifies to the patronage of Nur Jahan as an outstanding garden builder (her other creation at Agra is the tomb of I^ctimad-ud-Daula (no. 9), where her parents are buried).

The Nur Afshan garden is the earliest surviving Mughal garden of Agra, and it may have been laid out on the foundations of an even

older garden, built by Babur. It displays the earliest example of a scheme focused on the water, with a terraced area lining the river and a garden on the landward side [33, 34], although the configuration does not yet have the strictly planned symmetrical form of the later Shahjahani examples [e.g. 39, 48, 67]. No detailed documentation has ever been published on it. Sketch plans of the general layout go back to a British map of 1923–24 indicating its planting with fruit trees.[91] I prepared a plan of its pavilions in 1986.[92]

In the middle of the landward side is the main gate, which was rebuilt in the British period. From this a central walkway leads towards the terraced area at the riverfront. The walkway is accented by platforms, which, where fully preserved, show on both sides water chutes with a fish-scale (mahi pusht) pattern, flanked by steps. The third platform from the gate marks the beginning of the riverfront area, which is also signalled by two towers in the enclosing wall. This part is quite complex, because the uneven terrain is here levelled out

by a rectangular system of intersecting walkways of brick masonry. At the river end these are raised to form a rectangular grid, three units wide (parallel to the river) and two units deep, which crosses sunken sections that vary in depth from 2.5–2.7 m (8 ft 3 in.–8 ft 11 in.) on the garden side to 0.4–2 m (1 ft 4 in.–6 ft 7 in.) near the river. The walkways contain water channels, and at the points of intersection there are square platforms. The outer platforms of the raised 3 x 2 unit grid have steps leading down into the garden, again cut through by a water chute with a fish-scale pattern [35]. On one of these platforms a chhatri is set. In line with it, facing the river, a solid platform runs across two quadrants of the grid, and here the main garden buildings stand. This placement intensifies the south-centred, asymmetrical arrangement of the garden.

The garden buildings consist of two narrow rectangular pavilions set end-on to the river, forming an open court with a sunken pool between them [36, 38]. Below is a large tahkhana or underground

Nur Afshan garden/Ram Bagh, completed before 1621

33 *above* The garden seen from the bridge of the bypass of National Highway No. 2. (Photograph taken in 2002)

34 *below* Plan before restoration. The six squares at the bottom comprise the terraced area, reached by steps. The court and pavilions are right of centre; the large *tahkhana* is below the left-hand riverfront square.
• *Unless otherwise indicated, in all plans of gardens the riverfront is at the bottom.*

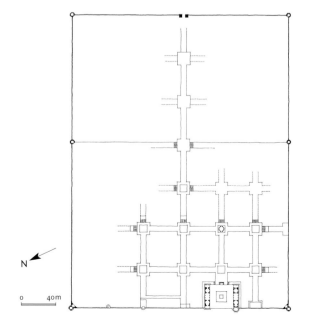

chamber for the hot summer months; its vaults show traces of a net pattern (*qalib kari*), a form characteristic of Jahangir's architecture, and, in a less deeply moulded form, also of Shah Jahan's [cf. 183]. To the north is another platform, below which is a much larger *tahkhana*. Among the rooms here is a *hammam* or baths, composed of the usual three units: disrobing chamber, hot room, and cold room; other rooms include a large hall with pools and a waterfall, covered by a *bangla* vault – a rectangular vault with 'downdrawn' corners derived from Bengali roofs. Where the decoration of the vaults is preserved, it shows patterns similar to those in the southern *tahkhana*.

At the riverfront are wells which provided water for the garden. The ends of the terrace are accentuated with towers topped by *chhatris* [33], each containing a vaulted chamber on the ground floor.

The two main pavilions on the terrace consist of open verandahs alternating with enclosed rooms (*hujra*) [36]. Their rectangular design, until then unusual for Mughal garden pavilions, clearly comes from the wings of *zanana* enclosures in palaces: wings with a similar sequence of rooms were built in the Agra fort around the garden of the women's palace, now called 'Anguri Bagh' [85]. Perhaps these forms were deliberately taken from the palace and used for independent buildings to make a statement of female architecture in the context of a garden used by the imperial women.

The pillars of the verandahs have faceted shafts and capitals built up of small arched elements known as *muqarnas*, a columnar form which was to become predominant in Shah Jahan's architecture (it is used extensively in the subsidiary structures of the Taj Mahal [e.g. 157]). They support elaborate brackets in the shape of peacocks. Islam prohibits the depiction of living beings, but the prohibition was often ignored, especially in the informal and private setting of

35 Water chute with a fish-scale (*mahi pusht*) pattern, set between steps on the northern side of the terraced area. (Photograph taken in 2002)

36 *below* The northern pavilion, seen from the south. (Photograph taken in 1981)

throne.[93] The emperor and his wife, the builder of the garden, were thus celebrated as a second Solomon and a second Queen of Sheba. While the Solomon of the Qur'an was a role model for all Muslim rulers, the Mughals created distinctive Solomonic settings in their architecture and art. In Jahangiri interpretations, the Persianate iconography takes on an idiosyncratic character: here, for instance, several of the winged creatures appear as women of a Mughal–Rajput type, in Indian dress of *choli* (blouse), *ghagra* (skirt) and *dopatta* (veil), evoking female retainers at the court. The detailed depiction of the varied species of birds reflects Jahangir's interest in natural history.

The Nur Afshan garden was one of the sites taken over by the British after the conquest of Agra in 1803. When Lord Hastings, Governor-General of Bengal, visited the city in 1815, the garden was 'in the possession of Government': he mentions that it was 'put to national use of raising a quantity of forest or fruit trees [mostly oranges], which are delivered gratis to any of the zemindars [landowners] who apply for them'. He comments that the channels sunk in the grid of raised walkways were in working order and distributed water raised from the Yamuna by means of Persian wheels to the different parts of the garden.[94]

In the 19th century the pavilions were walled up and provided with an upper storey to serve as a place of retreat and recreation for the European residents of Agra, favoured by British honeymooners [38].[95] The American journalist Bayard Taylor, who visited Agra in 1853 (p. 246), noted that when demand was pressing no one was allowed to stay more than eight days, to give a chance to others.[96] In the early 20th century the southern pavilion was allotted to Indians and the northern one to Europeans.

The pavilions were returned to their original form in the 1920s,[97] and the paintings, which had been covered with lime plaster, were restored in a campaign starting in 1975.[98] The garden continues to be cared for by the Archaeological Survey of India: together with the tomb of I'timad-ud-Daula and the Taj Mahal, it is one of the most intensively restored in the city. The present campaign focuses on the riverfront terrace and the main walkway. The original garden area has not been reconstructed.

the women's quarters. Paintings on the walls and intricately patterned plaster vaults in both pavilions also included animals, human figures, winged beings and birds. Such decoration is found in most Jahangiri buildings, but this is the only surviving example at Agra. The birds, angels (partly after European models) and *paris* (fairies) on the vaults [37] are a favourite Jahangiri motif, alluding to Solomon's winged subjects who form a living canopy over his

Nur Afshan garden/Ram Bagh

37 *above* A winged *pari* holding a peacock, painted in the springing of an arch in the western *hujra* of the northern pavilion [36]. She forms part of the retinue of King Solomon on his flying throne, who carry creatures that cannot fly (the peacock cannot fly over long distances). In the Qur'an, Solomon is the patron of the visual arts. (Photograph taken in 2001)

38 *right* The northern and southern pavilions with British additions, seen from the river [cp. 33], showing how the *tahkhana* originally opened out to the river: albumen print on waxed paper by Dr John Murray, 1855.

4 Bagh-i Jahanara (garden of Jahanara), later Zahara, Zehra, or Zahra Bagh *partly preserved* [99]

The garden was not founded by a daughter of Babur, as is generally assumed, but by Mumtaz Mahal, the Lady of the Taj: we are told this by Kalim, Shah Jahan's poet, who gave it special space in his eulogistic poem on the city in his *Diwan*. It is the only architectural foundation that can be connected to her patronage.[100] After her death in 1631 it passed to her daughter Jahanara, and, in the course of time, the name Bagh-i Jahanara or Jahanara Bagh – still in use in the 19th century – was changed by popular pronunciation to Zahara, Zehra, or Zahra Bagh. Jahanara turned her inheritance into the most splendid garden palace of Agra, if we are to believe Kalim. Several of his verses provide information about the original architecture, the planting, and the founder.

> A boat trip will remove the sorrow from your heart:
> Pass by the garden of Jahanara!
>
> In this paradise is an alluring palace (*qasr*)
> Such that the sight becomes impatient to behold it.
>
> On three [of its] sides is the flower garden, and in front there is the river,
> Every wave of which is the curl of a delightful ringlet.
>
> Its walls and doors are painted to look like flowerbeds:
> There one should sit inside looking at the wall.
>
> In that [garden] is a pool full of the water of life
> Whose waves do not know its shore.
>
> The laying out of this flower garden and this sublime palace
> Was done by the Chosen One of the Age (*Mumtaz-i Dauran*)
>   [i. e. Mumtaz Mahal], the Most High Cradle (*Mahd-i ʿUlya*)
>   [another title of Mumtaz].
>
> Chaste as an angel and of the character of Bilqis [the Queen of Sheba],
> She was pure in her heart like [the Virgin] Mary.
>
> She was so distinguished among the people of the world
> That she became the spouse of Shah Jahan.
>
> When the exalted lady of the world, the Bilqis of the age,
> Went to Paradise from the assembly of Solomon [Shah Jahan],
>
> That very Paradise which she had made to flourish [the garden]
> She gave to her own world-adorning child [a play on the name
>   Jahanara, 'world adornment'],
>
> The eldest beloved daughter of the king, the exalted veiled lady,
> The cherished reminder of Her Majesty, the Queen.[101]

Kalim also praises the 'hundred flowerbeds', the plants and the trees of the garden.[102] He mentions *gulbun* (rose bushes), *lala* (poppies),[103] *gul-i khorshid* (sunflowers), *nargis* (narcissus), *gul-i hazara* (double poppy),[104] *khiri* (gilliflowers: *Viola alba* or *Althoea rosea*), *taj-i khorus* (cockscombs), *gul-i jaʿfary* (marigolds: *Tagetes patula*),[105] *keora / kewrah / kiyoʾra* (fragrant screw-pine, a small tree with fragrant flowers: *Pandanus odoratissimus*), *saman* (jasmine bushes), *sarw* (cypresses), *bed* (willows), *champa* (golden champ, a tree of the magnolia family, which bears a fragrant yellow flower:

Michelia champaca), *maulsari* (bulletwood, a tree with jasmine-like flowers: *Mimusops elengi*), and *nim* trees (neem, also called *babul*: *Azadirachta indica*). Persian poetics have their own conventions, so one does not know for certain whether these flowers really grew in the garden or whether Kalim speaks of some ideal poetic vegetation. But since he names indigenous plants, and since he is generally inclined to include realistic observations in his verses, we can assume that he gives us here a rare glimpse of the flowers that were to be seen in an imperial Agra garden in the second quarter of the 17th century. *Champa*, *keora*, *maulsari*, *sarw* and *bed* are also mentioned by Jahangir as growing at Agra.[106]

The garden was not restricted to the imperial family: Shah Jahan also used it to receive his court, and foreign dignitaries. In May 1638 he entertained the Iranian ambassador Yadgar Beg here, taking a walk with him and in the evening ordering illuminations and fireworks on the bank of the Yamuna below the pavilion (*ʿimarat*).[107] Prince Aurangzeb visited his sister Jahanara in her garden in 1652 when he stopped at Agra to inspect the condition of the Taj Mahal (p. 250).

The garden of Jahanara or Zahara Bagh is not protected by the Archaeological Survey of India, so its Mughal substance is increasingly built over and obliterated by unregulated construction.[108] The garden area is used as a nursery, into which huts and humble residential structures are encroaching. Some of its northern part has also been destroyed by the bridge of the bypass of National Highway No. 2, which cuts between it and the Nur Afshan garden/Ram Bagh (no. 3). What survives is part of the north-western corner tower and the northern wall of the garden, with a *hammam*, and the south-western corner tower [41].

The garden followed the riverfront design [39], but only traces remain of the terrace. Part of its foundations, which were supported by cylindrical wells [cf. 124, 206], have fallen into the river. A modern set of steps, the Shri Ram Ghat, was introduced by a private patron; and the main garden building, which stood in the centre of the terrace and which can be be made out in a photograph taken by John Murray

39 Plan of the garden of Jahanara/Zahara Bagh, based on surviving and recorded evidence. The *hammam* is the rectangular structure attached to the outside of the garden wall to the left.

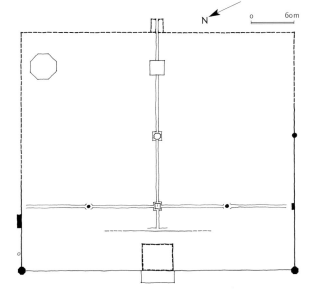

Garden of Jahanara/Zahara Bagh

40 *left* An albumen print by Dr John Murray, *c.* 1858–62, shows the central riverfront building – which no longer exists – on the right, and in the middle distance the garden's north-western tower. (Beyond that are the two towers of the Buland Bagh, and at the extreme left the Battis Khamba [32].)

41 *below* The south-western tower, 1620s–30s. (Photograph taken in 1986)

around 1860 [40], has been built over by a modern temple, the Mangaleshwar Mandir. Some brackets and *muqarnas* capitals from the pavilion lie scattered here and there on the riverbank. Several features recorded by the archaeologist Carlleyle in 1871–72 have disappeared since then, such as the enclosing walls, the gate on the landward side, the main walkway, accentuated by platforms, leading to the river, and an octagonal tank near the north-east corner.

Of the two red sandstone towers at the ends of the river frontage, the northern one – near the large pillar of the road bridge – has been turned into a shrine, the Kali Maha Temple, dedicated to the Hindu Great Goddess in her fearsome aspect: she is expected to protect the bridge, and in this way the female connotation of the garden is remembered even today.

The south-western tower is the best-preserved structure, and a splendid example of the garden towers of Agra [31, 41]. It has *chini khana* or 'China room' wall decoration, characteristic of Jahangir's time, where small niches are filled with pieces of porcelain – a motif here expressed in red sandstone relief. The main body of the tower seems to date from the first construction phase under Mumtaz Mahal in the late 1620s, when Jahangiri architectural forms were still in use. The *chhatri* at the top, with multi-cusped arches, appears to have been added when the garden was taken over by Jahanara. The tower was known in the first decades of the 19th century as the Kushak-i Sayyid or Burj-i Sayyid (pavilion or tower of the Sayyid), and according to Sil Chand people used to dive from it into the river.[109] The English traveller Fanny Parks in 1835 knew the garden as 'Syud [Sayyid] Bagh', and considered that with its red sandstone pavilion at the riverfront it was 'much finer than the Ram Bagh [Nur Afshan garden]'.[110]

Set into the northern wall of the garden close to one of the pillars of the modern road bridge is a ruined *hammam*, which has as yet not been noted. It is a rectangular building, originally with three vaulted units of which two and a half are preserved. Inside, the facing of the brick walls can still be seen, and the vaults have net patterns of the Shahjahani type (*qalib kari*). In 2002 the structure was occupied by a family.

5 **Un-named garden** *not preserved*

6 **Rauza of Afzal Khan** (tomb garden of Afzal Khan), known as **Chini-ka Rauza** (Chinese Tomb) *building preserved* [111]

Mulla Shukrullah as-Shirazi, given the title ᶜAllami Afzal Khan as-Shirazi, was an Iranian noble who had come in 1608 from his native Shiraz to the Mughal court. He served under Jahangir, and under Shah Jahan he held the office of *diwan-i kul* (finance minister) and reached the high rank of 7,000 *zat* / 4,000 *sawar*.[112] He was also a poet, astronomer and mathematician, and highly esteemed by Shah Jahan for his good character. He died in 1639 at the age of seventy at Lahore, and his body was brought to Agra to be buried in the tomb he is said to have built during his lifetime. His brother, ᶜAbd-ul-Haqq, who had come with him to India and there been given the title Amanat Khan, created the calligraphic inscriptions of the Taj Mahal (pp. 224–25), and probably also those on Afzal Khan's tomb, of which only fragments remain.

The tomb of Afzal Khan has lost its original garden setting. The northern riverfront tower survives, but its *chhatri* is missing [31, 43].

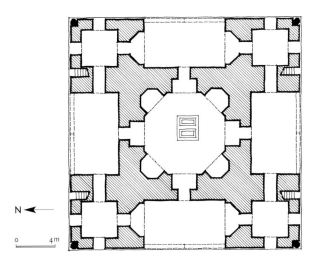

42, 43 The Chini-ka Rauza, before 1639: plan (*above*), on a basic *hasht bihisht* design [cf. 22], and view of the heavily restored tomb from the south-west (*below*); at the end of the wall is the stump of the northern riverfront tower, and beyond that the tall tower of the garden of Jahanara. (Photograph taken in 2002)

Chini-ka Rauza

44 *left* Company drawing by an Agra or Delhi artist, *c.* 1840. The interest in detail is typical of the Company school.

45 *below* 'The China Roza', painted by Sita Ram for Lord Hastings, *c.* 1815. Here, by contrast, the artist introduces a poetic atmospheric note into his view of the building; and although his record of it is earlier, the tomb appears in a state of decay.

46 *opposite* Detail of tile mosaic on the north wall. (Photograph taken in 1991)

7 Bagh-i Khwaja Muhammad Zakarya or Bagh-i Wazir Khan
(garden of Khwaja Muhammad Zakarya or of Wazir Khan)
riverfront buildings preserved but ruined [118]

The Jaipur map [17, 27] lists the garden as that of Khwaja Zakarya, and Raja Ram gives it as that of Khwaja Muhammad Zakarya, a noble of Jahangir;[119] he held a *mansab* of 500 in 1605/6.[120] Sil Chand and Carleylle, however, attribute the garden south of the Chini-ka Rauza to Hakim ʿAlim-ud-Din, with the title Wazir Khan (a title held successively by several different Mughal nobles), who was a physician and distinguished noble of Shah Jahan [47].[121] He was *wazir* in 1627/28 at the beginning of Shah Jahan' s reign, governor of Agra in 1628–31, then appointed governor of the Panjab in 1631/32, a post he held for an unusual length of time, until, in 1640/41, he was reappointed governor of Agra. He died in 1641, with a final rank of 5,000 *zat* / 5,000 *sawar* (1,000 x 2–3 horses).[122] Wazir Khan was held in high esteem by Shah Jahan, who chose him, together with Prince Shah Shujaʿ and one of the empress's ladies-in-waiting, to accompany the body of Mumtaz Mahal from Burhanpur to Agra (p. 20). He is described as a quiet man of simple habits, whose money went into building.[123] His great mosque and *hammam* at Lahore are famous;[124] he seems also to have had a *haveli* at Agra (no. 39). Wazir Khan appears frequently in darbars in the Windsor Castle *Padshahnama* [e.g. 2:7].[125]

In the garden of Wazir Khan Sil Chand mentions buildings of three and four storeys (perhaps the garden towers), a *tahkhana* or

47 Portrait of Wazir Khan, Mughal, 1630s or 1640s.

The tomb itself is placed at an angle to the riverfront [43], since the face of the deceased had to be turned towards Mecca, which in India is to the west. It derives its popular name, 'Chini-ka Rauza', or 'Chinese Tomb', from its facing with a mosaic of glazed tiles, a truly exotic element in the Mughal architecture of Agra [44–46]. The tiles form patterns of flowering plants and calligraphic inscriptions in the manner of Shahjahani buildings at Lahore. The tomb follows the traditional ninefold *hasht bihisht* plan (pp. 26–27), with large *pishtaqs* – monumental arched niches in rectangular frames – in the centre of each side. The interior has elaborate vaults; the main dome over the central chamber is built up in concentric tiers of *muqarnas*.[113] It is set on a platform with vaulted chambers, which are now walled up.

The Chini-ka Rauza is one of the few buildings of Agra mentioned by the Tyrolean Jesuit geographer Josef Tieffenthaler (p. 231), who saw it in the 1740s; he comments on its 'tegulis sinensi more incrustatis' – its inlay with tiles in the Chinese manner.[114] When the British took over Agra in 1803 the Chini-ka Rauza was noted as a building of architectural merit, so it appears as a subject of 'Company drawings' [44] – watercolours done with great attention to detail by Indian artists for British patrons. When Lord Hastings was in Agra in 1815, his artist Sita Ram made two views of 'The China Roza' in his characteristic soft and loose brushwork and aerial perspective[115] [45]. Fanny Parks in 1835 criticized the fact that the tomb's flanking buildings had been removed, that its decoration had been plundered for the gold components, and that farmers lived in it and tied their bullocks to the cenotaphs[116] (these have since been replaced by modern reconstructions). The situation had not changed much by 1899, when Lord Curzon, Governor-General and Viceroy of India, found 'this exquisite little tomb . . . in a shocking state of dilapidation', and ordered its restoration.[117] Since then the Chini-ka Rauza has been repeatedly restored, in particular the outer tile facing and the inner painted decoration, which have lost much of their original character.

underground chamber, and a *jilaukhana* or forecourt, and lauds their symmetry.[126] Carlleyle describes it as having a pavilion overlooking the river and, in the middle of the landward garden, a large octagonal platform beneath which was a *tahkhana*.[127] On the 1868–69 map of Agra [28] the garden appears under the name 'Jaggannath's Bagh', and has a circular feature in the centre. The area has now been built over by a residential colony.[128]

The surviving buildings, though ruined, are still the best-preserved riverfront ensemble of a non-imperial garden of Shah Jahan's time. The symmetrical arrangement is typical [48], with a pavilion in the centre of the riverfront, set above a *tahkhana*, and flanked by two towers at the ends of the terrace [49]. These towers are faced with red sandstone, and the ruined pavilion in the centre has sandstone arcades on the river and garden sides. The stylistic features of the architecture, such as the rectangular pillars of the arcade, point to the middle of Shah Jahan's reign or later, possibly the 1640s. It is thus likely that the garden buildings owe their present form to Wazir Khan.

Garden of Khwaja Muhammad Zakarya or of Wazir Khan, ?1640s

48 *below* Plan.

49 *bottom* View of the riverfront towers from the south-west. (Photograph taken in 2002)

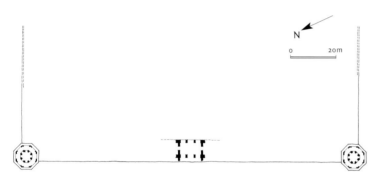

8 Bagh-i Sultan Parwiz (garden of Sultan Parwiz)
tomb only preserved [129]

Prince Parwiz, also called Sultan Parwiz [50], was the son of Jahangir and thus Shah Jahan's brother; his daughter, Nadira Banu Begam, was married to Shah Jahan's eldest son, Dara Shikoh. Pelsaert in 1626 lists this garden in his description of riverfront Agra, and we learn that in 1621 Jahangir resided for a time 'in the garden of Sultan Perwez on the upper bank of the river'.[130] Parwiz had a rank of 40,000 *zat* / 30,000 *sawar* when he died in 1626 at Burhanpur, of which he was governor.[131] His body was brought to Agra and buried in the garden he had built.[132] His family were ordered to present themselves at court and were allowed to continue to reside in the garden: Shah Jahan's official historian, Lahauri, mentions the residence of Prince Parwiz when he says that as part of the engagement ceremony of Dara Shikoh and Nadira Banu (in November 1632) presents were sent along the riverfront to the widowed mother of the bride.[133]

The garden is now covered partly by nurseries and partly by the residential colony of Moti Bagh. A modern shrine of a Muslim saint,

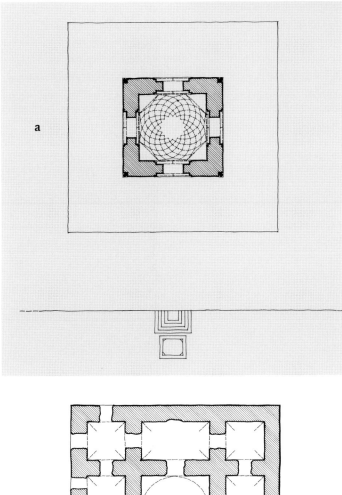

a

b

the Dargah of Dada Pir, has been built onto and with the remains
of the riverfront terrace. The main surviving building of the Mughal
garden is a tomb structure, locally known as Parwiz Khan-ka
Maqbara, 'the tomb of Parwiz Khan' [51], which is situated between
the river and the Aligarh Road, to the west of the police station.

The garden or *haveli* of Sultan Parwiz is mentioned in the early
19th-century records[134] but not in later descriptions of the city.
The tomb is not protected by the Archaeological Survey. The brick
structure is in a ruined condition, and its surroundings are not very
attractive. The cubical domed tomb stands on a substructure with
vaulted rooms, like most buildings of riverfront Agra. This in turn is
set on a larger platform with steps and a small pool, preserved on
the south side. The rooms of the substructure are arranged on a
basic *hasht bihisht* plan [52:b], while the tomb itself is raised over a
simple square with *pishtaqs* in the centre of each side and has an
inner dome set on eight arches and squinches [52:a]. The dome
has a plaster vault with a typical Shahjahani net pattern (*qalib kari*).
Originally the entire tomb, including its substructure, had painted
decoration, which survives only in small fragments [53]. The
structure is datable to the second quarter of the 17th century.

9 Maqbara of Iʿtimad-ud-Daula (tomb garden of Iʿtimad-ud-Daula) *well preserved* [135]

The mausoleum was built between 1622 and 1628 by Nur Jahan, Jahangir's powerful wife, for her parents. Her father, Ghiyas Beg Tehrani, with the title Iʿtimad-ud-Daula ('Pillar of the Empire'), was *wazir-i kul* and *wakil* under Jahangir [54]. As governor of Lahore he reached the high rank of 7,000 *zat* / 7,000 *sawar*. He is described as a pleasant and even-tempered man who was opposed to cruelty and held no ill-feelings towards anybody. Jahangir valued him as a capable official and as a kind and wise companion.[136] He died in 1622 of a broken heart, a few months after the death of his wife, when he accompanied the emperor on his way to Kashmir. Jahangir presented Nur Jahan with all the property of her father, and she buried him 'in his garden on the upper bank of the river'.[137]

The tomb that Nur Jahan built reflects her elegant taste, for her many talents included a pronounced interest in architecture. She built gardens at Agra and in Kashmir and caravanserais in the Panjab; and she also supervised the construction of Jahangir's tomb [108] and built her own tomb, both in Lahore.

Like most of the funerary, as opposed to pleasure, gardens of Agra (with the exception of the Taj Mahal), that of Iʿtimad-ud-Daula does not follow the riverfront design: instead it has the form of a classic *chahar bagh*, with the tomb structure at the centre where the walkways cross [56, 57].[138] A concession to the riverfront scheme is a pavilion which served as a gate towards the river, which is treated with particular elaboration [55]. In the middle of the northern and southern walls of the garden are narrower false gates that match each other: their composition, with a rectangular hall flanked by two

54 Iʿtimad-ud-Daula: detail of a painting by Balchand, Mughal, *c.* 1635, from the *Padshahnama*. (The complete painting shows Jahangir receiving Prince Khurram – the future Shah Jahan – on his return from the Mewar campaign.)

55 *below* The tomb of Iʿtimad-ud-Daula, 1622–28, seen from the other side of the river (top, in the plans opposite). (Photograph taken in 1986)

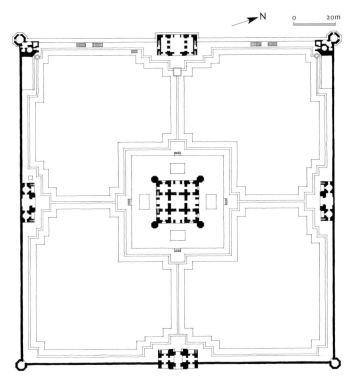

chambers, corresponds to one outer side of a *hasht bihisht* plan, the plan that appears in full in the tomb. The real entrance gate, to the east, displays another variation on the room arrangement. In this way the cross-axial garden plan receives a bilateral symmetrical accent, with emphasis on the axis in the centre – a device that would be realized on a grand scale in the Taj Mahal garden. Real gate, false gates, and riverfront pavilion are faced with red sandstone inlaid with white marble in *chini khana* patterns; their interiors have painted decoration. The riverfront terrace has staircases leading

Tomb garden of Iʿtimad-ud-Daula, 1622–28

56 *above left* Plan, drawn by an Indian artist for the Maharaja of Jaipur, 18th century.

57 *above* Plan, drawn today. Here the river is at the top, to conform to the orientation of the 18th-century plan: the entrance gate is at the bottom. The tomb has a basic *hasht bihisht* plan; the false gates, left and right, are on the pattern of the outer sides of that plan form.

The tomb of Iʿtimad-ud-Daula

58 *left* Detail of wall decoration in *pietra dura*. (Photograph taken in 2001)

59 *below left* The tomb in its garden setting, looking from the east towards the river. (Photograph taken in 2001)

60 *below* The tomb pavilion, with *pietra dura* decoration: Company drawing by an Agra or Delhi artist for Maria, Lady Nugent, *c.* 1812.

down to basement rooms, and the riverfront towers are enlarged by well chambers and ramps for water-lifts.

The tomb pavilion in the centre [59, 60] is an elaborate version of a form that became popular in Jahangir's period: the platform tomb, in which the low body of the building or platform supports individual structures (pp. 87–88).[139] The ninefold plan of the platform has the simplicity of a magic square, enriched with towers at the four corners. In the central chamber are the ochre-coloured cenotaphs of Iᶜtimad-ud-Daula and his wife, under an ornamental vault displaying network [62, 63]. The interior is, characteristically for the period, richly painted with a variety of designs. Above the geometrical dados are flowers and flower vases in real niches, a type of enlarged and embellished *chini khana* motif. Between the niches are single plants, alternately poppies and red lilies. Red flowers had a connotation of suffering and death in Persian and Turkish literature, and appear also inside the Taj Mahal (pp. 140, 170, 172–73).

On the main body of the tomb is a smaller superstructure in the form of a square vaulted pavilion which houses a further set of cenotaphs, set on a marble floor with an elegant interlacing scroll pattern of coloured stones set in white marble and [61].

The whole exterior of the building is faced with marble inlaid with different-coloured stones [58–60].[140] This anticipates the even more refined inlay of the Taj Mahal. Here, however, the once brilliantly polished surface has been rendered dull by recent chemical cleaning.[141]

At the top of the walls of the main body of the mausoleum and inside the roof pavilion there are Qur'anic inscriptions in marble relief. An inscriptional panel on the south-west corner tower bears the date '37', an abbreviation of 1037 AH (AD 1626/27), together with the name of the calligrapher, cAbd-un-Nabi al-Qarshi. The date 1036 AH (AD 1627/28) appears inside the roof pavilion, on the first panel from the west on the north wall.

Tieffenthaler in the 1740s had more to say about the tomb of Ictimad-ud-Daula than about the Taj Mahal. In his eyes it surpassed all Agra monuments 'if not in size, in art and ornamentation'. He was particularly impressed by its decoration of multi-coloured

The tomb of Iʿtimad-ud-Daula

61 *left* Upper cenotaphs of Iʿtimad-ud-Daula and his wife, set in paving with an inlaid interlacing pattern, in the pavilion on the upper level of the tomb.

62 *opposite* The inner chamber, with cenotaphs of Iʿtimad-ud-Daula and his wife: Company drawing by an Agra or Delhi artist, c. 1808–20.

63 *right* The inner chamber in the late 20th century. (Photograph taken in 1991)

stone inlay: 'This work of art, which deserves to be admired in all its aspects, is decorated with all kinds of vessels and pots and with flowers in natural colours. If one had not seen it with one's own eyes, one would hardly believe that it would have been possible to raise so much money, or to erect such an artistic work of such size and of hard marble, and to inlay it with such artistic designs and different colours.'[142] In the early 19th century the tomb became one of the monuments of interest to the British. Lord Hastings in 1815 noted that 'a branch of Eatimud's family' was failing to look after it properly, despite land grants allotted to them for the purpose:[143] they were told that if they did not repair the tomb it would be taken over by the British government. That happened in 1842 under Lord Auckland, and in 1843 Viscount Hardinge authorized the funds for the first repair.[144] The riverfront pavilion was adapted as a holiday bungalow for the European residents of Agra, who would occasionally stay there for a change of air.[145] Curzon visited the tomb in 1899 and was shocked that 'the paintings on plaster have been execrably restored by the Public Works Department'.[146] The conservation of the tomb has remained a controversial issue.

10 Bagh-i Musawi Khan Sadr (garden of Musawi Khan Sadr) *not preserved*

Musawi Khan served Jahangir and later Shah Jahan, who confirmed him as *sadr* (in charge of revenue and cash grants and appointment of judges) in 1636/37. He seems to have reached a rank of 4,000 *zat* / 750 *sawar*. Shah Nawaz Khan, the chronicler of the Mughal nobility (not to be confused with the owner of garden no. 1), writes about him that 'though he was not highly educated, he had through regular association with learned men picked up the essential etiquette for meetings, and could carry on a high-flown conversation'.[147] He died in 1644. He is often depicted in the Windsor Castle *Padshahnama* [2:13].[148] Raja Ram says that Musawi Khan's *haveli* on the river consisted of a palace 'with vaults underneath' and a 'very beautiful mosque'.[149] The site of the garden is now occupied by the Moti Bagh residential colony.

Lost imperial gardens (nos. 11–16) The garden of Musawi Khan Sadr (no. 10) was followed by a series of imperial gardens, which lined the bend of the Yamuna and the following straight stretch up to the Mahtab Bagh (no. 17), which also belonged to the emperor. Today the area has been built over up to the Iron Bridge by the modern residential colony of Moti Bagh – named after one of the lost gardens (no. 12) – while the remainder is used for cultivation. Only a few traces of the gardens remain in the fields, such as pieces of riverfront walls or wells. The most prominent surviving element of Mughal garden architecture is a large *baoli* or step-well called Gyarah Sidhi, situated in the bend of the river opposite the fort, built in red sandstone in the style of the 16th century [64].

11 Bagh Padshahi (Imperial Garden) *not preserved*

12 Moti Bagh Padshahi (Imperial Pearl Garden) *not preserved*

An imperial garden named Moti Mahal (Pearl Palace) 'on the other side of the river' is mentioned by Pelsaert in 1626.[150] Peter Mundy in

64 The Mughal *baoli* or step-well known as Gyarah Sidhi, 16th century, seen from the south-east. (Photograph taken in 2001)

1632–33 calls it 'Mootee ca baag' and says that it was built by 'Nooremohol' (Nur Mahal), that is Nur Jahan. He adds that it had many rooms painted with copies of European prints, including a 'picture of Sir Thomas Roe, late Ambassador heere, as it was told us'.[151] By the time of Sil Chand in the 1820s, it was thought the garden had been built by a wife of Shah Jahan called Nawab Moti Begam.

A painting in the Windsor Castle *Padshahnama* of a famous elephant fight in 1633 [65] shows part of the riverbank before the bend with a white building on a platform, which could represent the Moti Bagh. In form and style the pavilion resembles those of the Nur Afshan garden/Ram Bagh [33, 36].[152] The painter may have taken them as a model, or the Moti Bagh buildings may indeed have been similar, reflecting the personal taste of Nur Jahan.

13 Bagh Padshahi (Imperial Garden) *not preserved*

14 Lal Bagh Padshahi (Red Imperial Garden) *not preserved*

15 Second Chahar Bagh Padshahi (Imperial Chahar Bagh) *not preserved*

16 Chahar Bagh Padshahi (Imperial Chahar Bagh) or **Bagh-i Hasht Bihisht** (Garden of the Eight Paradises) *not preserved*

This garden was first called Bagh-i Hasht Bihisht, the Garden of the Eight Paradises, but eventually became known as Chahar Bagh (the Jaipur map adds 'Padshahi' – imperial).[153] It was a milestone in the development of the Mughal garden, because it was created by Babur in 1526 after he had vanquished the Lodi sultans of Delhi and established Mughal rule. Babur claimed that here he introduced Central Asian ideas of regularly planned gardens with intersecting walkways into Hindustan. It also marked the beginning of Mughal Agra as a riverfront city (p. 24).

In his autobiography, Babur enumerates the outstanding features of the garden, in the order in which they were built, but does not tell us how they were arranged:

> First was built the great well (*chah-i kalan*), from which the water for the bath house (*hammam*) came. Then the piece of ground where the tamarind trees and the octagonal pool (*hauz-i musamman*) are. After that the large pool (*hauz-i kalan*) and its court (*sahn*). After that the pool (*hauz*) which is in front of the stone buildings ('*imarat-i sangin*) and the wooden hall (*talar*). And then the small garden (*baghcha*) of the private chamber (*khilwat khana*) and its buildings. After that came the *hammam*. In this way, in unpleasant and disorderly India, regular and geometric gardens appeared. In every corner were beautiful plots, and in every plot were regularly laid out arrangements of flowers (*gul*) and bushes of white musk roses (*nastaran*).[154]

Only a few wells remain on the site of the garden, which is now used for agriculture. In the 1820s Sil Chand lauded its *ananas*

65 *opposite* Detail of a scene of Prince Aurangzeb facing a maddened elephant named Sudhakar in 1633, Mughal, c. 1635, from the *Padshahnama*. In the background is the riverfront in the area of Moti Bagh (no. 12). At the far right, on the other side of the river where it bends, is what might be the Haveli of A'zam Khan (no. 25).

(pineapples), *kaila / kela* (bananas), *anba* (mangoes), *anjir* (figs), *chakotra* (pomelo), various kind of *angur* (grapes), *shaftalu* (peaches), *nashpati* (pears), *seb* (apples), *zardalu* (apricots), *badam* (almonds), *girdugan* (walnuts), *amrud* (guavas), *limun* (limes), *anar* (pomegranates), *ray-yi jaman* (jamun or Java plum),[155] *fals'a*[156] (*Grewia asiatica*, used for sherbet), *amratban*[157] (plantain), and others. Since several of these fruit trees would not easily grow in the climate of Agra, it seems that Sil Chand wanted to paint the picture of an especially fertile garden, defying the laws of nature. In addition he lists *sarw* (cypresses), *'ar'ar* (junipers), *chinar* (plane trees) and *sandal* trees, flowers such as *gul-i surkh* (red roses), *gul-i zard* (marigolds) and *gul-i banafshar* (violets), and flowering bushes and trees including *gul-i yasmin* (jasmine), *gul-i atish* (flame-of-the-forest) and *champa* (golden champ).[158]

17 Bagh-i Mahtab Padshahi (Imperial Moonlight Garden), later Mahtab Bagh (Moonlight Garden) *partly preserved*[159]

What the Jaipur map calls 'bag mahaitab patisahi' in Hindi spelling, i.e. Bagh-i Mahtab Padshahi, was built by Shah Jahan. It is of the same width as the garden of the Taj Mahal, and situated exactly opposite it [17, 26] – facts that gave rise to the speculation that the emperor intended to built his own tomb here, as a counter-image in black marble of the mausoleum of his wife, linked to it by a bridge over the river. This story was reported by the French traveller Jean-Baptiste Tavernier, who was at Agra in 1640–41 and 1665, and has remained alive ever since (p. 249) [374]. Excavations carried out by the Archaeological Survey of India in the 1990s, however, found no evidence to substantiate that assumption. The garden historian Elizabeth Moynihan has suggested that the Mahtab Bagh was conceived as a place from which to view the Taj Mahal, of which the reflection would have been captured by a large pool in the centre of the now ruined riverfront terrace.[160]

The garden is only partly preserved because it is prone to flooding during the monsoon season, which lasts at Agra from July to September. Prince Aurangzeb, after a visit to the city in December 1652 to inspect the Taj Mahal, reported to Shah Jahan that the 'Bagh-i Mahtab' was 'completely inundated, and therefore has lost its charm, but soon it will regain its verdancy. The octagonal pool and the pavilions (*bangla-ha*) around it are in splendid condition.'[161]

Today the Mahtab Bagh has been planted with trees to provide a green background for the Taj Mahal. A reconstruction can be essayed, however, from what remains of the buildings, together

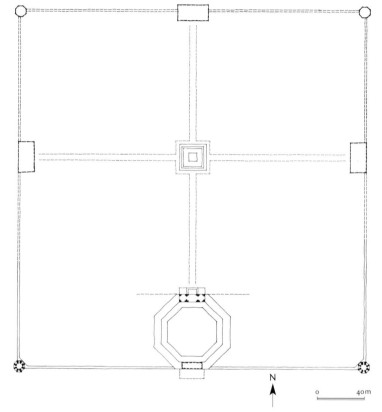

with 18th- and early 19th-century plans, including one in the Taj Museum that shows the entire Taj complex and the river frontage of the Mahtab Bagh (p. 103). The layout followed the usual scheme, with a riverfront terrace and a landward *chahar bagh* [67]. The central part of the terrace survives: instead of the usual pavilion, it displays an octagonal lobed pool with traces of twenty-five fountains. Attached to the pool there were two structures of which only the foundations remain. One, towards the river, took the form of a small, probably three-part, pavilion with a central *bangla* roof – a roof of curved form derived from traditional Bengali architecture. The other, on the garden side, was definitely of the tripartite form favoured for Shahjahani pavilions. Below it, the facing of the terrace step displays the arrangement for a 'sheet' waterfall (*abshar-i chadari*): this fell into a pool over a wall with tiers of tiny niches of *chini khana* type (in this context also called *taqcha*, 'small arches', in Shahjahani texts) [69].[162]

Mahtab Bagh, second quarter of the 17th century (photographed in 2001)

66 *left* The garden seen from the roof of the Taj Mahal. The south-eastern riverfront tower appears on the right.

67 *opposite, below* Plan.

The garden component had a classical cross-axial design, to judge from a central square platform with a pool, and foundations of gates or false gates in the centres of the eastern and northern sides, though evidence of the walkways is missing. The corners were accented with the usual towers, of which only the south-eastern one, at the riverfront, remains [66]. It provided a favourite 'repoussoir' in early picturesque views of the Taj [358]. Outside, to the west, are the remains of an aqueduct that brought water to the garden.

The Mahtab Bagh scarcely features in the 19th- and early 20th-century reports. Sil Chand repeats the story of the planned second mausoleum, like everyone else, and says that in his time (1825–26) there was only one small building in the garden and the rest was greenery and various trees.[163] Florentia Sale's *Notebook* of 1832–33 contains what purports to be an illustration of its riverfront, but this differs from the surviving architecture and from the elevation of the river frontage on the plan in the Taj Museum.

68 *right* Border of the large octagonal pool, with a pattern of multi-cusped arches, during restoration. The water would be on the right.

69 *below* The garden, looking across the river to the Taj Mahal. The vertical edge of the terrace in the foreground has *chini khana* or *taqcha* decoration, which would have been visible through a waterfall.

The gardens of the right bank

A. GARDENS FROM THE SOUTH-EAST UP TO THE FORT

18 Haveli of Khan-i Dauran *largely ruined and built over*

Khwaja Sabir, given first the title Nasiri Khan and then the title Khan-i Dauran Bahadur Nusrat Jang [2:11], obtained the high rank of 7000 *zat* / 7000 *sawar* (5,000 x 2–3 horses) at Shah Jahan's court.[164] As one of the emperor's great commanders, he distinguished himself in the Deccan campaigns and played a decisive role in the taking of the celebrated fortress of Daulatabad in 1633.[165] Khan-i Dauran was also instrumental in subduing the rebellion of the Bundela rajas in 1636.[166] He was a great builder, and raised a number of structures at Burhanpur, where he resided as governor of the Deccan. His son constructed a mosque for him at Gwalior.[167] He was however feared and hated for his cruelty, and was killed in 1645 by a Brahmin boy from Kashmir, whom he had taken into his service and converted to Islam. At the news of his death, the people of Burhanpur emptied the shops of sweets to give away in thanksgiving.

Khan-i Dauran's residence on the riverbank is referred to as a *haveli* (see p. 34). Sil Chand, writing in 1825–26, considered it the best building in the city.[168] An impression of how it looked originally, with its central riverfront pavilion and the arcaded openings of the rooms in the basement, can be had from topographical drawings and photographs. It appears in two early 19th-century drawings in the Taj Museum that give rare views of the Taj and its flanking buildings [72].[169] One of the illustrations in Florentia Sale's *Notebook* of 1832–33 shows it – though, because she was misinformed, or misspelt the name, it is called the 'Tyur Khana [*tahkhana*] of . . . Dowlat Khan'. The ruins of the *haveli* appear frequently in early photographic views of the Taj, as a picturesque foreground motif to set off the perfect splendour of the mausoleum [70]. What is left of the garden has been built over by the Taj Tannery, and visitors are not welcome. The most visible remains are the riverfront wall in red sandstone, constructed in Mughal bond (p. 96), and the western tower, which can be seen from the terrace of the Taj Mahal [71]. If one takes a boat at the Dassehra Ghat, not far from the Haveli of Khan-i Dauran on the eastern side of the Taj Mahal, one can contemplate the remains from the river [377].

70 *left* View of the Taj Mahal from the east: albumen print by Dr John Murray, 1850s. The wall and tower in the foreground are those of the Haveli of Khan-i Dauran (no. 18); beyond is the Haveli of Agah Khan (no. 19).

71 *right* The remains of the Haveli of Khan-i Dauran, seen from the roof of the Taj Mahal. The tower is that shown in Murray's photograph [70] and a Company drawing [72].

72 *below* The gardens of the right bank of the Yamuna, from the east (left) up to the Taj Mahal and beyond, as recorded in a Company drawing by an Agra or Delhi artist in the Taj Museum, early 19th century. From left to right are the Haveli of Khan-i Dauran (no. 18), the Haveli of Agah Khan (no. 19), the Taj Mahal, the aqueduct of the Taj, and the two elements of the garden of Khan-i ʿAlam (no. 21 [cf. 77]).

19 Haveli of Agah Khan *not preserved*

Agah Khan was a eunuch (*khwajasara*) in the service of Mumtaz Mahal. He held the post of *faujdar* (commandant in charge of law and order) of Agra until 1652 and then of its suburbs, and also the post of *mutawali* (trusteeship) of the Taj Mahal. In 1652 he supervised the construction of a hunting palace for Shah Jahan at Samugarh near Agra. He died in 1657 with the rather low rank of 1,500 *zat* / 1,500 *sawar* (2–3 horses).[170]

That this garden immediately to the east of the Taj Mahal held the *haveli* of Agah Khan is indicated by the Jaipur map [17, 27]. The building appears in two Company drawings in the Taj Museum [72].[171] A view in Florentia Sale's *Notebook* of 1832–33 also shows it, but she refers to it as 'Doulah Khan's Palace'.[172] The remains of this garden are still visible next to those of the Haveli of Khan-i Dauran (no. 18) in the foreground of the earliest photographic views of the Taj, beginning with those of John Murray of the 1850s [70]. In 1860 the Shri Daoji Maharaj Mandir (temple) was established here,[173] and the site is now called Dassehra Ghat. If the level of the water allows it, one can take a boat across the river to the Mahtab Bagh (no. 17).

20 Rauza of Shah Jahan (tomb garden of Shah Jahan): Taj Mahal
see Chapters II–IV

With its central building placed on a raised terrace, its flanking towers, and its *chahar bagh*, the Taj Mahal [72, 74] expresses the riverfront garden in its most monumental and ideal form (see p. 103). To the west are its waterworks, with a large aqueduct that brought water from the Yamuna into the garden [322, 323].

★ ★ ★

In Mughal times the entire riverbank between the Taj Mahal and the fort (no. 28) was lined with the residences of nobles. Their ruins are visible in an early 19th-century drawing in the Taj Museum [73]. Only two survive. Those beyond the Haveli of Asalat Khan were demolished in the British period (nos. 23–27). In 1837 the strand road (now Yamuna Kinara Road [89]) was constructed as famine relief work, during which 'old houses and foundations, sometimes as much as ten feet thick, were encountered and had to be removed by gunpowder'.[174] What remained was removed to provide work on

the occasion of another famine: MacDonnell Park – now Shah Jahan Park – was begun in 1897 and completed in 1901; the new landscaping included the construction of a channel to bring water from the Agra Canal to the park and to the Taj garden.[175]

In 1914 the idea was entertained of building a dam downstream below the Taj Mahal and creating an artificial lake between the mausoleum and the fort, with 'strand drives' running on each side of the Yamuna, the dam acting as connecting link.[176] The latest attempt to change this part of the historical landscape of Agra was made in

2003 by the government of Uttar Pradesh, with a proposal for a complex to contain a shopping mall: the idea was abandoned after fervent opposition.

21 **Bagh-i Khan-i ᶜAlam** (garden of Khan-i ᶜAlam) *riverfront buildings and parts of garden preserved but ruined*[177]

Immediately to the west of the waterworks of the Taj Mahal is the garden of Khan-i ᶜAlam[178] – a Turani (Central Asian) noble, who received his title from Jahangir in 1609. Two years later he was sent as ambassador to the court of Shah ᶜAbbas of Iran, with a retinue of eight hundred men, several large Gujarati bullocks, and ten elephants with gold and silver trappings, which greatly impressed the Iranians. Khan-i ᶜAlam also served Shah Jahan early in his reign, but in 1632 he retired at the rank of 6,000 *zat* / 5,000 *sawar* because of old age and his addiction to opium, and 'spent the remainder of his days in tranquillity and comfort' at Agra, presumably in his garden near the Taj Mahal.[179] He appears in the Windsor Castle *Padshahnama* [2:10].[180]

73 *above* Remains of the gardens of the right bank of the Yamuna between the Taj Mahal and the fort, as recorded in a fragile Company drawing by an Agra or Delhi artist in the Taj Museum, early 19th century. They correspond to what according to the Jaipur map [27] are the Haveli of Asalat Khan (no. 22) [cf. 79], the Haveli of Mahabat Khan (no. 23), the Haveli of Hoshdar Khan (no. 24), and at the right what must, from its position, be the Haveli of Aᶜzam Khan (no. 25) [cf. 80].

74 The Taj Mahal complex, seen from the river. The Mihman Khana or assembly hall (left), mausoleum, and mosque are set on the riverfront terrace, which is framed by towers. Originally, open arches in the middle of the terrace lit a *tahkhana*. (Photograph taken in 1985)

The design followed the standard scheme, with the main building on a terrace, overlooking the river on one side [76–78] and the garden on the other. This building is preserved but ruinous; below it is the usual *tahkhana*, flanked by two polygonal towers in the riverfront wall. The garden has an extension to the east, towards the Taj Mahal: here the riverfront terrace houses a large *tahkhana*, of which two rooms are preserved, one of them a spacious hall with a curved ceiling in the manner of a monumental *bangla* vault, similar to the one in the northern *tahkhana* in the Nur Afshan garden/Ram Bagh.

Like several of the gardens of Agra, this was later used as a burial place for its owner. The main building was not replaced, however: instead of erecting a mausoleum, as in the garden of Iᶜtimad-ud-Daula (no. 9) or the Chini-ka Rauza (no. 6), a platform with cenotaphs was raised on the central axis, inland from the river [75].

Early views of the riverfront building and the terrace can be found in Company drawings in the Taj Museum[181] [72] and among the illustrations in the *Notebook* of Florentia Sale of 1832–33 [77].

Garden of Khan-i ʿAlam

75 left, above The platform with cenotaphs. (Photograph taken in 2001)

76 left, below The riverfront buildings in the early 20th century; on the left is part of the lower extension to the east, housing a further *tahkhana*.

77 above The riverfront buildings as recorded in a Company drawing by an Agra artist from the *Notebook of Florentia, Lady Sale, 1832–33*. In the centre is the raised pavilion above a *tahkhana*; to the left of the left-hand tower is the eastern extension.

The ruins also feature in early photographs of Taj Mahal seen from the river, performing the same function as a repoussoir on the west as the *havelis* of Khan-i Dauran and Agah Khan did on the eastern side.

The garden of Khan-i ʿAlam is now used as a nursery by the Horticultural Department of the Archaeological Survey of India.

78 below Plan of surviving Mughal structures. From top to bottom, the features in the central area are what appear to be a small platform and then a larger platform, the platform with cenotaphs [75] extended to the east, the riverfront platform, and the riverfront pavilion [76, 77]. On the left, the garden is bordered by the aqueduct of the Taj garden, with ruined structures that formed part of the waterworks, and a temple built over the original water inlet [cf. 322, 323, 366].

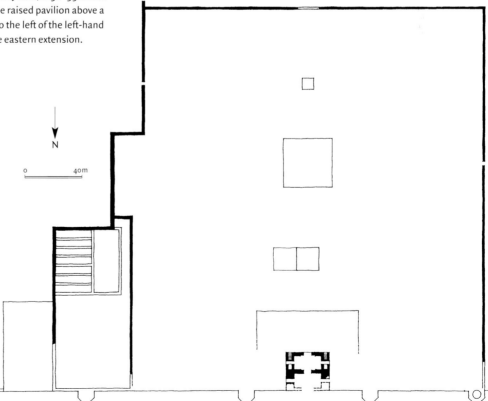

N

0   40m

22 Haveli of Asalat Khan *part of riverfront wall and towers preserved*

Asalat Khan was the title of Mir ʿAbdul Hadi, the descendant of a noble from Yazd in Iran. He distinguished himself in Shah Jahan's campaigns in the Deccan and served from 1644 to 1647 as *mir bakhshi* (in charge of *mansabs* and intelligence). He then took part in the emperor's unsuccessful Balkh and Badakhshan campaign, and died at an early age in the winter of 1647 at Balkh, from a cold caught while taking a bath in the open. At the time of his death Asalat Khan had a rank of 5,000 *zat* / 4,000 *sawar*. Shah Nawaz Khan tells us that he was famed for his good qualities and virtuous life, and was unmatched in his time for gentleness and modesty. Shah Jahan regretted his death and said he would have had a bright future.[182]

Only part of the riverfront wall of Asalat Khan's garden is preserved, with fragments of two projecting towers [79]. A depiction of the riverfront terrace with openings (of a *tahkhana?*) in the centre can be made out in one of the early 19th-century drawings in the Taj Museum [73]. This has been replaced by a temple dedicated to Shiva, the Kala Bhairon Mandir, built into the terrace. To the west is the Shamshan Ghat, where the dead are burned and their ashes put into the river. Beyond the burning *ghat*, inland, is the Dargah of Sayyid Jalal-ud-Din Bukhari (p. 250).

23 Haveli of Mahabat Khan *not preserved*

Mahabat Khan was one of the most powerful nobles of Jahangir and of Shah Jahan in the early years of his rule [2:9]. His father had migrated from Shiraz to Kabul. He himself, then still called Zamana Beg, entered the service of Akbar's son Salim as *ahadi* (cavalry trooper) and rose to the rank of 500. After Jahangir's accession in 1605 he received the title Mahabat Khan and held the governorships of the Deccan, Kabul and Bengal. When Prince Khurram rebelled against his father in 1622 (p. 19), Mahabat Khan was entrusted with the task of quelling the rebellion. In 1625/26 he was made *wakil*

79 The remains of the riverfront buildings of the Haveli of Asalat Khan: the bases of two projecting towers, and part of the wall of the terrace. Visible beyond are the taller polygonal towers of the garden of Khan-i ʿAlam, and the Taj Mahal. (Photograph taken in 2001)

(chief minister) at the highest possible rank for a noble, of 7,000 *zat* / 7,000 *sawar* (2–3 horses). Soon after, however, he held Jahangir prisoner for a while because he feared an intrigue by his greatest antagonist, the powerful Asaf Khan, brother of Nur Jahan. After Jahangir's death Mahabat Khan became reconciled with Shah Jahan, who appointed him governor of Ajmer, the Deccan and Delhi, and in 1628 made him commander in chief: *khan-i khanan sipahsalar*. In 1632 he was sent again as governor to the Deccan, where in 1633 he conquered the fort of Daulatabad with Khan-i Dauran (see no. 18). Mahabat Khan did not favour the Iranians (despite his own origin) or the Turanis, but chose his troops largely from indigenous Rajputs. He was skilled in astronomy and astrology; in his old age he became a *shiʿa* and used to wear the name of the *imams* engraved on costly jewels round his neck.[183] When he died in 1634 his sons were allowed to keep his movable property – all but the elephants, which had been his special favourites, and which he used to feed with lotus-rice and Persian melons: the emperor wanted these for himself.

In December 1652 when Prince Aurangzeb was at Agra on his way to take charge of the Deccan, he did not stay in his own riverfront residence (see nos. 33–35) but took up quarters in the *manzil* (mansion) in the *bagh* (garden) of Mahabat Khan. He visited his sister Jahanara in her garden (no. 4), and she returned his visit. During his stay he wrote to his father about necessary repairs at the Taj Mahal and the Mahtab Bagh (p. 250).[184] The garden residence of Mahabat Khan is mentioned in the 1620s by Pelsaert, and features in most of the 19th-century descriptions of Agra.[185]

24 Haveli of Hoshdar Khan *not preserved*

The noble who held this garden was most likely Hoshdar Khan Mir Hoshdar, son of Multafat Khan. He entered court service late in Shah Jahan's reign, and since he had always sided with Aurangzeb, he rose fast after the latter's accession. In 1663 he had the rank of 4,000 *zat* / 3,000 *sawar*. He became governor of Delhi, then of Agra (1664), and two years later he was also made *faujdar* (commandant in charge of law and order) of the adjoining territory. Aurangzeb approved of his good service and religious principles and kept him as governor of Agra until 1672, when he was transferred to Burhanpur where he died a year later. He was considered the best shot of his day and for a time instructed Aurangzeb's son Muhammad Aᶜzam in that art.[186] He must have built the garden during his tenure at Agra with an increase of 1,000 in his rank.

25 Haveli of Aᶜzam Khan *not preserved*

Aᶜzam Khan was one of the titles of Mir[za] Muhammad Baqir (the other was Iradat Khan) [2:15]. He came from Iran to the Mughal court in Jahangir's reign and became close to Asaf Khan, the emperor's brother-in-law. At the beginning of Shah Jahan's reign, at the request of Asaf Khan, he was made *mir bakhshi* (in charge of *mansabs* and intelligence) and *diwan-i kul* (finance minister), thus one of the foremost administrators. Aᶜzam Khan became governor of the Deccan in 1629/30 and took the fort of Dharur in the emperor's Deccan campaign (1631).[187] After that he became successively governor of Bengal (1632/33), Gujarat (1637) and Bihar (1646/47). He died with a rank of 6,000 *zat* / 6,000 *sawar* in 1649 in Jaunpur, the place of his last appointment, which he had preferred to Kashmir because he felt he would not be able to stand the cold of

that region. It was said that he had excellent qualities but that he was overly strict in financial matters.[188]

The background of a painting of an elephant fight in the Windsor Castle *Padshahnama* shows the Yamuna where it makes its great bend [65]; here, on the right bank, is a white building which might be the Haveli of Aᶜzam Khan.[189] The building also seems to feature in a view of the riverfront drawn by the English artist Thomas Daniell from the Haveli of Islam Khan (no. 27) in 1789 [80],[190] and its remains seem to be shown on the right in an early 19th-century Company drawing in the Taj Museum [73].

26 Haveli of Mughal Khan *not preserved*

This was probably the residence of Mughal Khan, whose father, Zain Khan Koka, descended from a family of Herat and was a foster-brother of Akbar. He served under Jahangir and, at the beginning of Shah Jahan's reign, became *qilᶜadar* (commandant) of Kabul. During the Deccan campaigns he was attached to Khan-i Dauran (see no. 18) and took part in the conquest of the fortress of Udgir, of which he was made *qilᶜadar*.[191] In 1652/53 he had a rank of 3,000 *zat* / 2,000 *sawar*, and became governor of Thatha. He fell into disfavour, however, for failing to assist Dara Shikoh in his Qandahar campaign; he was demoted, and only at the end of Shah Jahan's reign did he get an annual allowance of 1,500 rupees. He was fond of hunting, loved music, and kept a large establishment of musicians and singers.[192]

27 Haveli of Islam Khan *not preserved*

The owner of the *haveli* in the prestigious position next to the fort is given on the Jaipur map [17, 27] as 'Islam Khan'. This could be one of several people. Most 19th-century sources opt for Islam Khan Rumi – the title of Husain Pasha, who was governor of Basra and subject to the sultan of Turkey (Rum), but fell out with the sultan, migrated to India, and in 1669 came to the court of Aurangzeb at Delhi, where he was well received and given the title Islam Khan.[193] But from the

80 View of the riverfront by Thomas Daniell, drawn from the Haveli of Islam Khan (no. 27) in 1789. In the distance is the Taj Mahal; the building in the centre must be the Haveli of Aᶜzam Khan (no. 25).

sources of Shah Jahan's time it appears that the owner was Islam Khan Mashhadi (Mir ᶜAbd-us-Salam, who earlier had the title Ikhtisas Khan) [2:18]. Under Shah Jahan he served as second *bakhshi* and then as *mir bakhshi*, in charge of *mansabs* and intelligence (1634/35), and became governor of Bengal (1634/35), after which he was called to the court in 1639/40 and made *diwan-i kul* (finance minister). In 1645/46, after the death of Khan-i Dauran (see no. 18), Islam Khan Mashhadi was appointed governor of the Deccan and obtained the rank of 7,000 *zat* / 7,000 *sawar* (5,000 x 2–3 horses). He died soon after reaching his new assignment at Aurangabad in 1647/48.[194] Islam Khan Mashhadi's *manzil* on the riverbank at Agra is mentioned by Lahauri in April 1635, when Shah Jahan honoured it with a visit because it had been recently completed.[195]

The Haveli of Islam Khan was used by Thomas and William Daniell in 1789 to take a view of the fort,[196] and another of the riverfront looking towards the ruined Haveli of Aᶜzam Khan (no. 25) and the Taj [80]. It also seems to appear in one of the early 19th-century Company drawings in the Taj Museum.[197] Some fifty years later, Carlleyle recorded it as still standing about 'half a mile below the fort', 'decidedly the largest, loftiest, and noblest looking ruin about Agra, and well worthy of a visit'.[198]

28 **Agra fort** *palaces well preserved*

The main accents of the riverfront landscape of Agra are the Taj Mahal and the great fort of the emperors. Like the mausoleum, it assumed the position of a garden in the urban scheme, and in their layouts its palace garden and main courts followed the riverfront garden design.[199] The fort is here discussed under that aspect.

The Mughal fortress palace stands on the site of a Lodi mud-brick fort. Akbar began to rebuild it in 1564 as his main seat of government, and gave it the splendid fortifications in red sandstone that we see today. Contemporary observers felt that it looked like a city: the Jesuit Antonio Montserrate, who saw it in 1580, noted that in addition to the buildings of the emperor's palace there were 'the mansions of his nobles, the magazines, the treasury, the arsenal, the stables of the cavalry, the shops and huts of drug-sellers, barbers, and all manner of common workmen'.[200] The fort was altered by Akbar's successors, in particular by Shah Jahan, who rebuilt the three main palace courtyards between 1628 and 1637, with characteristic facings of white marble and polished stucco. The fort remained the main imperial residence until 1648, when he moved his court to his new capital at Delhi. When Aurangzeb deposed Shah Jahan in 1658, he kept him prisoner in the Agra fort and, to improve security, built an additional wall around it (1659–62).

During the 18th century, when the Mughal empire was on the wane, the fort changed hands several times between the Mughals, the Jats and the Mahrattas. The British established their garrison here when they conquered Agra in 1803, and the buildings were used for military purposes: the great courtyard of the Diwan-i ᶜAmm, for instance, functioned as an arsenal. Many of the Mughal structures were built over or pulled down and replaced by barracks, but the main palace courtyards survived. From 1876 the chief historic buildings were cared for by an officer of the Public Works Department. At the beginning of the 20th century, Curzon devoted a major restoration campaign to them which freed most from their military additions.[201] In 1923–24 the Archaeological Survey of India fenced off the area

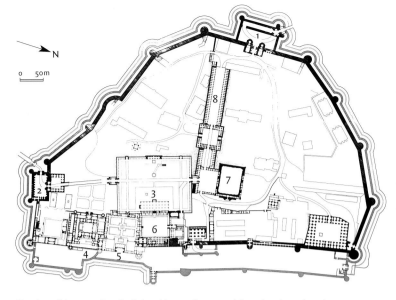

81 Plan of the Agra fort, built by Akbar 1564–70s, with major alterations by Shah Jahan in 1628–37 and by the British. 1 Delhi Gate and Hathi Pol, 2 Amar Singh Gate and Akbari Gate, 3 courtyard of the Diwan-i ᶜAmm, 4 Jahangiri Mahal, 5 'Anguri Bagh' and 'Khass Mahal', 6 'Machchhi Bhavan', 7 Moti Masjid, 8 bazaar street.

comprising the palaces and the Moti Masjid and made it accessible to visitors through the Amar Singh Gate.[202] The greater part of the fort is still under military administration, because after India's independence in 1947 it was taken over by the Indian army; but the area set aside represents a unique ensemble of 16th- and 17th-century Indian and Islamic palace architecture.[203] In 1982 the fort became, together with the Taj Mahal, a UNESCO World Heritage Site.

The fort has the shape of an irregular bow about 2.5 km (1.6 miles) in circumference; its straight eastern side, some 725 m (800 yds) long, lines the Yamuna [27, 81, 82, 299]. The double fortification wall and gates have a spectacular facing of red sandstone which is a hallmark of imperial Mughal architecture and which impressed viewers from the very beginning. Shah Jahan's historian Kanbo, who wrote in highly ornate prose, felt that its arched battlements looked as if 'flames of light were turning their face towards the sky'.[204] The two main gates in Akbar's wall, reached through lower gates in Aurangzeb's wall, both have barbicans or protective enclosures. On the west the Delhi Gate leads to the Hathi Pol (Elephant Gate) [81:1], while on the south the Amar Singh Gate

leads to the Akbari Gate [81:2]. The Hathi Pol was the public entrance in Mughal times, but now it is used only by the army. It leads to a long bazaar street of Akbar's period [81:8] which gives access to the large courtyard of private and public audience with the hall of the Diwan-i ᶜAmm [81:3]. The public entrance is now through the southern gate complex, which was originally used by the imperial family. From it a ramp ascends to the courtyard of the Diwan-i ᶜAmm.

To the east of the ramp are two compact courtyard complexes of Akbar's time, the Jahangiri Mahal [81:4] and the Akbari Mahal (only partly preserved); it seems Shah Jahan did not alter them because they were meant for the use of lesser imperial women. But between 1628 and 1637 he reconstructed the courtyard of the Diwan-i ᶜAmm, the heart of the palace, and the two courtyards between it and the river – what are now called 'Anguri Bagh' (with the 'Khass Mahal') to the south [81:5], and 'Machchhi Bhavan' to the north [81:6]. All three courtyards are organized in a similar way and follow the scheme of the riverfront gardens [85]. Three of their sides are formed by narrow wings of one or two storeys, while on the east side, nearest to the river, are pavilions which served for the main ceremonial

functions of the court and the personal use of Shah Jahan and the women of his household.

The courtyard of the **Diwan-i ᶜAmm**[205] is surrounded by narrow galleries with multi-cusped arches. Projecting into it on the east side is the great audience hall, the Daulat Khana-i Khass-u-ᶜAmm, literally 'Palace Building for the Special Ones and for the Wider Public' – commonly referred to as the Diwan-i ᶜAmm, or Hall of Public Audience [83, 84]. Here the emperor would hold court twice a day and personally attend to the administration of his empire. His courtiers had to stand according to rank in the hall and in the courtyard, in spaces sectioned off hierarchically by railings; foreign delegates too were received here [cf. 2, 114].

This type of large pillared audience hall was introduced into Mughal palace architecture by Shah Jahan. Its other designation was Chihil Sutun ('Forty-Pillared') – the name by which the ruins of Persepolis were then widely known. The building epitomizes Shah Jahan's concept of rulership. By recreating their famous audience halls, the Mughal emperor claimed the status of the ancient kings of Iran, considered as exemplary rulers in the Islamic world. Unlike the

Agra fort

82 *above* View from the south-east. The white marble complex right of centre is the 'Khass Mahal', where Shah Jahan appeared to his subjects every morning [81:5; cf. 87]. (Photograph taken in 1985)

83 *left* The Diwan-i ᶜAmm, or Hall of Public Audience, completed in 1637. (Photograph taken in 1984)

84 *right* The *jharoka*, or window of imperial appearance, in the Diwan-i ᶜAmm, with floral *pietra dura* inlay in the manner of the Taj cenotaphs and their surrounding screen [233]. (Photograph taken in 1980)

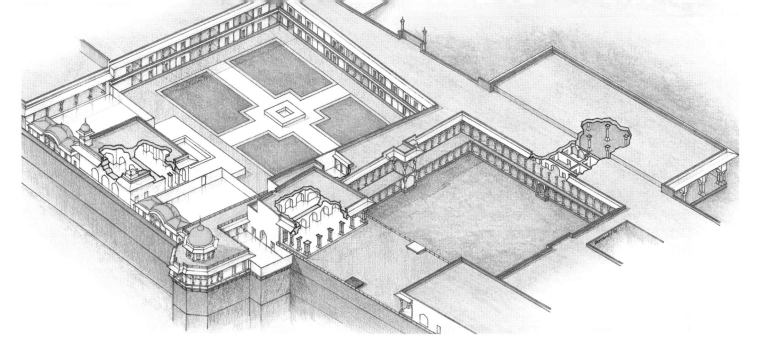

Iranian prototypes, in plan the Mughal halls followed a mosque scheme, with a wider aisle in the centre. But while in a mosque the central aisle leads to the *mihrab*, the niche that shows the direction of Mecca, here it leads to the emperor's *jharoka*, his loggia-like window of appearance in the back wall [84]. Thus the Mughals combined their re-creation of Persepolis with a revival of the connections between mosque and audience hall of earliest Islamic architecture, to signify that Shah Jahan's authority was not only worldly but also spiritual. The reference is reinforced by a mosque of five domed bays integrated opposite the audience hall in the centre of the west wing.[206]

The emperor's *jharoka* is distinguished by highly elaborate decoration. Its walls have *chini khana* niches which originally held porcelain vessels. The Mughals did not consider it a weakness to borrow from other art traditions, and the poet Kalim viewed this as a tribute of China to the court of Shah Jahan.[207] The walls and pillars also display flowering plants in *pietra dura* inlay. The decoration is similar to that of the central tomb chamber of the Taj Mahal [233], and the same artists must have been at work. The naturalistic plant decoration brings in a further symbolic accent: it stands for the bloom

brought about by the just rule of Shah Jahan (pp. 222–24).

While the Diwan-i ͨAmm was widely accessible for the reception of the court, the emperor kept the privileged riverfront for the imperial circle [85]. Here he constructed the 'Machchhi Bhavan', still semi-official, and the 'Anguri Bagh', part of the most inaccessible area, the private courtyards reserved for the emperor, his family and the imperial women. The buildings were, however, highly visible from outside [82, 87], and although screens closed the open spaces towards the river, the arrangement contradicted general notions of the public and private spheres in Muslim culture.

The **'Machchhi Bhavan'**,[208] which lies behind the Diwan-i ͨAmm, is a courtyard enclosed by two-storeyed arcaded wings with Shahjahani columns and multi-cusped arches [81:6, 85, 86]. It is now known as Machchhi Bhavan (Fish House), but in Shah Jahan's time it was referred to as the 'ground-level courtyard' of the Hall of Private Audience (the Daulat Khana-i Khass, or Diwan-i Khass), the upper level being the central part of the riverfront terrace.[209] From its southern wing a marble baldachin projects which housed Shah Jahan's golden throne: this is supported by baluster columns with

Agra fort

85 *above* Bird's-eye-view of the imperial riverfront zone. The hall of the Diwan-i ͨAmm, a public space, is top right. Between it and the river is the 'Machchhi Bhavan' courtyard; there on the riverfront terrace the Diwan-i Khass [86] faces the outer hall of the *hammam* (shown in reconstruction). The Shah Burj projects towards the river. Beyond it are the 'Khass Mahal' and 'Anguri Bagh'.

86 *left* South-east corner of the 'Machchhi Bhavan', completed in 1637. At the riverfront is the Diwan-i Khass or Hall of Private Audience; projecting on the right is the throne baldachin of Shah Jahan [cf. 133, 134]. (Photograph taken in 1981)

naturalistic acanthus decoration [133, 134], inspired by European engravings, of a type first used exclusively in the architecture framing the appearances of Shah Jahan (p. 222). The ranges housed the treasury, and in the open court the emperor would view his hunting animals – hounds, hawks and cheetahs – and watch his horses working out. It was also used for animal fights.

The courtyard has a raised terrace along the side nearest to the river, on the pattern of the riverfront gardens. At the southern end is the Diwan-i Khass [86]. This is a large pavilion faced with white marble which was used for meetings of the private council, as a law court, and for musical performances; here too the emperor would inspect the work of his artists on a daily basis. It has two halls with coved ceilings – the inner called *tanabi khana*, the outer one, with pillars, the *iwan*. (The components are typical of imperial pavilions in the time of Shah Jahan, though their arrangement may vary.) Opposite, on the north side of the terrace, is Shah Jahan's *hammam*, a suite of vaulted rooms, which has lost its marble facing and its outer hall. Parts of it were taken down by Lord Hastings in 1815, and its pillars are scattered (p. 143); the facing, and perhaps some of the pillars, were sold at auction by Lord William Cavendish Bentinck when he was Governor-General (1828–35), giving rise to the rumour that he wanted to take down and sell the Taj Mahal (p. 241).[210]

The **Shah Burj** or Royal Tower projects towards the river between the 'Machchhi Bhavan' and the 'Anguri Bagh', on one of the bastions of the red sandstone walls [82, 85, 87]. In it the typical riverfront garden tower [cf. 32, 55] is transformed into an imperial pavilion, clad in white marble and roofed with a gilded copper dome. Here the emperor would meet the highest dignitaries and his sons in secret council, and also work with his main historian, first Qazwini, then Lahauri, on editing the official history of his reign.

The courtyard now called **'Anguri Bagh'** (Grape Garden) is referred to by Lahauri simply as *bagh*, and in his time it was the only garden in the main palace complex.[211] Its design is that of the classic riverfront garden [81:5, 85]. On a terrace by the Yamuna is a group of three marble buildings now called the **'Khass Mahal'** (Special Imperial Palace), which forms a distinct group from inside [88] as well as from outside [82, 87]. The central building is the Aramgah,

or Imperial Sleeping Pavilion. It is flanked by two identical buildings with gilded *bangla* roofs: on the left (north), the Bangla-i Darshan or Imperial Viewing Pavilion, and on the right (south) the Bangla of Jahanara, Shah Jahan's daughter, which had no ceremonial function but demonstrated her status at court and provided imperial symmetry (*qarina*: pp. 104–5). In the Bangla-i Darshan the emperor showed himself every morning at sunrise to his subjects, assembled below the fort: the historians tell us that they perceived two suns, the heavenly one in the sky and the imperial one here on earth.[212]

The garden has the form of a rectangular *chahar bagh* divided by marble walkways which meet in the centre at a marble pool.[213] The quadrants have unique bed-dividers forming cartouches, which, when planted with flowers, look like a carpet. The garden is enclosed – and this is specific to its palace context – by two-storeyed wings formed of a modular sequence of open pillared verandahs and small enclosed rooms (*hujra*). This *bait* configuration (p. 118) is typical of the wings of Mughal residential courtyards. It appears in the Khawasspuras of the Taj Mahal [157], and also inspired the pavilions of Nur Jahan in the Nur Afshan garden/Ram Bagh [36].

At the end of the southern wing, near the Bangla of Jahanara, were her apartments, for which the northern rooms of the Jahangiri Mahal had been adapted [81:4]. Here in April 1644 her delicate muslin garment caught fire from a lamp standing on the floor, and she was badly burned.[214] The accident upset Shah Jahan so much that he did not appear in *darbar*, something he had failed to do only once before, when Mumtaz died (p. 20). Opposite, in the northern wing, is the entrance to a group of basement rooms with waterfalls and pools, called *tahkhana* by Lahauri.[215] Since the 19th century these rooms have been known as Shish Mahal (Mirror Palace),[216] from their facing with mirror mosaic set in white stucco relief (*ayina bandi* or *ayina kari*).

87 *below* Part of the river frontage: from left to right are the Aramgah, Bangla-i Darshan (where Shah Jahan appeared to his subjects in the morning), Shah Burj and Diwan-i Khass, all completed in 1637. (Photograph taken in 1978)

overleaf
88 'Anguri Bagh' and the buildings of the 'Khass Mahal' – Bangla-i Darshan, Aramgah, Bangla of Jahanara – completed in 1637. (Photograph taken in 1982)

It is uncertain how much remains of the garden residences lining the river between the fort and the tomb garden of Jaᶜfar Khan (nos. 29–44), because the area has been absorbed by the city of Agra and is densely built over. Yamuna Kinara Road runs on the line of the old riverbank, and it is here, about 800 m (½ mile) north of the fort in the city quarter called Belanganj, that the most visible remains survive [29]. Two towers topped by *chhatris* in Shahjahani style, set 40 m (130 ft) apart, formed the riverfront corners of a garden; locally called Khuni Burj (Blood Towers), they belonged to a complex now known as Puttariya Mahal [89].²¹⁷ Beyond, set back from the road, is Aurangzeb's 'Mubarak Manzil' (no. 35), which the British turned into the Custom House. Finally, where the road turns towards the west, there is a large ruined building now known as Sheron Wali Kothi or 'Library of Dara Shikoh' (see no. 39).

29 Haveli of Dara Shikoh *not preserved*

The *haveli* of Shah Jahan's son Muhammad Dara Shikoh occupied a privileged site immediately north of the fort [17, 27]. Pelsaert in the 1620s lists the site as that of 'Rochia Sultan Begam', by which he obviously means Ruqaiya Begam, Shah Jahan's foster-mother.²¹⁸ Dara Shikoh [2:2, 90], given the title Padshahzada-i Buland Iqbal ('Imperial Son of High Fortune'), was the eldest and favourite son of Shah Jahan. At the end of the emperor's reign, in 1657/58, he held the highest rank ever obtained in the Mughal empire: 60,000 *zat* / 40,000 *sawar* (30,000 x 2–3 horses).²¹⁹ The prince was a mystic and a philosopher and the spiritual heir of Akbar in his endeavour to unite the two chief religions of India, Hinduism and Islam: he translated the ancient Indian text of the Upanishads from Sanskrit into Persian, and brought out a comparative study of the Vedas and Sufism. He lacked the political, administrative, and military skills necessary to succeed in the Mughal system, however, and although Shah Jahan tried in every way to secure the throne for him, Dara

89 The two *chhatri*-topped towers known as Khuni Burj, which emerge from later buildings in Yamuna Kinara Road in Belanganj, seem to be the riverfront corner towers of a Mughal *haveli*. The site is known as the Puttariya Mahal. (Photograph taken in 1986)

Shikoh was defeated in the struggle for succession by his younger brother Aurangzeb, who had him executed for heresy in 1659.²²⁰

Dara Shikoh was a calligrapher and patron of painting and architecture.²²¹ His mansion (*manzil*) at Agra was built or rebuilt in the early 1640s. Shah Jahan honoured it several times with a visit, first on the occasion of its completion in March 1643, when the prince presented his father with the ceremonial gifts (*pishkash* – a form of tax) offered on such occasions. In September 1643 Shah Jahan visited the house again to see his newly born grandson, Sultan Mumtaz Shikoh, and presented the child with a rosary of pearls and rubies. A longer stay followed in June 1644: Shah Jahan's daughter Jahanara had not recovered from the severe burns she had suffered in April (p. 69), and he took her to the house of her brother for a change of scene.²²² On 27 December 1654 Shah Jahan came to Agra with Dara Shikoh to show him the recently completed Moti Masjid in the fort. Afterwards he went by boat to the 'Tomb of Paradisiacal Design' – the Taj Mahal – and then had a meal at the house of Dara before leaving the city.²²³ The emperor's last visit occurred in November 1657, when, recovering from the illness that had occasioned the rebellion of his sons (p. 13), he moved from Delhi to Agra in the hope that a change of residence would improve his condition. He arrived by boat and proceeded directly to the house of the prince, referred to as *daulat sara* (imperial palace). The inhabitants of Agra, who had assembled on both sides of the river, cheered him enthusiastically, 'as those who have been fasting greet the new moon that shows the end of Ramazan'.²²⁴

After Aurangzeb had defeated Dara Shikoh at the battle of Samugarh near Agra, he occupied the city, and made it a point to take up quarters not in his own *haveli* but in his brother's mansion (*manzil*): this he did on 28 June 1658, after it had been 'swept clean from the dust of non-splendour' supposedly left by his brother, and gave robes of honour to the nobles of the empire.²²⁵ Aurangzeb stayed here again when he visited Agra in February 1666 on the occasion of Shah Jahan's death (p. 101).

Dara Shikoh's *haveli* was plundered in 1761 by Suraj Mal, leader of the Jats from Bharatpur (p. 232). A fanciful view dated 1774 [91] shows a long low platform on which are set pavilions with *bangla*

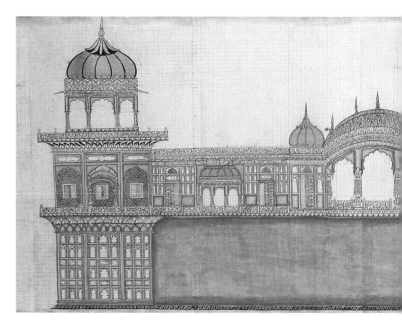

roofs supported by baluster columns, framed by corner towers.[226] The English artist William Hodges drew part of it in 1783 as a foreground of his view of the fort and the Taj [355] and found it dangerous to walk among its ruins.[227] The palace still existed in the early 19th century. Sil Chand in 1825–26 claimed that it was the best mansion of Agra, and noted that it had a wide courtyard and buildings of stone which were decorated with *parchin kari* (inlay work) and painted 'with portraits of the past kings' and other motifs, and that its *jilaukhanas* (probably vestibules) were decorated with mirror work (*ayina bandi*)[228] – modes of architectural decoration reserved for the emperor and the highest court circles. A ruinous wing of the palace, with two arcaded storeys, is depicted under the name 'Dara Sheko's Palace' in Florentia Sale's *Notebook* of 1832–33. At that time it was also known as Jamna Bagh or Jamna Haveli.[229] A plan of the fort and its immediate surroundings which dates from the first half of the 19th century shows the palace inscribed with this name as a large courtyard enclosure with pavilions on the riverfront.[230] According to the *Agra Gazetteer* of 1921, the remains of the Haveli of Dara Shikoh were taken down in 1881 to make space for the Town Hall.[231]

30 Haveli of Khan-i Jahan Lodi *not preserved*

Khan-i Jahan Lodi [50] was one of the most esteemed *amirs* of Jahangir, who made him governor of the Deccan. At the beginning of Shah Jahan's reign he had the high rank of 7,000 *zat* / 7,000 *sawar* (2–3 horses).[232] Because of irregularities, however, and because he had failed to support Shah Jahan's succession to the throne, he fell from favour and started a rebellion, which ended in his death in 1631 at the hands of Shah Jahan's troups, an event depicted with gruesome realism in the Windsor Castle *Padshahnama*.[233] His house in Agra is mentioned in reports of his flight in October 1629; De Laet in 1631 lists the palace of 'Chan Sian' (Khan-i Jahan) north of and close to the fort.[234]

31 Haveli of Hafiz Khidmatgar *two enclosures, not preserved*

This noble has not been identified.

90 Dara Shikoh (with his youngest brother, Murad Bakhsh), from a scene of the presentation to him of wedding gifts, painted by Balchand, Mughal, *c.* 1635, from the *Padshahnama*.

91 The river frontage of the Haveli of Dara Shikoh, as fancifully depicted in a drawing dated 1774. The once exclusively imperial *bangla* forms [cf. 87, 88] and baluster columns accentuate the façade.

32 Haveli of Asaf Khan *not preserved*

Abu'l Hasan, with the title Asaf Khan [2:6], was the most powerful *amir* of Shah Jahan, closely related to the imperial family. He was the son of I'timad-ud-Daula (Jahangir's esteemed father-in-law and *wazir*), the brother of Jahangir's wife Nur Jahan, and the father of Shah Jahan's wife Mumtaz Mahal (pp. 18–19). Asaf Khan secured the succession for Shah Jahan, who showed his gratitude by making him *wakil*, the highest office in the Mughal government, with the unusually high rank of 9,000 *zat* / 9,000 *sawar* (2–3 horses) and the title Yamin-ud-Daula ('Right Hand of the Empire').[235] When Mahabat Khan (see no. 23) died in 1634 Asaf Khan became commander in chief in his place.

Asaf Khan had a splendid establishment, liked good food and drink, and his servants were devoted to him and well cared for. The sumptuous *pishkashs* and *nazars* (tax in the form of presents) that he gave the emperor, the princes and the imperial *begams* were famous.[236] He was a good writer, a skilled accountant, and a noted patron of architecture: indeed, he was himself 'well versed in the subtleties of this craft',[237] and was employed in the planning and realization of imperial projects. His own buildings, notably the Nishat Bagh of nine terraces in Kashmir, rivalled those of the emperor.[238] He died in 1641 of chronic dropsy at Lahore, where he was buried in an octagonal tomb faced with tiles in a *chahar bagh* next to the tomb of Jahangir.[239]

Asaf Khan's riverfront mansion (*manzil*) is mentioned by Jahangir in his memoirs. The emperor visited it several times, and came there with his ladies for the Persian New Year in March 1621. He particularly admired its *hammam*, completed in 1619, where he bathed and had a wine party.[240] Sil Chand in 1825–26 describes the house in eulogistic terms: he says that it was like an imperial palace (*daulat khana*) and that it had a pillared hall (*iwan*) exactly like the Diwan-i 'Amm of Shah Jahan in the fort [83], but that Asaf Khan was disappointed when he saw it finished because he had wanted it even bigger.[241] Carlleyle in 1871–72 records that it was in such good condition before the Great Indian Uprising ('Mutiny') of 1857 that Dr Playfair, Deputy Inspector-General of Hospitals, Agra Circle, lived there with a friend, but that the British authorities blew it up because they feared 'it would afford a cover for any native force coming to attack the fort'.[242]

33–35 Complex of Aurangzeb with 'Mubarak Manzil' (Blessed House) *partly preserved*

The Jaipur map [17, 27] shows two enclosures named as the Haveli of 'Alamgir (the title taken by Aurangzeb on his accession), and north of them another enclosure named as Masjid-i Mubarak Manzil (Mosque of the Blessed House).

Aurangzeb [2, 65] was the third and least favourite son of Shah Jahan. On the other hand he was the most capable of the princes, and because of his military and administrative skills he was entrusted with important assignments from an early age, beginning with the nominal command of the campaign against the rebellious Bundela Rajputs in 1635, when he was only seventeen. A year later he was appointed governor of the Deccan. In 1657/58 Aurangzeb had the rank of 20,000 *zat* / 15,000 *sawar* (2–3 horses).[243] When Shah Jahan fell ill in 1657 Aurangzeb outmanoeuvred his brothers, and proclaimed himself emperor in 1658. He imprisoned Shah Jahan

in the Agra fort, resided at Delhi, and spent much of his reign in the Deccan, leaving Agra to the memory of its imperial days.

The history of the site of Aurangzeb's complex is a telling example of changing landownership in the Mughal system. We can trace its owners back to the 16th century. At the beginning of Akbar's reign the riverfront property belonged to Khan-i Khanan Bairam Khan Turkoman, *wakil* (chief minister) and guardian of the emperor, who was then a minor. When Bairam Khan fell from power in December 1560 Akbar gave his title and office, as well as his residence at Agra, to Mun'im Khan.[244] Upon the latter's death in 1575, the property reverted to the crown. After Jahangir came to the throne he granted it to his eldest son, Khusrau, together with one *lakh* of rupees to rebuild it.[245] The next owner was Shah Jahan, who, to ensure his own succession, had ordered the murder of Khusrau. De Laet in 1631, three years after Shah Jahan's accession, lists a house north of the fort, almost in the position of Aurangzeb's complex on the Jaipur map, not as that of Khusrau but as that of 'prince Sultan Khrom' – Khurram, i.e. Shah Jahan (De Laet gives this name to the fourth plot north of the fort; but he may not have got the position of the garden quite right, since he was working as a compiler and not as a first-hand recorder).[246]

In February 1628 Shah Jahan, still a prince, stayed in his residence, which was then called *daulat khana*, 'imperial palace', for twelve days while he awaited the auspicious hour (calculated by his astrologers as the 14th of the month) for his formal entry into the fort for his accession ceremony.[247] In March 1633 Prince Shah

92 'Mubarak Manzil' or 'Tara Niwas', part of the complex of Aurangzeb, with British additions of 1817 and later. The Mughal building consisted of the arcaded lower storey, flanked by towers of which one appears here on the left. (Photograph taken in 2004)

Shuja^c, Shah Jahan's second son, resided there on the occasion of his wedding.[248] The emperor continued to use it: later that year, in June, when plague had broken out in Agra, he moved there 'because of its spaciousness, closeness to the water and purity of air'.[249] The description of a historic elephant fight that took place while he was there confirms the position of Shah Jahan's princely residence north of the fort.[250] Eventually the property came to Aurangzeb.[251]

Of the three enclosures shown on the Jaipur map, what survives is a Mughal building, much altered in 1817, when a second storey was added [92]. Known variously since the 19th century as the Mubarak Manzil, Custom House, Permit Kothi, and now as Tara Niwas, it was used from 1810 to 1877 as the Custom House or Head Office of the Salt Department in Agra (the map of 1868–69 shows it at the head of the pontoon bridge [28]), and was sold by the British government in 1878.[252] In 1902 the Muslim community claimed it as a place of worship, but since no evidence of mosque architecture could be found, their petition to Curzon was denied.[253] A year later, A. C. Polwhele, Executive Engineer, Agra, reported that the 'Mubarak Manzil' was used as the East Indian Railway goods depot, and bore a marble tablet reproducing the local tradition that it had been erected by Aurangzeb after the battle of Samugarh.[254]

The most detailed description of the 'Mubarak Manzil' is that of Carlleyle in 1871–72. He mentions as a prominent feature 'a beautiful colonnade or pillared verandah on the east side of the building . . . with fluted pillars' and 'engrailed arches';[255] but he failed to discern the overall shape of the original Mughal building.

It consisted of a large flat-roofed pillared hall with towers at the four corners topped by small domes.[256] The hall has a grid of bays with coved ceilings demarcated by multi-cusped arches supported on Shahjahani columns – 116 freestanding columns, and 12 half-columns where the walls are solid near the towers. But for the unusual corner towers, the 'Mubarak Manzil' has its closest parallel in the Diwan-i ^cAmm of the fort [83].

36 Haveli of Sasat Khan (Haveli of Shayista Khan) *not preserved*

The garden appears on the Jaipur map as that of 'Sasat Khan'. This seems to be a corruption of Shayista Khan, because Sil Chand lists Shayista Khan's *haveli* next to the 'Mubarak Manzil'.[257] Mirza Abu Talib, given the title Shayista Khan (Worthy Khan) by Jahangir [2:16], was the son of Asaf Khan, nephew of Nur Jahan, and grandson of I^ctimad-ud-Daula. As Mumtaz Mahal's brother, he was Shah Jahan's brother-in-law. Under Shah Jahan he held several governships, including that of Malwa in 1657/58 when he was promoted to the rank of 6,000 *zat* / 6,000 *sawar* (5,000 x 2–3 horses).[258] When the struggle for succession broke out Shayista Khan sided with Aurangzeb, and deliberately advised Shah Jahan not to lead his troops into battle at Samugarh but to put Dara Shikoh in command, resulting in the disastrous defeat of the imperial army.

Aurangzeb gave him the high rank of 7,000 *zat* / 7,000 *sawar* (2–3 horses)and the prestigious title *amir-ul-umara* (head of the *amirs*). He was appointed governor of the Deccan, fought not very successfully against the Mahratta leader Shivaji, and was transferred to Bengal. In 1678 he was removed from that post and went on pilgrimage to Mecca. In the following year he presented the emperor with enormously valuable gifts, after which he was granted the rare privilege of bringing his palanquin into the Diwan-i Khass and beating his drum after that of the emperor. In the same year he was appointed governor of Agra, where he died in 1694. His legendary wealth was escheated to the crown and filled the Mughal treasury, kept in the Agra fort. Shayista Khan was famous for his good works and raised buildings for the common good in all parts of India.[259] Tieffenthaler, who was in Agra in the 1740s, credits him with the first construction of the city wall, which was renewed and extended by Jai Singh in the 18th century (p. 232).[260]

37 Haveli of Ja^cfar Khan *not preserved*

For the life of Ja^cfar Khan, see the description of his tomb, which survives (no. 44). Shah Jahan honoured his mansion (*manzil*) with a visit on 3 September 1637, on the occasion of its completion, and took part in a moonlight gathering.[261] When Sil Chand wrote his account in 1825–26 the *haveli* had been almost completely destroyed.[262]

38 Rauza of Sasat Khan (tomb garden of Shayista Khan) *preservation uncertain*

The building appears as the tomb of 'Sasat Khan' (cf. no. 36) on the Jaipur map [17, 27], and it is mentioned by Sil Chand.[263] The map shows it as a square domed structure in red sandstone on the river-front. A building of similar appearance, known as the tomb of Mir Jumla, still exists further up the river, overlooking the bypass of National Highway No. 2 before it reaches the Yamuna bridge, near the mosque of Ja^cfar Khan [95], west of the tomb of Ja^cfar Khan (no. 44). Perhaps the artist of the map erred in the placement of the tomb.

93 *top* The Haveli of Wazir Khan, across the river from the tomb of I͗timad-ud-Daula; both buildings are named in Devanagari script [see 56]. Detail of a drawing by an Indian artist, 18th century.

94 *above* The 'Library of Dara Shikoh', possibly a fragment of the Haveli of Wazir Khan. (Photograph taken in 2001)

39 Haveli of Wazir Khan *partly preserved?*

Hakim ᶜAlim-ud-Din, with the title Wazir Khan [47], was *wazir* (finance minister) under Shah Jahan. It is likely that he also had a garden on the left bank of the Yamuna (see no. 7). A drawing datable to the 18th century [93] shows the Haveli of Wazir Khan immediately opposite the tomb of Iᶜtimad-ud-Daula (no. 9). (On the Jaipur map [17, 27] it is shown too far upstream.) The situation opposite the

tomb of Iᶜtimad-ud-Daula corresponds to that of a large building where the Yamuna Kinara Road bends westward: now known as Sheron Wali Kothi, or 'Library of Dara Shikoh' [94],[264] this incorporates a Mughal structure of which an arcade with Shahjahani columns and multi-cusped arches is still visible from the road on the side facing the river.

40 Haveli of Muqim Khan *not preserved*

The owner was perhaps Muqim Khan, a noble of Akbar, who gave him the rank of 700[265] and the title Wazir Khan. Under Jahangir he was made co-*wazir* with another noble, and his rank was raised. He then served as *diwan* (finance minister) in Bengal, and later was sent with Prince Parwiz to the Deccan. He died in 1620.[266] Sil Chand and Raja Ram mention the ruins of the *haveli*.[267]

41 Haveli of Khalil Khan *not preserved*

Khalil Khan seems to be identical with Khalilullah Khan, a *mansabdar* of 5,000 zat / 5,000 sawar (2–3 horses) at the court of Shah Jahan, who went over to Aurangzeb in the war of succession.[268] Traces of his palace still existed in the first half of the 19th century.[269]

42 Bagh-i Rai Shiv Das (garden of Rai Shiv Das) *not preserved*

The presence of the garden of 'Rai Shiv Das' enables us to date the Jaipur map. Rai Shiv Das, or Rai Shivadasa, was a close associate of Maharaja Sawai Jai Singh of Jaipur, and acted as deputy governor after the latter had been appointed governor of the province of Agra in 1722 (p. 232). In the later 18th century the garden became one of the popular recreational spots along the Yamuna: the poet Nazir Akbarabadi describes the 'garden of Shivdas' as a place where people gathered to eat sweets, dance and swim (p. 33).[270] The garden was still planted with fruit trees in 1825–26,[271] and traces of it existed in 1891.[272]

43 Bagh-i Hakim Kazim ᶜAli (garden of Hakim Kazim ᶜAli)
not preserved

The identity of the garden owner has not been established. Nazir Akbarabadi mentions the 'Bagh-i Hakim' (garden of the doctor) together with the 'garden of Shivdas' as a popular recreation place for the people of Agra (see no. 42).[273] Sil Chand reports that in his time, in 1825–26, the garden of Hakim Kazim ᶜAli Khan was taken over by a Briton named 'Joras' (?George), 'son of Colonel John Sahib';[274] but it was still referred to as 'Hakimji-ka-Bagh' in the later 19th century,[275] and is one of the few riverfront sites that still feature as such, and with their original name, on the Agra map of 1868–69 [28].

44 Rauza of Jaᶜfar Khan (tomb garden of Jaᶜfar Khan) *preserved*[276]

Jaᶜfar Khan [2:14] was married to Farzana Begam, the sister of Mumtaz Mahal, and was thus the brother-in-law of Shah Jahan. The Venetian traveller Niccolao Manucci reported that after the death of Mumtaz, Shah Jahan sought the company of her sister so intensely that it gave rise to rumours in the bazaars.[277] In addition to his close ties to the imperial family, Jaᶜfar Khan distinguished himself by devoted service. He held the positions of governor of the Panjab (1646/47), mir bakhshi, in charge of mansabs and of intelligence (1647/48), and governor of Delhi (1649/50), Multan (1650), and Bihar (1650/51). Finally, at the end of Shah Jahan's reign he became *wazir-i kul* (finance minister), at a rank of 5,000 *zat* / 5,000 *sawar* (2,500 x 2–3 horses).[278] He is often depicted in the Windsor Castle *Padshahnama*.[279] When Aurangzeb won the battle of Samugarh in 1658 Jaᶜfar Khan went over to him, was made governor of Malwa, and was given an increase in rank to 6,000 *zat* / 6,000 *sawar*. He was one of the few nobles privileged to build a riverfront house in Delhi.[280] Jaᶜfar Khan died in 1670 in Delhi after a long and severe illness, and Aurangzeb sent two of the imperial princes to present condolences personally to Farzana Begam and her sons.[281]

Three buildings are connected with Jaᶜfar Khan on the right bank of the Yamuna: his *haveli*, which is not preserved (no. 37), his *rauza* or tomb (no. 44),[282] and a mosque, now called Lal Masjid, which still stands on the northern side of the bypass of National Highway No. 2 before it reaches the Yamuna bridge, next to a tomb known as that of Mir Jumla [95].

95 The 'tomb of Mir Jumla' and the ruined mosque of Jaᶜfar Khan, or Lal Masjid. (Photograph taken in the 1970s)

Tomb garden of Jaʿfar Khan

96 *left* The tomb pavilion, recorded in a Company drawing by an Agra artist from the *Notebook* of Florentia, Lady Sale, 1632–33. The corner towers were already in ruin, and are barely sketched in.

97 *left, below* The south front of the tomb pavilion as it appeared in 1999, with the arcade filled in.

98 *right* Plan.

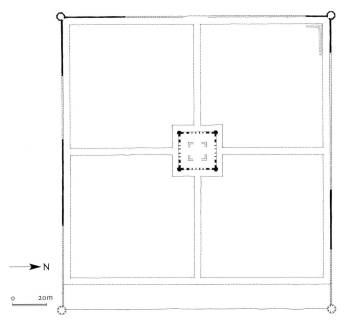

N

0   20m

The tomb garden of Jaʿfar Khan is situated on the riverbank immediately north of the highway bridge, opposite the Nur Afshan garden/Ram Bagh (no. 3); the Jaipur map [17, 27] shows it too far north. The tomb stands on a platform, in the centre of what was a large square walled garden with towers at each corner [98].[283] Parts of the garden wall and corner towers remain, although they are encroached upon by new structures. There is a fine view of the tomb itself in Florentia Sale's *Notebook* of 1832–33, inscribed 'Tomb of Nawau Jaffeer Khan' and 'Jaffer Khan's Roza', which shows it more or less as it is today [96, 97]. It is a square, flat-roofed building with towers, now ruined, at its corners, and a verandah in the centre of each side that communicates with an ambulatory surrounding an inner hall: thus it revives, in the idiom of the later 17th century, a tomb type which was popular in Jahangir's period [108].[284] Each verandah has five multi-cusped arches supported by rectangular pillars topped by a flame-like arrangement of acanthus leaves – a motif that first appeared in the palace of Shah Jahan in the Red Fort of Delhi (completed in 1648) and became popular in later Mughal architecture. The arcades are framed on each side by a further cusped arch, set off by vertical strips with superimposed stylized *chini khana* panels. The arrangement gives the elevation a *hasht bihisht* accent (p. 26). The tomb of Jaʿfar Khan is now used as a government store room, and all the arches are filled in.

The garden was the scene of great activity during the Triveni festival in the rainy season, when Muslims and Hindus gathered there to swim (p. 33).

45 Chhatri of Jaswant Singh (memorial pavilion of Jaswant Singh)
well preserved

Jaswant Singh Rathor of Jodhpur was confirmed by Shah Jahan as his father's heir and *raja* in 1638/39, and since he came from one of the noblest Rajput families of India, the emperor treated him with many favours. He was given splendid presents, such as an elephant from the imperial stables, received a Mughal rank of 4,000 *zat* / 4,000 *sawar*, and was given assignments in the administration, including a temporary governorship of Agra in 1646 when Shah

Jahan moved to the north for his Balkh and Badakhstan campaign. In 1653/54 he was accorded the title *maharaja* and an increase in rank. When the war of succession broke out, Shah Jahan gave him the governorship of Malwa and an increase in rank to 7,000 *zat* / 7,000 *sawar* (5,000 x 2–3 horses), to bind him to the imperial side. Jaswant Singh kept changing sides between Dara Shikoh and Aurangzeb, however; and when Aurangzeb became emperor he was confirmed in his position and given assignments in Gujarat and in the Deccan. He probably died in 1678.[285]

For Rajputs, a *chhatri* was a memorial structure, raised instead of a tomb, since Hindus do not bury their dead. The most usual form for a funerary *chhatri* was a domed pavilion, but other forms were also possible. The Chhatri of Jaswant Singh[286] lies about 1 km (just over ½ mile) north of the tomb garden of Jaʿfar Khan (no. 44), beyond the scope of the Jaipur map. Sil Chand gives Rajwara as the name of this northern stretch, which contained the residences of Rajput nobles who served in the Mughal administration, and the village where the Chhatri stands is today called Rajwara.[287] The memorial structure was originally set in a rectangular enclosure with corner towers, of which the ornamental wall on the riverfront

The Chhatri of Jaswant Singh (d. 1678)

99 *above* The pavilion. (Photograph taken in 1999)

100 *opposite* The riverfront wall, with flanking towers, seen from the bridge of the bypass of National Highway No. 2. (Photograph taken in 2002)

survives [100]. It is a flat-roofed pavilion built of red sandstone, with three openings on each side, in the form known as *baradari* (a structure with twelve doors) [99]. The openings have corbelled heads rather than true arches, and are partly filled with *jalis* or stone screens, composed of square panels with tracery in geometrical patterns. In its ornate style and its sandstone fabric the building looks back to the architecture of Fatehpur Sikri, built for Akbar in the 1570s [336], which in turn absorbed older motifs of Indian architecture, such as the corbelled openings, pillars with stone chains and bells (which had their origin in Hindu temples), and brackets in which are set lotus rosettes. These motifs were obviously used here to declare that the structure honoured the memory of a Rajput prince. The tomb of Jaswant Singh is protected by the Archaeological Survey of India.

Mughal workers and construction techniques, depicted in the *Akbarnama* (see caption 101).

At the bottom, below the strip of text which tells us about the founding of the fort, labourers clad in white loincloths (*dhoti*) and turbans unload large pebbles (*sang-i ghalula*) brought by boat from Delhi, probably to be used in the foundations. On the left stonemasons (*sangtarash*) split blocks of sandstone by cleaving them like logs with irons; as skilled workmen they are better dressed, in a simpler version of Mughal court attire – a tunic tied at the side with strings, a cloth sash, pants, and a turban. Behind them, a female worker in blouse, skirt and veil, the dress of Indian country women, holds a bowl with sand or lime on her head, while other masons carry long heavy blocks up a timber ramp by means of rope slings attached to thick bamboo poles. Below the ramp, workers lever a block of stone up with a stick. In the middle, oxen carry bags of lime. To the right a scribe notes something in a ledger while an ordinary labourer faces him with one hand outstretched, perhaps negotiating his payment. The ramp leads to the roof level of the gate, where a dome is being raised in concentric rings of brick by masons. To the right workers cup their hands as a water-carrier pours out water from a leather bag. Behind them, a female worker sieves lime, and a supervisor leaning on a stick raises his hand to give an order.

The spandrels of the gate, already finished, show a painted decoration of winged figures holding gazelles: these are *paris*, attendants of Solomon on his flying throne (relatives of the peacock-holding *pari* in the Nur Afshan garden/ Ram Bagh [37]).

II The construction of the Taj Mahal

Upon her grave – may it be illumined until the Day of Resurrection! –
The King of Kings constructed such an edifice

That since Destiny drew the plan of creation
It has not seen such an exalted building.

Abu Talib Kalim, *Padshahnama*, 1630s–40s[1]

Shah Jahan's architecture is closely linked to his form of governance. He conceived the Taj Mahal as the most magnificent building of all ages, and as the quintessential mausoleum for his deceased queen, represented not in a haphazard deployment of style but with careful consideration of specific Mughal forms developed over the 16th and 17th centuries. Its overall plan followed, on a much larger scale, the distinctive pattern of the riverfront gardens of Agra (p. 24). For the tomb itself the grandest, and from an orthodox Muslim point of view most daring, variant of a Mughal mausoleum was chosen: the monumental domed structure, which had been used only once before for an imperial burial, in the tomb of Humayun at Delhi (1562–71) [104]. The best builders and craftsmen of the empire were recruited and the finest materials employed. The white marble had to be carted from quarries hundreds of kilometres from Agra, and never before had so much of this precious and prestigious stone been used on an Indian building.

Despite the effort and the logistics that went into the planning and realization of this grand structure, no direct information is given about its architects, or about the details of its construction. It was understood that Shah Jahan was the conceptual force behind the venture: whatever architects were employed were merely agents who realized his designs. The progress of the construction, which went on over a period of twelve years, has to be pieced together from descriptions of the celebrations on the anniversaries of Mumtaz's death ('urs), held in different parts of the tomb complex. The completed building was worthy to be recorded, not the way in which it was achieved.

Shah Jahan and architecture

Under Shah Jahan the emperor assumed an absolute and centralized authority unparalleled in Mughal history. The hierarchic relationship was confirmed and acted out symbolically in a daily court ceremonial focusing on him. Hand in hand with the regulation of every detail of court life went an ever-increasing formalization of the court arts, which were represented as a necessary instrument of rule. The ruler who exerted himself in the sphere of the arts was sure of the loyalty, obedience and recognition of his subjects, as well as the esteem of rival rulers. This was put into words by the historian Kanbo:

Whenever the highest Wisdom of the Majesty exalted above all [God] – may His proof be exalted everywhere – out of concern for His servants and His countries finds it apt to choose a dynastic family of sultans of the world, He bestows special distinction on the lords of that God-given empire among all other masters of empires with perfect grandeur and majesty, and He gives whatever is necessary for [maintenance] of their rule. [Such matters] may belong [to the category] of beautiful and external things that are not so necessary for overall rule, but that are essential to give full distinction and spectacular display – the more so since it becomes a matter of increase of pomp and power, magnificence and elegance . . . It is evident that the increase of such things creates esteem for the rulers in the eyes [of the people] and augments respect [for the ruler] and [the people's own] dignity in [their] hearts. In this form the execution of divine injunctions and prohibitions, and the enforcement of divine decrees and laws which is the ultimate aim of rulership and kingship, are carried out in a better way.[2]

Shah Jahan and his advisers structured court proceedings with a rigid ceremonial which he himself followed to the minute in his daily routine. From morning to evening the emperor moved through the palace within the fort from one place of audience to another [see 85]. The most public was his appearance every morning before his assembled subjects in the viewing window or Jharoka-i Darshan in the outer wall of the palace [87]; next, he moved to the Hall of Public Audience or Diwan-i ʿAmm [83, 84]; then to the Hall of Private Audience or Diwan-i Khass [85, 86]; then to the Shah Burj [87], for secret councils; and finally to the *zanana*, most remote of all – the palace quarters of the imperial women [81:4, 85]. The appearance in the outer viewing window took place only in the morning at sunrise; the rest of the cycle took place in the morning and again in the afternoon.[3] The architectural setting was also standardized: the buildings were specifically designed for their ceremonial purpose, and followed, with slight variations, the same formal pattern – or showed the same components – in all the imperial palaces. Thus the form of a palace building tells us about its function.

In the Islamic world architecture and the arts had long been considered as the immediate expression of the ruler. The great 14th-century Arab historian Ibn Khaldun drew attention to the decisive role Muslim rulers played in the development of architecture and the crafts that expressed their status, and noted that their patronage was echoed by the nobility and the prosperous classes in the cities, the centres of power, religion, learning and culture.[4] In Europe such ideas manifested themselves widely only in the age of absolutism from the

101 The building of the water gate of the Agra fort, painted by Miskina with Sarwan and Tulsi Kurd, from the *Akbarnama*, 1590–95. The fort was begun in 1564 under the supervision of Qasim Khan, *mir barr u bahr* (lord of land and water), chief engineer.

16th century onwards, when the leading role of the church as patron of the arts was challenged by worldly rulers. Shah Jahan stands out for his consistent use of highly aestheticized form to express his specific state ideology – that centralized authority and hierarchy bring about balance and harmony. A counterpart, if not a follower, in the West would be Louis XIV of France (r. 1643–1715) – himself interested in 'Oriental rulers' – whose use of art as an instrument of absolute monarchy was in turn emulated by other European courts.[5]

The political role assigned to the arts, and the emperor's function as the supreme administrator of his court-led state, meant that Shah Jahan sought to assert as close control over his artists as over his court and administration. Mughal art was regulated as never before or after. All Shah Jahan's historians agree in saying that he made the personal overseeing of his artists a fixed part of his daily routine, thus acting – with typical perfectionism – as his own artistic director. Architecture was the imperial representational medium par excellence: as the most prestigious and useful art, it could represent the ruler and his state in the eyes of a wider public, and provide an everlasting memorial to his fame:[6] according to an Arabic saying, 'Our monuments will tell of us.' Shah Jahan had a personal interest in architecture (p. 89), and in his endeavour to explore and refine it as an imperial statement he employed a whole team of architects and advisers with whom he himself developed his building projects and established principles of construction. Qazwini writes:

> The superintendents of the imperial buildings together with the masterful architects (mi'mar-an) of excellent abilities bring architectural designs (tar-ha-yi 'imarat) before the exalted sight [of the emperor]. And since his most pure mind is inclined entirely towards building ('imarat) – which is the cause of the flourishing of the state and the adornment of the apparent world and which gives value and splendour to the material world – he attends to it fully by creating most of the designs himself and also by making appropriate changes to whatever the architects have thought out.[7]

Shah Jahan's buildings speak to us 'with mute eloquence', as his chief historian, Lahauri, put it in his account of the emperor's daily planning sessions with his architects:

> The mind [of the emperor], brilliant as the sun, pays great attention to lofty edifices and strong buildings, which, as the saying has it – 'Verily our monuments will tell of us' – long speak with mute eloquence (ba-zaban bizabani) of their master's high aspiration and sublime authority, and for ages to come are memorials to his love of land development, spreading of ornamentation, and nourishing of purity . . . In this peaceful reign the work of building has reached such a point that it astonishes even the world traveller who is hard to please and the magical masters of this incomparable art.[8]

The principles of construction that underlay the creations of Shah Jahan's reign were not put down in writing. The Mughals had no written architectural theory. None of the remarkable Sanskrit texts on art and architectural theory, the shilpa shastras and vastu shastras, was included in Akbar's extensive programme of translation; true, art theory was hardly a theme elsewhere in the Islamic world, but one would have expected the Mughals to be interested in the ancient Indian textual tradition – the more so since

(like the Muslim dynasties before them) they absorbed Indian traditions into their art and architecture, and even newly revived them. However, the fact that no texts exist does not mean that architectural theory was absent from Mughal thinking, certainly not in the time of Shah Jahan. And the buildings and formal gardens of Shah Jahan express the theories to which they owe their appearance so systematically that we can deduce the theories from the forms.

The strict formalization of construction served to express within each building, as in every other work of art of Shah Jahan, the hierarchy and timeless order of his rule. Particularly noteworthy is the emperor's own involvement in the organization of history, art and architecture to create his own personal ideology of power.

Shah Jahan was, after Akbar, the most tireless builder of the Mughal dynasty. His historians point out that already as a prince he had shown himself 'exceedingly fond of laying out gardens and founding buildings'.[9] He rebuilt the palace complexes in the Agra fort and the Lahore fort, built a new palace and city, Shahjahan-abad, in the old Delhi of the sultans, and founded a large number of suburban palaces, country houses and hunting palaces. Of the large formal gardens with which he was involved the most famous are the two Shalimar gardens, one in Kashmir and one at Lahore.[10] He commissioned, or caused others to commission, the construction of more mosques than any other Mughal emperor before him: largest is the Jami' Masjid at Delhi; most beautiful is the Moti Masjid in the Agra fort. His enormous building programme also encompassed a number of mausoleums, including the tomb of his father, Jahangir, at Lahore [108], the construction of which was supervised by Nur Jahan; his most ambitious mausoleum project was the Taj Mahal.[11]

Where the emperor led the way, the members of his family and the great nobles were expected to follow, and at times were even ordered to sponsor buildings conforming to the imperial taste. They were also employed in imperial building projects, in particular Asaf Khan, the father of Mumtaz Mahal and thus Shah Jahan's father-in-law, who had to write out the emperor's orders for the builders.[12]

The important position of architecture is reflected in the accounts of the imperial projects by the court historians and in the eulogies composed by the court poets. Shah Jahan supervised his historians personally, so the detailed recording of buildings must have been due to his specific order. While theory and symbolism were expressed by the buildings themselves, the texts provide information about dates, architectural terminology, forms, types and function, and clues to meaning.

Lahauri gives a comprehensive account of the entire complex of the Taj Mahal on the occasion of its formal completion, on the twelfth anniversary of Mumtaz Mahal's death, on 6 February 1643 (see below, pp. 97–99; translated on pp. 256–57).[13] Kanbo also provides a detailed description: his observations, in a highly ornate style, are less accurate, but they contain occasional reflections about meaning not found in the official history.[14] The court poets Abu Talib Kalim[15] and Hajji Muhammad Jan Qudsi (d. 1646) wrote descriptive eulogies on the Taj which also help to establish its meaning.[16]

The Taj Mahal complex is 'built architectural theory': it can be read almost like a literary text when one has mastered the grammar and vocabulary of the architectural language (pp. 104–5). Taken together, building and texts give us a fuller picture than of any other Indian monument of the Islamic period.

Imperial mausoleums –
a 'built tomb' controversy

The grand dynastic mausoleum is a paradigm of the imperial architecture of the Mughals. Akbar, Jahangir and Shah Jahan built monumental tombs for their fathers, and Shah Jahan in addition raised one for his wife. A great mausoleum was seen as the best memorial to the deceased. Jahangir says in his autobiography: 'A thousand blessings on a son who has made such a tomb for his father, "That there may remain a memorial to him upon earth."'[17] The mausoleum was also the favourite building type of the Muslim nobility, for whom erecting a tomb could be a way of establishing ownership of land (p. 28). With their interest in funerary architecture the Mughals continued and developed a tradition established by the earlier sultans of India. No other region of the world brought forth over the centuries so many monumental mausoleums.

Large tombs, however, contradicted both orthodox Islamic and Hindu regulations for how to deal with the dead. For Hindus dead bodies are impure, so a structure over a body is impure as well. The dead should be burned as quickly as possible and their ashes consigned to the purifying waters of one of the holy rivers. In the Islamic tradition, tombs were from the beginning a controversial issue. A large number of hadis – recorded sayings and actions of the prophet Muhammad, which with the Qur'an form the basis of Islamic law – declare tombs to be irreligious, heathen, and non-Islamic: they forbid praying at tombs as polytheism, are critical of distinguishing tombs by inscriptions, and speak against raising buildings over tombs because these might give rise to a cult of the dead and to idolatrous worship.[18]

For the majority of Muslims the fact that some cemeteries contain the tombs of individuals venerated in Islam sheds a light of sanctity on all. Visiting these tombs (ziyarat) is a means of associating oneself with the spiritual power (barakat) of the buried person, who is conceived as being present, in a sense, in his tomb. Those in favour of tombs regarded them as legitimate so long as they did not strive for vainglory and pomp. Structures over burials

were seen as a means to ensure paradisiacal conditions for the dead, as promised to the faithful in the Qur'an. They provided protective shade, and their height symbolized closeness to God and Paradise. Specific forms were symbolic: four-sided and eight-sided plans referred to the fourth and eighth stages of Paradise (p. 26), and the dome was at all times a symbol of heaven. Because of its ostentation, however, the dome was the most controversial feature in Muslim funerary architecture:[19] to orthodox eyes, large domed mausoleums were the most objectionable form of monument. This ambivalent attitude towards tombs explains why they could enjoy great popularity in certain periods and in certain regions of the Islamic world while in others they played only a marginal role.

The Mughals were outstanding tomb builders, but at the same time they were also highly aware of the controversial status of funerary structures. Apart from occasional remarks, however, they did not put down the pros and cons in writing: they expressed them in built form. The imperial tombs led the debate, and from Babur to Aurangzeb made opposing statements. This controversy over tombs testifies to the Mughals' capacity for using architecture and the arts as their specific form of expression.[20]

The Mughals came to India from Central Asia, where their ancestor Timur had been buried in 1405 at Samarqand in the underground chamber of a splendid tomb with a high double dome, faced with blue and green tiles [102]. Babur, however, the founder of the dynasty, was laid to rest at Kabul some time between 1539 and 1545 under a simple monument consisting of a stone block shaped like a sarcophagus and set on a plinth [103], a form often used for Muslim gravestones [cf. 16]: called by the Mughals surat-i marqad or surat-i qabr ('shape of a tomb'),[21] strictly speaking this is a cenotaph ('empty tomb'), because the body is not actually enclosed in it. Babur's monument was open to the sky, perhaps within a stone screen.[22] This form of burial in an open enclosure, called hazira, demonstrated orthodox minimalism.[23] A generation later, Babur's son Humayun was buried in a large domed mausoleum at Delhi [104]. These two extremes set the parameters for the funerary architecture of the Mughals.

102 The tomb of Timur, or Gur-i Amir, in Samarqand, 1400–1404. (Photograph taken in 1981)

103 The tomb of Babur at Kabul, in the Bagh-i Baburi. The terrace garden seems to have been laid out in 1589 by Akbar, to enclose an earlier cemetery where the body of Babur, who had died in 1530 at Agra, had been laid to rest. The additions to the tomb demonstrate the desire of later rulers to be associated with the founder of the Mughal dynasty. The stele with the inscription which praises Babur was put up by Jahangir in 1607, while the frame around the stele, the top of Babur's tomb chest, and the enclosures were added by the Afghan kings in the 20th century (Photograph taken in 2005)

The tomb of Humayun [104, 335] was erected by his son Akbar between 1562 and 1571.[24] It was a response to Timur's tomb at Samarqand [102], and at the same time to the tombs of the Delhi sultans, which had reached their apogee with the tomb of Humayun's rival Sher Shah Sur at Sasaram (1545) [105].[25] Humayun's tomb was set in the centre of a large *chahar bagh*, and the combination of tomb and formal garden established the prototype for the funerary garden of the Mughals. For the building, the architect, Sayyid Muhammad from Herat and Bukhara – exceptionally known by name – took inspiration from an idea of Humayun's and created an ambitious variant of the typical Timurid ninefold plan or *hasht bihisht* ('eight Paradises': see pp. 26–27) by multiplying the design four times within the overall plan figure [24], to achieve monumentality and

104 *above* The tomb of Humayun at Delhi, 1562–71, seen from the west. (Photograph taken in 1978)

105 *below* The tomb of Sher Shah Sur at Sasaram, 1545, seen from the east. (Photograph taken in 1981)

intensify paradisiacal symbolism. He placed the building on a large vaulted podium containing the actual grave: this arrangement of superimposed chambers also went back to Timurid antecedents,[26] and was to become the pattern for all monumental Mughal mausoleums. A cenotaph marks the grave in the lower chamber, and a similar cenotaph symbolizes it in the central hall above.

And the architect gave Humayun's tomb a facing of red sandstone and white marble which defines each structural element of the elevation. The highly symbolic colour dualism was derived from earlier Indian practices and was to become a characteristic feature of imperial Mughal architecture (pp. 215–17). With Humayun's tomb the Mughals set an example of successful architectural synthesis and made a grand imperial statement in Delhi, the old capital of the sultans. The monumentality and imperial splendour of the domed mausoleum ignored all orthodox concerns. Also, from the very beginning Humayun's tomb became a place of dynastic cult and was treated like the tomb of a saint. The emperors paid it a pious visitation whenever they came to Delhi and performed a ritual circumambulation (*tawaf*).[27] There could be no greater contrast to the simple tomb of Babur, the founder of the dynasty [103].

The tomb of Akbar in the suburbs of Agra, at Sikandra (then called Bihishtabad, or Abode of Paradise), was built by his son Jahangir and completed in 1612/13 [107].[28] It is even larger than Humayun's tomb, though of an entirely different shape, for which there is no precedent in Islamic funerary architecture: it consists of receding tiers of pillared sandstone galleries in the style of Indian post-and-lintel constructions. The feature it shares with Humayun's tomb, besides the studied use of red sandstone and white marble, is the vaulted masonry platform with surrounding vaulted bays on which it stands: this is here enriched with Timurid elements such as the tall centrally placed *pishtaqs* (arched niches in rectangular frames) and a vestibule with painted stucco decoration. However, despite its monumentality the mausoleum clearly aims at orthodox correctness. It has no dome, and the topmost storey consists of an open courtyard of white marble, enclosed with galleries [106]. The beautifully carved cenotaph in the centre is placed under the open sky, as it lawfully should be, like Babur's tomb at Kabul [103]. The entire structure below the cenotaph features as its 'plinth'. The actual grave, marked by another cenotaph, is, as in all major Mughal mausoleums, set within the platform and can be reached from the vestibule through a corridor.

This semantic tour de force of interpreting the plinth of a cenotaph as a monumental mausoleum can be attributed to Jahangir himself. He tells us in his memoirs that the architects had constructed his father's tomb according to their own ideas, while he was away from Agra, but that after his return in 1608, not liking the way it looked, he had had it pulled down in places and rebuilt.[29] Some scholars, intrigued by the unusual design, have felt that the building was incomplete, lacking a dome, which, they thought, must have been part of the original plan.[30] This is to misunderstand the ingenuity of the concept. Also, the interpretation of a mausoleum as a monumental plinth for a cenotaph did not remain an isolated phenomenon. It gave rise to a distinct tomb type of Jahangir's period, the platform tomb, where the cenotaph and small superstructures are placed on a flat substructure, the *takhtgah* (see p. 51).[31]

The tomb of Akbar at Sikandra, completed in 1612/13

106 *above* The open court on the top storey, with the emperor's cenotaph, seen from the south-east. (Photograph taken in 1999)

107 *below* View from one of the minarets of the gate. (Photograph taken in 1978)

108 The tomb of Jahangir at
Shahdara, Lahore, 1628–38.
(Photograph taken in 1979)

109 below The tomb of Aurangzeb at
Khuldabad near Aurangabad, 1707.
(Photograph taken in 1982)

This was used for the imperial family and the nobility: an elaborate example at Agra is the tomb of Iʿtimad-ud-Daula (1622–28), though there the notion of a dome was brought in again in the form of a baldachin [59].

Jahangir's tomb at Lahore [108] was built under the supervision of Nur Jahan between 1628 and 1638. The emperor had willed that his resting place should be according to the Sunni faith in the tradition of Babur's tomb [103], 'without the ornament of a building, and be entrusted to the Divine favour in an open space, so that it may always benefit from the countless clouds of Divine forgiveness without any obstacle'.[32] The dilemma of reconciling the imperial wish for an uncovered tomb and an appropriate imperial burial was solved by taking the cue from Akbar's tomb and from platform tombs, by then widely used. Jahangir's mausoleum was an extreme formulation of the type: a monumentalized bare plinth, but accentuated with high minarets at its corners. The marble cenotaph, now lost, was placed on top, open to the elements, to the blessing rain of the clouds as a symbol of divine mercy. The actual burial is again in a vaulted chamber in the platform, reached by a corridor.

Jahangir's contribution to imperial funerary architecture shows him in a new light. He is often portrayed as a hedonist, given to wine, women and artistic refinement. As a patron of architecture, however, he clearly took an active part in the debate on the lawfulness of mausoleums, and found a strikingly ingenious solution to the problem of how to reconcile orthodox considerations with imperial monumentality.

In the Taj Mahal Shah Jahan and his advisers reverted to the grandest possible form of funerary structure, the mausoleum with a dome. It was even to surpass the ancestral tomb of Humayun. There is however a slight bow to orthodoxy, in the use of a railing around the cenotaphs under the dome [233]: the hazira ensemble quotes the form of open burial used by Babur, the vault above representing heaven (p. 85).

Shah Jahan's son and successor Aurangzeb was the first Mughal emperor to speak out openly against visiting tombs and against mausoleums over graves. He forbade the roofing of buildings containing tombs, the lime-washing of sepulchres, and the pilgrimage of women to the graves of saints.[33] In this he distanced himself from his own early practice, for at the beginning of his reign he had raised a monumental tomb for his wife at Aurangabad.[34] Popularly called Bibi-ka Maqbara, this is a domed white structure inspired by the Taj Mahal. It was built by ʿAta Ullah Rashidi, the eldest son of Ustad Ahmad Lahauri, who has been named as architect of the Taj Mahal (p. 89). Completed in 1660/61, it represents the end of the imperial Mughal mausoleum tradition. Aurangzeb had himself interred at the Dargah (Shrine) of Shaikh Burhan-ud-Din in Khuldabad near Aurangabad under a simple stepped stone slab filled with earth and enclosed by a screen [109], like Babur. Similarly, Shah Jahan's daughter Jahanara, who died in 1681, was buried in the Dargah of Nizam-ud-Din Auliya at Delhi under a marble cenotaph the top of which was planted with grass, with an inscription that says: 'Let nothing cover my tomb save the green grass, for grass suffices well as a covering for the grave of the lowly.'[35] The later Mughals were laid to rest in Humayun's tomb or in the dargahs of Sufi saints.

The practice of building large tombs was, however, taken up and continued by the regional rulers of India. Even Hindu rajas were infected, and built, if not tombs (for their bodies were cremated and their ashes thrown into sacred rivers), empty structures to their own memory. The chhatris (the word can mean a funerary pavilion as well as a kiosk) of the rajas of Bharatpur near Agra, raised in the 19th century, reached monumental proportions.[36]

The architects of the Taj Mahal

The identity of the architect or architects of the Taj Mahal is not definitely known, because, as we have seen, the histories of Shah Jahan's reign emphasize the emperor's personal involvement. In the Islamic world a building was in the first instance associated with its patron. Several Mughal emperors did go so far as to influence the design of their buildings: Humayun invented new structures for his court (p. 11), and, as we have seen, Jahangir insisted on his own design for his father Akbar's tomb at Sikandra, rather than that proposed by his architects. Of all Mughal emperors, Shah Jahan showed the greatest interest in building, and he had himself represented as his own architect.

Unlike his painters, who were allowed to sign their works and to include their self-portraits, Shah Jahan's architects are only mentioned at random, and not a single portrait of a Mughal architect (mim'ar) is known. The supervisors (sarkar) of Shah Jahan's building projects are named more often, but the exact nature of their role in the process is not defined and remains to be established. Only one of the artists who worked at the Taj Mahal is known by name: the calligrapher ʿAbd-ul-Haqq from Shiraz, given the title Amanat Khan (pp. 224–25), who designed the formal Qur'anic inscriptions on the mausoleum [128–131, 224, 350–352]. Because of the high esteem in which the art of writing (as the medium of God's own word) was held in the Islamic world, he could sign his creations. The dates he inserted into his inscriptions greatly help to establish the history of construction (pp. 99–100).

What is recorded is that the planning of Shah Jahan's buildings was carried out by a team of architects who worked under his close supervision. He held daily meetings with them, and, Lahauri says, made 'appropriate alterations to whatever the skilful architects designed after many thoughts, and asked competent questions'.[37] The emperor's historians claim that most of the buildings were designed by his 'precious self'.[38] The credit for his buildings, even for their overall concept, had to go to Shah Jahan as the supreme architect. (Similarly, the work of the artists of Shah Tahmasp of Iran was subsumed in the expertise of their patron, who appeared as 'the ultimate arbitrator and source of cultural production'.[39])

Shah Jahan was in a figurative sense 'the architect of the workshop of empire and religion'.[40] The ruler had already been identified with architecture in ancient Mesopotamia: Gudea, ruler of the Sumerian city-state of Lagash (c. 2100 BC), had himself depicted holding on his lap a plan of one of his building projects, a temple.[41] Such parallels might evolve from analogous ambitions in a comparable social setting, but it is not the only instance where Shah Jahan, and his father Jahangir, pursued forms of self-representation which appear like revivals of ancient Near Eastern concepts.[42]

Two architects are, however, mentioned in connection with the Taj Mahal. One is Ustad Ahmad Lahauri – from Lahore, as his name tells us, like the historian Lahauri. He laid the foundations of the Red Fort at Delhi (1639–48), and was credited by his son, Lutfullah Muhandis – though not in the official chronicles – with building the Taj Mahal. The other is Mir ʿAbd-ul Karim, who had been the favourite architect of Jahangir. Lahauri mentions him as supervisor of the construction of the Taj Mahal, together with the administrator

110 Makramat Khan, supervisor of the construction of the Taj Mahal, seen among courtiers at the presentation of wedding gifts to Dara Shikoh: detail of a painting by Balchand, Mughal, c. 1635, from the *Padshahnama*.

Makramat Khan [110], who later supervised the building of the Red Fort at Delhi.[43]

The lack of information about the identity of the architect of the Taj Mahal has led to all kinds of fanciful speculation. In the 19th century, local informants of the British fabricated the story of an architect from Turkey named 'Ustad Isa', and came up with fictional lists of workmen and materials from all parts of Asia (p. 237). More attractive to the British was the claim of the Spanish Augustinian friar Sebastian Manrique, who saw the Taj under construction in 1640–41, that an Italian goldsmith named 'Geronimo Veroneo' had prepared the design (p. 249). Such an outstanding building could surely only have been created with European involvement. Even today speculations about the architect of the Taj Mahal can produce a worldwide echo in the media.[44]

Craftsmen, materials, and construction techniques

CRAFTSMEN

The craftsmen of the Taj Mahal are not named in the histories of Shah Jahan. We learn from Lahauri only that the best artisans came from all over India:

> And from all sides and parts of the imperial territories were assembled troop after troop of [skilled] men, stonecutters (*sangtarash*) of smooth work, inlayers (*parchinkar*), and those who do carving in relief (*munabbatkar*), each one an expert in his craft, who started the work together with the other labourers.[45]

The craftsmen working on the restoration of the Taj Mahal today use techniques that have not changed much since Mughal times [113, 115].

European observers give us unsubstantiated numbers for the workforce employed. Jean-Baptiste Tavernier, who was in Agra in 1640–41 and again in 1665, claimed that 'twenty thousand men worked unceasingly' on the tomb for twenty-two years.[46] Manrique says that a thousand men were employed on it every day.[47]

Stonecutters and bricklayers were called, respectively, *sangtarash* and *raj*.[48] The stonemasons at the Taj Mahal made their contribution known through numerous marks [111]. Most are scratched into the paving of the garden walkways and the slabs facing the walls of the buildings; some appear on the façade of the riverfront terrace. The marks have various shapes: there are graphic symbols such as stars, swastikas, fishes, flowers and intersecting figures, and numerals. There are also incised names, largely Hindu but also Muslim, respectively in Devanagari and in Arabic (Persian) letters [112]; but

Graphic symbols

Numerals

11	11	73

Devanagari inscriptions

क	Ka (first consonant)	वनरसी ५	Vanarsi 5/Banarsi 5
हीरा	Heera	व्यरमहसा	Dharamhassa/Gharamhassa
हमहर झ	Humhar	व्यनमहस	Dhanamhass/Ghanamhas
नटा	Natta	परसरामया २	Parasramayya 2
लोहम	Lohum	हरीदस	Haridus/Haridas
नेता	Neta	हिसा	Hissa/Hinsa
पेमेा	Pemay-a/Pemo [?]	ननठ	Nuntatt
रिटटछ	Tiyatay [?]	ठिगग	Tigagg [?]

Arabic inscriptions

	618	71
	(year)	
	Rak Charan [?]	ke darya Jaman
	Sak Charan [?]	

111, 112 *top and above* Masons' marks, and names and inscriptions in the Taj Mahal complex.

113 *left* Hajji Nizamuddin Naqshbandi, with other stonecarvers, using hammer and point chisel. After working at the Taj Mahal for over forty years, he was still employed on a daily wage when he died in 2005. (Photograph taken in 2001)

some of these might be graffiti by later visitors. The masons' marks have been largely ignored by scholars and are still not sufficiently understood.[49] They are not exclusive to the Taj: the same marks appear on contemporary or earlier Mughal buildings. They seem to denote the contribution of groups of hereditary stonemasons, to establish their wages (they were paid for each *gaz*, or linear yard, of stone cut).[50]

Stonecarvers (*munabbatkar*; in modern usage, also *sangtarash*) had, after the masons, the most important role in the construction.[51] Their work ranged from the carving of simple mouldings to the exquisite depiction of flowering plants in sandstone and marble on the dados of the mausoleum and flanking buildings.

How the carvers worked, squatting over the pieces of stone and using hammers and chisels, can be seen today, as damaged or deteriorating pieces are replaced with new work on the pattern of the old under the direction of men such as Hajji Nizamuddin Naqshbandi [113]. He was a follower of the Naqshbandi Sufis, keeping up the old tradition of the involvement of the mystic Sufi brotherhoods in the arts of building.

Craftsmen in stone inlay were called *parchinkar*. Simple stone intarsia, the inlay of a shape in one stone into a hollow in a stone of another colour, appears in some parts of the complex. It had been used over the centuries in India, a region abounding in attractive stones, and was known to the Mughals as *parchin kari*. They used the same term for the highly specialized form of inlay of hard or semi-precious stones into marble. This technique originated in Italy, in Florence. It is called *commesso di pietre dure* (composition of hard stones) – abbreviated to *pietra dura*[52] – because it involves the inlaying not of a single stone but of many. Extreme skill is needed to saw the stone, such as agate, jasper and heliotrope (bloodstone), into thin

pieces of various sizes and shapes, using bow saws with abrasives [115]. The pieces are fitted together so that the colours and natural markings form the desired image [117], and the composition is then fixed in the cavity with glue and polished, so that the joins become invisible.[53]

The Mughals knew *pietra dura* from European artists employed at the court and from Italian works which visitors brought as presents for the emperor [114]. (Also brought from Europe were herbals, which inspired the designs of the flowers in *pietra dura* and those

114 *above* Europeans bringing gifts to Shah Jahan: detail of a painting, Mughal, c. 1650, from the *Padshahnama*.

115 Inlay-workers in a marble craft shop in Taj Ganj, outside the south gate of the Jilaukhana of the Taj Mahal [cf. 307]. Those in the background are cutting hardstones with bow saws; in the foreground, a craftsman is fitting pieces into a table-top. (Photograph taken in 1997)

116 Detail of the back wall of Shah Jahan's throne in the Diwan-i ʿAmm of the Red Fort, Delhi: Florentine *pietra dura* panels, with black backgrounds, are set amidst Mughal *parchin kari* showing flowers and birds. (Photograph taken in 1979)

carved in low relief: p. 218.) Shah Jahan's love for gems was legendary. A group of Italian *pietra dura* tablets with the characteristic Florentine motifs of birds, flowers and flower vases is set in the back wall of his throne in the Diwan-i ʿAmm of the Red Fort at Delhi [116]; it is supplemented with bird and floral motifs made by Indian craftsmen, demonstrating the closeness between the Italian and the Mughal work.[54] The observant François Bernier noted of the Taj Mahal in 1659: 'Everywhere are seen the jasper, and *jachen* [*yashm*] or jade, as well as other stones similar to those that enrich the walls of the Grand Duke's chapel at Florence, and several more of great value and rarity, set in an endless variety of modes, mixed and enchased in the slabs of marble which face the body of the wall.'[55]

The technique was soon mastered to such perfection by the lapidaries of Shah Jahan that in its complexity, subtlety and elegance their *pietra dura* work far surpasses that of the Italian artists.[56] The most exquisite inlay appears in the cenotaphs and the surrounding screen in the tomb chamber, the heart of the Taj Mahal [230, 232–244]. H. Voysey, who untertook the first scientific study of the inlaid stones in 1825, noted that 'A single flower in the screen around the tombs, or sarcophagi, contains a hundred stones, each cut to the exact shape necessary, and highly polished; and in the interior alone of the building there are several hundred flowers, each containing a

like number of stones.'[57] The fineness of the Mughal *pietra dura* flowers was proudly pointed out by Shah Jahan's court poet Kalim:

> The inlayer (*naqqar*) has set stone into stone
> So [that even] the dark spot of the heart of the *lala* (poppy, tulip)
>   is without joints or fissures.[58]

The *pietra dura* inlay of the Taj Mahal has been frequently restored because of stones falling out, or being picked out by visitors (p. 251), so Voysey's early investigations are particularly valuable. He identified lapis lazuli or *lajward* (blue), chalcedonic quartzes such as jasper (reddish), heliotrope or bloodstone (dark green spotted with red), agate (brownish red), chalcedony, carnelian or ʿaqiq (brownish red), considered to be a stone of blessing power and therefore frequently used in seals and amulets,[59] sard (brown cornelian), plasma (a slightly translucent variety of quartz, either green, grey or blue), chlorite (green), jade (nephrite or jadeite), clay slate, yellow and striped marble, and yellow and variegated limestones. The stones occur in the Indian subcontinent and neighbouring countries – lapis lazuli in Afghanistan, and jade in Burma.[60] When the Taj was under construction, the workshop of the inlay workers may have been to the west of the garden wall, because early 20th-century reports say that pieces of semi-precious stone were found in that area.[61]

117 *opposite* Detail of the *pietra dura* on the platform of the upper cenotaph of Mumtaz Mahal [233]: flower type P (see p. 171), slightly less than actual size (the plant is 30 cm/11 3⁄16 in. tall). The banded, translucent stones are agate, the spotted, opaque ones are jasper, and the greens include chrysoprase.

Mughal *pietra dura* was closely linked to imperial patronage. At Agra the craft had almost died out by the mid-19th century; it was revived by Dr John Murray, the first photographer of the Taj (p. 251).

MATERIALS

The main construction materials of the Taj Mahal are brick, red sandstone, and white marble. Polished plaster was used as a surface finish.

The **bricks** (*ajir*, *khisht*) for the Taj Mahal were burned in kilns in the surroundings of Agra. The size of Mughal bricks was standardized. From Akbar's period they gradually became smaller, and in Shah Jahan's time they measured 18–19 x 11–12.5 x 2–3 cm (7–7½ x 4½–5 x ¾–1¼ in.).[62] That format has traditionally been called *lakhauri* brick, a term which has as yet not been fully explained; one interpretation holds that the name is derived from *lakh*, the Indian term for 100,000, because these bricks were such a common element in building.

The **sandstone** and **marble** – which, as we shall discover, had symbolic significance (pp. 215–17) – were brought from a great distance.

The sandstone (*sang-i surkh*), of a soft reddish to yellowish tint, came from quarries in the region of Fatehpur Sikri, some 40 km (25 miles) west of Agra, and Rupbas, some 45 km (28 miles) southwest of Agra, in a mountain range called the Vindhya system which throughout the centuries furnished building materials to the cities of the adjoining plains [118].[63] The sandstone is easily worked and susceptible of the most delicate carving: in the words of Akbar's historian Abu'l Fazl, 'clever workmen chisel it more skilfully than any turner could do with wood'.[64] Today the road between Jaipur and

Agra is lined with sandstone workshops where large blocks of 'Agra stone' – from the modern quarries of Dholpur and Rupbas – and Jaipur stone are cut into slabs with power saws, and then carved by hand in the traditional manner.

The white marble (*sang-i marmar*) came from quarries at Makrana in Rajasthan, more than 400 km (250 miles) away by road. It is white, streaked with grey or black, which gives it a lively character [215]. It is hard and yet easy to work, capable of taking both fine detail and a high polish, and its translucency makes it react very interestingly to atmospheric changes.[65] We do not know what

118 *above* Sandstone bed next to the road from Bari to Rupbas. (Photograph taken in 1993)

119 Marble quarry at Makrana. On the edge of the trench, to the right, are cranes used to raise the cut blocks of stone. (Photograph taken in 2002)

121 *below* A sandstone pilaster in the 'Fatehpuri Masjid' at the Taj Mahal is splitting because the stone has been laid on edge, with the grain vertical. (Photograph taken in 1997)

120 Cut marble slabs at Makrana transported on a cart drawn by a water-buffalo. (Photograph taken in 2002)

the Mughal quarries looked like, but hundreds of quarries in the region of Makrana today probably follow the historical form [119]. Canyon-like trenches, some as deep as 60–65 m (197–214 ft), are cut down from the surface into the bed of marble; blocks are cut manually with hammers, chisels and wedges, and by drilling with steel rods, and then hauled up by cranes.

Makrana was in the territory of the rajas of Amber (Jaipur), and the Rajasthan State Archives contain *farmans* (orders) from Shah Jahan to Raja Jai Singh – from whom the emperor had obtained the site for the Taj Mahal – about the transport of marble to Agra.[66] Both sandstone and marble were transported on carts drawn by bullocks or water-buffaloes [120]. In 1641 Sebastian Manrique came across such a cortege proceeding to Agra: 'Some of these blocks, which I met on the way . . . were of such unusual size and length that they drew the sweat of many powerful teams of oxen and of fierce-looking, big-horned buffaloes, which were dragging enormous, strongly made wagons, in teams of twenty or thirty animals.'[67]

At the construction site blocks were cleft with the help of iron wedges and sledgehammers, or cut into slabs with metal saws. It is vital that stone be quarried and cut according to its grain – the plane on which it breaks more easily – and laid so that the grain is horizontal. Stone laid against the grain ('edge-bedded') is liable to disintegrate under pressure. Soft sandstone is more vulnerable than marble: it flakes off or splits into layers [121].

Polished plaster (*chuna*, popularly *chunam*) was used as a less expensive alternative to marble facing to give imperial buildings the desired white and shining appearance. When the *chuna* of the 'Shish Mahal' in the Agra fort was analysed its ingredients proved to be 1 part burnt lime, 1 part ground shells, calciferous stone or marble dust, ⅛ part gum from the *babul* or neem tree (*Azadirachta indica*), ⅛ part sugar mixed with the juice of the fruit of the bael (bel) tree (*Aegle marmelos*), and a little white of egg. The mixture was strengthened with plant fibres and applied to the brick walls as a coating; when it was dry, it was polished with a shell (*kauri*) and chalk powder.[68] The historian of Shah Jahan's later reign,

Muhammad Waris, mentions that a calciferous stone from Gujarat, called *sang-i Patiali* (stone from Patiali) or *sang-i mahtabi* ('moonlight stone'), served as the main ingredient of Shahjahani *chuna*; it was white and soft, and the mixture obtained from it 'could be polished so highly that it reflected all things opposite it like marble'.[69] Lahauri says that the resulting plaster 'is better than marble-dust plaster in polish and purity'.[70] Similarly, the perceptive Dutch trader Pelsaert observed about Mughal plaster that it was

> very noteworthy, and far superior to anything in our country. They use unslaked lime, which is mixed with milk, gum, and sugar into a thin paste. When the walls have been plastered with lime, they apply this paste, rubbing it with well-designed trowels until it is smooth; then they polish it steadily with agates, perhaps for a whole day, until it is dry and hard, and shines like alabaster, or can even be used as a looking-glass.[71]

No architectural drawings are preserved. The only evidence of this type that we have is a few incised patterns on stone slabs re-used in buildings. There is very little written evidence about the actual construction of the Taj Mahal. From accounts of the building of the Red Fort at Delhi, slightly later, we learn that the head of the architects, with his assistants, would first chalk out the plan on the ground. Diggers (*beldar*) would then excavate the foundations.[72] At the Taj, the greatest technical challenge was to secure the foundations of the terrace in the unstable sands of the riverbank so that it would be able to support the domed mausoleum, of a total height of *c.* 68 m (223 ft). Kalim, an unlikely but here unique source for technical data, reports – in verse – that this was done by means of wells cased in wood and filled with rubble and iron.

> Since there is sand where there is a river, it is difficult
>   to lay down foundations:
> As sand is removed, it fills in again.
> They make a well (*chah*) to manage the work, from wood,
>   and set it firmly into the sand.
> Then they take out the sand from inside it, until solid earth
>   comes from its depth.
> In this well stone and iron are buried until they reach
>   the level of the surface.
> Then another well beside it is emptied of sand and filled
>   in the same way, so that the building may be erected.
> With this good method and powerful concept they raise
>   a mountain from the ground.[73]

Kalim's description was supported in the 1950s when excavation of the foundations revealed wells filled with rubble, placed at a distance centre-to-centre of 3.76 m (11½ ft) [124, 206].[74] Foundation wells of this type can be seen exposed in the riverbed in front of several of the gardens on the left bank of the Yamuna – the garden of Jahanara/Zahara Bagh, the Chini-ka Rauza, and the garden of Khwaja Muhammad Zakarya or Wazir Khan. The foundations of the

Taj proved so stable that they did not give way during the great floods of September 1978, when the river level almost reached the top of the platform of the mausoleum.

Lahauri tells us that the foundations were 'built of stone (*sang*) and [watertight] mortar or cement (*saruj*)', and that on them a terrace (*chabutra*) of brick (*ajir*) and mortar (*ahak*) was built, on which the main buildings were placed. Its exterior (*ru-yi kar*), especially the front to the river, was artistically faced with red sandstone.[75]

The facing of supporting walls with red sandstone in the entire complex was effected with a construction technique characteristic of Shahjahani architecture, which can be called 'Mughal bond' [122, 123].[76] Long sandstone slabs are used: in the Taj they are *c.* 125–200 cm (*c.* 49–79 in.) long, 60–80 cm (23½–31 in.) wide, and 10–15 cm (4–6 in.) thick. They are laid alternately horizontally and vertically; alternate vertical slabs run at right angles through the

brickwork in lime mortar

brickwork (shown without mortar): stretcher course

brickwork: header course
vertical sandstone slab
horizontal sandstone slab

sandstone facing slab

122 *top* Mughal bond in the western enclosure wall of the Taj Mahal: two of the facing slabs have come away, exposing the brick within. (Photograph taken in 2001)

123 *above* The structure of Mughal bond: a core of brick is faced, and tied, with sandstone slabs.

124 *left* Foundation wells below and beside the river frontage of the Taj Mahal [cf. 206].

opposite
125 Traditional bamboo scaffolding, erected for the repair of the south wing of the madrasa of Ghazi-ud-Din Khan, Delhi. (Photograph taken in 1996)

thickness of the wall and, with the horizontal slabs, form a permanent framework that is filled with rubble or bricks set in mortar.

All buildings of the Taj complex are built of brick. In a typical Shahjahani structure the bricks are laid in horizontal courses composed largely of stretchers, but alternating at times with headers, in a thick bed of mortar made with kankar, a nodular limestone.[77] The walls of the mausoleum are very thick – in places as much as several metres. Vaults are built up in concentric rings of brick courses, set in an even thicker bed of lime mortar [cf. 101]. This construction technique, and the excellent quality of the mortar, gave the masonry the strength necessary to support the curvature of the partly spherical shell of the inner dome and the high bulbous dome above it, which has no inner stiffening walls [221]. The structure of the outer dome is reinforced by a continuous series of relieving arches integrated in the brickwork of the drum.[78]

The brick masonry was faced with marble or sandstone slabs, which were firmly locked together with iron dowels and clamps. All domes of consequence in the Taj complex are faced on the outside with white marble [326]. In the mausoleum, the main inner dome of the tomb chamber is also faced with marble [228, 229], while the inner domes of the side rooms and the rooms of the upper storey are covered with white plaster [250]. (The domes inside the flanking mosque and Mihman Khana are covered with sgraffito decoration in red and white plaster [271].)

Tavernier says that all the scaffolding of the Taj Mahal, including the centering for the vaults, was made of brick, removed after completion of the structural work, and that this added greatly to the building costs.[79] It seems more likely, however, that old masons still working in the traditional techniques are right in thinking that the vaults were built without centering and that the walls were raised with the help of bamboo scaffolding. Such scaffolding is still used today in India [125], even for concrete constructions. We know from miniature paintings of Akbar's time that wooden ramps served to carry up heavy material [101].

The planning, and the logistical and physical manipulation of huge amounts of bricks, thousands of cartloads of stone, and many other materials involved in the creation of the monumental mausoleum, were an amazing work carried out with simple technical means. The construction was essentially completed in twelve years.

Construction history and celebrations of the anniversaries of Mumtaz Mahal's death (ʿurs)

The site chosen for the Taj Mahal lies on the right bank of the Yamuna, on the southern edge of the city [17, 26–29]. The property – one of the riverfront residences of Agra – had belonged to Raja Man Singh of Amber, and had come down to the raja's grandson, Jai Singh. Shah Jahan was drawn to it because, Qazwini says, 'from the point of view of loftiness and pleasantness [it] appeared to be worthy of the burial of that one who dwells in Paradise'.[80] Jai Singh was prepared to present the property to Shah Jahan, but the emperor, anxious to proceed without a shade of doubt in the sensitive matter of his queen's last resting place, insisted on giving him in exchange four other mansions at Agra.[81]

Work on the site had begun by January 1632, when the body of the dead queen arrived from Burhanpur. Her coffin had been accompanied by Shah Shujaʿ (the second eldest prince) [2:3], Wazir Khan [2:7, 47], and her chief lady-in-waiting, Satti-un-Nisa Khanum (p. 210), with an entourage of attendants and Qur'an reciters. All along the road food, drink and coins had been distributed among the poor and deserving, to ensure the favours of Heaven for the departed one. At Agra the body of Mumtaz was given a second temporary burial on the construction site, and a small domed building (gunbad-i mukhtasari) was quickly raised over it, to protect her chastity, as Kanbo explains, from the eyes of males who were na-mahram – those who did not have access to the haram, or zanana.[82] The place is thought to be marked by an enclosure in the western area of the garden near the riverfront terrace [146:6]. From other garden foundations of Shah Jahan, such as the Shalimar gardens at Lahore, we know that trees were planted when construction began, so that they would have grown to some height by the time work was completed.[83]

Construction of the Taj Mahal started with the foundations of the riverfront terrace. After that, work seems to have gone on simultaneously over the entire complex. Peter Mundy, in Agra in 1632–33, tells us that 'the buildinge is begun and goes on with excessive labour and cost' and that the surrounding grounds were levelled so as not to hinder the view of the mausoleum as it took shape. He also mentions that the bazaars and caravanserais of 'Tage Gunge' (Taj Ganj) were in the process of being built.[84]

Shah Jahan's historians report on progress only in the initial stages, in describing the celebrations of the first two anniversaries of Mumtaz Mahal's death. This event is called by Indian Muslims ʿurs – literally 'marriage', referring to death as the union of the soul with God – and is intended to ensure the 'lasting tranquillity' of the deceased. Shah Jahan's Iranian historian Jalal-ud-Din Tabataba'i witnessed the first one, and explained what was to him an unfamiliar ceremony: 'They spend one whole night and day in observances – such as keeping awake . . . reciting the Qur'an, the Fatiha [the first sura of the Qur'an (p. 229)] and prayers seeking forgiveness for the departed ones, feeding the poor and giving alms to the needy.'[85]

The first ʿurs, in the Jilaukhana

The first ʿurs of Mumtaz was held on the equivalent of 22 June 1632 (the Muslim calendar is lunar, so the date of the anniversary varies when expressed in the solar 'AD' calendar). Arrangements were made in the courtyard (sahn) of the mausoleum, which was later called the Jilaukhana (p. 116). On Shah Jahan's orders, the area was surrounded by tent enclosures and covered with fine floor-coverings (gustardani) and carpets (farsh), and sumptuous audience tents surrounded by awnings (shamiyana) of gold brocaded velvet were set up [126]. Here the emperor held an assembly for high and low, for his great amirs and mansabdars, men of religion, scholars, the elite of Agra, and ordinary citizens. He himself retired to spend the whole night praying for God's forgiveness of the soul of Mumtaz, having asked his father-in-law, Asaf Khan, and the Iranian ambassador, Muhammad ʿAli Beg, who happened to be at court, to preside over the gathering. Everyone was seated according to his rank, and after they had recited the Fatiha and other suras of the Qur'an, and offered prayers for the soul of Mumtaz, they were served exquisite refreshments from the imperial kitchen – 'beverages, sweetmeats and other tidbits, confections, fruits, aromatic essences and pan' (the popular Indian betelnut preparation). At the end of the gathering, 50,000 rupees were distributed to needy and deserving men.

After the assembly of the men, another was held for the women. It too was open to high and low, but it differed in that the imperial women walked around the tomb to honour the deceased. The same amount of alms, 50,000 rupees, was distributed to needy women.

Shah Jahan decreed that on every subsequent ʿurs his financial department should provide for charity 100,000 rupees (twice 50,000) when he was in the city, and if he was not present, 50,000 rupees. The figure of 100,000 rupees was a substantial sum: it corresponds to 2 per cent of the total construction costs of the Taj Mahal.

The second ʿurs, on the riverfront terrace and the platform of the mausoleum

The celebrations for the second death anniversary took place on 26 May 1633 on the riverfront terrace and on the white marble platform of the mausoleum, which housed the lower tomb chamber [cf. 217]. Arrangements were made to seat 1,000 participants. The paved surfaces were covered with carpets, on which were set large audience tents surrounded by awnings [127].

Bibadal Khan, superintendent of the imperial goldsmiths, had with his artisans completed a screen of pure gold decorated with inscriptions and floral designs in enamel work, as well as golden globes and lamps to hang around it. It had cost 600,000 rupees, almost 12 per cent of the cost of the entire mausoleum complex. The screen was installed around the upper cenotaph, which had been set on the platform over which the domed hall was to be raised. Peter Mundy noted in 1633 that 'There is alreadye about her Tombe a raile of gold'.[86] The golden screen was replaced in 1643 by the present marble screen with inlay work [230, 232], probably so as not to attract robbers.

In the evening the emperor, the princes, Princess Jahanara, and the imperial women arrived. They would have come by boat to the stepped landing below the terrace – visible in older photographs [206]

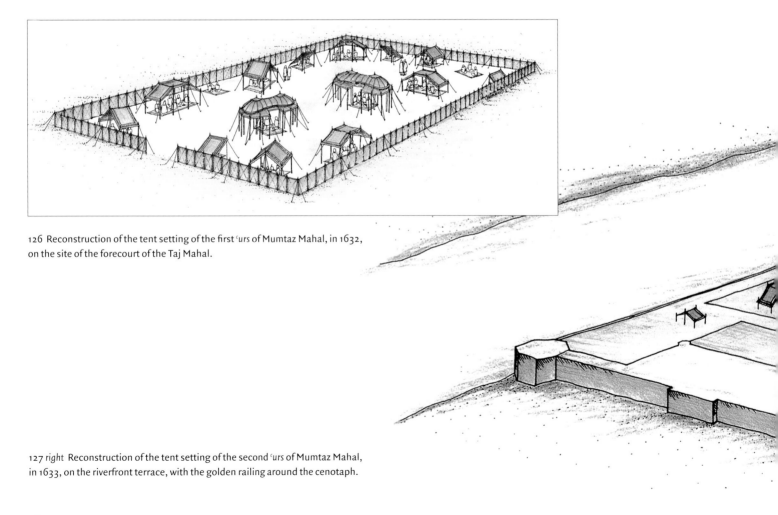

126 Reconstruction of the tent setting of the first ʿurs of Mumtaz Mahal, in 1632, on the site of the forecourt of the Taj Mahal.

127 *right* Reconstruction of the tent setting of the second ʿurs of Mumtaz Mahal, in 1633, on the riverfront terrace, with the golden railing around the cenotaph.

– and would have ascended temporary stairs to one of the postern doors near the towers, eventually reaching the Tahkhana, the gallery under the terrace (p. 148). They performed the ritual walk around the tomb to honour it, and said prayers for Mumtaz Mahal. Big assemblies were entertained as in the previous year, but now on the riverfront terrace. The emperor presented eminent religious men and Qur'an reciters, who had come from all parts of the empire, with garments and money. He also gave out charity to needy men and women, though – perhaps because of the special treatment of the religious sector – he only distributed 50,000 rupees, the amount designated for ᶜurs celebrations in his absence.[87] He observed this practice also in later celebrations of the death anniversary.

Subsequent progress

The celebrations in the following years are mentioned only intermittently and briefly, with no information about the construction until the twelfth ᶜurs, on 17 Zi'l Qaᶜda 1052 or 6 February 1643, when the complex was officially completed.[88] Progress can however be deduced from dated signatures of the calligrapher Amanat Khan, who created the inscriptions on the bands dividing the floors and framing the arches of the mausoleum and the great gate. The main inscriptions are passages from the Qur'an, hence in Arabic, and in formal *sulus* script (p. 224). Amanat Khan's signatures are in Persian, in *naskh* script, inserted in small letters at the end. All inscriptions read from right to left.[89]

The earliest dated signature appears inside the mausoleum at the end of the inscription band which surrounds the tomb chamber,

128 Detail of the inscriptions above the south arch in the tomb chamber of the Taj Mahal. The signature of Amanat Khan and the date 1045 (AD 1635/36) appear at the left below the upper band of *sulus* script; they are in *naskh* script, in cartouches; the date appears at the far left. (Photograph taken in 1981)

above the left spandrel of the south arch [128]. It reads 'Written by the son of Qasim as-Shirazi, ᶜAbd-ul-Haqq, with the title Amanat Khan, in the year 1045 Hijri' (AD 1635/36). The second date appears outside, in the west *pishtaq*, at the bottom of the left leg of the

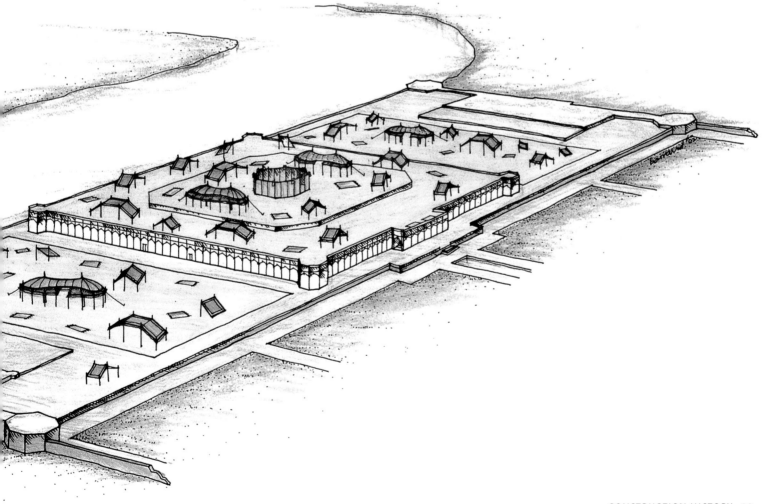

129 Inscription with the date 1046 (AD 1636/37) in the west *pishtaq* of the mausoleum. (Photograph taken in 2000)

130 *right* Inscription with the date 1048 (AD 1638/39) framing the south arch in the tomb chamber of the mausoleum. (Photograph taken in 1981)

131 Inscription with the date 1057 (AD 1647/48) on the north *pishtaq* of the great gate. (Photograph taken in 1996)

Construction history and anniversaries of Mumtaz Mahal's death

17 June 1631: temporary burial of Mumtaz Mahal in the Zainabad garden at Burhanpur

June–December 1631: selection of and negotiation for the site of the funerary complex at Agra

mid-December 1631: body of Mumtaz brought from Burhanpur to Agra

January 1632: laying of the foundations of the Taj Mahal

8 January 1632: second burial of Mumtaz in a 'small domed building' on the construction site, next to the riverfront terrace

22 June 1632: ceremonies of the first anniversary of Mumtaz Mahal's death (ʿurs) in the Jilaukhana

26 May 1633: ceremonies of the second ʿurs, on the white marble platform of the mausoleum which contains the third and final burial of Mumtaz, with installation of a gold screen around the upper cenotaph, made by the court goldsmith Bibadal Khan

1635/36: dated signature of the calligrapher Amanat Khan in the domed hall of the mausoleum, on the inscription band above the south arch

1636/37: date written by Amanat Khan at the bottom of the left leg of the calligraphic frame of the arched opening in the back wall of the west *pishtaq* of the mausoleum

1638/39: dated signature of Amanat Khan at the bottom of the left leg of the calligraphic frame of the south arch in the domed hall of the mausoleum

1640–41: Manrique observes the construction nearing completion and the planting of the garden

1643: officially recorded completion of construction

1647/48: dated signature of Amanat Khan at the bottom of the left leg of the calligraphic frame of the north arch of the great gate

December 1652: Prince Aurangzeb writes to Shah Jahan about repairs needed because of leakage in various parts of the mausoleum, the mosque and the Mihman Khana

inscription surrounding the arched opening in the back wall [129]: it reads 'In the year 1046' (AD 1636/37). In December 1637, according to both Lahauri and Kanbo, Amanat Khan was granted an elephant – the ultimate Mughal status symbol – for inscriptions inside the domed hall of the mausoleum.[90] The third date is inside again, at the bottom of the left leg of the band framing the south arch [130]: it reads 'Finished with His [i.e. God's] help; written by the humble *faqir* Amanat Khan as-Shirazi, in the year one thousand and forty eight Hijri, and the twelfth of His Majesty's auspicious accession'. This tells us that the main body of the mausoleum and its marble facing were completed in 1638/39.

In 1640–41 Manrique saw the Taj Mahal under construction and the garden being planted.[91]

Lahauri and Kanbo report that the entire building was completed at the twelfth ʿurs of Mumtaz Mahal, in 1643, and on that occasion they give a detailed description of all parts of the complex, including the subsidiary structures[92] (translated on pp. 256–57). Work on the decoration, however, seems to have gone on for several more years, at least to 1647/48. The last dated signature of Amanat Khan appears on the north (garden) front of the great gate, at the bottom of the left leg of the rectangular inscriptional frame of the large arch [131]; it reads: 'Finished with His help, the Most High, 1057' – AD 1647/48.

Expenditure and maintenance

The cost of construction of the entire complex, including materials and labour, had been estimated in 1631 as 20–40 *lakhs* of rupees; in the end it cost 50 *lakhs* or 5,000,000 rupees.[93] A sense of what such a figure meant is given by the fact that in 1637–39 an Indian servant of the Dutch East India Company in Agra earned 3 rupees a month or a little more, and a *mansabdar* of 20 *zat* (p. 28) 750 rupees a month.[94]

To finance the upkeep of the complex, Shah Jahan established an endowment (*waqf*) of 3 *lakhs* or 300,000 rupees. One-third came from the annual revenues from thirty villages of the district of Agra, and the other two-thirds came from the income of the bazaars and caravanserais which formed the southern part of the Taj Mahal complex.[95] In 1691 Aurangzeb ordered the governors of every province to send 2,000 rupees 'as a standing practice' (yearly?) to Khwaja Khidmat Khan, whom he had installed as caretaker.[96] Since the Mughal empire at the time had twenty-one provinces, the additional amount came to 42,000 rupees.

The *waqf* covered all the necessary repairs of the buildings, the annual charities, and the monthly salaries and expenses for food and drink of the tomb attendants (*khadim*) and the reciters of the Qur'an who prayed day and night inside the mausoleum for the soul of Mumtaz Mahal – who had their quarters in the Khawasspuras in the outer courts (pp. 118–20).[97] The surplus went to the emperor, who held the trusteeship of the tomb, and had a local representative. The post was first held by the eunuch Agah Khan, whose garden palace was immediately east of the Taj Mahal (p. 59).[98]

The *waqf* was finally abolished by the British in 1803,[99] and they took on the upkeep of the tomb (p. 251). Major Henry Hardy Cole, in his *First Report of the Curator of Ancient Monuments in India for the Year 1881–82*, noted that 'In 1840 the local agents at Agra reported that the Taj revenues from villages yielding Rs 4,200 per month were at the time of the British occupation [i.e. 1803] applied to the general purposes of the State'; and 'In 1816 the pensions of the deceased kadims [sic] at the Taj were discontinued, and the fruit grown in the garden was sold for the benefit of [the British] Government.'[100] The institution of the *khadim* was, however, not entirely given up: there were in 1905 still '18 hereditary care-takers or *khadims* who receive Rs 3 per mensem from funds at the disposal of the garden committee, and who take it by turns to look after the buildings, six being always on duty at time'.[101]

Death and burial of Shah Jahan

After the Taj Mahal was completed, Shah Jahan's historians mention briefly that he presided over two more assemblies on the anniversary of Mumtaz's death, on 27 January 1644 and 15 January 1645.[102] In 1648 the emperor moved his main residence from Agra to Delhi, and after that his historians record only one more visit to the tomb, in December 1654: after showing his son Dara Shikoh the newly built Moti Masjid in the fort, he took a boat from the landing below the Shah Burj to the Taj Mahal, where he said the *Fatiha*.[103]

Four years later, in 1658, Shah Jahan was deposed by his son Aurangzeb. He was held captive in the Agra fort, and deprived of his writing materials, favourite objects, jewels and precious stones. No-one was allowed to see him without Aurangzeb's special permission.[104] The deposed emperor spent his days in religious readings and meditations, the Taj Mahal before his eyes. Jahanara, who after the death of Mumtaz Mahal had been his favourite companion, shared her father's captivity.

On 17 or 18 January 1666, shortly after his seventy-fourth birthday, Shah Jahan fell ill with strangury and dysentery. He was confined to bed for two weeks and became weaker and weaker, despite all the efforts of his physicians.[105] He felt his end was near, and made arrangements for his funeral and burial. On the evening of 31 January 1666, lying in the Shah Burj, he commended the ladies of the imperial *zanana*, in particular Akbarabadi Mahal, the esteemed consort of his later life (p. 120), to the care of Jahanara, and recited with her the *kalima* (the Islamic profession of faith) and verses from the Qur'an, after which he died. In the words of Aurangzeb's historian Muhammad Kazim, 'the bird of the graceful spirit of that exalted monarch . . . flew away with the intention of . . . taking its eternal seat in the heavenly house'. Jahanara and the other ladies broke into tears and laments, began beating their faces and tearing their hair, and donned mourning dresses.

Jahanara planned a grand burial for her father, but Aurangzeb was against public honours for Shah Jahan. Kanbo, a partisan of the emperor, gives us an image of the funeral as it would have been according to Jahanara's wishes[106] – the body taken 'with honour and dignity' to the 'illumined tomb' (the Taj Mahal), the great nobles of the court carrying the bier on their shoulders, the distinguished citizens of Agra, men of religion, and learned men gathered round the corpse calling the *kalima* and traditional religious phrases, and the officials of the imperial household scattering coins along the way of the procession as a token of the bounty of the dead emperor.

What actually happened was that the governor of Agra, Hoshdar Khan, sent for two eminent religious men, Sayyid Muhammad Qannauji, who had been Shah Jahan's spiritual guide during his captivity, and Qazi Qurban, the chief religious judge of Agra, to help with the funeral arrangements and the burial. The corpse was taken to one of the halls near the Shah Burj, washed according to the rites of Islam, and placed in a coffin of sandalwood. The coffin was carried down the stairs of the Shah Burj, and the door at the bottom, which had been closed during Shah Jahan's imprisonment, was specially opened for this occasion. From the gate in the fort's outer wall the coffin was taken by boat to the mausoleum. There Sayyid Muhammad Qannauji and Qazi Qurban spoke the funeral prayers with some of the dignitaries of Agra, and the coffin was laid in the lower tomb chamber next to that of Mumtaz Mahal.

Aurangzeb's son, Prince Mu'azzam, who had been sent to Agra from Delhi when the emperor learned of his father's illness, did not arrive until 1 February, shortly after the funeral. He presented his condolences to Jahanara and the other ladies, then held the ceremonies of distributing alms and reading the Qur'an for the forgiveness of the soul of the deceased.

On the evening of the following day runners bringing the news of Shah Jahan's death reached Aurangzeb. He expressed his regrets at not having been present at his father's last hour and ordered the court to wear mourning; but he did not set out for Agra until 14 February. Since he did not want to stay in the fort where Jahanara and the women of Shah Jahan's household were residing, he gave orders to have the Haveli of Dara Shikoh prepared for him (p. 72). He arrived on 25 February, went to the tomb, performed the ritual walk around it, recited the *Fatiha* and other prayers for the souls of his parents, broke down in tears, and gave 12,000 rupees to the tomb attendants. He then offered afternoon prayers in the mosque of the mausoleum, after which he went to see his sister and the women in the fort. In the following days Aurangzeb visited the tomb regularly, and each time inside the mausoleum held the ceremony of giving alms to the poor and presents to the pious and learned. He ordered that Shah Jahan should have the posthumous title Firdaus Ashyani, 'Abiding in Paradise'.[107]

Eventually Aurangzeb decided to turn his stay of mourning at Agra into a demonstration of power, and ordered that the festival of 'Id al-Fitr (marking the end of Ramazan, the month of fasting), which in 1666 fell on 6 April, should be held in the old capital of his father. He sent to Delhi for his women and for the famous Peacock Throne of Shah Jahan, for a big celebration, as undisputed emperor at last.

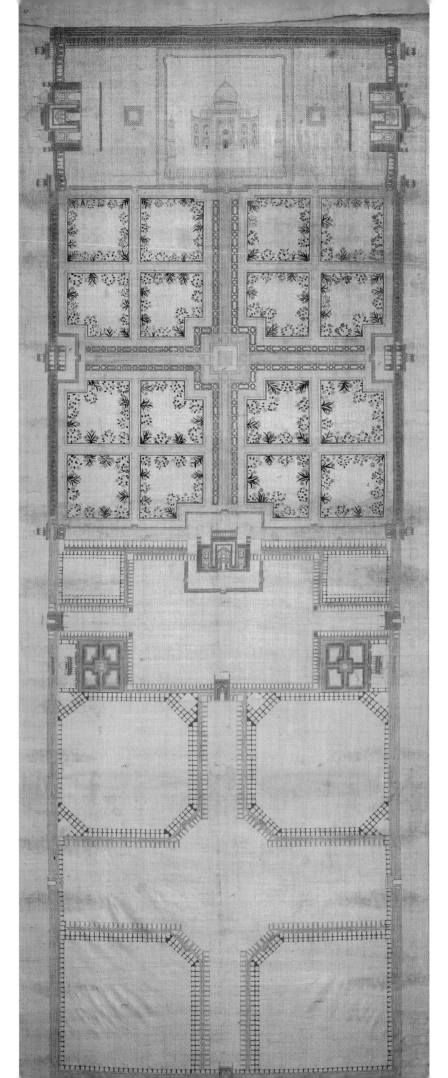

II More than a tomb: the parts of the Taj Mahal

They drew up the plan for a magnificent building and a high-built dome which for its loftiness will until the Day of Resurrection remain a memorial to the sky-reaching ambition of His Majesty, the Second Lord of the Auspicious Conjunction of the Planets Jupiter and Venus, and its strength will represent the firmness of the intentions of its builder.

ᶜAbd-ul-Hamid Lahauri, *Padshahnama*, 1630s–54[1]

The grandiose structure of the Taj Mahal is not just a mausoleum set in a garden, marking the culmination of Mughal funerary architecture: it was designed as part of a large complex with many buildings of varying purpose, so systematically planned that it epitomizes the principles of Shahjahani architecture [144–148]. A funerary ensemble of this size, strict planning and intricacy is unique in South Asia; in the Islamic context it can only be compared to the *külliyes*, the great mosque complexes of the Ottomans which included the tombs of the builders. They were however smaller and laid out in a more informal way.

The oblong site of the Taj Mahal is divided into two main zones, the funerary and the 'worldly', reflecting the dialectics of the Islamic concept of *din wa dunya*, the domain of the spiritual and the domain of material life. The funerary zone consists of the mausoleum with its flanking mosque and assembly hall, set in a garden and reached through a monumental gate [146:A,B]. This is preceded by the transitional zone of the Jilaukhana or forecourt, flanked by the quarters for the tomb attendants, subsidiary tombs, and bazaar streets [146:C]. To its south was the entirely mundane large bazaar and caravanserai complex [146:D], which served the funerary complex in a way that was not only functional but also formal, as the servant area echoed the plan of the area served. By providing quarters here for foreign travellers and merchants visiting the monument, the designers ensured that 'the whole world should see and admire its magnificence', as Tavernier observed in the mid-17th century.[2] The reception of the Taj Mahal by the viewer forms an integral part of its concept.

THE DESIGN

The historians and poets of Shah Jahan state that the Taj Mahal was to represent an earthly replica of the house of Mumtaz Mahal in the gardens of Paradise (pp. 20, 144, 152, 215). This must not be dismissed as Shahjahani court rhetoric: it truly expresses the programme of the mausoleum. In order to realize the idea of the eschatological garden house as closely as possible, the canonical layout of previous imperial mausoleums, where the building stood in the centre of a cross-axially planned garden or *chahar bagh* [19:a], was abandoned, and the riverfront design that had become the

132 Plan of the Taj Mahal complex, drawn by an Indian artist (perhaps after the Daniells' plan [147]), early 19th century. The main buildings are depicted in elevation rather than plan. At the north (top) is the riverfront terrace, where the mausoleum is flanked by the mosque on the left and Mihman Khana on the right; south of this is the garden, with the garden-wall pavilions at either end of the transverse axis; in the centre is the great gate; south of it is the Jilaukhana or forecourt; furthest south is the bazaar and caravanserai complex, or Taj Ganj, and the gate known as Dakhnay Darwaza. (For a key, see p. 112.)

prevailing residential garden type of Agra [cf. 30] was chosen instead, and raised to a monumental scale [132]. The interaction between residential and funerary genres had characterized Mughal architecture from the beginning.[3] In the Taj Mahal the aim was to perfect the riverfront garden and enlarge it to a scale beyond the reach of ordinary mortals, to create here on earth and in the Mughal city a paradisiacal garden palace for the deceased.

The mausoleum is set at the northern end of the main axis of a vast oblong walled complex which descends in hardly noticeable terraced steps towards the Yamuna river [144, 145]. The overall composition is formed of two major components: the mausoleum and its garden [146:A,B], and two subsidiary courtyard complexes to the south [146:C,D]. The garden shows the characteristic combination of a rectangular raised riverfront terrace [146:A] on which are placed the main buildings, and on the landward side, at a lower level, a *chahar bagh* [146:B].

The two subsidiary complexes echo the configuration of the garden; but here the elements are open courtyards surrounded by shallow arcades, characteristic of the residential and utilitarian architecture of the period. The rectangular unit to the north [146:C] is formed of the Jilaukhana or forecourt, framed by two residential courtyards, the Khawasspuras, for the tomb attendants [146:10a,10b], and two tombs for lesser wives of Shah Jahan ('Saheli Burj'), which have miniature riverfront garden plans [146:13a,13b]. This connects to an ancient principle of Indian architecture where a constituent element may reflect the overall structure (p. 27). The subcourts are separated by open bazaar streets [146:12a,12b] which lead in to the Jilaukhana.

The squarish unit to the south [146:D] has been built in and over by the city quarter called Taj Ganj, and the original Mughal fabric can only be made out in places. It consisted of two cross-axial open bazaar streets [146:12c–12f] and four caravanserai courts [146:16a–16d], echoing the *chahar bagh* plan of the garden. To date four large plans are known that show the complex with this southern element: the Jaipur plan [17], a plan drawn by Thomas and William Daniell in 1789 [147]; an early 19th-century plan on view in the Taj Museum, measuring 132 x 352 cm (roughly 4 x 10 ft), on which the main elements of the architecture, and fruits then grown in the Taj garden, are indicated [193] (sadly, it has so far proved unphotographable as a whole);[4] a simpler version of it, also in Agra;[5] and a plan of similar date in the Museum für Indische Kunst in Berlin [132].

Thus the entire Taj complex consisted of two components, each following the riverfront garden design: the *chahar bagh* and terrace – a true riverfront garden – and a landlocked variant in the configuration of the two subsidiary units, where the rectangle of the

Jilaukhana corresponded to the riverfront terrace, and the cross-axial bazaar and caravanserai element to the *chahar bagh*. That lost complex was an integral part of the Taj Mahal, forming its counter-image, according to the basic Shahjahani architectural principle of symmetrical correspondence.

THE PRINCIPLES OF SHAHJAHANI ARCHITECTURE

The complex of the Taj Mahal explores the potential of the riverfront garden as both an ideal funerary and a utilitarian worldly construct. And it also expresses in canonical form the architectural principles of the period. Theory was laid down in the architecture itself, and we note here the purest expression of a consistent formal systematization which characterizes all the art of Shah Jahan – a distinctive and outstanding contribution, specific to this period. The principles of Shahjahani architecture interact closely with each other. We can identify them as follows:

1. Geometrical planning
2. Symmetry. Particularly favoured was bilateral symmetry, for which we even get a term in contemporary descriptions of buildings: *qarina*.[6] This Arabic word expresses the notion of pairing and counterparts, but of integration too, thus it fits conceptually into the ideas of universal harmony that played a great role in the imperial ideology of Shah Jahan. In a typical Shahjahani *qarina* scheme two symmetrical features flank a dominant central feature.
3. Hierarchy. This is the overriding principle that governs all the others.
4. Proportional formulas expressed in triadic divisions
5. Uniformity of shapes, ordered by hierarchical accents
6. Sensuous attention to detail
7. A selective use of naturalism
8. Symbolism

133, 134 *below and above right* The imperial baldachin, in the south wing of the 'Machchhi Bhavan' in the Agra fort (completed in 1637), and one of the capitals of its baluster columns, seen when still intact before restoration. (Photographs taken in 1980 and 1982)

One side of the courtyard of the 'Machchhi Bhavan' in the Agra fort illustrates these principles very clearly [86, 133, 134]. It consists of uniformly shaped arcades. The emperor's marble baldachin in the centre, and the identical arcades on either side, together express bilateral symmetry, or *qarina*, in a triadic division. The baldachin sets its hierarchical accent by the use of marble, a nobler material. Its organic baluster columns, decorated with three-dimensional acanthus leaves, are shaped with sensuous attention to detail and stand in stark contrast to the plain arcades in the rest of the courtyard. The plant forms of the baldachin display selective naturalism and serve as a symbol that the emperor, whose throne stood below it, generates bloom and well-being (pp. 222–24). This is emphasized by the pot with overhanging leaves out of which each of the four columns grows: it represents a *purna-ghata* or *purna-kalasha* (vase of plenty), an ancient symbol of Indian architecture standing for growth, fecundity and prosperity [347].

These principles govern the entire architecture of Shah Jahan. They are expressed most grandly and most consistently in the Taj Mahal.

THE PRINCIPLES AS EXPRESSED IN THE TAJ MAHAL

1. Rational and strict geometry This is ensured by the use of grid systems based on the Shahjahani *gaz*, or *zira'*, of an average length of 80–82 cm (*c.* 32 in.). As Richard Barraud explains (pp. 108–9), different modules are used for the garden and the subsidiary complexes, and even individual buildings have their own grid. The unit of the riverfront terrace and the garden is based on a 23-*gaz* module, and the unit of the Jilaukhana and bazaar and caravanserai complex on a 17-*gaz* module. In the planning of the mausoleum a 7-*gaz* module is used, and in that of the great gate a 3-*gaz* module.
2. Perfect symmetrical planning, with an emphasis on bilateral symmetry (*qarina*) along a central axis on which the main features are placed The main north–south axis runs through the garden canal and the bazaar street. On it are set the dominant features: the mausoleum [146:1], the pool [146:5], the great gate [146:9], the Jilaukhana [146:11], the southern gate of the Jilaukhana [146:15], and the *chauk* (square) of the bazaar and caravanserai complex [146:17]. These elements are flanked by pairs of identical buildings: the

mosque [146:2] and Mihman Khana (assembly hall) [146:3], the two pavilions in the garden wall, now called 'Naubat Khana' [146:7a,7b], and, to accentuate the corners of the enclosing wall and the raised terrace, three pairs of towers (burj) topped by chhatris [146:4a–4f]. The elements of the subsidiary units are arranged with the same mirror symmetry.

Integrated into the overall qarina symmetry are centrally planned elements: the four-part garden [146:B], the four-part bazaar and caravanserai complex [146:D], and the miniature chahar baghs of the inner subsidiary tombs. The mausoleum [146:1] and the great gate [146:9] have centralized plans. Each element plays an indispensable part in the whole: if just one part were missing, the balance of the entire composition would be destroyed.

Bilateral symmetry dominated by a central accent has generally been recognized as an ordering principle of the architecture of rulers aiming at absolute power, as an expression of the ruling force which brings about balance and harmony, 'a striking symbol of the stratification of aristocratic society under centralized authority'.[7]

3. A hierarchical grading of materials, forms and colours down to the most minute ornamental detail Particularly striking is the hierarchical use of colour. The only building in the whole complex entirely faced with white marble is the mausoleum. All the subsidiary structures are faced with red sandstone; special features, such as domes, may be clad in white marble. This hierarchic use of white marble and red sandstone is typical of imperial Mughal architecture, but it is here exploited with unparalleled sophistication. It represents the clearest link to Indian concepts set out in the shastras, and expresses social stratification (p. 215).

4. Triadic divisions bound together in proportional formulas These determine the shape of plans, elevations and architectural ornament. A leitmotif is a tripartite composition consisting of a dominant feature in the centre flanked by two identical elements – a configuration that relates to hierarchy as well as to qarina symmetry.

5. Uniformity of shapes, ordered by hierarchical accents Only one type of column, for instance, is used in the entire complex: it was chosen by the emperor's builders from the repertoire of earlier Mughal architecture, and may be called the Shahjahani column [187].[8] It has a multi-faceted shaft, a capital built up from miniature arches and concave elements (muqarnas), and a base with four multi-cusped arched panels. Within uniformity there is hierarchy, for the proportions and details of the columns vary according to their position in the complex – simplest in the bazaar streets, larger and richer in the funerary area. They usually support a multi-cusped arch: another typical feature of Shahjahani architecture, this emerged in the 1630s and was referred to by Muhammad Waris, the historian of Shah Jahan's later reign, as taq-i marghul or taq marghuldar, 'curled arch' or 'arch with curls'.[9] The basic shape of the panelling of the walls, with shallow multi-cusped arches and cartouches, and the treatment of vaults are again governed by uniformity. A particular type of decoration is used for the main vaults and half-vaults of the mausoleum and the great gate – a net pattern developed from points in concentric tiers, which Shahjahani authors call qalib kari (p. 131).

6. Sensuous attention to detail This is expressed most notably in the dado flowers of the mausoleum and in the exquisite pietra dura decoration of the cenotaphs and the screen that surrounds them [e.g. 117, 226, 233].

7. A selective use of naturalism Naturalism expresses hierarchy. The most naturalistic decoration appears in the chief building of the entire complex, the mausoleum. Here the lower wall zone is carved with realistic flowering plants and flower vases [e.g. 225, 230, 339], and the corner colonnettes of the tomb chamber have acanthus bases and capitals [230]. The cenotaphs and the screen that encloses them are covered with colourful flowers and floral ornament in pietra dura technique, which produces highly realistic effects [117, 233–240]. The flanking buildings, the mosque and Mihman Khana, display less naturalistic and less refined ornament [276–295]; in the garden buildings it is used only sparingly; and none appears in the Jilaukhana or the bazaar and caravanserai complex.

8. A sophisticated symbolism in the architectural programme – used to present the mausoleum as the earthly realization of the mansion of Mumtaz in the garden of Paradise (pp. 20, 52, 215).

Prelude: the mausoleum throughout a day

The mausoleum is entirely clad in white marble. Alluding to the stone's luminosity, the Mughal poets compared it to early dawn or to a cloud. Kalim wrote:

> It is a [piece of] heaven of the colour of dawn's bright face,
> Because from top to bottom and inside out it is of marble –
>
> Nay, not marble: because of its translucent colour (ab-u-rang)
> The eye can mistake it for a cloud.[10]

And Kanbo refers to 'the illumined tomb (rauza-i munauwara) . . . on whose every stone slab from early morning until late evening the whiteness of the true dawn is reflected, causing the viewer to forget his desire to move towards the highest heaven'.[11] Because of its capacity to transmit and refract light, the white marble reacts to atmospheric changes, enhancing the mystical and mythical aura of the building. The mausoleum's appearance alters from hour to hour. An early Western observer who described the effect at different times of day is Captain William Sleeman (see p. 240), who visited the Taj Mahal on 1 January 1836, and noted:

> after going repeatedly over every part, and examining the tout ensemble from all possible positions, and in all possible lights, from that of the full moon at midnight in a cloudless sky to that of the noonday sun, the mind seemed to repose in the calm persuasion that there was an entire harmony of parts, a faultless congregation of architectural beauties, on which it could dwell for ever without fatigue.[12]

overleaf
135–140 The mausoleum seen from the upper level of the great gate on 13 November 1996 at 9:15 a.m., 11:30 a.m., 4:03 p.m., 5:00 p.m., 5:15 p.m., and 5:30 p.m.

Modular planning of the Taj Mahal

RICHARD ANDRÉ BARRAUD

THIS SECTION presents, as briefly as possible, the modular planning of the Taj complex. So far, the only attempt to explain the planning has been that of Begley, who assumed that 'odd'-looking figures given by Shah Jahan's historians Lahauri and Kanbo were incorrect, and used an overall 400 gaz as the basis for his layout.[13] Our investigations showed a scheme that is almost the complete opposite.

That the complex is designed on a grid is obvious.[14] The question is: how was this plan developed? One method involves using a fixed grid, on which a plan is superimposed – similar to the process of designing on standard graph paper. Another method involves planning a layout directly on a 'generated' grid. In this system a specific length can be divided into modules or subdivisions in various ways – by halving them, e.g. 16, 8, etc., or by using tripartite divisions, e.g. 9, 12, etc., or by employing the decimal system, e.g. 10, 20, etc.[15] This forms the basis of the grid, and, though the module thus obtained may not be a convenient 'round' gaz figure, the layout can be worked out so that features match such a grid. A thorough examination of the available material revealed that the Taj complex was designed using this latter method. Inspiration may also have been derived from ancient Indian planning principles, the vastu shastras.[16]

In the course of this study, gaz figures given by Shah Jahan's historians were correlated with our measurements. Comparisons were made with various proposed equivalents for the gaz, including Hodgson's 79.9 cm (31.456 in.)[17] and the generally accepted 81.28 cm (32 in.). Several earlier drawings of the Taj, including those prepared by the Archaeological Survey of India, were also studied. Hodgson's work on the equivalent of the gaz has also served as a reliable comparative source.

Basically, it was discovered that several seemingly 'odd' dimensions in the histories were accurate, while many apparently precise figures were, in fact, rounded-off and hence not accurate (of the figures given, we shall see that 368 for the garden and 204 for the Jilaukhana court are accurate, while 140 for the riverfront terrace is not). There are several reasons for this. It is, of course, impossible to design a building in which all dimensions are round figures.

Several figures often turn out to be fractions, which the historians rounded off since they were too unwieldy to be used in a transcription. There is also the possibility that a third person gave figures to the historians, and errors crept in. Finally, it is a fact that the workmanship was not always very good, resulting in varying measurements for a particular gaz dimension.[18] It is thus of great importance to realize that in working out a system of planning the precise gaz equivalents for a particular measurement are not as relevant as the proportions these measurements are supposed to represent.[19] The Mughals found that certain figures had a geometrical convenience in planning terms. For instance, a regular octagon with a diameter of 5 has a side of 2, one with a diameter of 17 has a side of 7 [141:a], and one with a diameter of 70 has a side of 29. There can be no justification for simply dismissing 'odd' figures in the sources such as 204, 368 and 374 gaz. Also, since tripartite proportional divisions play a dominant role in Mughal planning, one can assume that the Mughals were aware of the sexagesimal system of numeration.[20] These are among several assumptions made in arriving at the planning procedure outlined below.

1. The overall concept, supporting the tripartite connotation, is a rectangle composed of three squares of 374 gaz [141:b]. Lahauri and Kanbo give 374 gaz as the width of the entire complex. This figure is a multiple of 17, and 17 gaz is the module used for the planning of the Jilaukhana and the bazaar and caravanserai complex. However, the garden and riverfront terrace, being the setting of the tomb, have a more refined 23-gaz module with a clearer definition of features [142].

2. The detailed planning begins with the cross-axial garden, which as a perfect square represents the focus of the geometric planning. This section is designed on a module of 23 gaz. Though at first glance an arbitrary figure, this proves to have a solid basis. The width of the garden given by the historians is 368 gaz. It is divided into a grid of 16 x 16 squares, each of which is thus 23 gaz to a side. The length of the platform of the garden-wall pavilion is recorded by Lahauri and Kanbo as 46 gaz (23 x 2), while the length of the paved walkway alongside the platform in front of the great gate is 92 gaz (23 x 4) when converted from our measurements. These figures are among several recorded in the garden which are multiples of 23 gaz.[21]

3. The riverfront terrace section is also based on a 23-gaz module. The width of the terrace given by the historians, 140 gaz, has been measured as 111.89 m. When we measured the body of the mausoleum, given by the historians as 70 gaz, we found a width of 56.76 m. According to that measurement, 140 gaz should be not 111.89 but 113.52 m – a difference of 1.63 m. This implies that one of the two gaz figures given might not be correct. If 56.76 m = 70 gaz, then 111.89 m = 137.99, effectively 138 gaz (divide 111.89 by 56.76 and multiply by 70). Amazingly, 138 is precisely 23 x 6! Similarly, the measurement for the platform or kursi of the mausoleum, 95.69 m, was given as 120 gaz, but when it is compared proportionately in the same way it works out as 118 gaz.[22] Here again, the proportional equivalent is more important than the neat figure in the histories.

On working out the spacing and dimensions of various features in the garden and on the riverfront terrace,[23] it was found that they fit perfectly into the 23-gaz grid, and consequently into a sub-module of 11.5 gaz. The length of the complex along the N–S axis from the terrace to the 23-gaz transition zone of the southern gallery and walkway between the garden and the Jilaukhana is 529 gaz, exactly 23 x 23! The E–W axis of the terrace measures 300 m, or 373 gaz – a deviation from the overall 374 gaz.[24] The sunken courts in front of the mosque and Mihman Khana are 57.5 gaz wide (23 x 2.5 – the 11.5 sub-module x 5), and their axes are perfectly aligned with the secondary walkways in the garden.

4. The Jilaukhana is planned on a 17-gaz module. The lesser importance of this space is evident in its slipshod execution. Here the 204 gaz given by the historians for the length of the courtyard is accurate. Their figure of 150 gaz for its width, however, is not:[25] using comparisons similar to those used for the terrace, the courtyard was found to be 153 gaz wide. The total width of the Jilaukhana complex, 374 gaz, proves to be the 17-gaz module multiplied by 22. The 153 gaz width of the courtyard is 17 x 9, and its 204 gaz length is 17 x 12. Both 9 and 12 are ideal numbers for tripartite planning. The figure given in the sources for the Khawasspura is 76 gaz: the actual measurement is 76.5 gaz – 17 x 4.5.

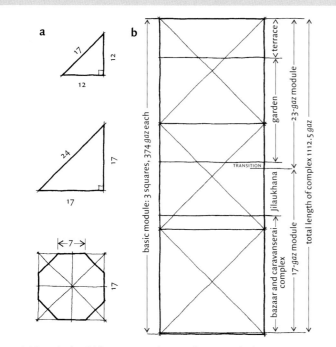

141 (a) Seemingly odd figures can make sense in geometric shapes:
e.g. in a right-angled triangle with two equal sides of 12, the hypotenuse is 17. If the sides are 17, the hypotenuse is 24.
(b) The scheme of the Taj Mahal is a basic 1:3 ratio rectangle made up of three squares, each theoretically having a side of 374 gaz, which is a multiple of 17 gaz. The four main sections of the complex are laid out on this rectangle, in their respective modules of 17 gaz or 23 gaz.

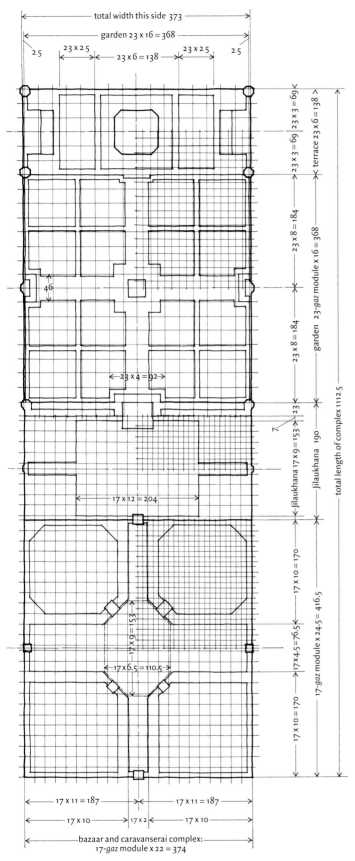

5. The bazaar and caravanserai complex is also planned on a module of 17 *gaz*. Evidence comes essentially from the remnants of the gates to the four caravanserais, the southernmost gate of the entire complex ('Dakhnay Darwaza'), and fragments of residential wings and shops. Each of the caravanserais is planned as a square of 17 x 9.5 *gaz*, giving sides 161.5 *gaz* long (Lahauri and Kanbo give the length as 160). With the addition of the rows of rooms opening onto the bazaar streets, each caravanserai measures 170 *gaz*, or 17 x 10. The E–W bazaar street is 76.5 *gaz* wide, i.e. 17 x 4.5. Thus the total N–S length of the bazaar and caravanserai complex is 170 + 76.5 + 170, or 416.5 *gaz*, which is 17 x 24.5. The central *chauk* itself measures 110.5 x 153 *gaz* – both figures again multiples of the 17-*gaz* module.

Thus the planning of the garden and the riverfront terrace is based on a 23-*gaz* grid, while the Jilaukhana and the bazaar and caravanserai complex are planned on a 17-*gaz* grid. Individual buildings are designed on smaller grids, which are then superimposed on the overall scheme. The mausoleum, mosque and Mihman Khana are designed on a 7-*gaz* grid. The great gate is designed on a 3-*gaz* grid, which is superimposed on the 17-*gaz* grid of the Jilaukhana [143].[26] The total length of the complex is thus 138 + 368 + 190 + 416.5 = 1,112.5 *gaz*. The metric figure for this length is, according to our measurements, 896.1 m, resulting in a *gaz* equivalent to 80.55 cm.

Each space is not entirely symmetrical about both axes. In the bazaar and caravanserai complex the northern caravanserais have larger gates than the southern ones. In the Jilaukhana section the Khawasspuras lie to the north of the courtyard and the subsidiary tombs to the south. In relation to the garden, of course, the mausoleum is to the north while the great gate is to the south.

The entire complex was conceived on modular grids not only in plan but also in elevation. Individual elements and features, in the outer buildings as well,[27] are skilfully integrated into the overall scheme, combining various grids with remarkable dexterity. The results of our investigations show that the planning of the Taj Mahal cannot be reconstructed by putting a decimal grid over the whole complex and explaining away the features which do not fit into it, but that it was a much more complex procedure deeply rooted in indigenous building traditions.

142 This drawing shows, in detail, the development of the individual grids for each of the four sections [cf. 146] in the overall planning. It indicates how critical elements in each section relate to their grids, whether the 17-*gaz* or the 23-*gaz* module. Note also the alignment, for instance, of axes of pathways and of squares or octagons in each section.

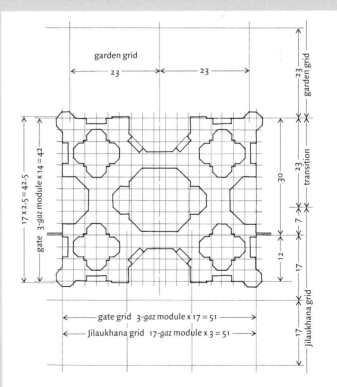

143 The 3-*gaz* module of the great gate is superimposed on the 17-*gaz* module of the Jilaukhana, to the south. Note also the transition from that 17-*gaz* module to the 23-*gaz* module of the garden, to the north.

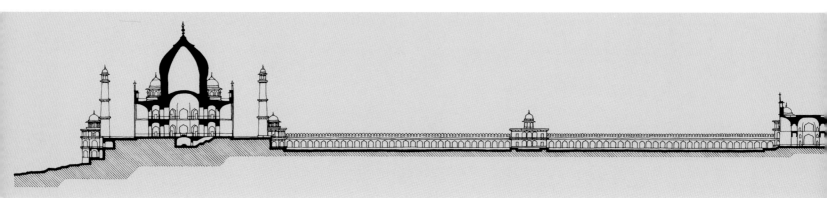

144 Schematic reconstruction of the complex as it looked in the time of Shah Jahan. From the river end at the north (left), the elements are: the mausoleum, flanked by the mosque and Mihman Khana or assembly hall; the garden, with the garden-wall pavilions on the transverse axis; the great gate; the Jilaukhana or forecourt, with the Khawasspuras or quarters of the tomb attendants nearer the great gate, and two subsidiary tombs further away; and the bazaar and caravanserai complex. The latter has all but vanished today, but it was an essential element, and its traces can still be found.

145 Section of the entire complex, from the riverfront at the north (left) to the south (right), with the east gate and ranges of the bazaar and caravanserai complex partly reconstructed. This, the first section ever prepared, shows how the complex falls in terraced steps towards the river.

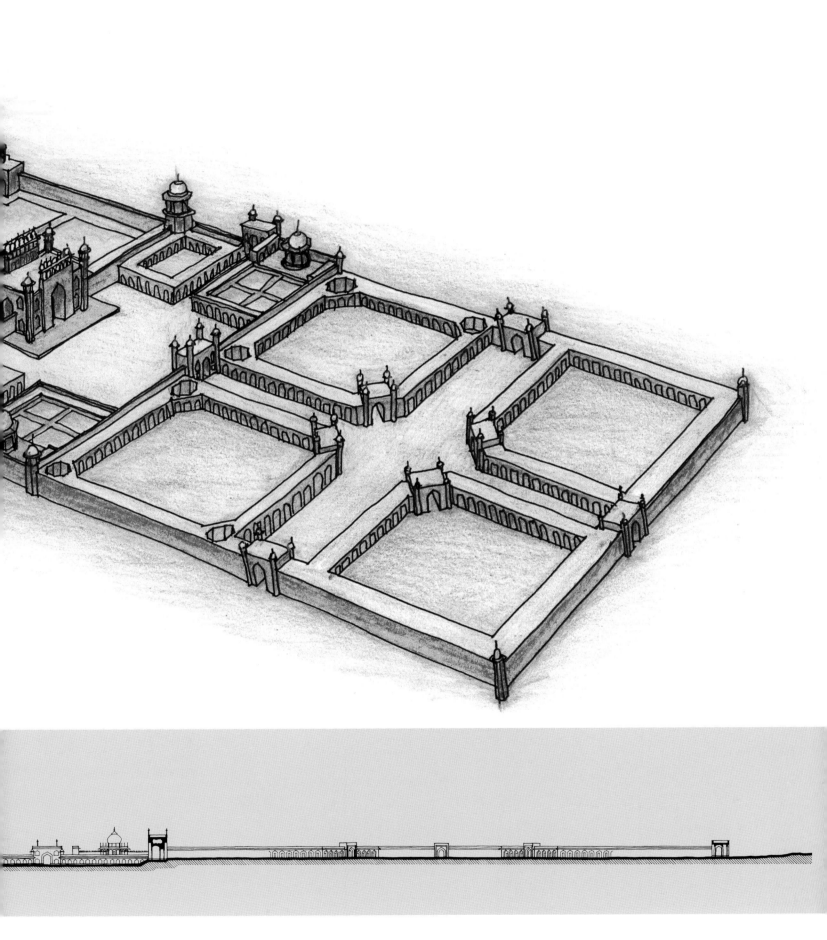

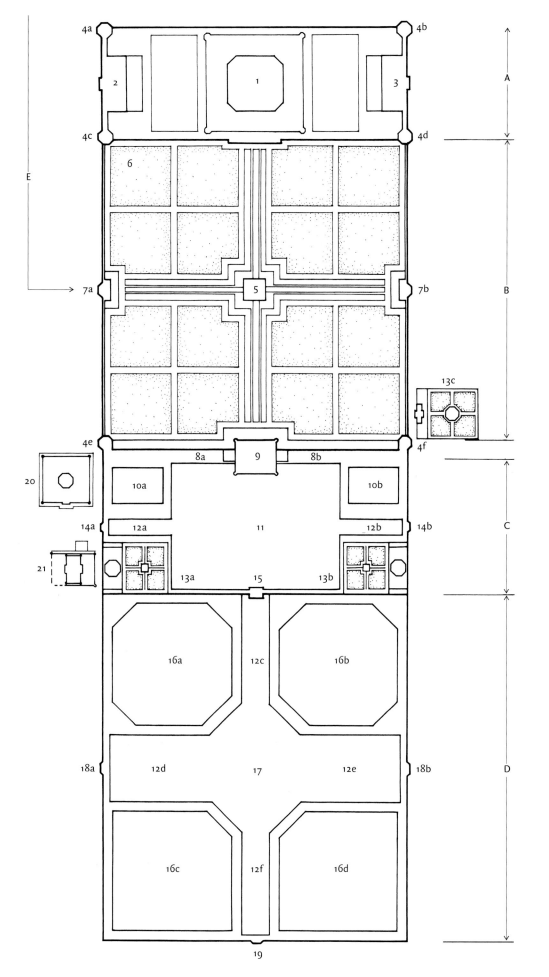

146 *left* Site plan of the complex, including buildings outside the walls.

A Riverfront terrace
B Garden
C Jilaukhana (forecourt) zone
D Bazaar and caravanserai complex
E Waterworks

1 Mausoleum
2 Mosque
3 Mihman Khana (literally 'guest house'; presumably used as assembly hall)
4a–f Wall towers
   c *baoli* tower
   d latrine tower
5 Central pool
6 Site of the first burial of Mumtaz
7a,b Garden-wall pavilions ('Naubat Khana')
8a,b Southern galleries
9 Great gate
10a,b Khawasspuras (quarters of the tomb attendants)
11 Jilaukhana (forecourt)
12a–f Bazaar streets
13a–c Subsidiary tombs ('Saheli Burj')
   a Inner western subsidiary tomb
   b Inner eastern subsidiary tomb
   c Outer eastern subsidiary tomb with the 'Sandli' or 'Kali' Masjid
14a,b West gate ('Fatehpuri Darwaza') and east gate ('Fatehabadi Darwaza')
15 South Gate ('Sirhi' or 'Sidhi' Darwaza)
16a–d Caravanserais
   a Katra Omar Khan
   b Katra Fulel (Perfume Market)
   c Katra Resham (Silk Market)
   d Katra Jogidas
17 *Chauk* (market square)
18a,b West and east gates of the bazaar and caravanserai complex
19 South gate of the bazaar and caravanserai complex ('Dakhnay Darwaza')
20 Outer western subsidiary tomb, of 'Fatehpuri Begam' (probably of Satti-un-Nisa Khanum)
21 'Fatehpuri Masjid'

opposite
147 *left* The first plan of the Taj complex, prepared by Thomas and William Daniell in 1789 and published in 1801.

148 *right* The complex seen from a satellite, before 2000. The bazaar and caravanserai area at the bottom is densely built over, in the district called Taj Ganj, but its outline can still be made out.

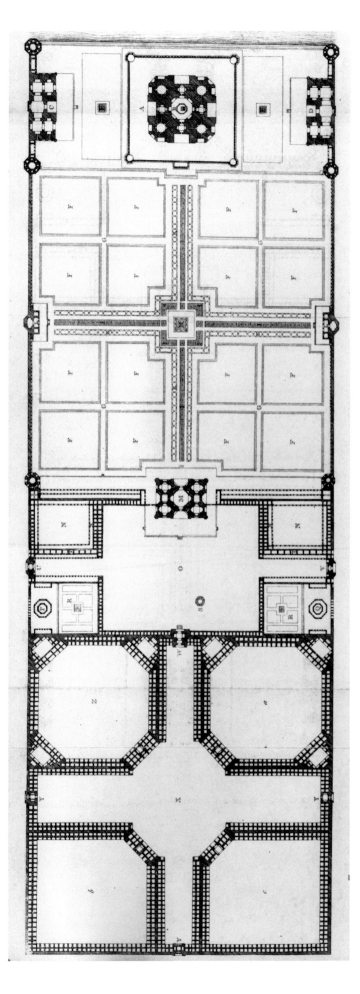

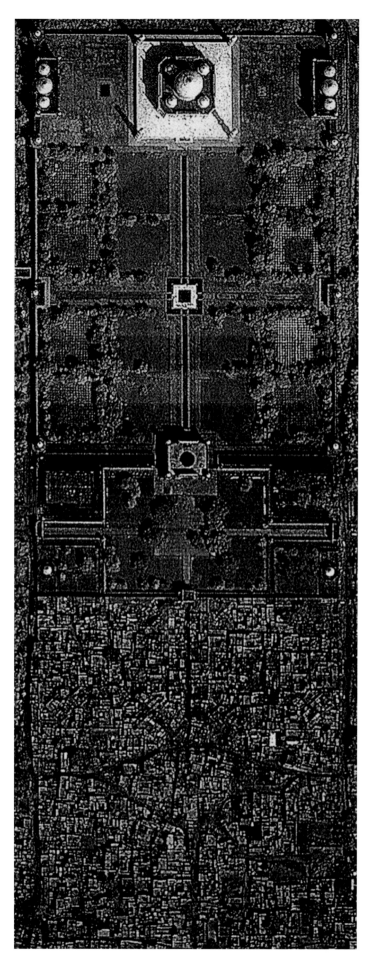

A WALK THROUGH THE TAJ MAHAL COMPLEX

This analytical walk takes its cue from the 'ambulatory descriptions'[28] by Lahauri and Kanbo on the occasion of the official completion of the Taj Mahal on 6 February 1643 (for a translation of Lahauri's text see pp. 256–57).[29] They lead the reader from north to south, starting with the mausoleum and ending in the bazaar and caravanserai complex. That area was already in ruin in the late 18th century, and largely disappeared in the course of the early 20th-century restoration;

what little remains is buried in the Taj Ganj district [148]. We proceed, as the present-day visitor does, in the opposite direction, from the gates of the Jilaukhana [146:14a,14b] to the riverfront terrace [146:A]. (Indeed, it has been suggested that a 'scripted path' is the basis for reading the Taj: moving from the mundane world to the spiritual climax of the mausoleum, the visitor's perception is directed by perspective effects devised in sequences along the main axis.[30]) We then turn back to consider the bazaar and caravanserai zone, the waterworks, and the adjoining buildings outside the walls.

Mughal terms and names of buildings are used whenever they are available; later popular names are printed in inverted commas.

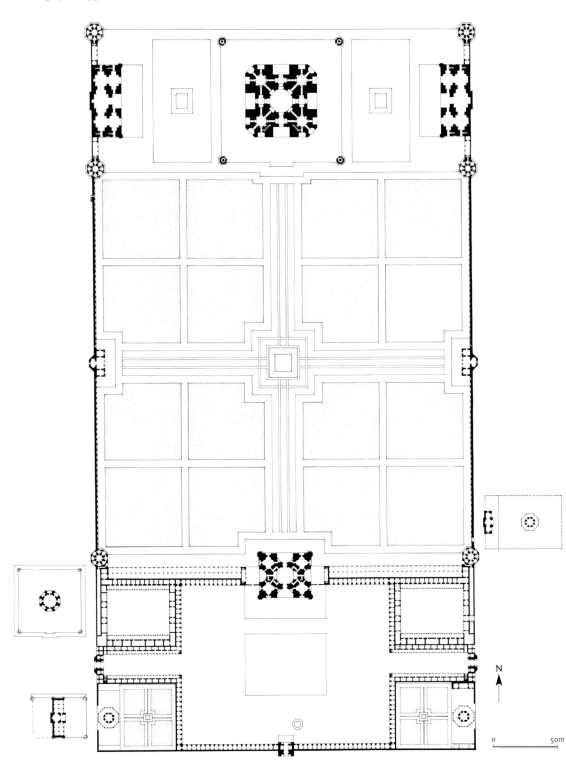

149 *left* Plan of the complex as preserved today (A, B and C on the plan p. 112). At the bottom (south) is the Jilaukhana zone. Its courtyard is reached by bazaar streets left and right, which separate the Khawasspuras (quarters of the tomb attendants) to the north from the subsidiary tombs to the south. From the Jilaukhana the great gate leads to the garden, which is bordered on the line of the gate by the southern galleries. At its centre is a pool, with balancing garden-wall pavilions to east and west. At the top is the riverfront terrace. Here the mausoleum is at the centre, surrounded by the four minarets and flanked by the mosque (left) and Mihman Khana. Outside the walls, to the west are a subsidiary tomb and a mosque, and to the east a tomb with mosque.

opposite
150 *above* The outer face of the west gate to the Jilaukhana, or 'Fatehpuri Darwaza', as it appears in a Company drawing by an Agra artist from the *Notebook* of Florentia, Lady Sale, 1832–33. On either side there are two arched niches with rectangular doors leading to inner rooms. There are significant differences between the gate's appearance here and after restoration [151]: the walls flanking it are stepped down, mediating the transition between gate and wall, whereas now they have a curved form foreign to Mughal architectural aesthetics, and less red sandstone facing is shown. (Inside the wall to the right is the western subsidiary tomb, partly screened by a *jali* of red sandstone [cf. 166].)

151 *below* The outer face of the west gate as restored. (Photograph taken in 1996)

The Jilaukhana (forecourt) zone

The complex of the Taj Mahal is now entered through one of three gates leading into the Jilaukhana, or forecourt [146:C]. The east and west gates [146:14a,14b] are those commonly used by tourists. The south gate [146:15, 307], from Taj Ganj, is more difficult to reach. The arcaded ranges along the south side of the Jilaukhana, and the bazaar streets leading to it, were restored between 1905 and 1922 (p. 116).

The approach road to the west gate is flanked by two somewhat later buildings, the 'Fatehpuri Masjid' [146:21] and an anonymous tomb [146:20], which is probably that of Satti-un-Nisa Khanum, the chief lady-in-waiting of Mumtaz Mahal.

THE EAST GATE ('FATEHABADI DARWAZA') AND WEST GATE ('FATEHPURI DARWAZA')

The east and west gates are identical.[31] Their outer façades [150, 151] have a broad centre with a *pishtaq*, here taking the form of a pointed archway in a rectangular frame, set between engaged polygonal shafts topped by *guldastas* (ornamental pinnacles extending above roof level) which mark the centre off from flanking angled sections of wall. At the top is a parapet carved in relief with a characteristic Mughal pattern of multi-cusped *kanguras* (crenellations). This is a simple design in the wide repertory of Mughal gateways; the inner façades [152, 156, 163] are richer, with a central arch flanked by two tiers of niches. Here we first encounter the triadic composition that determines most façades in the Taj complex, including that of the mausoleum [e.g. 135]. The differentiation between outer and inner façades is an expression of architectural hierarchy: the inner face is more elaborate because it is closer to the mausoleum. The decoration is restrained. The main accent is given by the buff sandstone spandrels that contrast with the overall facing with red sandstone, and the edging of the central arch with a triple rope moulding – a newly introduced quotation from Timurid architecture which appears also on the great gate, the mausoleum, and its flanking buildings.

152 The inner face of the east gate, or 'Fatehabadi Darwaza', and the eastern bazaar street before its rebuilding in 1907 [cf. 163, 366]; on the right is the eastern subsidiary tomb.

THE SOUTH GATE ('SIRHI' OR 'SIDHI' DARWAZA)

The design of the south gate is a vertically elongated version of that of the outer façades of the east and west gates. Both its faces have a simple *pishtaq*, flanked by engaged shafts terminating in *guldastas*. Because of the overall slope of the site [145], it stands 2.4 m (7 ft 10 in.) above the level of the Jilaukhana [155], and is reached up a short flight of stairs. Outside [307], a further short flight leads up to the bazaar and caravanserai complex, the Taj Ganj, which lies at a level 1 m (3 ft 3 in.) higher.

THE BAZAAR STREETS

Two identical bazaar streets lead from the east and west gates to the Jilaukhana [146:12a,12b]. The income from goods sold here paid for part of the upkeep of the mausoleum. (In the 20th century, until 1996, the bazaar streets were used to sell souvenirs and handicrafts.[32]) The streets are lined with rows of small unconnected rectangular cells (*hujra*) without windows, fronted by an arcaded verandah [153, 163]. In the arcades, typical multi-cusped arches are supported by columns of distinctive Shahjahani type (p. 105), which appear here in their most basic form. Above the arcades sloping sandstone slabs supported by voluted brackets project from the wall as a protection from rain or sun: this feature, known as *chhajja*, is the Mughal version of a form that had been popular in Indian architecture for centuries.

153 The north arcades of the western bazaar street, looking towards the Jilaukhana. (Photograph taken in 2000)

THE JILAUKHANA, OR FORECOURT

The two bazaar streets lead into the great ceremonial forecourt, referred to by the historians of Shah Jahan as *Jilaukhana* (literally, 'in front of the house') [146:11].[33] Here visitors to the tomb would get down from their elephants and horses and assemble in style before entering through the great gate. The Jilaukhana was also used for the ceremonial gathering on the first anniversary of the death of Mumtaz Mahal (p. 98). The *chauk-i jilaukhana* ('courtyard in front of the house') or *jilaukhana* for short, was an element that had been introduced on a grand scale into Mughal architecture under Shah Jahan. Court etiquette and proper ceremonial behaviour had become increasingly important, and required an adequate architectural framing. The lack of a forecourt was bemoaned as one of the serious deficiencies of the Agra fort: when the nobles came to court in great numbers they had no place to dismount, leading to congestion and traffic problems.[34] A *jilaukhana* had been incorporated in the complex of the tomb of Jahangir at Lahore a few years earlier.[35]

The Jilaukhana consists of a large courtyard with gates to north and south. In the centre of the north range is the great gate to the garden [146:9, 154, 170, 351], preceded by a platform (called *chabutra* by Lahauri and Kanbo). Opposite is the south gate [146:15, 155]), which led to the bazaar and caravanserai complex. The courtyard is surrounded by 128 *hujra* rooms which open onto it directly through multi-cusped arches supported by pilasters, topped by a continuous *chhajja*. Originally the ground seems to have been paved (excavations carried out under Lord Curzon found evidence of brick paving); the present paving, lawns, trees and hedges were put in during later restorations. There is a Mughal well near the south gate.

The Jilaukhana still served for accommodation at the end of the 18th century – for the men of the British Resident at the Maratha court (p. 232), as noted by 'Major J. H.': 'Beyond this gate [the great gate] there is a spacious court, called the jellaul kaunah, built of red stone, with arched apartments for servants, and those attached to the king [Shah Jahan]; it now serves as a barrack for Major Palmers sepoys.'[36] A plan drawn in 1828 shows the imperfect state of the court by that time [366]. By the beginning of the 20th century the southern ranges and the eastern bazaar street were largely ruined [152]. The eastern street had 'become a receptable for debris and dirt and was overgrown with rank jungle';[37] and when Sir Anthony MacDonnell, Lieutenant-Governor of the North-Western Provinces and Oudh, wrote to Curzon in 1900 suggesting that this area should be included in the Viceroy's grand restoration scheme for the Taj (pp. 251–52), he commented that parts 'were used as a municipal poor house'.[38] Curzon had the ranges of the Jilaukhana and the bazaar streets reconstructed between 1905 and 1908 on the pattern of the original architecture, which survived in places; the missing arcades of the southernmost ranges were restored in 1922.[39]

The Jilaukhana is flanked by two pairs of courtyard enclosures. On the north, adjoining the garden wall, are the two Khawasspuras, the quarters of the tomb attendants. On the south are two tomb complexes, traditionally known as 'Saheli Burj'.

154 *opposite, above* Looking across the Jilaukhana to the great gate [cf. 351]: Company drawing by an Agra artist from the *Notebook of Florentia, Lady Sale*, 1832–33.

155 *opposite, below* Looking back across the Jilaukhana from the roof of the great gate. Beyond the south gate lies Taj Ganj. (Photograph taken in 1997)

THE KHAWASSPURAS (QUARTERS OF THE TOMB ATTENDANTS)

Both Khawasspuras housed the people who looked after the tomb (the *khadims*) and those who performed the funerary services. The latter included the *hafiz*, the Qur'an memorizers, who – we are told by the 17th-century French observers Bernier and Tavernier – sat in the mausoleum and recited day and night the verses of the holy book to redeem the soul of Mumtaz Mahal (p. 229).

The two courtyards with their surrounding rooms and arcades each fit within a rectangle [146:10a,10b, 149]. To the north they are bounded by the wall of the garden, and to the outside by a stretch of the enclosing wall; on their two other sides they abut arcaded ranges of the Jilaukhana to east and west and the bazaar streets to the south (giving the effect on plan of doubled ranges). They were entered in the corners where the Jilaukhana meets the garden wall. The forms of their wings are those used in the palace courtyards of Shah Jahan, in particular *zanana* quarters. They introduce an intimate residential element in a part of the Taj complex which functions as a transitional zone between the formal funerary area and the 'worldly' area. In plan the Khawasspuras mirror each other, on the principle of symmetrical correspondence (*qarina*), and the same principle informs their internal organization: east and west wings are identical, and north and south wings are similar.

On the east and west wings [157], verandahs fronted by three multi-cusped arches supported on full and half Shahjahani columns alternate with square *hujras*, to which they are connected; all have flat ceilings. The pattern of an open verandah flanked by two *hujras* conforms to the triadic principle in Shahjahani architecture. It served as a modular formula for the wings in Shah Jahan's large palace complexes (e.g. the 'Anguri Bagh' in the Agra fort [85], and had appeared earlier in Nur Jahan's pavilions in the Nur Afshan garden/Ram Bagh (though with pillars and brackets, not arches) [36]. In building up residential wings from modular units Shah Jahan's architects revived a concept of early Islamic architecture, the *bait* system, seen in the palaces of the Umayyads and ͨAbbasids and last realized on a grand scale in the courtyards of the palace of Lashkari Bazar in Afghanistan (10th–12th century). The Mughals might have known that now ruined complex, since the region was at times part of their territory: the adoption of the *bait* system would thus be easier to explain than other intriguing revivals in Shah Jahan's art and architecture (p. 89).[40]

The north and south wings are not identical, but they are organized in a similar way: rows of rooms (with coved ceilings) lie behind continuous verandahs, again shaded by deep *chhajjas* (an arrangement similar to that of the bazaar streets). This system too may be used for palaces, as in the west wing of the 'Machchhi Bhawan' in the Agra fort. In the north wings [158] the *hujras* are all of equal size; in the south they are arranged in a triadic *qarina* pattern, with a larger oblong room in the centre flanked by three rooms of decreasing size.

In the outer southern corners of the Khawasspuras are larger rooms which gave access to the latrines, which were inserted in a narrow 'strip', open to the sky, between the backs of the outer wings and the enclosing wall. Their 'furnishing' is not preserved, but from surviving latrines of Shah Jahan's period we know that it consisted of a continuous low platform with alternate rectangular openings, below and in front of which ran channels to receive the waste [159].[41]

opposite

156 The western Khawasspura, seen from the great gate. Note the difference between the wings: on the west (the far side) and east triple arcades alternate with enclosed rooms [157], while on the south (left) and north is a continuous verandah [158].

Outside the Khawasspura to the left is the bazaar street, leading to the west gate, and to the right is one of the wall towers. Beyond the enclosing wall are the 'Fatehpuri Masjid' (partly visible to the left of the gate) and the outer subsidiary tomb of 'Fatehpuri Begam'. (Photograph taken in 1995)

157 *right* The east wing of the western Khawasspura. (Photograph taken in 1995)

158 *below* The north wing of the western Khawasspura. (Photograph taken in 1995)

159 *below right* The latrine in the main complex of Shah Jahan's palace at Bari, known as the Lal Mahal, 1637: this gives an idea of the latrines of the Khawasspuras. (Photograph taken in 1982)

By the late 18th century the Khawasspuras had fallen into disrepair (p. 251), but the institution of the *khadim* survived into the 20th century (p. 101). Between 1900 and 1908 under Curzon the buildings were restored. Until recently the western one was called the 'Nursery' because it was used by the Horticultural Department of the Archaeological Survey of India to grow plants for the garden; another modern name is 'Fatehpuri Gate Courtyard'. The eastern Khawasspura, known since at least the early 20th century as the 'Gaushala', functioned until 2003 as cow stables;[42] it is now known also as 'Fatehabad Gate Courtyard'. Both courtyards are being restored to function as the new Visitor Centre (p. 254).

THE INNER SUBSIDIARY TOMBS ('SAHELI BURJ')

The two enclosures that flank the Jilaukhana on the south are funerary complexes held to be those of lesser wives of Shah Jahan [146:13a,13b, 149]. They are not mentioned in official descriptions: their absence from the 1643 description, which mentions the Khawasspuras, may mean that they had not yet been built; but they may have been ignored because they were the tombs of women. They bear no inscriptions, so it is not certain which women are buried here or in the two tombs outside the main complex [146:13c,20]. All four tombs are known as 'Saheli Burj' ('Tower of the female friend'). On the earliest detailed plan of the Taj Mahal so far known, which was prepared by the English artists Thomas and William Daniell in 1789 [147], the eastern tomb is identified as that of Akbarabadi (Mahal) and the western one as that of Fatehpuri (Mahal).The same designations are given by Fanny Parks in 1835.[43] Shah Jahan's historian ᶜInayat Khan noted in 1650 that Fatehpuri Mahal and Akbarabadi Mahal were then especially favoured by the emperor; he explains that since the names of the wives of the Mughal emperors should not be on the tongue of common people, they were called after the place of their birth or the country or city in which the eye of the emperor had first fallen on them.[44] 'Akbarabadi' referred to Akbarabad (Shah Jahan's name for Agra), and 'Fatehpuri' referred to Fatehpur Sikri, Akbar's short-lived residence west of Agra. Florentia Sale was told in 1832–33 by her local informants that the eastern tomb was that of 'Aberabadee Begum'; but the western one she gives to 'Sistee [Satti-un-Nisa] Khannim Begum', the lady-in-waiting of Mumtaz (p. 20) who was buried 'west of the Jilaukhana'.[45] To add to the confusion, the large plan in the Taj Museum identifies the western tomb as that of Akbarabadi Mahal, and the eastern one as that of 'Sirhindi Mahal'.

Akbarabadi Mahal is the best known of the imperial women supposedly buried here. She rose in favour as Shah Jahan's 'beloved consort' in the last years of his reign. He gave her a garden at Delhi which she rebuilt between 1646 and 1650 as a copy of its namesake, the famous Shalimar gardens of Kashmir. Akbarabadi Mahal assembled so much wealth that on the emperor's sixty-fourth birthday she was able to present him with a diamond ring worth 30,000 rupees[46] – almost two-thirds of the cost of the *pietra dura* screen around the cenotaphs in the mausoleum. On his deathbed Shah Jahan recommended her especially to his daughter Jahanara (p. 101). Akbarabadi Mahal died in 1677.

The tomb enclosures are placed in perfect mirror symmetry within rectangles bordered by the southern sides of the bazaar streets, the south-east and south-west ranges of the Jilaukhana, the

extension of the southern wall of the Jilaukhana, and the outer enclosing wall. They stand on a raised level, and each is reached by steps leading up from the bazaar street at the inner corners. The complexes form miniature replicas of the mausoleum and garden: each tomb, originally flanked by two buildings and thus forming a tripartite group, stands on a raised rectangular terrace overlooking a small *chahar bagh* [163]. In the centre of the garden is a square pool (*hauz*) at the intersection of paved walkways (*khiyaban*). In the walkways are sunk channels which were fed from the central pool over waterfalls with a fish-scale (*mahi pusht*) pattern. (Such water features were a popular element in Mughal gardens [e.g. 35], but they do not appear in the main garden of the Taj Mahal.) The gardens are also surrounded by a paved walkway. Both tomb complexes were restored under Curzon in the first decade of the 20th century; during the restoration the architectural elements of the *chahar baghs* were excavated, and where necessary rebuilt. Three of the four *chhatris* on the inner corners of the enclosures were renewed at the same time.[47]

The tombs have the form of a single-storey octagon surrounded by a pillared verandah [160]. Each face of the octagon has a door filled with a *jali* composed of small hexagons – a pattern that recurs

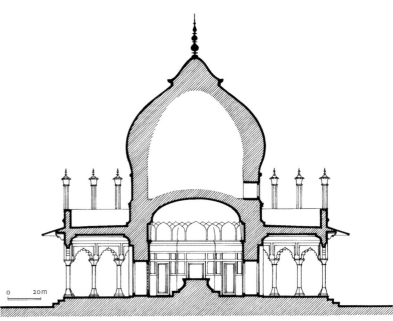

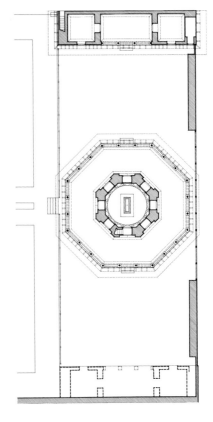

The eastern subsidiary tomb or 'Saheli Burj'

160 *left* View of the tomb and its northern flanking building. (Photograph taken in 1995)

161 *above* Section of the tomb.

162 *right* Ground plan of the tomb and its flanking buildings, of which the northern one survives.

for the filling of doors or arches in the entire complex. Each face of the verandah is formed of three multi-cusped arches on Shahjahani columns. The red sandstone structure is topped by a dome clad in white marble, which sets a hierarchical accent. The dome is surrounded by *guldastas* above the columns. The verandah has a flat ceiling edged with a cavetto moulding. A door on the south side (from which a narrow staircase leads up to the roof) gives access to the inner chamber [164]. This is an octagonal room, covered by a dome on eight shallow squinches and eight arches. The colour dualism of the outside is here reversed, probably for the sake of variety: the wall facing and the *jalis* are of white marble, whereas the inside of the dome is faced with red sandstone. The dome is built up of curved slabs in Mughal bond (p. 96), and has no decoration: such smooth vaults were favoured in later Shahjahani architecture, and form a stark contrast to the intricately patterned vaults of the great gate and the mausoleum.

The two complexes differ only in the decoration of the cenotaphs. The marble cenotaph of the eastern tomb had floral decoration in *pietra dura*, but most of the stones have been picked out and only the empty cavities remain. The flowering plant at the foot

and solar motif at the head are smaller, simplified versions of the corresponding designs on Shah Jahan's cenotaph [243]; this bespeaks special closeness to the emperor, and seems to confirm the burial as that of Akbarabadi Mahal (the cenotaph would have been added when she died in 1677, after the tomb was built).

overleaf
163 Looking towards the eastern subsidiary tomb or 'Saheli Burj' from the roof of the great gate. Between the domed tomb and the bazaar street is the tomb's surviving flanking building. To the left of the street, which leads to the east gate, is the eastern Khawasspura. In the foreground is part of the Jilaukhana, surrounded by arcades. (Photograph taken in 1995)

The cenotaph in the western tomb [164] does not have *pietra dura* inlay, which in Shah Jahan's time was reserved for members of the imperial family: instead, it has a pattern of cartouches, panels and mouldings carved in relief. The tablet on its top was the sign in India of the tomb of a female Muslim.

Each subsidiary tomb was originally flanked on the terrace by two rectangular buildings, but only one of these, to the north of the eastern tomb, survives fully [165]. The building south of the western tomb was deliberately removed under Curzon in 1906 because it was

164 *above left* Interior of the western subsidiary tomb, with its centrally placed cenotaph. (Photograph taken in 1995)

165 *above* The northern flanking building of the eastern subsidiary tomb [cf. 160, 162]. Its outer wall is decorated with a *chini khana* motif in relief and painted. (Photograph taken in 1995)

166 *below* Part of the geometric *jali*, topped by floral crenellations, in the enclosing wall of the terrace of the western subsidiary tomb [cf. 150, 151]. Visible outside is the top of the 'Fatehpuri Masjid'. (Photograph taken in 1995)

ruined, but he had it recorded in drawings.[48] These side buildings are composed of a verandah flanked by two *hujras*: the popular tripartite *bait* module used for residential wings, seen in the Khawasspuras [156, 157], here forms an independent structure. The walls are covered with shallow *chini khana* motifs of white vessel shapes countersunk in fields painted red, blue, and green, setting a colour accent in the otherwise strict red and white scheme of the architecture.

The part of the enclosing wall that forms the back of the terraces with the subsidiary tombs is expressed by fine *jalis* composed of hexagons and six-pointed stars filled with minuscule hexagons [166]. These are topped by *kanguras*, which alternate with baluster elements and are linked to them by interlocking volutes, all carved in relief; flowers inside the *kanguras* heighten the organic character of the ornament. The geometrical designs belong to an older stream in Islamic architecture, whereas these organic three-dimensional topping elements show a new type of ornament developed for Shah Jahan. Their form seems to be inspired by the crenellations of the screen around the cenotaphs of Shah Jahan and Mumtaz Mahal inside the mausoleum, which is dated 1643 [232].

The style of the inner 'Saheli Burj' tombs points to the last construction phase of the Taj Mahal complex, in the 1640s.

Descendants of the Dome of the Rock

The type of the domed octagonal tomb surrounded by an arcaded ambulatory has a long ancestry in Islamic architecture. Ultimately it goes back to the Dome of the Rock in Jerusalem, built in 691–692 [167]. Scholars of Islamic architecture have paid little attention to the fact that the first monumental building of Islam was copied throughout the centuries in various regions of the Muslim world.[49] The earliest known copy is the Qubbat-as-Sulaibiya at Samarra near Baghdad (probably 862); two outstanding later examples are the tomb of Qala'un in Cairo (1284–92) and the tomb of the Mongol Il-Khanid Öljaitu (d. 1316) at Sultaniya in north-western Iran.[50] But it is in India, in Sultanate and Mughal architecture, that the Dome of the Rock engendered its most remarkable offspring.[51] The series begins at Delhi in the period of the Tughluq sultans, with the tombs of

167 *top* The Dome of the Rock in Jerusalem, 691–692. (Photograph taken in 1998)

168 *above* The tomb of Sikander Lodi in Delhi, 1517. (Photograph taken in 1984)

Zafar Khan (1323–35), the son of Sultan Ghiyas-ud-Din Tughluq, and of Firuz Shah Tughluq's *wazir* Khan Jahan Maqbul Tilangani (d. 1368/69).[52] The building type continued with the tombs of the Sayyid rulers (Muhammad Shah Sayyid, d. 1445/46), was maintained in the Lodi period (tomb of Sikander Lodi, 1517 [168]), and was brought to its apogee in the Sur period (tomb of Sher Shah at Sasaram, 1545 [105]).[53] It was adopted with some stylistic changes by the early Mughals, in the tomb of Adham Khan at Delhi (1562), after which it ceased to be used for funerary architecture. It then emerged in a lighter trabeate idiom as a pavilion in residential architecture, and also, combined with a *chhatri*, as a topping element of the garden towers of Agra and the Taj [e.g. 32, 299]. Finally the type in its new lighter shape, with an ambulatory of Shahjahani columns and multi-cusped arches, was restored to sepulchral architecture in three of the subsidiary tombs of the Taj Mahal [160, 325].[54] They form the endpoint of the series.

The great gate
(*darwaza-i rauza*)

The Jilaukhana complex is dominated by the great entrance gate set in the centre of the southern wall of the funerary garden [146:9, 154, 170]. Lahauri calls it *darwaza-i rauza*, 'gate of the mausoleum'.[55] It is in a long tradition of grand Mughal gateways – its most recent predecessor was the gate of Akbar's tomb at Sikandra (1612–13) [169][56] – and a worthy counterpart to the mausoleum, built on a variation of its plan. The monumental structure sets a formal accent and mediates the transition between the area of the Jilaukhana and the funerary garden. It prepares the visitor for the grandeur of the mausoleum that awaits within. The great gate is preceded on the south and north by platforms paved with geometrical patterns [337:a].

The south front of the great gate faces the Jilaukhana as a splendid introduction to the imperial architecture of the domain of the mausoleum [170, 351]. It is a monumental version of a Mughal elevational formula that also appears in the mausoleum, that of a large *pishtaq* flanked by two tiers of niches. The triadic design had been announced within the Jilaukhana area in a more modest form on the inner faces of the east and west gates [152]. The design has its roots in the Sultanate architecture of Delhi, beginning with the ᶜAla'i Darwaza (1311) of the Quwwat-ul-Islam Mosque [334]. It brings to mind Roman triumphal arches, but no obvious connection can be established. The Mughal version is remarkable for the harmonious proportional relationship of the parts and the elegant architectural ornament. The corners of the building are accentuated by engaged towers – Lahauri calls them minarets – that project as five sides of an octagon: they give it a look of fortification, which differentiates it from the mausoleum.

169 *below* The gate of Akbar's tomb at Sikandra, of 1612–13, prefigures the composition of the great gate of the Taj Mahal. (Photograph taken in 1983)

170 *right* The great gate, seen from the south-west. From this angle its oblong plan, with longer façades to north and south centred on tall *pishtaqs*, and shorter façades to east and west, is clear. (Photograph taken in 2001)

171 One of the leaves of the south door of the great gate, leading in from the Jilaukhana. (Photograph taken in 1986)

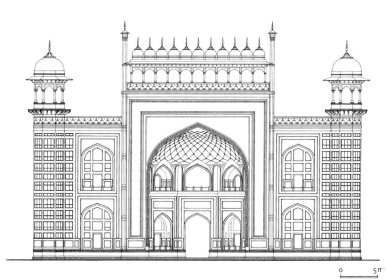

172 The great gate: elevation.

The entire façade is clad in red sandstone and white marble. The studied handling of the two colours underscores the hierarchical importance of the elements (pp. 216–17). White marble frames the dominant portal arch in the centre and then decreases towards the corner towers, where it is reduced to thin margins around rectangular panels. In the intermediate zones, it outlines groups of multi-cusped blind arches and cartouches in a reductive form of the *chini khana* motif, with 'niches' but no vessels. This type of wall ornament is found throughout the complex. The central arch is further highlighted by a triple rope moulding, a quotation from Timurid architecture which also appears in the Jilaukhana gates, the mausoleum and its flanking buildings. Further accents are provided by flowery scrolls of stone intarsia (of a simpler type than the *pietra dura* inside the mausoleum) which fill the marble spandrels of the arch, and by the inlaid inscription band in large formal *sulus* script (p. 224) surrounding its rectangular frame [351]. This displays *sura* 89 of the Qur'an, *al-Fajr*, 'Daybreak', which invites believers to enter Paradise and serves as a motto for the funerary garden behind (for the text, see pp. 225–28). This type of precious decoration – inlaid ornament and inlaid script – reappears only in the mausoleum and, in a reduced form, in its flanking buildings.

The north front of the great gate, facing the garden [189], is almost identical to the south front. One of the differences is in the inscriptions framing the *pishtaq*, which contain different passages from the Qur'an, though all deal with the end of time, in keeping with the eschatological programme of the mausoleum (p. 225). At the bottom left end of the frame is the signature of the calligrapher Amanat Khan and the Hijri date 1057, which corresponds to AD 1647/48 [131] – the latest date to be found in the entire complex (p. 100). Steps negotiate the drop into the garden, which lies about 2 m (6 ft) lower than the gate and the Jilaukhana [145].

The great gate does not have an outer dome, which in Mughal architecture is reserved for mosques and tombs. Instead, the roof

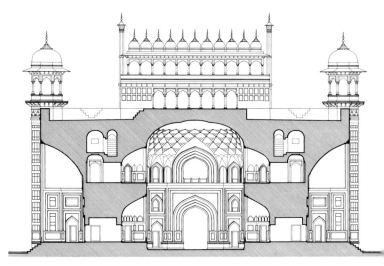

173 The great gate: section from west (left) to east.

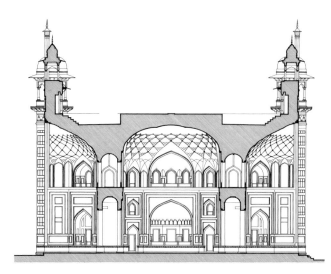

174 The great gate: section from north (left) to south.

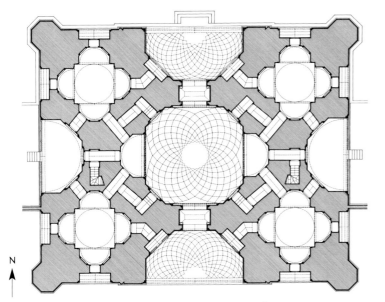

175 The great gate: plan of the ground floor, showing vaults.

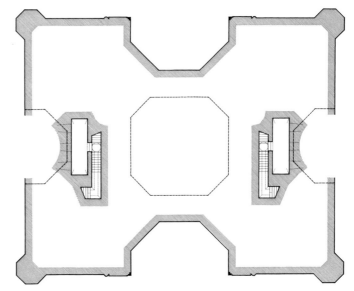

178 The great gate: plan of the staircase level below the roof.

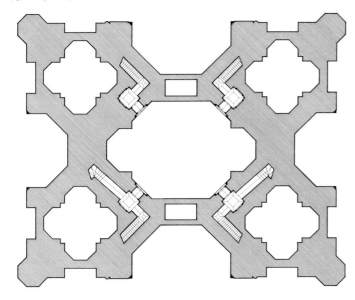

176 The great gate: plan of the mezzanine level.

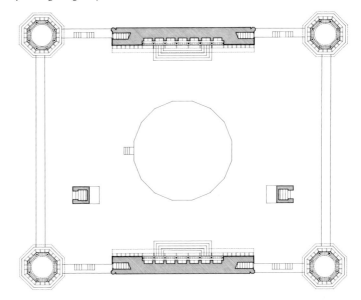

179 The great gate: plan of the roof level.

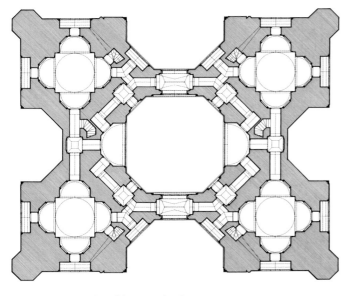

177 The great gate: plan of the upper level.

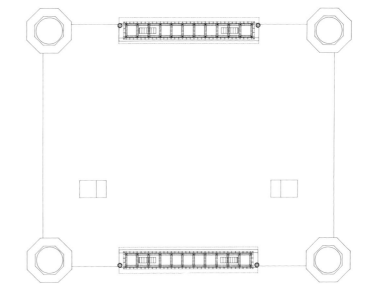

180 The great gate: plan of the topmost level.

zone is accentuated with small white marble cupolas: the north and south *pishtaqs* are each topped by a row of eleven cupolas (called by Lahauri and Kanbo *chaukhandi*[57]), set between the freestanding *guldastas* of the engaged colonnettes that frame the central part of the façades, and the corner towers are topped by marble-domed *chhatris*.

The great gate is built on an oblong version of the ninefold *hasht bihisht* plan [22–23, 175]. Thus, although its four elevations are similar in principle, the building has an orientation: the main façades are the longer ones to the south and north [170, 189]. Perfect centrality and perfect symmetry were reserved for the chief building, the mausoleum.

Entrance is through the monumental vaulted niche of the *pishtaq*, which is raised over a half-octagonal plan. In its back wall is an impressive wooden door sheathed in bronze plates with a pattern of cartouches in relief [171]. Once inside the gate, the visitor has his or her first sight of the white marble mausoleum, at the end of the

central canal of the garden [135]. The striking image diverts attention from the splendour of the central domed hall in which the viewer stands [181, 182]. It is an irregular octagon in plan, following – as Lahauri points out – a favourite Mughal figure called *musamman baghdadi* or 'Baghdadi octagon':[58] its form, a square with chamfered corners, announces the plan of the mausoleum [175, 220]. On the east and west sides the hall is extended by half-octagonal niches, which Lahauri terms *nashiman*, 'seat'. The central hall and the two half-octagons of the portals form the main axis of the building. Because the ninefold plan here has an oblong shape, these three voids move close together and form a grand passageway to which the flanking rooms are subordinated. That, in turn, brings about a strong triadic accentuation, in keeping with the overall principles of the design.

Another of these principles, uniformity of shape, determines the elevation of the central hall [173, 174, 181]: its organization and

The great gate

181 *below* The central hall, looking west. (Photograph taken in 1997)

182 *right* Vault of the central hall. The bronze lamp, commissioned by Curzon from the Mayo School of Art at Lahore, was installed in 1909. (Photograph taken in 1997)

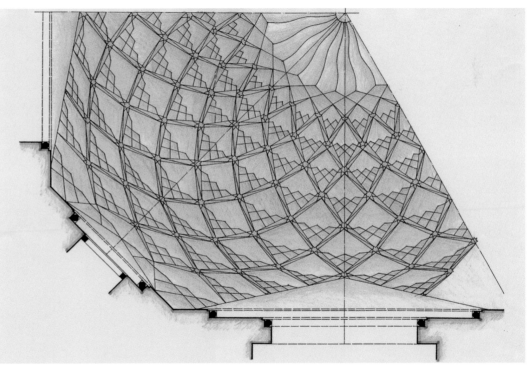

183 *above* The central vault of the great gate is developed from points, either five-pointed stars or partial stars, arranged in concentric circles. The stars form the knots of the geometrical network of the vault which creates kite-shaped compartments. The lower part of each compartment shows three intersecting arches linked to the points of the stars. Closer to the apex the kite shapes become compressed and contain only two intersecting arches. The apex of the vault appears in a whirl pattern, resting on the tops of intersecting arches which form the transition from the main network below.

decoration repeat the forms of the external façades. A plinth with cartouches carved in relief supports the dado, composed of panels framed by chevron inlay in white marble. Above, on each of the four longer sides of the octagon, are two superimposed large arches; the shorter sides have superimposed niche motifs. All the spandrels are faced with white marble inlaid with flowery scrolls.

The central vault inside and the half-vaults of the *pishtaqs* are further accentuated and connected through their elaborate decoration [170, 175, 182]. The vault of the hall is faced with red and white painted plaster in a system of stars or partial stars arranged in concentric circles, linked by a network forming concave kite-shaped compartments [183]; in the centre is a star-shaped medallion in a whirl pattern. This type of vault decoration, which evolved out of earlier more plastic forms of Jahangir's period, is typical of Shah Jahan's buildings: it was called *qalib kari*, 'mould work',[59] because the shapes were pressed into the wet plaster with moulds.

The great gate

184 *left, above* Ventilation shaft of a chamber under the roof. (Photograph taken in 1997)

185 *left, below* A stairway. (Photograph taken in 1997)

186 *above* Roof level, looking north towards the mausoleum. In the foreground is the top of one of the two staircases that lead up from the floors below. The slightly raised area at the left lies above the central dome [cf. 173, 179]. Beyond it is the top of the north *pishtaq*, taking the form of a gallery. (Photograph taken in 1997)

The large bronze lamp that hangs from the apex of the dome [182] was presented by Curzon, who had it made in the Mayo School of Art (now the National College of the Arts) at Lahore. After being exhibited in England it arrived at Agra in 1909.[60]

In the corners there are square rooms extended by half-octagonal *nashiman* niches into a cruciform shape, vaulted with simple domes and half-domes [175]. All rooms are linked by an intricate system of angular corridors which makes the plan quite complex – a far cry from the balanced interconnection of rooms in the mausoleum [220]. Today the side rooms are used as offices of the Archaeological Survey of India for the administration of the monument and they are not accessible to visitors. The same is true of the upper levels of the great gate.

Above the ground floor there are the upper storey and roof terrace usual in Mughal gate buildings, mausoleums and pavilions on a *hasht bihisht* plan; but there are also two small intermediate levels [173, 176, 178]. This was perhaps done to lighten the construction; the effect is to make the gate more complex in section than the mausoleum [cf. 221]. From each of the two short corridors that link the central chamber with the *pishtaq* halls at the sides, a flight of stairs leads to a mezzanine; from there further flights lead to the main upper storey, and on via a further intermediate floor to the roof. The stairs are very steep, to accommodate them in the walls [185]. Stairways were not a theme of Mughal architecture, and whenever possible were made invisible. The scheme necessitated ventilation shafts [184].

On the southern side of the great gate both stairways lead to corridors on the mezzanine level [176] which widen into square rooms with coved ceilings, and give access to further stairs to the main upper storey. There are the same square rooms on the northern side, but these can only be reached from above. The four rooms open into the central hall through arched openings in the upper niches flanking the four large arches [181].

The main upper storey [177] consists of cruciform chambers in the corners, corresponding to the ones on the ground floor, and a system of small rooms and niches, linked by narrow angling corridors, which surround the main dome and open into it like balconies [182]. The two oblong rooms north and south open to the outside as well, into the vaults of the pishtaqs [170], and thus form 'bridges' on the upper level. They are covered with bangla roofs, at the time a prestigious form reserved for imperial architecture [cf. 88] This level is reached from below by stairs that lead to the inner apsidal niches of the four cruciform corner rooms. The stairs leading on up start from a corridor behind the east and west pishtaqs; on their way to the roof, they open into narrow rectangular chambers which form another intermediate floor [173, 178].

The roof level is conceived as a viewing terrace, providing impressive vistas of the mausoleum, the entire complex, and the landscape beyond [e.g. 135, 163, 186]. Exploring the potential of the top of a building for visual and recreational purposes was a special concern of Mughal architects. All the elements that extend up to or above roof level are integrated into this open terrace and interpreted as seats or pavilions. A surrounding parapet protects the space and binds the elements together. Where the stairs end there are stepped structures which, besides protecting the stair landings, may have served as seats. The large inner dome is masked by a sixteen-sided platform on which floor coverings and tents could be placed. The four chhatris topping the corner towers feature as gazebos. The parts of the pishtaqs that rise above roof level are the most elaborate elements of the scheme. Their inner faces have a central arcade of seven multi-cusped arches on Shahjahani columns, behind which there are seven niches, which seem to have functioned as places to sit. Between that level and the row of eleven small domes is an open gallery made up of the same elements, which is accessible from both sides by steep stairs set into the narrow sides of the pishtaqs [180]. From this vantage point the viewer can survey the entire garden and the mausoleum from above, without being seen easily from below.

THE SOUTHERN GALLERIES ('IWAN DAR IWAN')

The north front of the great gate is flanked by two arcaded galleries which form the southern end of the garden [149, 187–189]; they are recessed between the towers that mark the corners of the garden wall (echoing those of the riverfront terrace) [156, 327],[61] and preceded by platforms with paving in a geometrical pattern [337a]. Bernier is the only source to tell us their function: 'Into this gallery the poor are admitted three times a week during the rainy season to receive the alms founded in perpetuity by Shah-Jahan.'[62] It appears that the charities endowed by Shah Jahan for the redemption of the soul of Mumtaz Mahal were not confined to the annual 'urs celebration (pp. 97–99) but also took place seasonally in this part of the monument. In keeping with the religious importance of the act, the architecture of these galleries has an imperial character.

The two wings have double arcades, called iwan dar iwan ('pillared hall with pillared hall') by Lahauri.[63] The arches are multi-cusped. The columns are of Shahjahani type, but they are larger and more massive than the ones in the Jilaukhana area and on the roof of the great gate. Those of the front row are distinguished by more elaborately decorated bases, with multi-cusped arched panels containing naturalistic flowering plants in relief. They give a foretaste, at the farthest end of the garden, of the naturalistic plant decoration which finds its culmination in the mausoleum, and which to a lesser degree appears in the mosque and Mihman Khana. Each wing terminates at both ends in transversally placed rooms. At the inner ends, these take the form of tripartite bait units of a verandah flanked by two narrow hujras, and face onto small courtyards between them and the gate [149].

187, 188 Galleries with double arcades flank the great gate at the southern end of the garden (the side of the gate is visible below on the left) [cf. 189]. Here in the rainy season the poor were given alms endowed by Shah Jahan. The importance of this imperial gesture is reflected in the galleries' stately architecture: they have cusped arches, and faceted Shahjahani columns with carved floral bases in the outer row. (Photographs taken in 1995)

The garden
(bagh-i firdaus-a'in)

The garden is the heart of the Taj Mahal complex [146:B]: it 'is to the buildings what the soul is to the body, and the lamp to an assembly' (as the main inscription on Shah Jahan's palace at Delhi put it several years later).[64] Its symbolic function is announced in the name which the historians Lahauri and Kanbo give it – *bagh-i firdaus-a'in*, 'Paradise-like garden', the perfect setting of Mumtaz's paradisiacal house.[65] It was intended as a replica (*namudar*) of the Qur'anic 'gardens beneath which rivers flow'.[66]

The connection between architecture and nature which generally characterizes the Mughal garden is epitomized at the Taj Mahal in an ideal form. The architectural nature of the design means that the 17th-century plan is well preserved. The planting, however, is uncertain, since it does not feature in contemporary descriptions.

ORGANIZATION

Strict planning determines the organization of the garden component of the riverfront scheme, the cross-axial *chahar bagh* [142, 149]. The large square is divided by two main walkways (*khiyaban*) into four quadrants; each quadrant is in turn subdivided by narrower cross-axial walkways, so that sixteen sub-quadrants are formed; and the garden as a whole is surrounded by a walkway which connects with all the sub-walkways. The main walkways [189] consist of several elements. In their centre runs a shallow canal (*nahr*) containing a line of fountains (*farwara*). This is framed by strips of sandstone paving and by ornamental borders with a geometrical pattern of alternating regular and oblong stars. These in turn are framed by wider strips of sandstone paving 'arranged entirely in a geometrical design (*girih bandi*)', as Lahauri tells us. Such geometrical patterning had been characteristic of early Mughal architectural decoration; in the Taj Mahal, when floral designs became the nobler form of ornament, it was demoted and used for floors and for *jalis* [e.g. 337].

At the crossing of the walkways in the centre of the garden is a raised platform (*chabutra*) of white marble with an ornamental pool (*hauz*) containing five fountains [190]. Kanbo claimed eulogistically that it held the water of the celestial Kausar, the Prophet's river in Paradise, which fills the pool at which believers quench their thirst on arrival. He also lauds the 'novel design' of the pool with its lobed and voluted corners. The pattern reflects the increasing preference in Shahjahani architecture for curved and organic forms. The four marble benches around the tank were put up in 1907–8 on the order of Curzon.[67]

189 *opposite* The garden, seen from the south-eastern minaret. The central walkway starts on the south at the platform of the great gate. Where it crosses the east–west walkways there is an ornamental pool set into a white marble platform [190].

Flanking the gate are the southern galleries [187, 188]; beyond it lies the Jilaukhana. The domes visible top right are those of an inner subsidiary tomb, of the 'Fatehpuri Masjid', of a garden tower, and of the outer western tomb. (Photograph taken in 2001)

190 *right* The corners of the central pool are inset with a pattern of organic lobes, waves and volutes. (Photograph taken in 2000)

The four main walkways are identical [337:b], but they are differentiated through their context. The north–south walkway connects the principal buildings – the great gate and the mausoleum – and represents the dominant axis of the complex to which the cross-axial plan of the *chahar bagh* is subordinated. The perceptive Bernier noticed its role in the *qarina* symmetry, writing that 'it divides nearly the whole of the garden into two equal parts'.[68] This walkway also provides the perfect viewpoint: only along its axis do the mausoleum and its flanking buildings present a balanced composition [e.g. 135].

The east–west walkway has a subsidiary function. It links the two pavilions which project from the centre of the garden wall on each side in mirror symmetry, and widens out in front of them to integrate two platforms paved with a different geometrical pattern.

The enclosing wall is lined by a peripheral walkway and articulated by large pointed arches which support a narrow elevated walk running in front of ornamental crenellations [191]. These elements of fortification architecture give the garden wall substance and a character of display.

At the place where the subsidiary walkway of the south-western quadrant meets the garden wall, a drinking fountain of a design 'in accord with its surrounding' was put up in 1909–10 by the British government 'for the use of soldiers and other visitors to the mausoleum'.[69] It is not in use today.

In the north-western quadrant, near the north-west corner, is an enclosure supposed to mark the site where Mumtaz Mahal was first buried [146:6], before her body was moved to its final resting place inside the white platform of the mausoleum.

The garden was supplied with water from the Yamuna through an aqueduct [146:E, 322, 323, 366]: this brought water up to the middle of the west wall, whence it was distributed through earthenware pipes (p. 208). The fountain system of the central tank consisted of copper vessels connected through copper pipes with the main supply pipe.[70] According to Colonel Rowlatt, who undertook their first repair in 1867, the earthenware pipes were embedded in solid masonry 6 ft (1.8 m) underground (p. 251).

191 The wall enclosing the garden – seen here from inside, along the eastern edge – has a raised walkway bordered by ornamental crenellations. The trees visible here include banyan or *Ficus benghalensis* and *maulsari* or *Mimusops elengi*. (Photograph taken in 1995)

PLANTING

The original planting is the least known aspect of the garden. The present lawns, flowers and trees, maintained by the Horticultural Branch of the Archaeological Survey of India, go back to reconstructive efforts of the British which were intensified under Curzon. He reported to the Legislative Council at Calcutta in 1904 that 'Every building in the garden enclosure of the Taj has been scrupulously repaired, and the discovery of old plans has enabled us to restore the water-channels and flower-beds of the garden more exactly to their original state.'[71] An ongoing concern since then has been to keep the cypresses lining the walkways small, and to confine trees to certain areas, so as not to obstruct the view of the mausoleum.

In our present state of knowledge, we can only guess at the Mughal planting to a certain extent. Lahauri and Kanbo describe all the architectural features of the garden, but mention only 'various kinds of fruit-bearing trees (*ashjar mewadar*) and rare aromatic herbs (*riyahin badi' a'in*)'. Shah Jahan's poet Qudsi eulogizes its sweet-smelling roses of abundant bloom.[72] European observers in the 17th century say not much more. Bernier speaks only of 'garden walks covered with trees and many parterres full of flowers'.[73] The possible organization of planting is suggested by contemporary miniatures: in a manuscript dated 1663 a garden in Kashmir is shown with *chahar bagh* plots structured by ornamental dividers, into which are set cypresses, plane trees, poplars and almond trees; in between grow flowers such as irises and tulips [192]. The cypresses of the Taj garden were arranged more formally, lining the walkways in straight rows.

In the early 20th century it was believed that some of the oldest trees in the garden dated from the Mughal period. Muhammad Moin-ud-Din, who wrote a pioneering *History of the Taj* in 1905, claimed that a cotton tree (*senbal, simbal: Bombax heptaphyllum*) 48 ¾ ft (*c.* 15 m) in circumference near the eastern wall was then 425 years old.[74] A number of old trees have been numbered and labelled with their Latin and Hindi names by the Archaeological Survey of India. Most common is the Indian medlar tree, also called bulletwood (*maulsari, maulshree: Mimusops elengi*),[75] which Kalim mentions as

growing in Jahanara's garden, in the course of a description that gives us an idea of what grew in an imperial Agra garden in Shah Jahan's time (p. 41). Another important source is the English observer Peter Mundy, who described a typical grand Agra garden that he saw in 1633: the walkways were lined with cypress trees, and the squares of the subdivisions were planted with

> litle groves of trees, as Apple trees (those scarse), Orenge Trees, Mulberrie trees, etts. Mango trees, Caco [cocoanut] trees, Figg trees, Plantan trees, theis latter in rancks, as are the Cipresse trees. In other squares are your [i.e. English] flowers, herbes, etts., whereof Roses, Marigolds . . . to bee seene; French Mariegolds aboundance; Poppeas redd, carnation and white; and divers other sortes of faire flowers which wee knowe not in our parts, many groweinge on prettie trees, all watered by hand in tyme of drought, which is 9 monethes in the Yeare.[76]

The roses, marigolds and poppies mentioned by Mundy were Mughal favourites and are often depicted in paintings; they are also among the flowers which, according to Kalim, grew in Jahanara's garden. We can assume that they were among the original flowers in the Taj garden – though it is also possible that different plants were grown in a funerary garden. From the account of a visit of Iranian envoys in 1621 we learn that *lala* (poppy: see p. 140) grew in the garden of Akbar's tomb at Sikandra.[77] The naturalistically rendered flowers in *pietra dura* work which decorate the cenotaphs of Mumtaz

192 Beds of *chahar bagh* form in a Mughal garden in Kashmir: detail of a painting in the *Masnawi* of Zafar Khan, Mughal, 1663. The tall trees are planes, the evergreens cypresses; fruit or almond trees are just coming into flower.

Mahal and Shah Jahan and the surrounding screen, and the flowers in marble and sandstone relief which appear on the dados of the mausoleum and its flanking buildings, indicate which plants the Mughals considered ideal in a funerary context – or, more specifically, which plants were specially selected in view of the taste of Mumtaz Mahal. Spring flowers inspired by lilies, irises, tulips and poppies, of which irises and tulips grow not in Agra but in the Himalaya region,[78] feature prominently (pp. 158, 218, 221).

Cypress trees are the most certain feature of the garden; they were a characteristic lining of Mughal garden walkways. Mundy depicts them in his sketch of the garden of Akbar's tomb,[79] and they are also seen in the earliest drawings and photographs of the Taj garden, from the end of the 18th to the mid-19th century [354, 360, 367].

The poet Nazir Akbaradi, who lived at Agra from the mid-18th century, describes what he saw in the garden in an Urdu poem on the Taj Mahal:

> The straight cypresses (*sarw-i sahi*) and bushes of white musk roses (*nastaran*)[80] stand symmetrically.
> The turtledoves pour sugar by their cooing.
> All of the garden's flowerbeds are full of *raibel* (*Jasminum zambac*), *sewati* roses, carnations (*gulnar*),[81] poppies (*lala*), flowers (*gul*), and *nasrin* and *nastaran* roses.[82]

Nastaran roses had been planted by Babur in the Bagh-i Hasht Bihisht (p. 54), thus it is quite likely that they also grew from the beginning in the Taj garden.

Fruit trees were observed in the garden by travellers at the end of the 18th century and in the 19th century; Thomas Twining, for instance, saw 'thousands of orange trees' there in 1794 (p. 233), and another visitor noted an 'abundance of grapes'.[83] The large plan in the Taj Museum (p. 103; one of several discovered and used under Curzon) identifies in Persian script in the subdivisions of the garden (labelled *takhta*, 'bed') fruits including pineapple (*annas*) or pomegranate (*anar*), banana (*kila*), orange (*sang-tara*) [193], pomelo (*chakotra*), lime or lemon (*limu*), guava (*amrud*) and apple (*seb*).[84] The *Handbook of the Taj at Agra* (1854 and 1862) notes Bombay mangoes, guavas, oranges, limes, loquats, palms, banyan and feathery bamboo, and points out that the fruit trees were let out by the British Government to 'native gardeners who derive a thriving trade during the season'.[85] In this the British were continuing an earlier practice.[86] In 1815 mango trees obstructed Lord Hastings' view of the mausoleum (p. 238). Early 19th-century paintings and the earliest photographs of the Taj garden show it overgrown with various kinds of trees [367].

Favourite Mughal plants

The cypress (Pers. *sarw*) appears in Persian poetry as a popular simile for the slender elegant stature of the beloved; it is often related to a watercourse, like the canals which divide the *chahar bagh*.[87]

The rose (Pers. *gul*) [194] was the preferred flower of Persianate culture, to the extent that *gul* also meant 'flower' as such. Sufi mystics regarded it as a manifestation of divine glory, and as a symbol of the initiated soul of the mystic; for the poets, it represented the face of the beloved, and the classic pairing of rose and nightingale was a metaphor for worldly as well as mystical love.[88]

193 Detail of a large plan of the complex in the Taj Museum, by an Indian artist, early 19th century, inscribed in Persian with the names of the buildings and plants. Here we see the subsection of the garden north-east of the central pool. The artist depicts flowers, and records the elaborate paving of the walkway areas [cf. 189]. The inscription in the centre says 'sang-tara', meaning that oranges were grown in this plot.

194 *below left* A large pink rose between a yellow daisy and a small iris, from the *Dara Shikoh Album*, Mughal, 1641/42.

195 *below right* A poppy, inscribed 'gul-i lala' ('poppy flower'), from the *Small Clive Album*, Mughal, late 17th or early 18th century.

Lala is a loose term: in classical Persian and Turkish poetry it is basically any wild flower with red petals and a black area at the centre of the blossom, so it could refer to poppy, anemone, or tulip. Its use to mean tulip is not consistent until the 18th century. In India *lala* was widely used to mean poppy.[89] Two depictions of poppies in the *Small Clive Album* (late 17th–18th century) are inscribed *gul-i lala*, 'poppy flower' [195], and *lala-i rasmi* (regular poppy); a red tulip is described there as *lala-i jughashu*, the name under which Jahangir knew the red tulips growing on the roofs of the buildings of Kashmir.[90] In Persian and Turkish poetry the red flower with a black mark in the centre symbolizes the suffering heart and death. It is associated with Majnun, and his burning desire for union with his beloved Laila [16], which in a figurative sense stands for the mystical quest of the soul for God.[91] Poppies would thus be highly appropriate as flowers in a tomb garden for a lost beloved.

The marigold (Pers. *gul-i jaʿfari*: *Tagetes patula*) was and still is a popular garden flower in India, used for decoration and garlands.

THE GARDEN-WALL PAVILIONS ('NAUBAT KHANA')

The two pavilions placed in mirror symmetry in the enclosing wall at the ends of the east–west walkway are an important accent in the overall *qarina* scheme [146:7a,7b, 149, 196–204]. Apse-like extensions projecting outward beyond the line of the wall emphasize their orientation inward, to the garden. They are in the same position as the false gates in earlier imperial funerary *chahar baghs*, but are less emphatic, so as not to distract from the buildings on the central axis. The pavilions are now known as 'Naubat Khana' (Drum House). Lahauri and Kanbo do not give any specific name for them: they merely list the main rooms of one storey.[92] Each of the two storeys consists of an open verandah [197] framed by square closed rooms (*hujra*); all three rooms have coved ceilings, the central one with a deeper surrounding cavetto. Behind the verandah, in the extension, is a room (*tanabi khana*[93]) of tripartite form, consisting of a central square covered with a shallow dome between two niches with half-domes.

The tripartite configuration of the fronts of the pavilions is based on the standard unit of Shahjahani residential architecture, the *bait* (p. 125), which we have met for instance in the flanking buildings of the inner 'Saheli Burj' tombs [165]; here, however, that formula is monumentalized by being doubled, with one set of rooms above the other. A pillared *chhatri* on top of the 'apse' acts as an informal version of a dome.

To use a basic form repeatedly and with variations in its size and proportions is a characteristic procedure in Shahjahani designing: it creates correspondences, and conforms to unity, one of the principles of Shah Jahan's architecture. The formula of an oblong pavilion with a bilaterally symmetrical plan is in line with a trend that had begun in the pavilions of the Nur Afshan garden/Ram Bagh [36]. For residential architecture it gradually superseded pavilions built on the ninefold *hasht bihisht* plan, which had been popular under Akbar and in the early reign of Jahangir. The connection was not given up completely, however, since the tripartite plan of the garden-wall pavilions corresponds to one side of a basic ninefold plan [22, 202].

The pavilions stand on platforms paved with red sandstone and white marble in a lobed in-and-out pattern [337:c]. These are reached by two flights of steps that lead up to a central landing.

The garden-wall pavilions

196 *above* The eastern pavilion, seen from the garden. (Photograph taken in 1997)

197 *left* The upper verandah of the eastern pavilion. Like the lower one, it is accentuated with coupled columns and double arches. (Photograph taken in 2000)

198 *right* Detail of the brackets under the eaves of the *chhatri* at the top of the western pavilion, showing vases set in interlacing stems. (Photograph taken in 1999)

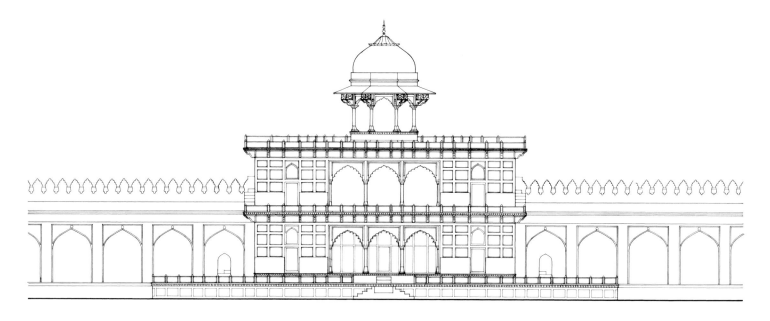

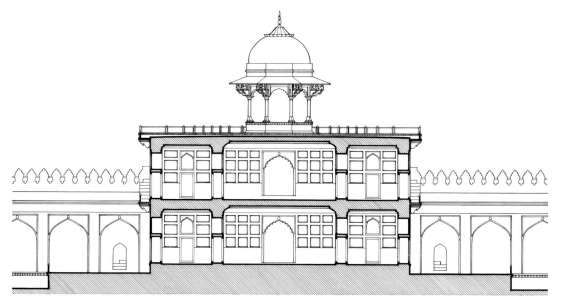

There, between the steps, is a slit through which water fell in a sheet into the canal of the walkway. The pavilions thus declared themselves as pieces of garden architecture. The platforms are enclosed by low balustrades filled with *jalis* composed of small hexagons and octagons, between posts topped with lotus buds. Similar balustrades surround the balconies of the upper floor and the roof.

The tripartite elevation of the pavilions is organized with triadic subschemes. The central superimposed verandahs are fronted by three multi-cusped arches supported on Shahjahani columns. The columns and arches are doubled in depth on both floors to give them additional emphasis [197], which underlines the stately character of the buildings. The lower verandah arcades are closed by *jalis* filled with tiny hexagons. The front walls of the *hujras* on either side also show a division into three: on each storey, a central door topped by an arched window is flanked above dado level by superimposed panels filled with multi-cusped blind arches and cartouches. The openings have been partly walled up, or closed with *jalis* also filled with hexagons.

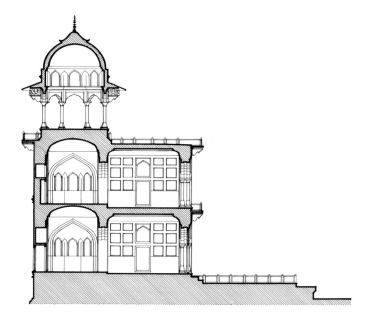

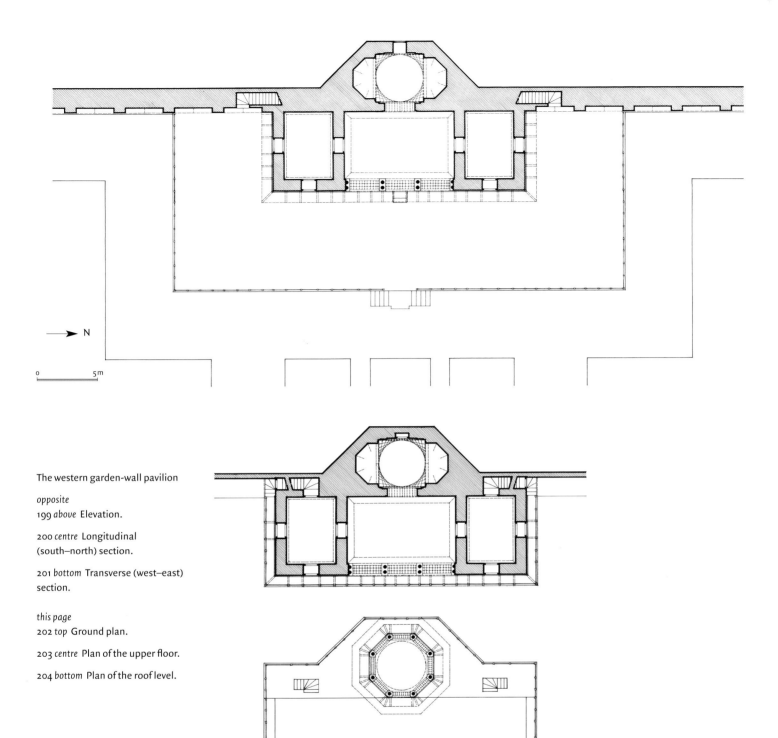

The western garden-wall pavilion

opposite
199 *above* Elevation.

200 *centre* Longitudinal (south–north) section.

201 *bottom* Transverse (west–east) section.

this page
202 *top* Ground plan.

203 *centre* Plan of the upper floor.

204 *bottom* Plan of the roof level.

The roof terrace is reached by steep staircases, which also give access to an elevated wall-walk along the *kanguras* of the enclosing wall [191]. The dome of the octagonal *chhatri* is supported by eight Shahjahani columns and multi-cusped arches, and at each corner three elaborate brackets project to support the *chhajja* [198]. These brackets have voluted lower parts, on top of which is placed an openwork component of interlacing stems with hanging buds, enclosing a flower vase. The vase is the sculpted version of a motif that appears again in grand style in the mausoleum and the riverfront terrace.

The western garden-wall pavilion houses the Taj Museum.[94] It contains a collection of old paintings, sheets of calligraphy, Persian manuscripts, imperial *farmans* (written orders), coins, jade objects and porcelain, several rare 19th-century views of the riverfront [e.g. 72, 73], and one of the Agra fort.[95] Of particular interest is the large plan of the entire Taj Mahal complex and part of the Mahtab Bagh (p. 103) [193]. There are also two large marble columns with inlay work which come from the porch of Shah Jahan's *hammam* in the 'Machchhi Bhavan' in the Agra fort, which was dismantled on the orders of Lord Hastings in 1815 (p. 69).

The riverfront terrace and the marble platform of the mausoleum

On the riverfront terrace stands the group of buildings that forms the architectural climax of the entire complex [135, 146:A]. The mausoleum, surrounded by its four minarets on its platform in the centre, is flanked on the left by the mosque, and on the right by the Mihman Khana or assembly hall. The principle of triadic division here reaches its apotheosis. The hierarchy of elements in a tripartite scheme is applied to the grouping: the commanding position of the mausoleum is underlined by its flanking elements, which relate to it in perfect mirror symmetry. This hierarchy also dictates the viewpoint: the observer must stand directly opposite the mausoleum, or distortions arise in the relationship of the parts to each other. A strictly frontal view is needed to grasp the unity of the design.

THE RIVERFRONT TERRACE (*chabutra, kursi*)

The terrace of the Taj Mahal is the most ambitious ever built in a Mughal riverfront garden scheme, unprecedented in size and decoration, and one of the most impressive platforms in the history of architecture. From the landward side it is hardly noticeable: since the site slopes down towards the river [145], the terrace rises only 1.22 m (4 ft) above the level of the garden – just high enough to announce itself [205]. Its full splendour is displayed towards the river, where it forms an uninterrupted red sandstone band 8.7 m (28 ft 6 in.) high from the lowest visible plinth and 300 m (984 ft) long, with elaborate decoration in relief and inlay work [frontispiece, 74, 207–209].

The riverfront terrace was the first part of the Taj Mahal complex to be built (p. 97). Lahauri described it thus:

> And on top of the foundation the platform (*kursi*) of the exalted mausoleum, which imitates the gardens of Rizwan [the guardian of Paradise] and gives an impression (*nishan*) of the holy abodes, was raised like a terrace (*chabutra asa*) of brick and mortar in one solid block . . . and in the centre of this terrace of the rank of the Throne of God (*kursi-yi ʿarsh martaba*) was raised another solid platform (*kursi*) . . . faced with white marble . . .[96]

205 *opposite* The mosque, mausoleum and Mihman Khana seen from the garden: Company drawing (wrongly inscribed 'The Taj, from the opposite side of the river') from an album of Lady Hastings, *c.* 1815. All three buildings stand on the red sandstone riverfront terrace. The mausoleum is further raised on a white marble platform.

206 *right* Foundation wells similar to those that underly the riverfront terrace [cf. 124] are seen here in 1958, after they had been exposed by excavation. They supported steps leading down to the river below the mosque and the north-west tower. Steps and foundations are now invisible.

207 *below* The riverfront terrace. In the foreground is the north-west tower. The shoreline today is higher than it was originally [cf. 206]: the door beyond the tower, now blocked, was probably reached by temporary stairs to give access to the complex from a boat. Further along, in the centre of the terrace (the area between the two minarets), seven of the large arches alternating with smaller ones were originally open and lit a cool gallery, the Tahkhana [211–213]. (Photograph taken in 1985, before the restoration of 2004–5.)

opposite

208 *above* Detail of the right-hand end of the river façade of the terrace, of red sandstone carved with flower vases and inlaid with white marble. Here the rhythm changes. (Photograph taken in 2004, before the restoration of 2004–5)

209 *below* The south-western face of the north-west tower [cf. 207]. Where the wall bends, the arches contain not a flower vase but two separate tripartite groups with palm trees. (Photograph taken in 2001, before the restoration of 2004–5)

210 *right* One of the entrances to the Tahkhana, in the sandstone-paved area in front of the mosque, seen from the roof of the mosque. (Photograph taken in 2001)

Lahauri uses the word *kursi* for the terrace, for the platform on which the mausoleum stands, and for its low plinth, treating all three semantically on equal terms. *Kursi* also means throne, and this leads to the comparison of the terrace with the ultimate throne, the Throne of God. The importance of the terrace is expressed in its linguistic treatment, in its grand form, and in its elaborate decoration.

The façade to the river is framed by two octagonal tower pavilions of which five sides project [74]. As endpoints, they are integrated into the elaborate decorative scheme of its facing with red sandstone, highlighted with white marble. This decoration is divided into two bands. The lower band is built up in simple Mughal bond [cf. 122,123]. It is separated from the upper band by a strongly projecting moulding with pendant leaves, traditionally called *dasa*, though the term does not appear in Mughal texts. The upper band is articulated by a repetition of decorative units expressed in relief and marble inlay, on which Kanbo commented in 1643: 'The exterior of this [terrace] was decorated with cut red stone in which much skill has been employed with regard to relief work (*munnabat* [*kari*]) and inlay work (*parchin kari*).'[97] Throughout the main length of the terrace, large units containing a blind arch, itself subdivided into eight panels, alternate with narrower units that contain an arch below and a rectangular field above. These elements are framed by bands with oblong cartouches inlaid in white marble.

The alternating wide and narrow units form sequences which read as the familiar tripartite façade formula of a major arch flanked by two superimposed niches. Each major arch shows in turn a tripartite subdivision of *qarina* symmetry: a large flowering plant set in a blind door in the centre is flanked by superimposed symmetrical vases, and topped by a vase between further flowering plants. The narrow units have a large flower vase in the lower arch and a field with arabesques above. At each end of the façade, near the towers, the pattern changes [208]: the major unit is flanked by additional narrower strips with three superimposed panels. The facing of the towers introduces a further variation [209]: the major arch appears in the centre of each face, and the dividing units are 'bent' around the corners. To avoid bending the vase motif, it is replaced by tripartite groups of palm trees flanked by flowering plants, one group in each half of the angle.

While articulation with arches is a usual feature of funerary platforms in Mughal architecture, there is no precedent for filling the arches and panels with flowery arabesques and large naturalistic flowering plants, flower vases in relief, or palm trees. The decoration takes up and magnifies a motif of the buildings above, where naturalistic flowers appear on the dados of the mausoleum, the mosque and the Mihman Khana, and flower vases in the mausoleum only.

The arches in the centre were originally open, lighting rooms along the river front, the Tahkhana (see below). Judging by the style of the decoration, they were filled in in Shah Jahan's time; it is also doubtful that Aurangzeb would have paid for such elaborate carving after he had deposed his father.

There are two doors, now blocked, in the lower band at each end of the façade, near the towers [207]. They led to stairs and rooms inside the towers [306] and from there to the upper level, giving access to the Taj Mahal when one arrived by boat, as Shah Jahan did several times. They are quite high up, and were probably reached from the water by temporary stairs.

Below the terrace there were landings in the form of wide flights of steps (*ghats*), which are now covered with sand and silt but which are visible in photographs of the 1950s when part of the front foundations were excavated [206].

The terrace is paved with geometrical patterns – of lighter and darker sandstone slabs, and, around the mausoleum, of sandstone and marble [210, 216, 337:a,d].

The Tahkhana

The gallery inside the terrace is not mentioned in the official descriptions, but Aurangzeb refers to it in his report of 1652 (p. 250) as *tahkhana-i kursi haftadar*, 'the terrace *tahkhana* of seven arches'.[98] It lies below the white marble platform, and is reached at either end by steps leading down from the paved floor of the terrace, near the base of the two riverfront minarets [210]. The upper openings of the stairways are now closed with an iron railing, and form an attraction for visitors who look down into the dark and speculate how far the tunnel below will reach – up to the Agra fort, or perhaps even to Delhi; guides also tell them that this is how Shah Jahan had the architect and the workers brought to the dungeons of the fort so they would not be able to build another Taj Mahal.

The Tahkhana was first recorded by J. W. Alexander (p. 251), who had the passage that had been filled in opened in 1874 and had a plan drawn of it.[99]

The gallery consists of a series of rooms arranged in line along the riverfront [211]. They are reached on their landward side by a narrow corridor [212] which terminates at each end in a bend following three sides of an octagon. One would expect these part-octagons to correspond to the bases of the minarets above, but they are slightly off-centre: clearly the builders at the higher level deviated from the plan laid down in the Tahkhana.

The rooms comprise seven larger chambers extended by niches on each side, alternating with six square rooms; at each end is a group of two octagonal rooms linked by short corridors to a rectangular chamber between them. The outer octagons form the link to the stairways. Short passages connect all rooms and provide links to the corridor. The seven larger rooms originally looked out to the river through generous arches, a feature that allows us to identify the gallery with Aurangzeb's 'terrace *tahkhana* of seven arches'. It must have been a beautiful airy space, which served the emperor, his women and his entourage as a cool place of recreation when visiting the tomb. It now has no natural light. Such galleries in a substructure are known from Mughal palace fortresses: in the fort of Lahore, for instance, below the courtyard of the Shah Burj (Shish Mahal) at the north-west corner a series of vaulted rooms is set into the riverfront.

The rooms [213] show traces of painted decoration under their present whitewash, especially in the dado zone, and a *qalib kari* facing of their vaults in the form of netted patterns arranged between concentric circles of stars with a medallion in the centre. The patterns are highlighted with painted lines.

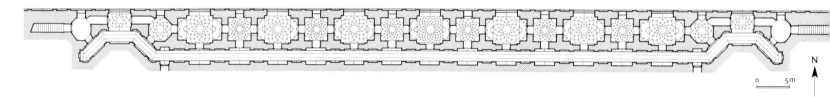

N

0   5m

The Tahkhana

211 *above* Ground plan. The river frontage is at the top. The vaulted rooms, alternately large and small, opened to the Yamuna through alternately wide and narrow arches.

212 *far left* A view along the corridor that runs to the south of the rooms. The white dot in the distance is the light of a torch. (Photograph taken in 2001)

213 *left* One of the seven main rooms, showing the walled-up arch on the left that once opened to the river, and remains of the *qalib kari* vault. (Photograph taken in 2001)

The marble platform of the mausoleum
(takhtgah, kursi)

Monumental platforms housing the tomb chamber, above the actual burial, had been a conspicuous feature of Mughal mausoleums since the beginning; in Jahangir's tomb, built about the same time as the Taj Mahal, the platform became the mausoleum itself [108]. The designation of funerary platforms as *kursi*, which as we have seen also means throne, or *takhtgah*, which can mean a platform on which a throne stands, was emphasized by Lahauri for the riverfront terrace and played on by Shah Jahan's poet Kalim in his celebration of the tomb of Humayun [104]: 'From its podium (*kursi*) men of vision have recognized that an enthroned one reposes here.'[100] The platform of an imperial mausoleum was thus associated with kingship, and emphasized the status of the person buried.

The platform is square, and its corners are accentuated by the bases of the four minarets which project as five sides of an octagon [cf. 149, 217]. It is set off from the paved surface of the terrace by paving with an interlocking pattern of white marble octagons into which are set four-pointed sandstone stars, surrounded by a border with alternating long and short cartouches [210, 216, 337:d], a lobed variant of the angular pattern that frames the garden walkways [189].

On the occasion of the celebration of the second death anniversary of Mumtaz Mahal, when the platform stood alone before the mausoleum was raised on it [127], the historian Tabataba'i referred to it as 'that platform (*takhtgahi*) which forms the actual podium (*kursi-yi asl*) of the building of that holy mausoleum'.[101] In their later descriptions Lahauri and Kanbo point out especially that it was entirely faced with white marble.[102] This was a new feature for a funerary platform of this size. The decoration of the marble facing does not appear elsewhere in the Taj Mahal complex: it consists of a row of rectangular panels into which are set trefoil-headed blind arches topped by a leaf, with medallions in the spandrels showing an interlacing leafy pattern [215].

In the centre of the southern side of the platform, towards the garden, are two flights of stairs, partly covered by tunnel vaults, which provide the only access from the terrace up to the level of the mausoleum [216]. In the centre of the other three sides a tripartite *bait* in the form of an open oblong room flanked by two square *hujras*, all

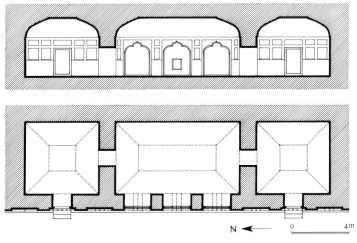

214 *above* Section and plan of the tripartite unit of rooms that occurs within the west, north and east sides of the platform (here, the west). Doors at either end lead into windowless rooms; in the centre is a longer room lit by *jalis*.

covered with coved ceilings, is set into the platform [214, 217, 218]. The central room has three arched openings corresponding to the trefoil-headed blind arches, filled with *jalis* in the hexagonal pattern found everywhere in the complex; a small rectangular window is cut into the central *jali*. The *hujras* are reached through doors. Today used for storage, these rooms probably originally served visiting members of the imperial family as a place to retire and rest; or perhaps the Qur'an reciters stayed here when they were not on duty.

215 *below left* A detail of the platform, showing the blind arches and the figure of the marble. (Photograph taken in 1995)

216 *below* Looking down one of the two flights of stairs in the southern side of the marble platform, which link the levels of the mausoleum and riverfront terrace below. The area here [cf. 210] is paved with sandstone and marble and bordered by a band of alternating cartouches (only partly visible) similar to that of the garden walkways and the tomb chamber [189, 230]. (Photograph taken in 1995)

overleaf
217 The mausoleum seen from the east. At the centre of the platform are three screened arches between two doors: the doors lead to windowless cells and the *jalis* light a central room. (Photograph taken in 2000)

The mausoleum

(*rauza-i munauwara, rauza-i muqqadas, rauza-i mutahhara*)

The mausoleum dominates the entire Taj complex: the architectural effect is that of a strictly ordered progression of elements towards the overwhelming climax of the white marble building [135]. The historians and poets of Shah Jahan apply the word *rauza* ('garden', used for tombs in a garden and, in India, for tombs of persons of standing or Sufi mystics) to the entire Taj Mahal complex, as well as

to the mausoleum itself, which is styled ʿimarat-i rauza-i munauwara, 'the building of the illumined tomb', *rauza-i muqqadas*, 'holy tomb', or ʿimarat-i rauza-i mutahhara, 'the building of the pure tomb'.[103] The phrases have strong religious connotations: *rauza-i mutahhara* is used to designate the tomb of the prophet Muhammad at Medina. The mausoleum was conceived as a pure and holy building, as an image here on earth of the house of Mumtaz in Paradise, a heavenly garden building within a heavenly garden (see Chapter IV). The architecture was to express this concept through perfect symmetry, harmonious proportional relationships, and the translucent white

218 Cutaway perspective view of the mausoleum, seen from the north-east. Also shown partially in cutaway form are one of the tripartite units of rooms in the marble platform [cf. 214], and the Tahkhana in the centre of the riverfront terrace [cf. 211].

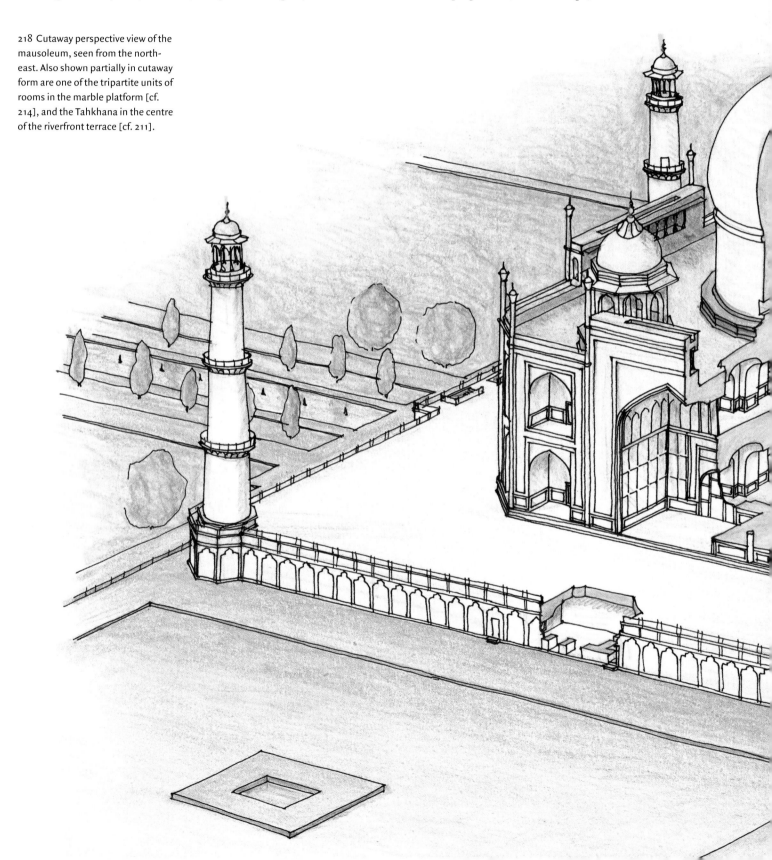

marble facing which gives the purity of the geometrical and rational planning the desired unworldly appearance.

The mausoleum is raised over an enriched version of the nine-fold *hasht bihisht* plan favoured by the Mughals for tombs and garden pavilions (pp. 26–27) [220]. Simpler versions of the plan can be seen in other Agra riverfront buildings: the Chini-ka Rauza [42], the podium of the 'tomb of Parwiz Khan' [52:b], the tomb of Iᶜtimad-Daula [57], and the Rauza of Jaᶜfar Khan. A variant is used in the great gate [175]. In the mausoleum the *hasht bihisht* plan is expressed in perfect cross-axial symmetry, so that the building is focused on the central tomb chamber. And the inner organization is reflected on the façades, which present a perfectly balanced composition when seen from the extensions of the axes which generate the plan.

The plan is inscribed in the figure of a square with chamfered corners – what the Mughals called a *musamman baghdadi* or 'Baghdadi octagon', with four longer and four shorter sides (p. 130). It is the radial variant of a *hasht bihisht*, with two cross-axes, into which additional features are introduced to generate a richer design. The basic cross pattern (+) is formed by the domed octagonal hall in the centre, connected to the rectangular *pishtaq* halls on the cardinal

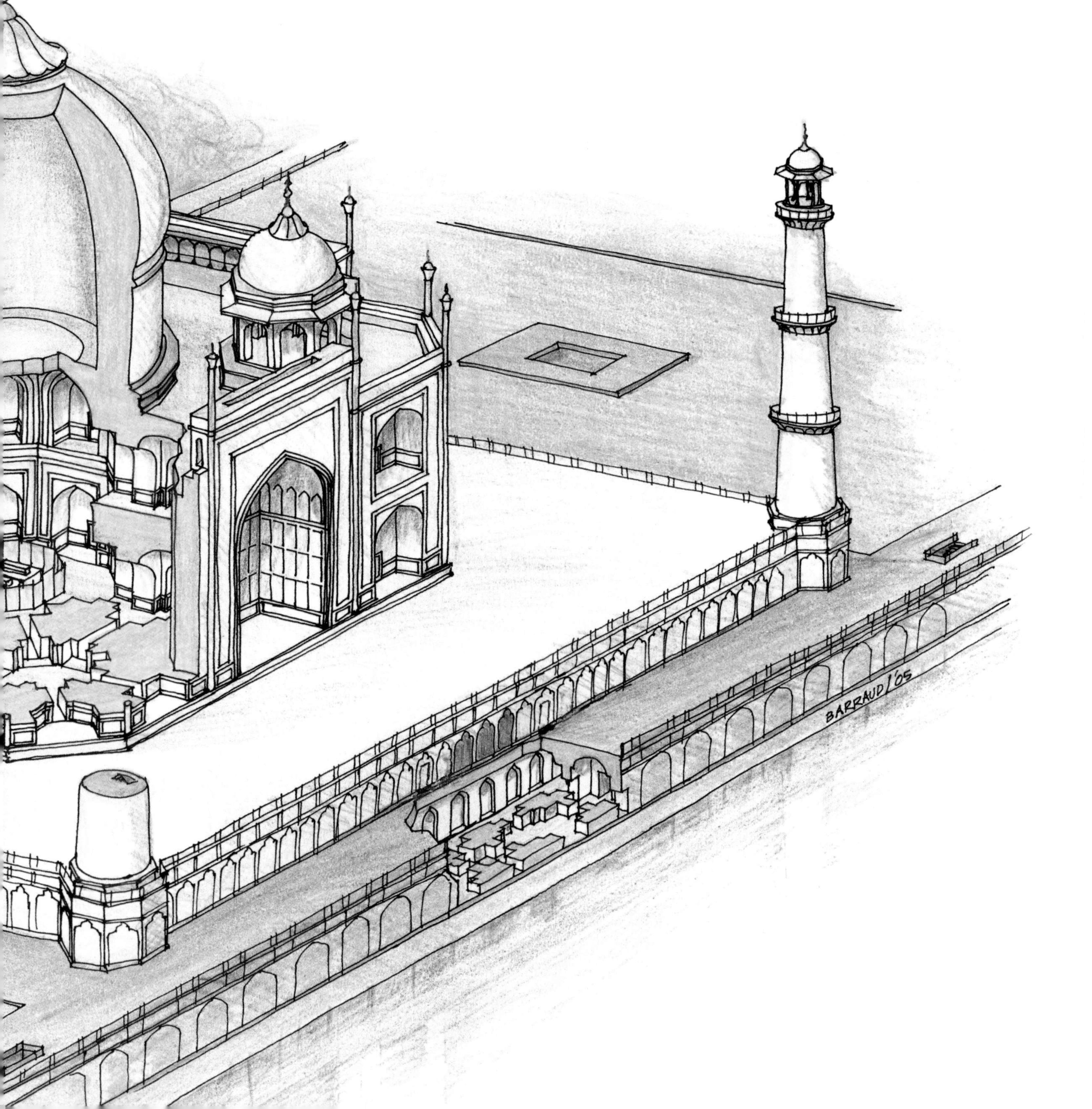

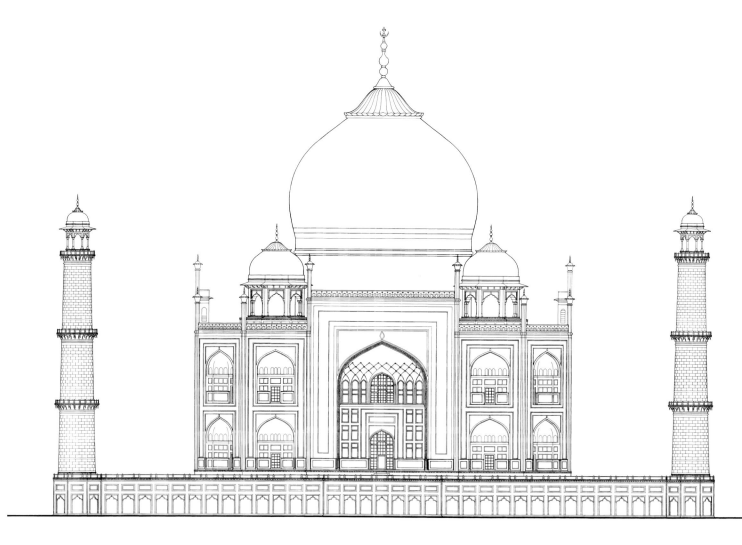

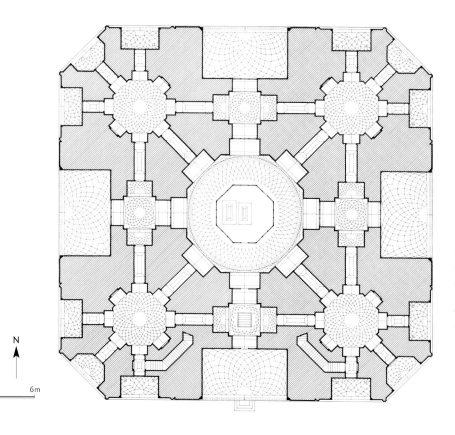

The mausoleum

219 *above* South elevation of the mausoleum, with its marble platform and flanking minarets. The seven central bays in the platform project forward and house the stairs that connect the levels of the riverfront terrace and the mausoleum.

220 *left* Plan of the ground floor. The perfect geometry of the architecture is rendered fairly precisely in the plan: the measurements of the *pishtaq* halls and the four corner rooms were found to be the same within a few centimetres, and the tomb chamber in the centre is a precise regular octagon. The plan as drawn here shows, for the first time, the geometric projection of the vaults, highlighting their role in the composition.

221 *opposite* Section from south (left) to north.

N

0   6m

axes. The second cross pattern (x) links the central hall to the corner rooms, which are also octagonal. The connection is fully realized only in the case of the southern entrance: otherwise *jalis* filled with panes of glass are inserted, which allow one to see but not pass through.

The corner rooms are not, as in a basic radial *hasht bihisht* design [23], simple rooms on the diagonal axes: they display a more complex configuration. The chamber in each corner is moved in towards the centre, and three passages radiate from it to the exterior, where they widen into niches on the façades. This configuration represents a quarter of a *hasht bihisht*, and is clearly inspired by the design of Humayun's tomb [24]. There, however, the corners have the form of full *hasht bihisht*s and consequently project outwards, whereas at the Taj they remain within the outline of the chamfered square and the integrity of the *musamman baghdadi* is preserved. Furthermore, because the corner rooms are moved in beyond the line of the backs of the *pishtaq* halls they are able to function as corners of a square ambulatory, which is inserted by means of short corridors around the central domed hall. On the cross axes, between the *pishtaq* halls and the central hall the ambulatory system opens out into cruciform rooms. Thus the inner square forms in itself a perfect *hasht bihisht* scheme.

The plan of the ground floor is repeated on the upper floor [252] and is also reflected at roof level [253], though there the individual rooms are represented by freestanding elements.

The exterior of the building displays four identical elevations on the principal façades and four identical elevations on the chamfered corners. The principal façades are a grandiose expression of the favourite Mughal triadic formula of a dominant central *pishtaq* flanked by pairs of superimposed niches. (The latter are also termed *pishtaq* by Lahauri and Kanbo,[104] but for clarity these sub-*pishtaqs* may be called niches.) The paired niches appear also on the corners, with the effect of unifying the elevation and intensifying the effect of the central *pishtaqs* and the dome above them, which acts as the climax of the composition. The structural planning of the elevation is highlighted by its linearity and two-dimensionality. All niches are kept within the plane of the wall, and the flat wall elements are 'hinged together' with thin engaged shafts, which terminate above the roof level in freestanding *guldastas*.

The designing binds plan and elevations together: all major elements of the plan are represented in the elevation. The rectangular forehalls appear in elevation as the vaulted niches of the *pishtaqs*, the smaller niches appear as features on two storeys, the outer dome corresponds to the inner dome, and the four octagonal roof *chhatris* represent the octagonal corner rooms of the inner *hasht bihisht* figure.

The clarity which characterizes the overall planning of the building is also at work in the details of the architecture. Although only a few basic forms are used, each element and each ornamental detail is carefully differentiated according to its role in the overall composition, to conform to the principles of symmetrical correspondence, hierarchical schemes, triadic proportional configurations, uniformity of shapes, sensuous attention to detail, selective naturalism, and elaborate symbolism (pp. 104–5).

Exterior

THE PLINTH

The mausoleum sits on a plinth, decorated with delicate relief carvings (*munabbat kari*) of plant elements [222]. This type of ornament, conforming to the principles of sensuous attention to detail and selective naturalism, is reserved for the lowest zone of the building, where it could be immediately appreciated by the viewer. Naturalistic ornament also appears above the plinth, in the spectacular flowering plants of the dados of the *pishtaq* halls [223, 225, 226].

The top of the plinth is accentuated by a moulding showing a row of hanging leaves (*dasa*). In a simple schematic form it is a common pattern of decoration for the bases of Mughal buildings [e.g. 153], but here it is embellished by the naturalistic treatment of its constituent elements: the leaves, hanging from interlacing stems, alternate with pendant acanthus buds. At the bottom is a related pattern, with rows of hanging flowers and buds. In between

is a band formed of interlacing cartouches with mirror-symmetrical acanthus leaves, which reinterprets in plant forms and in relief a popular Mughal border that was previously expressed in geometric forms. (Inlaid versions of the formula appear in the star patterns lining the walkways of the garden [189] and the border of lobed cartouches of alternating size around the marble platform [216].)

THE *PISHTAQS,* OR MONUMENTAL PORCHES

Each *pishtaq* [224] is accentuated by a large inscription in *sulus* script in a band on its rectangular frame. The texts are carefully selected passages of the Qur'an which relate to the eschatological programme of the building – references to the Last Judgment, divine forgiveness, and the reward of the faithful in Paradise.

The large arch within the frame is topped by an inlaid flower and lined with three cable mouldings, which rise from three short engaged corner colonnettes in the dado zone that grow out of plain vases and are topped by simple *muqarnas* capitals [223]. (This revival of Timurid rope moulding also occurs in the arches of the gates and the flanking buildings of the mausoleum.) The spandrels are filled with flowery arabesques in red, green and dark yellow inlay, forming diagonally set lyre patterns. The inner walls of the *pishtaq* halls are patterned with symmetrically arranged multi-cusped blind arches alternating with cartouches set into rectangular panels in a framework of bands.

222 *below* Detail of the plinth. (Photograph taken in 2000)

223 *right* Engaged bundled colonnettes and rope mouldings framing the *pishtaq*. (Photograph taken in 1995)

224 *opposite* The east *pishtaq*. Both *pishtaq* and inner door are surrounded by inlaid texts from the Qur'an. (Photograph taken *c.* 1990)

The *pishtaqs* embrace two storeys, and in their back walls are superimposed arched doors, larger below and smaller above. Both doors are filled with a rectangular framework containing *jalis* formed of tiny hexagonal elements in a honeycomb pattern. The setting of the door on the ground floor echoes that of the outer *pishtaq* arch: it is framed with an inscription band, and its spandrels show a simpler version of arabesques. The door of the upper floor is integrated into the transition zone of the half-vault, formed of arches from which the network or *qalib kari* of the vault is developed. The *qalib kari* is here removed from its plaster origins and rendered in marble carving – a feature specially pointed out by Lahauri and Kanbo in their description of the inner main dome. Irregularities in the netted patterns of the vaults tell us that the craftsmen were grappling with the problem of having to translate the complex patterns from plaster into marble; this is particularly noticeable in the corners. They were not able to achieve the desired uniformity – or perhaps they did not take enough care. Irregularities appear also in the superimposed niches.

The dado flowers in the *pishtaqs*

The naturalistic decoration of the exterior of the mausoleum culminates in the flowers which cover the dados (195 cm/ 76¾ in. high) of the three inner walls of the *pishtaq* halls, transforming them into ever-blooming paradisiacal flowerbeds. These appear at eye level and above to a person standing below on the platform outside the niche, and present themselves as rows of individual flowering plants, standing on little hillocks.

The dado flowers are carved in sensuous detail, but they are highly ambivalent creations. Their style of representation is inspired by European herbals of the 16th and 17th centuries which Jahangir's painters had consulted for floral miniatures (pp. 218–21).[105] Characteristic of the flowers in the herbals is the symmetrical composition and the botanical detail, the use of front and side views of the blossoms to display stamens and carpels, and a sense of movement in the petals, leaves and stems. But while providing their plants with apparently naturalistic detail, Shah Jahan's artists depicted identifiable species only exceptionally: rather, they adapted the herbal style to compose flowers of their own invention, even grafting blossoms and leaves of different species together onto one plant.[106]

Such naturalistic plant forms were a new feature in Mughal architectural ornament. In the 1630s they had begun to make their appearance in a strictly controlled way to designate imperial spaces. This new style of architectural ornament was inspired not only by herbals but also by other types of European print which Mughal artists had explored for realism and naturalism since Akbar; to transfer forms inspired by them into architectural ornament was a special concern of the artists of Shah Jahan (pp. 222–24). While the models for these naturalistic flowers were derived from European sources, the arrangement of individual marble plants in tiers can be traced back to Gujarati tombs of the 14th century.[107]

The delicate beauty of the marble flowers of the Taj appeals to our senses and captivates our mind so that we do not realize that we are here confronted with a strict and complex expression of the Shahjahani system. The flowers, partly symmetrical in themselves, are arranged in a perfect order, based on triadic divisions and subdivisions. This working of two contrasting principles –

225 Dado panel on the back wall of the north *pishtaq* of the mausoleum. Large flowers, of types A–B–C–B–A, alternate with smaller flowers. (Photograph taken in 1980)
A flower with tulip-shaped blossoms
B flower with blossoms inspired by tulips and narcissus, the leaves perhaps derived from anemones
C flower with tulip-shaped blossoms broader than those of A

naturalism and formalism – against each other to arrive at a harmonious synthesis is a characteristic procedure of Shahjahani art and explains, for instance, the intriguing effect of the paintings of the emperor's history in the Windsor Castle *Padshahnama* [e.g. 2, 65].

Each 'species' of the dado flowers always appears in the same form, according to the principle of unity. When it has asymmetrical elements, these are also used in reverse, according to the flower's position in the overall scheme. The dados of the back walls [225] display three different species, which we may call A, B and C. The side walls have only two, D and E [226]. E sets a special accent because it is a perfect mirror-symmetrical unit in itself.

The panels of carved flowers are outlined by a band inlaid with flowery scrolls set between narrow lines of black and ochre marble.

The dados of the superimposed niches and the outer dados are plain and, because of the compartmentalization of the façade, they appear as individual panels, 'assigned' to their respective wall elements. Their margin shows a simple inlaid chevron pattern of yellow and black marble. (This type of dado is also found, in sandstone, in the great gate, mosque and Mihman Khana, forming one of the unifying factors of the overall decoration.) Thus the dado hierarchy manifests itself in a progressive increase and elaboration of plant forms towards the interior, culminating in the tomb chamber.

226 Dado panel on a side wall of the west *pishtaq* of the mausoleum. The flowers are of types D–E–D. (Photograph taken in 1980)
D a variant of B [cf. 225]
E symmetrical plant, with blossoms inspired by lilies

overleaf
227 The south-east corner of the mausoleum, seen from the south-eastern minaret. (Photograph taken in 2001)

THE SUPERIMPOSED NICHES

The smaller side niches of the façade are uniform in shape, the main difference being that the ones flanking the *pishtaqs* are rectangular in plan while the ones on the chamfers are half-octagonal [227]. In line with the principles of hierarchy and uniformity of shapes, these 'sub-*pishtaqs*' are smaller and simplified versions of their larger counterparts. They have no surrounding inscription, the opening in their back wall is a straight-headed door, their walls have fewer ornamental blind arches, and the *qalib kari* of their half-vaults has fewer elements. The vaults differ in form because of the differences in plan of the two types of niche: those over a rectangular plan have to bridge a corner, which brings about a spacing of the arches at the base of the transition zone that is less even than in the half-octagonal ones. Here too we find irregularities in the execution of the vault patterns.

OTHER ELEMENTS

The engaged shafts which hinge the façade elements together all have the same chevron pattern in dark yellow and black inlay, similar to that in the margins of the outer dados. The surface of the inlaid stone has in many instances corroded: in particular, the black appears as grey, perhaps the effect of chemical cleaning (p. 252). The top of the body of the mausoleum is surrounded by a parapet. This is faced on the outside by an inlaid band featuring an in-and-out pattern of red and green voluted acanthus leaves highlighted with dark yellow leaves, which is separated by a prominent moulding from a narrower lower band which displays, as a subtle echo of the relief moulding of the plinth below, hanging red flowers alternating with yellow buds. Below the parapet and next to each engaged shaft projecting water spouts conduct the rainwater from the roof.

Interior

THE TOMB CHAMBER

Just as the mausoleum represents the culmination of the entire
Taj complex, so the inner domed hall represents the climax of the
mausoleum. It is the final station in the progress towards the tomb
of Mumtaz, and that of Shah Jahan. The large hall, together with the
lower tomb chamber over the actual burials below and the outer
dome above, forms the core of the building [221]. Here all the
elements, architecture, furniture, and decoration combine to create
an eschatological house for Mumtaz Mahal. Even sound was put to
the task of eternity, through one of the longest echoes of any
building in the world (pp. 228–29).

The hall has the form of a perfect octagon, 7.33–7.35 m (c. 24 ft)
to a side, with two tiers of eight radiating niches [228]. These niches,

228 *opposite* The tomb chamber: Company drawing by an Agra or Delhi artist,
c. 1820–30. The drawing combines several viewpoints to give a complete
impression of the interior. The screen that surrounds the cenotaphs is shown in
black, probably to make it stand out against the pattern of the floor.

229 *above* The upper niches of the tomb chamber, and springing of the dome;
its footline is formed of a band of *muqarnas*. (Photograph taken in 1999)

termed *nashiman* ('seat'), are equal in size but differentiated in their
elevations. In those on the cardinal axes the inner wall is open
and fitted with a screen which transmits light into the interior of
the hall. The screens are triadically structured and subdivided by a
framework filled with small rectangular *jalis*, which are in turn
fitted with panes of glass [cf. 365] – from Aleppo (or of Aleppo type),
the historians tell us. In the niches on the diagonal axes the back
walls are solid but for a simple rectangular door filled with a *jali* that
corresponds to the lowest central part of the 'transparent' niches.
The decoration of the ground-floor niches [230] reflects that of the
pishtaqs and niches outside: they are framed by inscription bands and
have flowery scrolls in the spandrels, and their walls are panelled with
registers of multi-cusped blind arches, here expressed in inlay with
black stone. They are covered by short pointed barrel vaults without
any decoration, in contrast to the *qalib kari* of the half-vaults on the
exterior and of the inner dome.

The two levels are separated by a large inscription band which
surrounds the entire hall. The upper niches [229] have the same
shape as the lower ones but no frames. They are integrated into the
transition zone of the dome: the ring marking its base rests on the
apex of their arches, and the pendentives that descend between
them are faced with *qalib kari*. The ring is formed of small *muqarnas*

230 The tomb chamber and screen surrounding the tombs. The niches are framed, and the room encircled, by inlaid inscriptions from the Qur'an. The dados display carved flower vases framed by *pietra dura* inlay, and corner colonnettes carved with plant motifs springing from pots with overhanging leaves – all evoking paradisiacal bloom. Plant ornament, including naturalistic flowers in *pietra dura*, appears on the screen. The floor, by contrast, has an inlaid geometric pattern surrounded by a border of lobed cartouches. (Photograph taken in 1992)

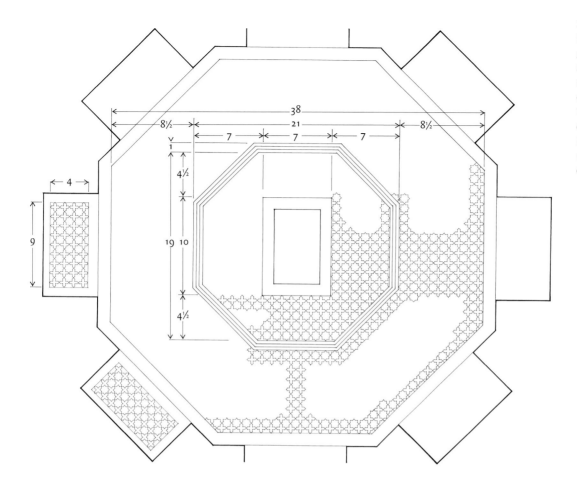

elements – the only instance of *muqarnas* in a vault of the mausoleum. This ornament, once part of the mainstream, was used by the Mughals only marginally, but its appearance on a structural element of the main dome of the mausoleum shows that it was still considered good for a special accent. Above the *muqarnas* band the dome is covered 'with marble cut in the design of *qalib kari*', as Lahauri and Kanbo point out. The apex is accentuated, as in the gateway, with a whirl pattern, here expressed in the more prestigious inlay technique. From the centre hangs a vase-shaped bronze lamp inlaid with gold and silver [233], a gift of Lord Curzon, who did not shy away from complex logistics to have it made in Cairo after a 'Saracenic design' he had 'found in a book' on the Islamic monuments of that city[108] (pp. 244, 252). The lamp, though of foreign design, recreates an original feature, because under Shah Jahan orbs (*kaukaba*) and hanging lamps (*qindil*) of gold with enamel work were suspended in the interior;[109] their shape is however not known.

The floor is paved in a geometrical pattern consisting of octagonal stars alternating with pointed cruciform shapes, formed by black marble inlaid in white [231]. Around the whole is a border of lobed cartouches of alternating size [230]. The same border surrounds the cenotaph of Mumtaz (but not the one of Shah Jahan, which was introduced later) [233]: it is a variant of a pattern used repeatedly in the Taj complex, most closely paralleled in the border of the terrace surrounding the platform of the mausoleum [216].

The concept of the hall as eschatological architecture is expressed in a geometrical way through its eight-sidedness, which according to Muslim cosmology evoked the eight levels of Paradise

(p. 26), and in an orthodox religious way through the Qur'anic inscriptions on the walls which again speak of the Last Judgment, divine mercy and Paradise. The same theme is conveyed more immediately to our senses through the paradisiacal vegetation in the dados, which are roughly as tall as the viewer (1.75 m/5 ft 9 in.) [230]. Luxurious vases filled with flowers appear here instead of the individual flowering plants of the *pishtaq* halls outside. The flowers follow botanical species more closely, and one can identify the Mughal favourites – irises, tulips, daffodils and narcissus. They are naturalistic and seductively beautiful, but at the same time they convey the order of the Shahjahani system. All vases have the same general shape and all are set on little hills with small flowering plants in mirror symmetry on each side. All bouquets follow the same basic tripartite arrangement, with a dominant flower in the centre flanked by mirror-symmetrical groups on each side. Variations are in the number and species of the flowers, and in additional decorative elements, which occur according to the position of the vases in the hall.

The dados of the side walls of all the niches display triadic vase groups with dominant tulips. The central vase (I) is distinguished by a voluted ornament attached to its upper body and a different flower arrangement: the central tulip of the bunch has its outer petals curved down, and it is flanked by daffodil-like flowers and lilies with curved-back petals. The side vases (II) have a central tulip flanked by daffodil-like flowers combined with anemone-like leaves and narcissus.

In the diagonally placed niches a different, plain, vase appears on each side of the door in the back wall, with a single flower in the centre, flanked by flowers showing elements of anemones, carnations and lilies with curved-back petals (III). This vase is flanked by plants with three blossoms.

Yet another variant appears on the dados in the eight corners of the main hall: the vases here are garlanded by a ribbon and have a curved lip, and they are filled with an exuberant arrangement of various flowers, patterned on daffodils, narcissus with anemone-like leaves, daisies and tulips, dominated by a splendid iris (IV) [339]. The iris has a funerary connotation: in Kashmir and elsewhere in the Islamic world, it is grown on graves.[110]

The flower vases set a special accent in the Paradise symbolism of the hall. Their Europeanizing form is used for an elegant Shahjahani reinterpretation of an ancient symbol of Indian architecture, the pot with overhanging leaves (purna-ghata), which symbolizes prosperity and wellbeing [347];[111] the motif appears again, closer to its original form, at the corners of the dados, as pots out of which the engaged colonnettes grow together with acanthus leaves [230, 346]. The colonnettes are not plain, as they are outside, but enriched all over with naturalistically carved acanthus leaves and flowering creepers, in keeping with the emphasis on plants in the tomb chamber.

The screen and the cenotaphs

The naturalistic decoration of the interior culminates in the central ensemble of the cenotaphs of Mumtaz and Shah Jahan and the screen that surrounds them [230, 232, 233]. It attracts all visitors today with its spectacular flowers and plants inlaid in semi-precious stones.

The idea of cenotaphs surrounded by a screen in a tomb chamber was new: usually Mughal cenotaphs are placed by themselves in the centre of the building [61, 164]. The combination of 'tomb' and screen represents the most minimal form of burial, least offensive to orthodox concerns, and resembles what appears to have been the original form of that of Babur at Kabul. Perhaps at the Taj it testifies to orthodox conscientiousness within the unorthodox, a typical Mughal sophism which would separate screen and cenotaphs conceptually from the surrounding hall. According to this construct, the dome would be what it symbolically signifies – heaven.

The perforated marble screen (mahjar-i mushabbak) was set up in 1643 to replace the original one of enamelled gold made by the goldsmith and poet Bibadal Khan on the occasion of the second anniversary of Mumtaz Mahal's death in 1633 (p. 98), which was obviously deemed too precious. It took ten years to make and cost 50,000 rupees – less than one-tenth of the cost of the gold screen. Since 1994/95 it has been protected from the hands of visitors by an ungainly aluminium grille in a wooden frame.[112]

The screen is octagonal, reflecting on a smaller scale the octagon of the surrounding hall [228] and intensifying the paradisiacal symbolism of the number eight. Overall arrangement and detail follow the principles of Shahjahani system. Each side of the octagon is divided into three by marble frames [232]. The corners are fortified by posts ending in kalasha finials (globes surmounted by a pointed element), an adaptation of a feature of older Indian architecture. The frames are filled with jalis, in which elegantly and intricately wrought plant elements are composed

232 Elevation of the south side of the octagonal inlaid marble screen surrounding the tombs, with the entrance arch: Company drawing by an Agra or Delhi artist, c. 1808.

overleaf
233 The centre of the tomb chamber, seen from the north-east. Within the screen are the cenotaphs of Mumtaz Mahal (left) and Shah Jahan – the latter interrupting the border of alternating cartouches round that of Mumtaz. The bronze lamp inlaid with gold and silver was a gift of Lord Curzon, who had it made in Cairo after an early 14th-century lamp in the tomb of Sultan Baibars II there. (Photograph taken in 1992)

around a central axis – the only instance in the Taj Mahal where *jalis* are formed of organic plant arabesques rather than geometric forms. The Indian *jali* tradition is here brought to one of its highest points.[113] The screen is topped with ornamental crenellations, *kanguras*, consisting of vase-shaped elements alternating with openwork formed of volutes of acanthus leaves, crowned at their juncture by small vase elements [240]. The entrance arch in the centre of the south side [232, 233] and a corresponding closed arch opposite it in the centre of the north side [230] rise above the screen; they have semicircular heads lined by a moulding terminating in hanging acanthus buds. Together with the acanthus elements of the crenellations and the *jali* panels, the arch form belongs to the new organic and curvilinear vocabulary of Shah Jahan as it had first appeared in the baldachin of the 'Machchhi Bhavan' of the Agra fort [133, 134]; within the Taj complex it is seen in elements of the subsidiary tombs [166] and in the 'Fatehpuri Masjid' [331], which are, like the screen, datable to the last construction phase. According to Lahauri and Kanbo, the open archway held a door of jasper or agate (*sang-i yashm*) 'in the Turkish style' (*tarhbandi-yi rumi*), closed with gilded fasteners which alone cost 10,000 rupees.

Within the screen are the upper cenotaphs of Mumtaz Mahal and Shah Jahan – what Lahauri and Kanbo call *surat-i qabr*, 'the likenesses of tombs' [233]. As usual in imperial Mughal mausoleums, the actual burials are below, in the lower tomb chamber, under cenotaphs of similar design [246].

The cenotaph of Mumtaz is exactly in the centre of the hall. The larger cenotaph of Shah Jahan was added on its western side, and thus from a formal point of view appears as an afterthought. This placing gave substance to the rumour of the emperor's burial having been planned not within the Taj Mahal but on the opposite side of the Yamuna in a black marble tomb (pp. 56, 249).

The cenotaphs are aligned north–south, with the head to the north. The bodies were laid in their graves below on their side, with their face turned towards Mecca – which in India is to the west – so that they would rise in the correct position at the sound of the trumpets at the Last Judgment.[114] Each cenotaph consists of a single block of stone, shaped like a sarcophagus, set on a stepped plinth which is placed in turn on a wider platform. The cenotaph of Shah Jahan is characterized as a male tomb by the symbol of a pen case on its top. While the cenotaphs conform to an established Mughal type, no other Mughal, nor any other personage in the Islamic world, was commemorated with such exquisite decoration. The lower cenotaph of Jahangir at Lahore is the only one that comes close; it was created at the same time as that of Mumtaz, probably by the same artists. The decoration of the cenotaphs with hardstone inlay was reserved for members of the Mughal imperial family.

The *pietra dura* decoration of the screen and cenotaphs

The glory of the screen and the cenotaphs is their ornamentation with inlaid semi-precious stones, in the technique known as *pietra dura* (pp. 91–93). Shah Jahan's historians and poets use the same term, *parchin kari*, for both the traditional simple stone inlay and the complex technique in which Mughal craftsmen surpassed their Florentine models, but it is clearly the *pietra dura* form that they laud in the mausoleum, in particular its most exquisite

expression in the cenotaphs and screen. Here is Lahauri:

> All over the interior and exterior of this mausoleum, artisans (*sanna*) creating wonders and magic designs have inlaid (*parchin namuda*) carnelian (*ʿaqiq*) and other kinds of coloured stones (*sang-ha-yi rangin*) and precious stones (*ahjar-i samin*) . . . in such a manner that the sharpest eye cannot grasp its subtleties and the keenest mental perception fails to comprehend its wonders.
>
> And a description of both the quality and quantity of the craftsmanship employed in the inlay work (*parchin kari*) of the platform of the resting place (*chabutra-i marqad*) and the screen (*mahjar*) around it . . . and the miracle which the magic-working carvers (*naqqar*) and artisans (*sanna*), producing work akin to that of Mani [the supreme artist, in Persian literature],[115] have accomplished could never be finished and brought to a close, even with trees for pens and oceans of ink . . .[116]

The poet Kalim tells us that the painterly effects obtainable with *pietra dura* made it possible to create naturalistic flowers that were permanent and thus superior images of their counterparts in nature:

> On each stone a hundred colours, paintings and ornaments
> Have become apparent through the chisel's blade.
>
> The chisel has become the pen of Mani
> Painting so many pictures upon the translucent marble
>   (*ab-i marmar*).
>
> Pictures become manifest from every stone;
> In its mirror behold the image of a flower garden.
>
> They have inlaid flowers of stone in the marble,
> What these lack in smell they make up with colour.
>
> Those red and yellow flowers that dispel the heart's grief
> are entirely [made] of carnelian (*ʿaqiq*) and amber (*kahruba*).
>
> When of such stones the surface of a tomb is made
> The deceased will [want to] clasp the flower pictures to
>   her heart.[117]

The surfaces of the screen and cenotaphs are covered with flowers, plants and flowery arabesques. The *pietra dura* flowers had to create more realistic images than the flowers carved in marble, and the designers again drew on illustrations in European herbals (pp. 218–21). But, true to the principle of selective naturalism, they too did not necessarily have to represent precise botanic species. Identifiable species [345] and imaginary 'naturalistic' flowers [117] intermingle in the decoration, the latter outnumbering the former. Red and yellow dominate in the colours. Red flowers have in Persian and Turkish poetry the connotation of blood and death (p. 140), which gives an additional funerary connotation to their main task to represent paradisiacal bloom. At the same time, even they follow Shahjahani principles, and appear in a strict system of formal relationships and symmetrical correspondences.

The decoration of the screen

Fanny Parks in 1835 'had the curiosity to count the number [of pieces] contained in one of the flowers [of the screen], and found there were seventy-two; there are fifty flowers of the same pattern'.[118]

The decoration is organized around the favourite Mughal border scheme of oblong cartouches alternating with squarish or round ones. On the uprights they are arranged in vertical bands. The oblong cartouches contain seven types of flowering plants (F–L) [234–240], among them one with poppy blossoms (L) and the ever-popular lily with curved-back petals, perhaps inspired by a martagon lily (F). Most of the plants have a form like candelabra, with a blossom at the top and two pairs of blossoms in reverse symmetry below. Two types – F and G – consist of a stem around which thin stalks with hanging blossoms twine. A bend in a stalk, stem or blossom may be used to set reverse symmetrical accents in the overall context.

The outer faces of all the uprights have sequences of two types of flowers alternating vertically [230]: these are F and G (inspired by columbine), except on the corner posts, which display H and I (with blossoms like honeysuckle). The inner faces [233] display another alternating pair – J and K – again except on the corner posts, which show only poppies, L. The sides of the doorposts, where they project above the top of the screen, have the same decoration as the inner faces (J and K).

On the outer faces, the cartouches in the horizontal framing elements at the top of the screen contain scroll compositions with chrysanthemum- or lotus-like flowers in the centre and a spray of three miniature tulips on each side. The solid 'vase' elements of the *kanguras* above show two alternating types of plant standing on little hills [240]: one has a stem that grows out of a single serrated leaf, and a large blossom, surmounted from behind by a smaller opening bud (M); the other has a stem that grows out of two leaves, and a blossom formed of a single upstanding calyx, the five petals of which intertwine with four stamens (N). On the inner faces, the horizontal elements show a horizontally expanding spray with seven flowers of type I, while the vase elements of the *kanguras* show a variant of the flowers on their outer faces, this time with three blossoms, O.

The decoration of the upper cenotaph of Mumtaz Mahal

The cenotaph of Mumtaz [233, 241, 350], dated 1632 in an epigraph, is less affected by Shahjahani flower mania than the screen and the cenotaph of the emperor, both of which came later. The main decoration consists of inlaid Qur'anic inscriptions. Naturalistic plants are confined to the platform, where two types alternate, between borders of hanging blossoms: one has asymmetrically arranged erect funnel-shaped calyxes and buds (P) [117], the other a perfectly symmetrical arrangement of seven smaller blossoms and buds (Q); both seem to be inspired by lilies. The upper surface of the platform has a framed flowery scrollwork pattern.

The oblong sarcophagus-like block is placed on a stepped base which displays registers of interlacing hanging flowers [241]. Inscribed on the top and the sides of the block are Quran'ic verses in formal *sulus* script [233, 350]; their common theme is to comfort the soul (of Mumtaz) with the prospect of Paradise. The programme begins at the north (head) end with the invocation, 'In the name of God, the Lord of Mercy, the Giver of Mercy, O Living O Eternal, I beseech Thy mercy! Said the Blessed and Great God', and continues with verse 30 of *sura* 41, *Ha Mim* or *al-Fussilat*, 'The Explanation': 'As for those who say, "Our Lord is God," and take

the straight path towards Him, the angels come down to them and say, "Have no fear or grief, but rejoice in the good news of Paradise, which you have been promised."' At the south (foot) end, in the lowest element of the plinth, is the epitaph, in small characters in the less formal *naskh* script, which reads: 'The illumined grave of Arjumand Banu Begam, entitled Mumtaz Mahal, who died in the year 1040 [AD 1631].'[119]

The decoration of the upper cenotaph of Shah Jahan

The cenotaph of the emperor, installed more than thirty years later, in 1666, is similar to that of Mumtaz in shape and decorative organization, but larger, and entirely covered with flowers and scrollwork without any formal inscriptions [233, 242, 243, 361, 362]. The only inscription is the epitaph, positioned like that of Mumtaz [244].

The decoration is distinguished by its use of identifiable and botanically quite accurate flowers. On the platform two types of flowering plant are set within cartouches formed of baluster arcades: double-tiered crown imperial (*Fritillaria imperialis*), a species that grows in the Himalaya region (R) [345],[120] alternates with a lily-derived plant with small star-shaped flowers and lanceolate leaves (S). All sides of the cenotaph block have tiny baluster arcades which contain a botanically accurate red poppy (T) alternating with a yellow flower with erect blossoms resembling lilies (U). The covering of the emperor's cenotaph with recognizable poppies might be intended to give heightened realism to red flowers as symbols of suffering and death. The poppy as a funerary flower on tombs was evoked by the Turkish poet Ahi (d. 1517):

> May the clouds undo their hair, may sighs reverberate
> like thunder,
> And until the Day of Judgment may poppies (*lala*) burn
> on my tomb.[121]

The top surface [243] shows a composition of unsurpassed refinement in the interaction of naturalistic plants, flowery scrolls and symbolic elements. The head panel displays a splendid sunburst, alluding to the solar symbolism which played an important role in the imperial ideology of Shah Jahan: he was a sun king in the Persian as well as in the Indian tradition (p. 69). In the larger section in the centre, the pen case is flanked by two mirror-symmetrical scrolls with delicate 'cornucopias' from which emerge ornately wrought flowers, among them again funerary poppies. The cornucopias symbolize abundance, and relate in meaning to the vases and *purna-ghata* – vases from which foliage emerges – of the dados. At the foot end a single large bushy plant with multiple red blossoms and buds and two types of botanically incompatible leaves – linear lanceolate and small serrated – (V) is set within delicate interlocking scrollwork enriched with miniature flowers and bunches of grapes, an imperial motif which also appears in the baldachin of the throne of Shah Jahan in the Red Fort at Delhi.[122]

The epitaph at the south end of the base [244] reads in *nasta'liq* script: 'This is the sacred grave of His Most Exalted Majesty, Dweller in Paradise (*Firdaus Ashiyani*), Second Lord of the Auspicious Conjunction (*Sahib-i Qiran-i Sani*), Shah Jahan, Padshah; may it ever be fragrant! The year 1076 [AD 1666].'[123]

K

Flowers on the screen

234–239 *above* On the uprights:
K, G ('columbine'), H, I
('honeysuckle'), J and L ('poppy').

240 *right* On an upright at the
level of the cresting, F ('lily'),
and on the cresting, M and N.
Detail of a Company drawing by
an Agra or Delhi artist for Maria,
Lady Nugent, *c.* 1812.

G   H   I   J   L

F   M   N

241 The east side of the upper cenotaph of Mumtaz Mahal: Company drawing by an
Agra or Delhi artist for Maria, Lady Nugent, *c.* 1812. The decoration includes flowers (on
the platform, P [117] and Q) and inscriptions from *sura* 83 of the Qur'an, verses 22–28.

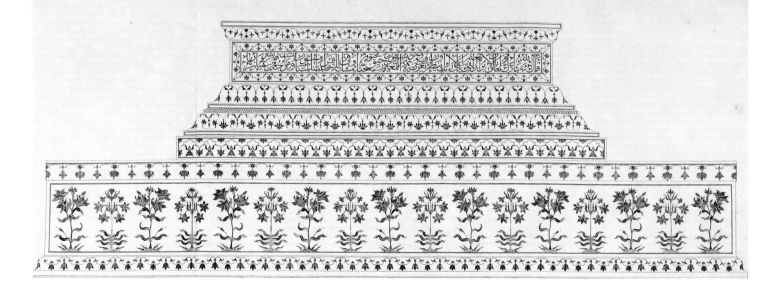

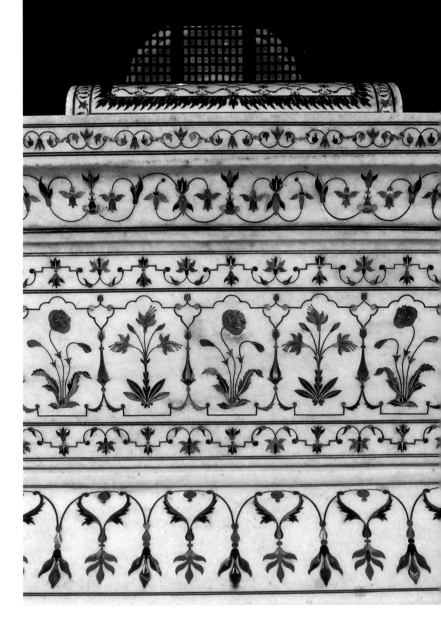

The decoration of the upper cenotaph of Shah Jahan

242 *above* Detail of the side, with the symbolic pencase at the top. The flowers are alternately poppies (T) and lily-like plants (U). (Photograph taken in 1992)

243 *left* The top: Company drawing by an Agra or Delhi artist for Maria, Lady Nugent, *c*.1812. The blank space represents the pencase, on a higher level.

244 *below* The epitaph: 'This is the sacred grave of His Most Exalted Majesty, Dweller in Paradise, Second Lord of the Auspicious Conjunction, Shah Jahan, Padshah; may it ever be fragrant! The year 1076 [AD 1666].'

From the southern entrance room a stairway covered with a pointed barrel vault leads down to the lower tomb chamber [245–247] (not accessible to visitors). The rectangular room is entirely faced with marble and has an undecorated coved ceiling. In the centre stand the two cenotaphs that cover the actual graves; they are similar to those above [233] but have different motifs in their decoration.

The lower cenotaph of Mumtaz Mahal has an almost undecorated platform. Its top is again covered with passages from the Qur'an, expressing related themes, promising God's mercy and forgiveness. On the sides are tiny cartouches containing the Ninety-Nine Beautiful Names of Allah, which express divine attributes (such as O King, O Holy, O Peace) and play an important part in private Muslim prayers.[124] The Ninety-Nine Names had been used on the upper cenotaph of Akbar at Sikandra, and in a similar arrangement to that of Mumtaz's also on the one of Jahangir at Lahore.[125] They appear again on the simpler cenotaph of Asaf Khan, the father of Mumtaz, also at Lahore (1641). This seems to be a Mughal peculiarity: otherwise they are not a frequent feature of cenotaphs and tombstones.

The entire south end of the sarcophagus element is occupied by the epitaph set within a cartouche. It is given more space than that on the upper cenotaph, but the words are the same.[126]

The lower cenotaph of Shah Jahan is also a more simply decorated version of his cenotaph above. The same flowers, namely poppies and plants with yellow lily-like blossoms, appear on the side walls of its sarcophagus element; they are however smaller, and set individually in tiny red cusped cartouches [349], reflecting the arrangement on the cenotaph of Mumtaz. The south end displays the epitaph, which is more comprehensive than the version on Shah Jahan's upper cenotaph [244]:

This is the illumined grave and sacred resting place of the emperor, dignified as Rizwan, residing in Eternity, His Majesty,

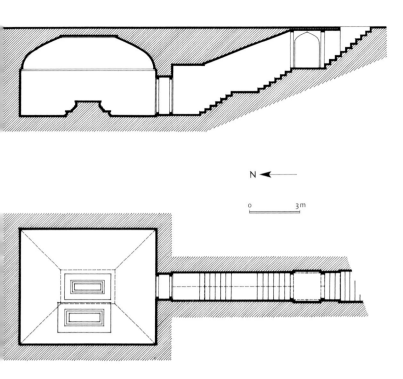

The lower tomb chamber

245 *opposite, above* Looking up the staircase that leads down from the entrance room, to the south [cf. 221]. All the staircases within the mausoleum have this form. (Photograph taken in 2001)

246 *opposite, below* The lower cenotaphs of Mumtaz Mahal (foreground, with offerings) and Shah Jahan. (Photograph taken in 1981)

247 *above* Section and plan.

having his abode in [the celestial realm of] ʿIlliyun, Dweller in Paradise (*Firdaus Ashiyani*) [posthumous title of Shah Jahan], the Second Sahib-i Qiran, Shah Jahan, Padshah Ghazi [Warrior for the Faith]; may it be sanctified and may Paradise become his abode. He travelled from this world to the banquet hall of eternity on the night of the twenty-sixth of the month of Rajab, in the year one thousand and seventy-six Hijri [31 January AD 1666].[127]

THE AMBULATORY ROOMS ('SHISH MAHAL')

The central tomb chamber is surrounded by ambulatory rooms on two storeys [220, 221, 252], which on all but the southern, entrance, side are separated from it by *jalis* filled with panes of glass [cf. 365] – whence the later name, 'Shish Mahal' ('Mirror Palace'). These rooms are not accessible to visitors. Cruciform rooms are set on the cardinal axes and octagonal ones on the diagonal axes. Each cruciform room [248] consists of a square chamber (*khana–i murabbaʿ*) extended by four arms, called *nashiman* by Lahauri and Kanbo, like their larger counterparts in the tomb chamber; the central space is covered by a sail vault between four pointed arches, the arms on the cardinal directions by deep pointed arches (which may also be read as short pointed barrel vaults), and the niches leading to the octagonal corner rooms by half-vaults. The octagonal rooms [250, 251] have eight niches, reflecting on a smaller scale the plan of the tomb chamber; their central space is domed, while the niches are covered with deep pointed arches.

248, 249 A corner of one of the cruciform rooms in the ground-floor ambulatory of the mausoleum, and a detail of its dado. *Above:* Flower types Y (similar to X, between two small flowers), X–W–X in a single panel (see below), and, in the opening to the *pishtaq* on the right, Z (loosely based on irises). *Below:* Types X (with bending stalks supporting pairs of blossoms except at the top, where one of each pair is left out so as to create reverse symmetry), W (botanically correct single-tiered *Fritillaria imperialis*), and X. (Photographs taken in 2002)

and carved with less refinement, and different flowers are represented. In the arms leading towards the octagonal corner rooms, the side walls display a tripartite group: a single-tiered *Fritillaria imperialis* with long stamens in the centre (W) is flanked by flowers with bending stalks supporting pairs of blossoms except at the top, where one of each pair is left out so as to create reverse symmetry (X); and the narrow sections flanking the doors have a similar plant, between two small flowers (Y). In the arms on the cardinal directions the dado panels have a flower loosely based on irises (Z). The corners of all the arms and niches are accentuated by engaged colonnettes, which demonstrate the progressive increase of plant decoration towards the interior: they are not as plain as the colonnettes of the *pishtaqs*, but not as intensely decorated with plants as the ones of the central hall. Their shafts and bases are plain, but they have an acanthus capital and stand on an element of doubled acanthus leaves.

In the ambulatory rooms, where marble is not used the walls and vaults are faced with plaster of a later date; it is possible that originally polished plaster (*chuna*) was employed, which in imperial buildings served as an alternative to marble. In the arms of the cruciform rooms, above the dado there are multi-cusped blind arches in plaster relief [248]. All the main vaults are faced with plaster *qalib kari*. The linking corridors are covered with coved ceilings, also faced with *qalib kari*.

The southern niches of the south-eastern and south-western octagonal corner rooms give access to angled staircases with fairly comfortable steps, covered by a pointed barrel vault, which lead to the upper floor. They are not accessible to visitors.

The upper floor corresponds in plan [252] to the ground floor [220], though the corner rooms are slightly larger. In construction it is less exactly built and less carefully finished. In this respect the mausoleum compares to its disadvantage with the great gate, where the greater complexity of the plan necessitated a careful execution on all levels. Here there are considerable variations

251 Octagonal corner room on the upper floor of the mausoleum. (Photograph taken in 1999)

250 The south-eastern octagonal corner room in the ground-floor ambulatory of the mausoleum. Only the dados and door frames are faced with marble; the walls and the vault are plastered. (Photograph taken in 1981)

The ground-floor ambulatory rooms are more simply decorated than the tomb chamber, and the octagonal rooms [250, 251] are given less attention than the cruciform ones [248, 249]. Marble is used only for the floors, for the dados, as lining of the arches of the cruciform rooms, and for all door frames. The floors of the octagonal rooms are based on that of the tomb chamber but without a border; the remaining rooms are paved with square slabs. The dados of the octagonal rooms are plain and surrounded by an interlocking leafy relief pattern set off by a margin with a yellow stripe framed by black stripes.

The dados of the cruciform rooms show individual flowering plants carved in low relief, surrounded by an inlaid border [248, 249]. They conform in arrangement and stylistic treatment to the flowers in the dados of the *pishtaqs* [225, 226], but they are somewhat stiffer

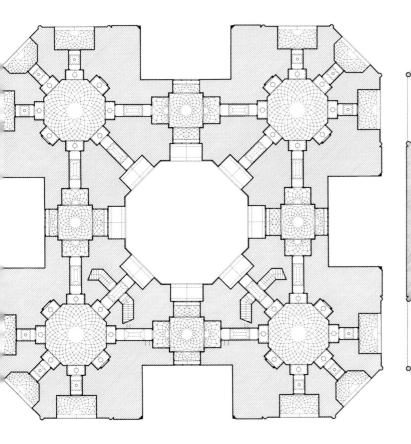

252 Plan of the upper floor of the mausoleum. It repeats the ground plan [220], but is less precise in execution.

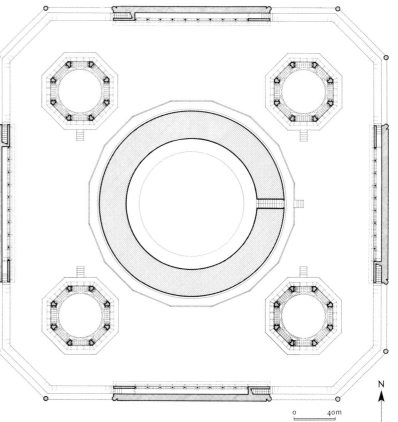

N

0   40m

253 Plan of the roof level of the mausoleum. In the centre is the dome, its drum pierced by a passage on the east. In the corners are four *chhatris*, and in the cardinal directions the tops of the four *pishtaqs*.

in the dimensions of the rooms, and no marble is used except in the niches that can be seen from the tomb chamber and from the exterior. Elsewhere the walls are faced with ordinary plaster of a later date, which gives a rather shoddy appearance [251] in stark contrast to the splendour of the hall within. Another main difference from the ground floor is in the treatment of the subsidiary vaults in the ambulatory rooms, all of which are faced with *qalib kari*.

THE ROOF TERRACE AND DOME

Staircases covered by pointed barrel vaults [cf. 185] lead from the ground floor to roof level. On the upper floor they set out from the corridors between the central hall and the two southern corner rooms, and emerge at the sides of the east and west *pishtaqs*. As in the great gate, there is a system of ventilation shafts.

Again as at the gate [186], the roof terrace is an architectural space on its own where the main elements of the plan are given freestanding individual expression [253–257], and where they become points from which to view the surrounding architecture and the landscape below, providing unforgettable vistas of the garden, the mosque, the Mihman Khana, and the sites of the Mughal gardens on the banks of the Yamuna up to the Agra fort [e.g. 261, 299].

The terrace is dominated by the outer dome, which rises with its high drum like an independent tower in the centre. The transition zone between drum and dome is ornamented with a moulding with

a twisted rope design in inlay, set between bands displaying inlay patterns; most prominent is the band above the moulding, which consists of arches the apexes of which are connected by inwardly bent stems to a hanging flower. The dome itself has a slightly bulbous profile which Lahauri and Kanbo called *amrudi-shakl*, 'guava-shaped', and which has been interpreted as a Deccani adaption of Timurid prototypes.[128] At its top is a crowning element formed of lotus leaves, which had become a standard motif of Indian Islamic architecture. From this rises a finial (*kalasha*) formed of superimposed gilded bulbs topped by a crescent. The pinnacle was regilded in 1874 by J. W. Alexander, Executive Engineer of the Public Works Department: he found, cut into it, an inscription by the first British restorer of the Taj Mahal – 'Joseph Taylor 1811' (p. 251). A silhouette of the pinnacle can be found in the paving of the riverfront terrace below, in front of the Mihman Khana [263].

The interior of the dome can be reached through a door in the eastern side of the drum. There one finds a hollow space between the outer shell, constructed of bricks and cement, and the floor rising in a curve that corresponds to the apex of the inner dome below [218, 221]. No other opening provides light and air to this dark and some-what mysterious interior, which is inhabited by swarms of bats.

The dome is surrounded by four *chhatris* which, as the Mughal historians tell us explicitly, form the third floor of the octagonal corner chambers, in the shape of octagonal pillared domed structures (*iwani musamman gunbadi saqf*) [221]. This demonstrates how closely the elements of the ground floor are related to the

254 *opposite* The roof level of the mausoleum, seen from a minaret. Here each part of the ground plan is represented as a freestanding element – the dome above the tomb chamber, the *chhatris* above the octagonal corner rooms, and the rectangular galleries on the inner face of the *pishtaqs*. (Photograph taken in 1992)

elevation. The arcades of the *chhatris* consist of multi-cusped arches supported on piers flanked by Shahjahani half-columns. Their inner marble domes rise from sixteen arches, the apexes and 'pendentives' of which are woven into a netted zigzag line pattern, forming the baseline of the dome [255]. This type of vault is found in most of the *chhatris* of the Taj complex. The whole pavilion-like structure sits on an octagonal plinth of red sandstone.

The roof terrace is surrounded between the *pishtaqs* by a high parapet, and its corners are accentuated by the *guldastas* terminating the shafts on the corners of the mausoleum.

The part of each *pishtaq* that extends above the roof forms a very narrow arcaded gallery with nine arches supported by Shahjahani columns [256], topped by a narrow walkway marked by *guldastas* at its ends [257]. Both galleries can be reached by stairs, and the highest level – regrettably, like all the mausoleum except for the ground floor, not accessible to the general visitor – provides the fullest view onto the surroundings of the mausoleum. In contrast to the *pishtaqs'* outer facing with marble, their inner face is built entirely of sandstone. Whether these parts were originally faced with *chuna* is a matter of debate (p. 95, n. 68); before its plastering in 1999 the red sandstone formed an attractive, and probably deliberate, contrast.

255 Looking up into one of the *chhatris* on the roof, in the form of an octagonal pavilion with multi-cusped arches and voluted brackets of a type used throughout the complex. (Photograph taken in 1996)

256 *below left* The gallery on the inner face of the west *pishtaq*, which frames one side of the roof-level terrace. Faceted Shahjahani columns support multi-cusped arches. The ends are accented by *guldastas*. (Photograph taken in 1981)

257 *below right* The walkway set into the top of the *pishtaq*, looking towards the point where the stairs come up from the gallery. (Photograph taken in 1996)

The minarets
(*minar*)

Four minarets are set at the corners of the platform of the mausoleum and complete the architectural composition [e.g. 135]. That platform, mausoleum and minarets form a whole is underlined by their exclusive facing with marble [333]. The minarets create a special aura around the mausoleum, and the Mughals interpreted them as mediators to the upper sphere. For Lahauri they were 'like ladders to the foot of the sky' and to Kanbo they appeared as 'accepted prayers from the heart of a pure person which have risen to heaven'.[129] (Later observers were more critical: pp. 244, 246.)

Minarets were not used by the Mughals for mosques or mausoleums until the 17th century. They were introduced only some twenty years before the Taj Mahal, in the mausoleum of Akbar at Sikandra; the four minarets on the roof of the southern gate there [169] are a close forerunner of the grouping at the Taj, but they are not yet freestanding.[130] The towers at the four corners of the tomb of Iᶜtimad-ud-Daula [60] reflect the idea. The source of inspiration seems to have come from Timurid, Deccani, or to an even greater extent Ottoman architecture, where the centrally planned mosques of the sultans of the 16th and 17th centuries were surrounded by minarets, their number indicating the rank of the mosque.[131] Under Shah Jahan minarets became a frequent feature: since they were considered as an architectural symbol of Islam, they may be seen as an expression of his increasingly orthodox attitude towards religion.

The overall shape of the minarets of the Taj is true to the specific Mughal type, but their facing and decoration are unique. They have a tapering cylindrical shaft set on an octagonal base, encircled by three balconies, and topped by a *chhatri*[132] with a *kalasha* finial [258]. Their exterior is formed of curved marble blocks, the joints of which

258 *right* The south-western minaret, seen from the south-eastern minaret. Beyond it lies the mosque. (Photograph taken in 2001)

259 *below* Detail of a balcony of the south-western minaret. It is supported by brackets ending in buds; note the pronounced three-dimensional treatment of the plant ornament. (Photograph taken in 2001)

are lined with black stone intarsia which creates the effect of rustication. The walls of the narrow winding staircase inside are built up with curved rough sandstone blocks which present a strong contrast to the neatly finished outer face. The staircase opens through rectangular doors onto the balconies, and windows provide light and ventilation. Although these are covered with grilles, the interior is full of bats, which makes the ascent difficult because they react with hysteria to a person's entrance. The minarets are now not open to visitors, but this was not always the case, and the *chhatris* are covered with inscriptions reaching back to the early 19th century. Maria, Lady Nugent, admits in her diary in 1812 to have left her name 'at the top of one of the minarets' (p. 238).[133]

The balconies (the railings of which are dangerously low) are supported by voluted brackets ending in hanging buds [259], another instance of the new organic vocabulary of Shah Jahan which is concentrated in the mausoleum and its flanking buildings. A direct reference to the mausoleum is the inlaid band below the balconies, which shows the same pattern as the lower band topping the main body of the tomb [224].

Investigations by the Geodetic and Research Branch of the Survey of India undertaken in 1984 showed that the minarets are slightly tilted outward, and it was assumed that this was for structural reasons, to protect the mausoleum in case one should collapse,[134] but it could have also be done for optical effect. The tilt of the minarets has recently been 'rediscovered', giving rise to alarm stories.[135]

The mosque and Mihman Khana, or assembly hall

The mosque on the west (left, when seen from the garden) and the Mihman Khana or assembly hall on the east are the complementary elements of the riverfront ensemble [205, 356]. The mausoleum is the dominant and unique feature in the centre of the tripartite composition of the *qarina* scheme, and the lateral buildings, exactly alike, are the mirror-symmetrical components. Still, the mosque [260] sets the tone, and as a religious building gives the riverfront group additional gravity. It is distinguished by a few elements related to the prayer ritual and the sermon. The Mihman Khana (literally 'guest house') [262] was created as its replica solely to balance the group, to provide a *jawab*, an answer, for the mosque. Its original function was to accommodate visitors, and it is likely that the celebrations of the death anniversaries of Mumtaz (pp. 97–99), held in the first years in tents, took place in this building once it was completed. This function had been forgotten by the late 18th and 19th century, when local people and discerning Western observers criticized its use by British officials and Indian princes for banquets to entertain visitors (p. 241).

Neither building stands alone: each forms the central accent in a composition which is in itself organized in a sub-tripartite system [264]. Central building and flanking wings terminating in towers set off the ends of the riverfront terrace, and give it the effect of a piazza around the mausoleum. Both mosque and Mihman Khana are preceded by a large platform or *chabutra*, 64 cm (25 in.) above the level of the terrace. On each side, the area between these platforms and the mausoleum is articulated as a shallow sunken rectangular 'court'. Here on the central axis, surrounded by a raised platform,

is a tank (*hauz*) with lobed corners which contains five marble fountains [261]. The tank is a ritual requirement of the mosque for the ablutions before prayer. (The tank of the Mihman Khana is a counter-image without any specific function.) The riverfront terrace thus integrates the elements and the function of a mosque courtyard (*sahn*): that it does so with minimal means is especially pointed out by Lahauri.[136] All the areas are differentiated by their paving in varying geometrical patterns of dark and light sandstone [337:e,f].

The Mihman Khana and its platform have two 'working drawings' scratched into their stone slabs. These are often found in buildings of Shah Jahan. One is in the floor of the central bay: it is not possible to make out which part of the building it relates to. The other, in the northern part of the platform, shows the silhouette of the finial of the dome of the mausoleum [263]. In 1888 the shape was infilled with black marble inlay on the orders of the British Magistrate at Agra, F. Baker.[137]

EXTERIOR

The mosque [260] establishes the form that the Mihman Khana [262] follows. It is based on a standard type which the Mughals took over from the Sultanate architecture of Delhi, namely that of an oblong massive prayer hall formed of vaulted bays or rooms arranged in a row with a dominant central *pishtaq* and domes. The elevation of mosque and Mihman Khana takes its cue from the great gate [351], the third monumental subsidiary building of the funerary garden (their relationship is also announced on the overall plan [149], where they form the points of a compositional triangle).

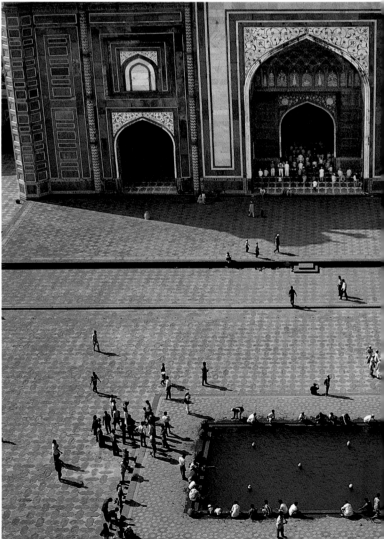

260 *left, above* The mosque.
(Photograph taken in 1978)

261 *left, below* The platform and court
of the mosque, with the ablution
tank, seen from the roof of the
mausoleum. The tank is surrounded
by men washing before prayer.
(Photograph taken in 1996)

262 *above* Moonrise over the Mihman
Khana. (Photograph taken in 1981)

263 *right* Looking down from the
south-west *chhatri* of the Mihman
Khana (right, in the image above) to
the pattern of the finial of the dome
of the mausoleum inlaid in the
platform. (Photograph taken in 1999)

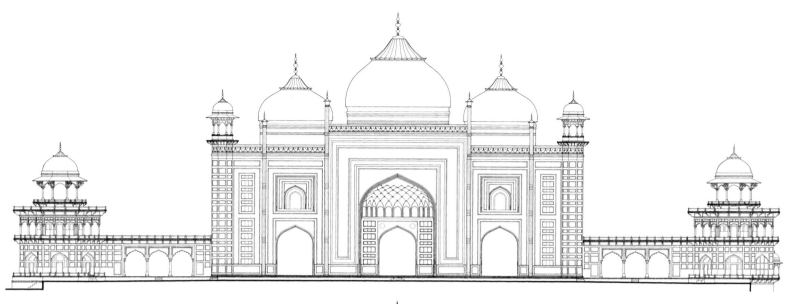

264 *above* Elevation of the mosque with its flanking wings and terminal towers.

265 Longitudinal section of the mosque.

266 Ground plan of the mosque. The three domed halls have half-octagonal vaulted *mihrab* niches in the back wall.

N

N

o   6m

267 Ground plan of the Mihman Khana. Here there are rectangular arched niches instead of *mihrabs*.

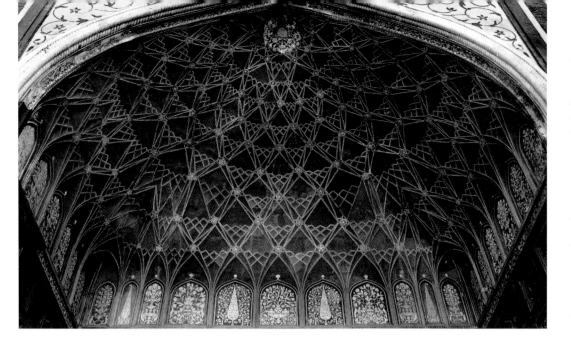

268 Vault of the *pishtaq* of the mosque, with *qalib kari* decoration. In the central arch a bowl supports a vase flanked by two miniature depictions of the mausoleum. (Photograph taken in 2001)

269 *below* Roof level of the Mihman Khana, looking north. The drums of the domes display a geometrical pattern in red sandstone and white marble similar to that of the platforms of the garden-wall pavilions [337:c]. (Photograph taken in 1999)

A large *pishtaq* is flanked by the standard superimposed niches, though those of the upper storey are blind. As in the gate, we find a similar focusing of marble and intensity of ornamentation in the centre of the façade, lessening towards the ends. The corners are emphasized by engaged towers topped by *chhatris* which read as a lesser form of minarets. The *pishtaq* has a half-vault faced with *qalib kari* [268], the only instance here of a feature employed extensively in the mausoleum and gate; below the vault, the arched panels of the transition zone – heavily restored – show symmetrically arranged flower vases on pedestals, cypresses entangled by blossoming creepers, and flowering plants, all motifs relating to the decorative programme of the mausoleum; at the mosque the panels include additional designs, such as tiny replicas of the mausoleum.

The three white marble domes are a specific mosque feature; that they are repeated in the Mihman Khana demonstrates the preference for symmetrical correspondence over the religious significance of forms. All the domes sit on drums decorated with a striking interlocking red and white inlay pattern [269], a variant of the paving of the platform of the garden-wall pavilions [337:c], topped by an inlaid band of hanging flowers and an inlaid rope moulding.

Other decorative features relate to the mausoleum and the great gate. Rope moulding appears around the arches, and also, in a mannerist transferral to another context, around the rectangular wall fields on the façades, a feature which occurs also on the side elevations of the gate. The walls are covered with the usual multi-cusped blind arches, and the dados are surrounded by an inlaid chevron pattern, a 'wave design' (*tarh-i mauj*), as Lahauri calls it, of black and white marble.[138] The same pattern appears on the engaged shafts terminating in *guldastas* that accent the façades [263].

The upper levels of mosque and Mihman Khana are not accessible to visitors. They offer impressive views of the mausoleum and the surrounding riverscape, and would also be the place to study the wildlife of the Taj Mahal, because besides the unavoidable bats they are frequented by parrots, pigeons, and hawks that hunt the pigeons. Occasionally also the mongooses who live in the area of the garden near the Mihman Khana make their way up to the roof.

INTERIOR

In their interiors, the mosque again set the pattern for the Mihman Khana, though as we shall see there are differences. In accordance with the all-permeating tripartite scheme of the Taj Mahal complex, the mosque has three domed bays. Lahauri uses the expression 'masjid . . . sih chashma'.[139] The bays or *chashmas* are of hall-like dimensions, and made cruciform by arched recesses. The central hall is the largest – a hierarchical grouping that is reflected outside by the dominant central dome flanked by two smaller ones. To enrich the design, the central *pishtaq* is deepened, which allows the insertion of flanking rooms connected by linking passages, doubling the row of rooms of the prayer hall proper. This doubling in the plan was taken up in several later mosques, first the Jami[c] Masjid of Agra sponsored by Jahanara and then Shah Jahan's great Jami[c] Masjid at Delhi.

The three main halls are covered by domes; the rooms at the front by coved ceilings, or more accurately by truncated domical vaults; and the linking passages with pointed barrel vaults. Four staircases lead up from points near the ends of each building – the two at the back up to the roof, the two at the front up to the roofs of the side wings, and from there to the upper level of the corner towers.

Each of the three domes rests on a transitional zone of four arches and four squinches; the resulting eight pendentives are covered with a decorative network of ribs [271]. The arches between the squinches are faced with the chief wall ornament of the Taj, multi-cusped blind arches; the squinches are filled with *muqarnas*, otherwise found only in the baseline of the dome of the mausoleum.

The domes themselves are covered with a diaper pattern; each central dome is more densely patterned, creating a whirling effect. The dome of the mosque is more densely patterned than that of the Mihman Khana, but in both cases a medallion in the apex is filled with an even more dynamic whirling pattern.

The arches flanking the main hall and their linking passages are covered with several designs of ornamental cartouches and interlacing floral scrolls, arranged in symmetrical correspondences [272]. The pattern that appears on the arches of the 'arms' of the main hall is made of a net of cartouches formed of arches supported on balusters, housing small flowers. The baluster column, even in a miniature expression, was a mark of special distinction (p. 104); the same motif appears, expressed more sophisticatedly in *pietra dura*, on the upper cenotaph of Shah Jahan [242]. Such designs here point towards the late 1630s and 1640s, when the new imperial plant ornament had established itself more widely.

270 *below* The mosque during noon prayers (Photograph taken in 2001)

opposite
271 *above* One of the side domes of the Mihman Khana. (Photograph taken in 1999)

272 *below* Arches in the mosque between the central hall (right) and side hall. (Photograph taken in 1995)

overleaf
273 The northern arch of the mosque, set off as an imperial prayer space by a marble railing. (Photograph taken in 1995)

274 The northern bay of the Mihman Khana, with coved ceiling, seen from the south. (Photograph taken in 1995)

The decoration of the domes and other vaults, and of the greater part of the walls, appears as white patterns on the red surface. The designs are however not created with marble inlaid in red sandstone, as elsewhere in the Taj complex, but with a sgraffito technique: a coat of red plaster is laid over a white one, then the top coat is cut away to expose the desired design in the white layer underneath. This technique appears only in the mosque and Mihman Khana. Another departure is that the vaults are built up with smooth curved stone slabs and given their pseudo-structural decor in sgraffito.[140]

Several features are found only in the mosque. Most important are the polygonal *mihrab* niches in the back wall of each of the three bays [266, 270, 276]. A *mihrab*, usually an arched niche, is an obligatory element to indicate the *qibla*, the direction of prayer, which is Mecca, the most holy city of Islam. In accordance with the triadic hierarchy of the Taj, the *mihrab* of the largest central bay is given special attention [272]: its polygonal niche and arched back wall are faced with marble and surrounded by Timurid rope mouldings resting on engaged colonnettes, as well by an inscription band inlaid with verses of *sura* 91, *al-Shams*, 'The Sun'; and within the arch is set a simple marble *minbar* (a pulpit for the imam to deliver the Friday sermon) of three steps. *Mihrab* and *minbar* reflect the colours and ornamental features of the mausoleum, in the white marble, the *qalib kari* of the vaults, and the white, black and yellow chevron band surrounding the dados. Also peculiar to the mosque is the floor, inlaid with a pattern of prayer mats to create individual spaces for the believers when calling their prayers. And the mosque is again alone in having a *maqsura*, a secluded compartment for the emperor, in a space set off within the northern arch of the northern bay by means of a beautiful marble screen formed of three-dimensionally carved baluster-shaped blossoms and buds [273]. The use of baluster elements for this space confirms its imperial connotation.

The Mihman Khana has no *mihrabs* in its back walls (instead there are rectangular niches [267]), no inscriptions, no *minbar*, and its floor is paved with a random pattern of sandstone flagging.

Floral decoration

All the dados inside as well as out have a display of flowering plants that recall their marble counterparts in the mausoleum; but since the sandstone is more susceptible to corrosion, they are not as well preserved, and many have been replaced by carved copies [275–295].

The floral decoration is more complex than that of the mausoleum, and a range of new species appears. Only two types of flowers of the dados of the mausoleum are repeated here, Y and Z [248]. Both occur in hierarchically prominent places: Y in the central niche of the Mihman Khana [278–295:14] and flanking the side *mihrabs* of the mosque [276], and Z within those *mihrabs* [276].

While in the mausoleum the flowers symbolized the eternally blooming gardens for the enjoyment of Mumtaz, they have an additional connotation in the mosque. Flowers and plants were a form of decoration specially sanctioned by Islamic theologians and were thus particularly appropriate for a religious building.[141] The five sides of the polygonal niche of the central *mihrab* are faced with plain white marble panels, but the dados of the side *mihrabs* [276], in red sandstone, are decorated with symmetrically arranged flowers, two of which as we have seen occur also in the mausoleum. Otherwise the floral system corresponds to that of the Mihman Khana, though the flowers tend to be carved with less refinement.

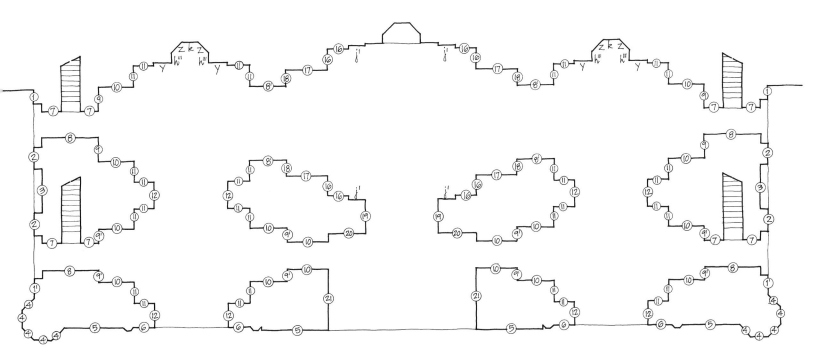

275, 276, 277 The flowers on the dados in the mosque appear in symmetrically arranged groups (indicated with figures) which are repeated according to their position in the architecture. They follow the same pattern as those in the Mihman Khana [see 278], except in the central and side *mihrabs* (where they are indicated with letters). (Photographs taken in 2004)

h''' simpler variant of h [see 278–295] with only one erect bud

k with iris-like blossoms and pairs of tear-shaped buds, flanked by tufts of three leaves on the same hill as the central plant

Y with bending stems supporting pairs of iris-like blossoms, between two small flowers (also in the cruciform rooms of the mausoleum [248])

Z loosely based on irises (also in the cruciform rooms of the mausoleum [248])

Y   h'''   Z   k   Z   h'''   Y   h'''

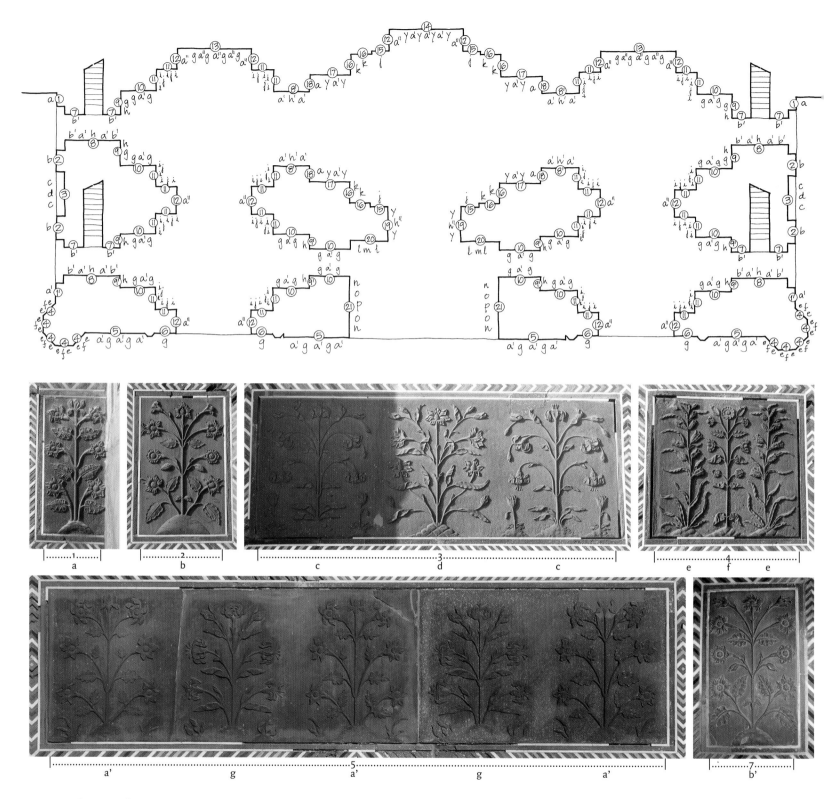

278–295 The flowers in the Mihman Khana (indicated with letters) appear on the dados in symmetrically arranged groups (indicated with figures) which are repeated according to their position in the architecture, as in the mosque. (Photographs taken in 2004)

a   plant topped by an iris blossom, below which are two pairs of anemone-inspired blossoms, the petals of the upper pair being arranged like a Catherine wheel; the pairs of blossoms alternate with two pairs of ribbed leaves; the main stem is flanked by another pair of blossoms and leaves on short stems

a'   variant of a with additional leaves on the flower stems, flanked by tufts of three leaves standing on their own tiny hills

a'' variant of a' with additional pendant buds

a''' identical to a'' except that buds here are open

b   with open blossoms and lobed petals and leaves

b'   variant of b with different blossoms flanking the top one

c   with pendant martagon-lily-like blossoms and pendant buds, flanked by two small tulips

d   with open blossoms and lanceolate leaves

e   elongated plant with tulip-shaped blossoms growing almost directly from the stem

f   elongated plant topped by a daisy-like blossom, with pairs of daisy-like blossoms and tulips in side view

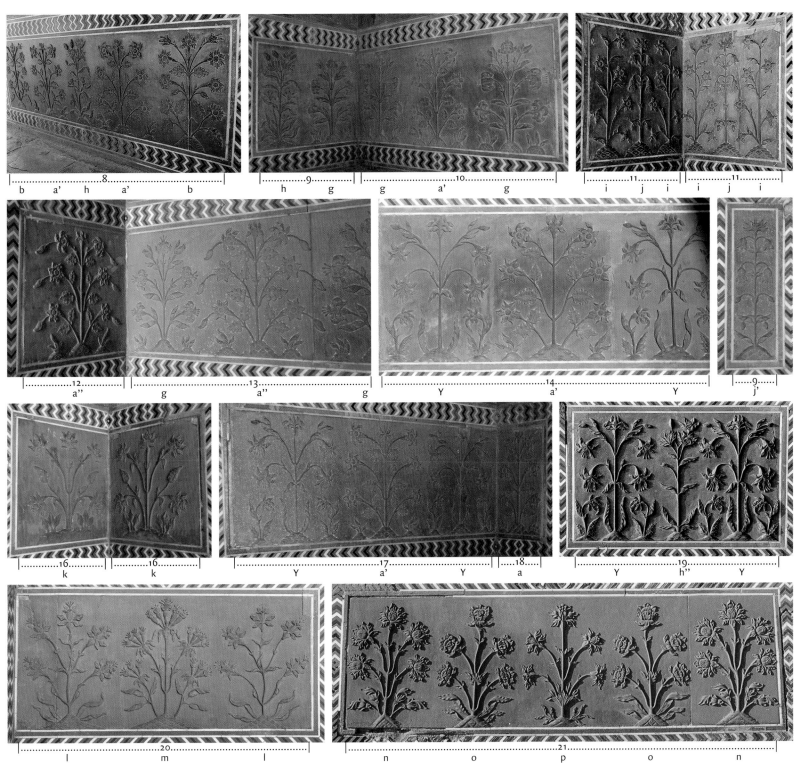

g   variant of c, of a more stocky structure and the paired blossoms not on drooping stems, flanked by tufts of three leaves on their own tiny hills

h   asymmetrical plant with lily blossoms, and two erect buds at the top

h' variant of h with an erect central bud flanked by two horizontal ones

h'' reduced variant of h with only one erect bud and no lower blossoms

h''' simpler variant of h with only one erect bud

i   elongated plant with open blossoms

j   elongated plant with iris-like blossom at the top and pairs of drooping buds

j' variant of j without buds, and with leafless tiny hills

k   plant with iris-like blossoms and pairs of tear-shaped buds, flanked by tufts of three leaves on the same hill as the central plant

l   plant with erect daffodil-like blossoms

m   plant with three separate stems carrying erect blossoms inspired by honeysuckle (similar blossoms appear as type I in *pietra dura* on the screen in the mausoleum [234–239], and in marble relief on the dados of the Diwan-i Khass in the Agra fort)

n   plant with rich open blossoms

o   plant with rich open blossoms, and leaves in the centre of the stem

p   variant of I

Y   plant with bending stems supporting pairs of iris-like blossoms, flanked by small flowers on individual hills (also seen in the cruciform rooms of the mausoleum [248])

296 Verandah of the southern wing of the mosque, looking towards its northern *hujra* and a side entrance to the mosque. (Photograph taken in 2000)

THE SIDE WINGS

The mosque and the Mihman Khana are flanked on both sides by tripartite *bait* units consisting, true to the Shahjahani system, of a triple-arched verandah flanked by two *hujras*, of which the outer ones provide access to the respective corner towers [264, 297–299].

The columns of the verandahs have bases with flower decoration [296], similar to those of the southern galleries [187, 188]. Over the doors to the *hujras* are arched panels filled with an unusual composition in sandstone relief of symmetrically arranged flowers and leaves growing out of interlacing stems.

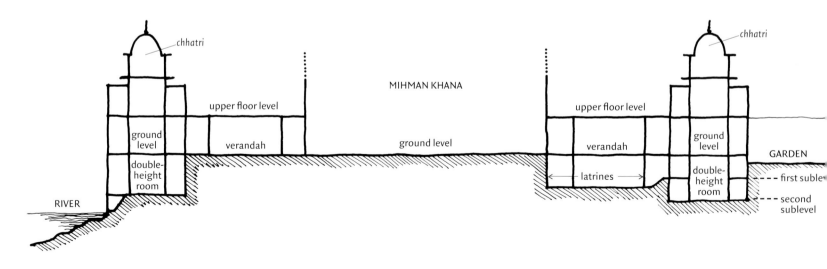

The towers of the riverfront terrace

The towers of the terrace [146:4a–4f, 74, 297–306, 333] are succinctly described by Lahauri: 'At the four corners of the terrace of red stone are placed four octagonal towers (burj) of three storeys, and the third storey has a domed roof. The inner shell of the dome (kulah-i gunbad) is of red sandstone, and the outside of white marble.'[142] There are two identical towers at the southern corners of the garden [156, 327]. They introduce into the funerary complex the type of the tower pavilion, a characteristic feature of the riverfront gardens of Agra [e.g. 32]. At the same time, their white marble cupolas echo the white cupolas and domes of the other buildings in the Taj garden, which all together create the impression of a floating level of domes among the trees.

Besides being indispensable accents of the architectural composition, the towers have a functional inner life: the one south of the mosque houses an elaborate well construction, a baoli [300–303]; the one south of the Mihman Khana contains chambers leading to latrines at a lower level [304]; and those to the north of both buildings have chambers at a lower level including a latrine (in the north-western tower), and stairs that lead down to exits in the river façade of the terrace [306]. (The towers are not open to visitors.)

All the towers have the same shape. They are regular octagons. Towards the terrace, they display the three storeys mentioned by Lahauri: their lowest storey has solid walls, above that is a storey with a surrounding gallery, and above that a chhatri [299]. Towards the outside, however, they show an additional basement storey [300]. In the case of the baoli tower there are two further subterranean levels [298].

The main floor has at its heart an octagonal domed chamber; from this eight octagonal rooms radiate, covered on the cardinal axes with coved ceilings and on the diagonal axes with small domes [303:d, 305:a]. In this way they form an octagonal variant of a hasht bihisht design, which reflects the plan of the mausoleum and the great gate in a different architectural context and on a smaller scale [cf. 149]. The surrounding rooms are connected by angled corridors so as to form an octagonal ambulatory. Towards the outside, each 'diagonal' room has a pointed opening, which with the exception of the entrance arch is typically screened with a jali, and each 'cardinal' room has a straight-headed door set in a panelled field enclosed by an arch. The walls are decorated with the usual multi-cusped blind arches and cartouches set in rectangular fields, outlined with white marble. Over each door is a panel with a naturalistic flowering plant in sandstone relief – a touch of prestigious imperial plant decoration to ennoble a peripheral component. Each terrace tower has an oriel window (jharoka) opening out from its main floor [74, 300], which provides views towards the river and the gardens outside (this feature does not appear in the towers at the southern corners of the garden).

The floor above the main level also has a central octagonal chamber. Here it is surrounded by a flat-roofed verandah, with on each face three multi-cusped arches on Shahjahani columns.

At the topmost level is the domed chhatri. Inside, this has a smooth sandstone dome set on arch netting over eight arches and eight squinches. The brackets over the eight columns which support the chhajja, or angled eaves, show the same composite form with a vase element – another floral touch in the decoration – as in the chhatris of the garden-wall pavilions [198].

Taken together, the two top storeys echo the form of the subsidiary tombs [e.g. 160].

The tower to the south of the mosque houses a baoli, or step well, built in red sandstone [146:4c, 300–303]. Elaborate underground well constructions with staircases and galleries are a characteristic

297, 298 *opposite and below* Schematic sections of the Mihman Khana and mosque, with their side wings and flanking towers The tower south of the mosque (*below*, left) contains a deep baoli, or step well [cf. 302].

overleaf
299 Part of the mosque, its northern wing, and the north-western riverfront tower, seen from the roof of the mausoleum. In the distance is the Agra fort, with the three marble domes of the Moti Masjid. Seasonal melon (*tarbuz*) is cultivated on the sandbanks. (Photograph taken in 1999)

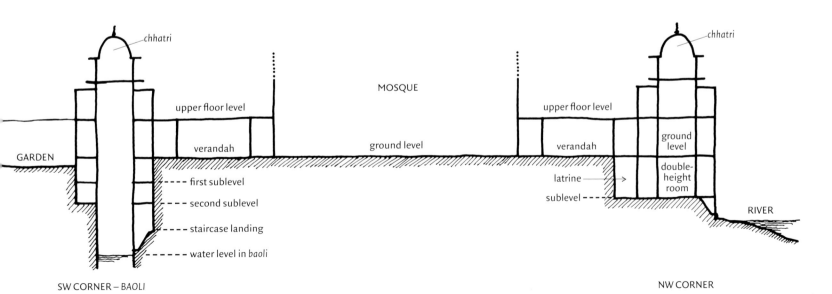

SW CORNER – BAOLI

NW CORNER

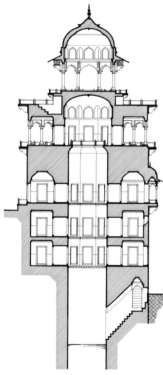

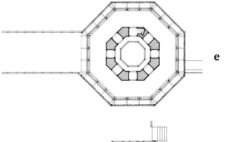

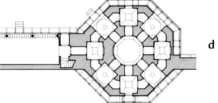

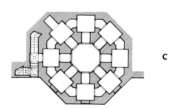

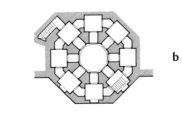

The *baoli* tower, south of the mosque

300 *above* The tower seen from outside the west wall. (Photograph taken in 2001)

301 *below* View up the well shaft. (Photograph taken in 2001)

302 *above* Section north–south.

303 *right* Plans (reading up) of (a) the lowest level, (b) the second sublevel, (c) the first sublevel, (d) the main floor, and (e) the upper floor. All main floors of the towers show an octagonal radially planned *hasht bihisht* design which is echoed in the sublevels.

N ←

0   5 m

e

d

c

b

a

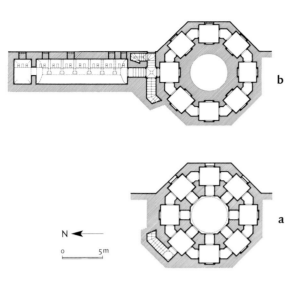

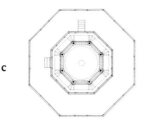

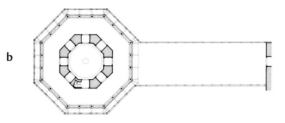

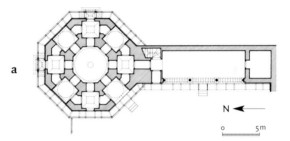

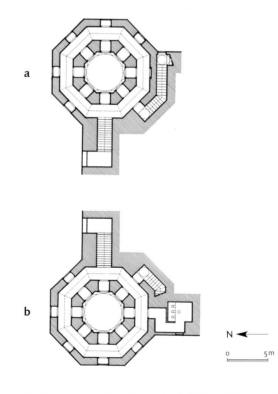

N ◄

0   5 m

304 *above* The tower south of the Mihman Khana: plans (reading up) of
(a) the lower sublevel and (b) the upper sublevel with latrine.

305 *right* The north-eastern riverfront tower, north of the Mihman Khana: plans
(reading up) of (a) the ground floor, (b) the upper floor, and (c) the roof level.

feature of Indian architecture throughout the centuries, and
were adopted by Muslim builders.[143] The Taj *baoli* provided water
independently of the waterworks outside the complex (p. 208). It
may also have had some symbolic connotation as a connection to
the underworld, or to the mythical figure of Khwaja Khizr (p. 33),
who is associated with wells, because according to Muslim lore
he found the water of life and gained immortality.

The *baoli* tower [298, 300–303] has the same shape as the other
towers, but below the octagonal chamber of the upper floor an open
well shaft, executed in simple undecorated forms, cuts through all
floors, taking the place of the inner chamber and descending to
three additional levels below ground. The first and second
correspond to the ground floor but are flat-roofed. At the lowest
level the shaft turns from octagonal to circular and runs deep into
the ground. A stairway reached from a door in the *hujra* of the wing
between the tower and the mosque leads down to the floors below
ground and to a landing above water level.

The tower to the south of the Mihman Khana [146:4d, 297, 304]
has two levels below the main floor: they take the form of ambulatory
rooms around a central octagonal chamber which extends through
both floors, being walled in on the upper. The upper level connects
with an oblong latrine room, placed under the verandah of the wing
linking the tower with the Mihman Khana. The latrines have a
continuous bench pierced with rectangular openings along the wall
[cf. 159]. The whole arrangement was reworked at some point.

The two towers next to the river have only one level below the
main floor, but it is as deep as the two lower levels of the latrine
tower [297, 298, 306]. Both have an octagonal room in the centre,
connected to a surrounding ambulatory by eight short passages.
In the north-western tower the ambulatory leads to a small latrine
room through a corridor with a double bend in it. From the lower
level of both towers stairs lead down inside to the now-walled-up
doors in the riverfront terrace (p. 147) [207].

306 The two riverfront towers, (a) north-east, by the Mihman Khana, and
(b) north-west, by the mosque: plans of the basement level, with stairs leading to
postern doors in the riverfront terrace, and, in the north-western tower, a latrine.

The bazaar and caravanserai complex
(Taj Ganj)

Having walked through the complex from south to north as the modern visitor does, from the Jilaukhana zone to the riverfront terrace, we must now go back to the area south of the Jilaukhana, and consider its layout.

Here we come to the bazaar and caravanserai complex, which originally formed an integral part of the Taj Mahal [144, 146:D]. It has been almost obliterated by the city quarter known as Taj Ganj, 'Taj Market' [148]. The visitor who steps out of the south gate or 'Sirhi Darwaza' does not realize that the narrow street ahead, lined with small shops trading in inlaid marble work and other souvenirs, was once the main bazaar street of the utilitarian complex [307, 310].

With its novel architecture, and the encouragement of imperial patronage, the complex set a new accent and became the main commercial centre of Agra. Lahauri and Kanbo tell us that 'different kinds of merchandise from every land, varieties of goods from every country, all sorts of luxuries of the time, and various kinds of necessities of civilization and comfortable living brought from all parts of the world' were bought and sold here. Outside the imperial commercial complex, merchants built substantial houses and their own caravanserais (called in Mughal India *sara'i*), so that the surrounding area became like another city, called Mumtazabad, the city of Mumtaz.[144] Kalim devotes twenty-six verses of his great poem on Agra to the bazaars of the city, giving us a glimpse of the attractions of the trading that went on there. He is conforming to the Persian poetic genre of the *shahr-ashub* ('disturber of the city'), 'with its playful inventories of the urban marketplace with all its commercial wealth and winsome shopkeepers':[145] typical of this genre is the fusing of the personal attractions of the merchant with those of his product, so that both arouse desire in the buyer's heart.

> The streets of its bazaars are heart-cheering,
> Craftsmen are engaged every day in the business of pleasure.
>
> An old man gets free of cost
> From these shops the merchandise of youth.
>
> From the shop of the druggist he can buy
> Health for the sick person instead of medicine.
>
> Among the beauties in its bazaars
> You will find a rosebush in blossom at every step.
>
> The fabric of the ravishing cloth merchant
> Is proud to be superior to fine Chinese silk. . . .
>
> Do not set your heart on the promise of a betel (*tanbul*) seller
> For there is nothing to be gained from him except grief.
>
> One cannot rely on their promises:
> Their job is to roll betel leaves.
>
> The moon-like jeweller, ravisher of one's senses –
> The jewel has become enslaved as his earring.
>
> Why should he care if his admirer is smitten?
> What is it to the pearl, if the oyster's breast is torn? . . .
>
> The handsome Rajputs and the descendants of shaikhs are such
> That the lovers have thrown patience to the wind.
>
> The Afghan [Pathan] youths present a good spectacle to
>   their admirers,
> One hand on their tresses and a dagger in the other.[146]

307 *opposite* The south gate, or 'Sirhi Darwaza'. The Jilaukhana lies beyond; in the foreground is the beginning of the main bazaar street. (Photograph taken in 1999)

308 *right* A betel (*pan*) seller preparing his wares, made of areca nut and lime rolled up in a betel leaf: Company drawing by a Panjabi artist from *Tashrih al-aqwam: An account of the origins and occupations of some of the sects and castes and tribes of India*, written for Colonel James Skinner, 1825.

309 *far right* One of the shops in the bazaar street south-west of the south gate. A vaulted verandah fronts an enclosed room, or *hujra*. (Photograph taken in 2002)

In the 1640s the bazaar and caravanserai complex is mentioned in various corrupt spellings such as 'Tage Gunge'[147] or 'Tadgundy', and praised as 'the chief place of the piece-goods [textiles cut in standard lengths] wanted by the English factors', but by the 1650s trading had already deteriorated.[148] It was however still functioning at a local level when the first colonial travellers arrived. In December 1794 P. F. Juvenal, by then the only priest remaining in the Catholic Mission at Agra, hired armed guards 'in Tagy Ghung' to accompany Thomas Twining to Delhi after he had visited the Taj Mahal[149] (p. 233).

Because the bazaar and caravanserai complex served commercial purposes its architecture was from the beginning treated with less respect than the formal part of the forecourt and garden, and over time it has been increasingly altered. At the beginning of the 20th century the original fabric had disintegrated to the extent that it was not recognized as historical architecture worthy to be preserved, and under Curzon it was even robbed of its bricks, which were used to rebuild the ruined wings of the Jilaukhana zone (p. 252).

Today no greater contrast to the formal architecture of the funerary garden and the forecourt of the Taj Mahal can be imagined than the agglomeration of haphazard constructions of Taj Ganj, built with and within the remains of Shah Jahan's architecture. A writer who undertook an analysis of tourist practices at the Taj was, like most people, not even aware of the fact that it formed part of the Taj Mahal; he noted: 'The area is a mixture of domestic dwellings, public offices and commercial establishments, and shops, hotels and restaurants serving the tourist trade. The small shops and stalls typical of urban India are here: sweet shops, bookbinders, pharmacies, tailors, cassette vendors.'[150] There is even a large buffalo stable in what was the north-eastern caravanserai [146:16b, 312], and the roofs and trees of the entire area are inhabited by a substantial monkey population which is inclined to attack foreign visitors to obtain edibles from their bags. The contrasting development of the formal and the utilitarian parts of the Taj Mahal is in keeping with a general dualistic aspect of South Asian cities.[151]

The Taj Ganj is inhabited by Hindus and Muslims and is also frequented by low-budget and backpack tourists. To cater for these travellers a number of cheap hotels and restaurants have been built which despite the narrow plots have several storeys so as to provide the desired view of the Taj Mahal. Here foreign visitors have a chance to intermingle with the local population, for which there is less occasion in the formal area of the monument.

While the tourists do not know that the Taj Ganj was originally part of the Taj Mahal, the local people living in it have an uneasy awareness that they encroach on forbidden historical ground. A judgment of the Indian High Court in 1996 (p. 252) ruled that no building must be raised within 200 m (some 220 yds) of the Taj Mahal – and even those who pronounced the judgment did not realize that this involved every modern building in Taj Ganj.

The original fabric of the complex survives only in fragments. It can however be reconstructed with the help of the descriptions of Lahauri and Kanbo, 18th- and early 19th-century plans [132, 147], and the surviving evidence. All tell us that beyond the southern wall of the forecourt was a large square divided into four quadrants by two

310 View from the south gate of the Jilaukhana southward down the axis of the bazaar and caravanserai complex. (Photograph taken in 1999)

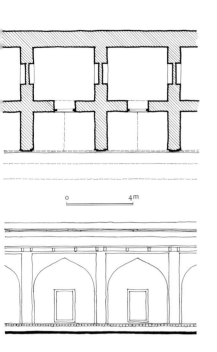

bazaar streets of unequal width [146:12c–12f,12d–12e] that crossed in the middle (charsu bazar).[152] In the quadrants, according to Lahauri and Kanbo, there were four caravanserais (sara'i), built of baked brick (khisht-i pukhta) and chuna, which indicates that they were faced with plaster or even with polished plaster (chuna). Their inner corners, at the crossing of the streets, were chamfered and pierced by a large gate [314–317]. Each had four wings around an open square, the two northern ones with chamfered corners forming an irregular octagon, or musamman baghdadi [146:16a–16d]. These wings contained 136 hujra rooms fronted by a verandah [311], which is the usual unit of which Mughal caravanserais and bazaars are composed. The surviving remains show that each hujra was roofed by a small dome, and that the verandahs were larger and much simpler than those in the bazaar of the Jilaukhana complex, with plain sections of wall supporting large pointed arches [313]. In the three outer corners of the caravanserais there were small open subcourts.

Lahauri and Kanbo describe the two northern caravanserais and point out that they were built by the imperial establishment (sarkar-i padshahi); of the southern ones they say only that they were the mirror image (qarina) of those to the north. This could mean that the southern pair was not financed by the emperor, since only structures sponsored by the emperor or the imperial family were described in detail. Despite the claim to qarina, even with what little evidence there is one notices differences in the architectural vocabulary. The gates of the southern pair of caravanserais were simpler, and the outer corners of their courtyards had no chamfer.

The central open space, or chauk, had the shape of a doubly irregular octagon [146:17], with four closed short sides (containing the gates of the caravanserais), two shorter open sides (where the north–south streets came in), and two longer open sides (where the wider east–west streets came in).

The architecture of the bazaar streets is not described by Lahauri and Kanbo, but the surviving fabric [309] indicates that they consisted of hujras and verandahs of the type used in the caravanserais [311, 313].

According to my survey undertaken since 1999, the chief remains of the bazaar and caravanserai complex are the four gates

The north-eastern caravanserai, Katra Fulel (Perfume Market)

311 *above left* Plan and elevation of two bays.

312 *above* Part of the site, now occupied by a buffalo stable. The wall separating the caravanserai from the Jilaukhana, to the north, would have been lined with a series of verandahs and *hujras* [cf. 311]. The white marble dome is that of the eastern subsidiary tomb. (Photograph taken in 1999)

313 Part of the east wing. The left-hand bay has been turned into a private house. The right-hand bay shows the original verandah-plus-*hujra* arrangement – of which the vaulting system can be made out in the ruined bay at the far right. Seated on the *charpa'i* (an Indian multifunctional bed) is Richard Barraud, preparing the sketch for the measurements of the plan and elevation [311]. (Photograph taken in 1999)

of the central *chauk* and the south gate, called 'Dakhnay Darwaza' [314–321]. The bazaar street leading from the south gate of the Jilaukhana, which formed the north–south axis, still exists, though narrowed, with modern shops and houses built into and in front of the original verandahs and *hujras* [307, 310]. The original fabric of three of these units on either side of the 'Sirhi Darwaza' was cleared by the Archaeological Survey of India in 2002 [309]. The *chauk* also survives, though only in an ill-defined, reduced form.

Since the early 18th century, when the Jaipur plan [17] was prepared, the north-western caravanserai has been known as Katra Omar Khan (Market of Omar Khan) [146:16a], the north-eastern one as Katra Fulel (Perfume Market) [146:16b], the south-western one as Katra Resham (Silk Market) [146:16c], and the south-eastern one as Katra Jogidas [146:16d]. The present quarters preserve these names. Their population consists of Hindus and Muslims, with the exception of the Katra Jogidas, where only Hindus live.

All four caravanserai gates are built of brick and faced with red sandstone. The gate of Omar Khan is best preserved [314, 315, 317:a] and allows one to reconstruct the appearance of the others. Towards the *chauk* each gate has a large pointed archway set in a rectangular frame; above the arch is a *chhajja*, and at the top is a row

314 *opposite, above* Gate leading from the central *chauk* to the north-western caravanserai, Katra Omar Khan. (Photograph taken in 1981)

315 *opposite, below* Passage within the gate leading to Katra Omar Khan. (Photograph taken in 1999)

316 *above* Gate leading from the *chauk* to the north-eastern caravanserai, Katra Fulel, seen from a neighbouring rooftop restaurant. In the distance are the great gate, the mausoleum and the Mihman Khana. (Photograph taken in 1999)

317 *right* Plans and elevations of the surviving fabric of the caravanserai gates opening from the *chauk*:
(a) north-west, Katra Omar Khan
(b) north-east, Katra Fulel
(c) south-east, Katra Jogidas
(d) south-west, Katra Resham

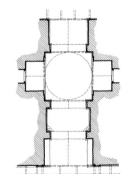
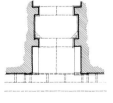

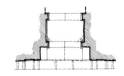

0   4m

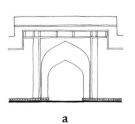
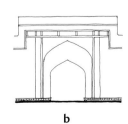
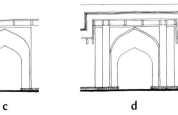

a   b   c   d

318 Gate of the south-western caravanserai, Katra Resham. (Photograph taken in 1999)

319 *below* Gate of the south-eastern caravanserai, Katra Jogidas. (Photograph taken in 1999)

320, 321 'Dakhnay Darwaza', the gate at the southern end of the north–south axis: view of the inner face, plan and elevation. Here the bazaar and caravanserai complex ended. (Photograph taken in 1999)

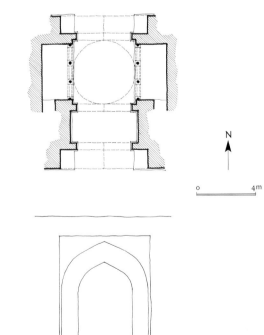

of *kanguras*, in the simple form of small pointed arches. In all the gates the entrance arch, or arched entrance niche, leads to a rectangular flat-roofed passage. The gates of the two northern caravanserais, however, were more elaborate than those to the south: there the passage led to a domed chamber with flanking niches (only preserved in Omar Khan [315, 317a] – where there are also remnants of the flanking caravanserai wings). This architectural distinction between the northern and southern pairs of gates tallies with the way Lahauri and Kanbo described the caravanserais.

The 'Dakhnay Darwaza', at the southern end of the north–south street, is the southernmost gate of the entire Taj Mahal complex [146:19, 320, 321]. It is similar in design to the gates of the northern caravanserais, with an additional elaboration: the niches flanking the domed chamber in the passage are set off with a tripartite arcade of multi-cusped arches and Shahjahani columns.

All the gates are protected by the Archaeological Survey of India.

The waterworks

The waterworks, which brought water to the Taj garden from the Yamuna by means of an aqueduct supported on arches, are situated outside its western wall and still preserve their original design [146:E, 322, 323]. The inlet from the river [72] is no longer visible (a temple complex dedicated to Shiva, now called Khan Alam Basai Ghat Mandir, has been built over it).[153] From it a channel conducted the water into an oblong reservoir sunk into the ground along the east wall of a rectangular building containing storage tanks (now ruined) [78, 366]. From the reservoir the water was lifted by means of animal hides attached to pulleys, or Persian wheels turned by bullocks, to tanks at the top of the building. This fed an open channel along the top of the aqueduct wall. The large aqueduct runs south, with two bends, up to the level of the western garden-wall pavilion. Here it turns east and forms a wider arm with three tanks on its top and meets the garden wall. The water was then conducted in a pipe through the wall and down to the level of the channels in the walkways of the garden. The wall is here 9.47 m (31 ft) tall, and the drop gave the water the necessary pressure to keep the fountains playing and the garden plots irrigated. The pipes were made of earthenware and copper and laid into the masonry of the walkways.[154]

The Mughal aqueduct, operated with manual pumps, was in use until 1903, when under Curzon the old earthenware conduits were replaced by cast-iron pipes and connected to the irrigation main from the reservoir of the MacDonnell Park, now Shah Jahan Park (p. 60).[155] Part of the present water supply still uses the tanks of the old aqueduct, which are filled from wells by electric pumps.

The arches of the wider arm of the aqueduct that runs west–east have been filled in to house offices for the Horticultural Department of the Archaeological Survey of India, which also uses the area west of the aqueduct extending into the garden of Khan ᶜAlam as a nursery.

322, 323 *above and below* The waterworks looking south, from the roof of the mosque, and north, from the roof of the western garden-wall pavilion looking back towards the mosque. From the raised tanks next to the pavilion a pipe leads through the wall to the garden. (Photographs taken in 2001 and 1999)

Buildings outside the wall

Three structures are situated outside the large rectangle of the Taj Mahal complex [146]: to the east is a tomb garden with an integrated mosque [324, 325], and to the west a tomb and a mosque [326–332].

Like the subsidiary tombs inside the Taj complex, the two tombs are known as 'Saheli Burj' ('Tower of the female friend'). Their form and style show that they were built after the main complex was completed. The structures are not mentioned by the historians of Shah Jahan, and they are not shown on the Jaipur plan of the 1720s [17], on that of the Daniells made in 1789 [147], or on the early 19th-century plan in Berlin [132]. The western tomb and mosque feature in the plan in the Taj Museum (p. 103) and in the Hodgson plan of 1828 [366]. The tombs were first written about in the early 19th century by women travellers, who were especially interested to explore the monuments dedicated to their gender.

THE OUTER EASTERN TOMB WITH THE 'SANDLI MASJID', ALSO CALLED 'KALI MASJID'

This small tomb complex is situated outside the south-eastern corner of the garden and can be reached from the east gate of the Jilaukhana [146:13c, 324, 325]. It lies north of the main office of the Horticultural Department of the Archaeological Survey of India. The identity of the person buried here is not known, but since the design is based on that of the subsidiary tombs inside the Taj complex [160] it was probably built for a female member of Shah Jahan's household.

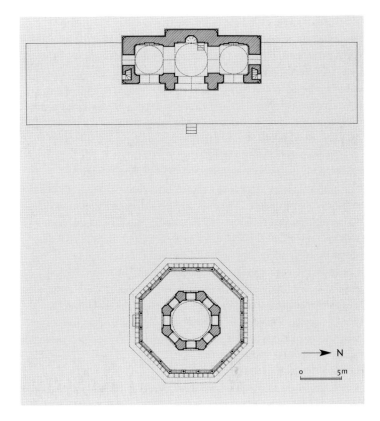

324, 325 The outer eastern tomb and 'Sandli Masjid': plan showing the two buildings and their relationship (*above*), and view of the tomb with the mosque beyond (photographed in 1995). When Fanny Parks saw the mosque, in 1835, it was of red sandstone with white marble domes. It is now plastered.

Florentia Sale called the building 'the Tomb of the Sirhinde Begum' and commented that when she saw it in 1832–33 it was 'much fallen to decay' and showed evidence of having been used as 'a Bakery', that it was very dirty, and seldom visited. She included a picture of it in her *Notebook*. When Fanny Parks saw it three years later she was shocked that a cowherd fed 'his cattle on the marble pavement within the tomb; and sacrilegious hands have picked out all the precious stones with which the white marble sarcophagus was inlaid'.[156]

The plan of the group is, like those of the inner subsidiary tombs, a miniature landlocked version of a riverfront garden, combining a *chahar bagh* with a rectangular terrace. It introduces a variation on the design, however, and demonstrates that after the main complex was finished, the builders of the Taj started playing with the concept of the riverfront garden. The tomb here is in the centre of the garden, and the building on the terrace is a small mosque. Only traces of the *chahar bagh* remain, but it can be reconstructed on the basis of the surviving evidence. The tomb is of the same octagonal pillared form as the subsidiary tombs. It has a marble cenotaph in its inner chamber which had *pietra dura* decoration, but most of the stones are missing and the design is only represented by the empty cavities. There is no inscription to enable the identification of the person buried.

The mosque, known as the 'Sandli Masjid' (Sandalwood Mosque) or 'Kali Masjid' (Black Mosque), is a simplified version of the type of the Taj mosque [260, 266] and Mihman Khana: it consists of three domed bays, of which the larger central one is preceded by a *pishtaq*. It was originally, according to Fanny Parks, of red sandstone 'ornamented with white marble, and surmounted by three white marble domes'. It is now covered by thick layers of plaster.

326 The Taj Mahal complex from the west, in a 19th-century photograph. Outside the wall, with a dark dome below that of the mausoleum, is the outer western tomb, of 'Fatehpuri Begam' [327]. Also outside, to the right, is the 'Fatehpuri Masjid' [329], seen from the back. (Inside the wall, from left to right, are the mosque, mausoleum, Mihman Khana, inner western tomb – sometimes identified as that of Fatehpuri Begam – and great gate.)

THE OUTER WESTERN TOMB (TOMB OF 'FATEHPURI BEGAM', PROBABLY THAT OF SATTI-UN-NISA KHANUM)

This tomb [146:20, 326–328] has been known as that of Fatehpuri Begam (one of the wives of Shah Jahan: p. 120), and the plan in the Taj Museum identifies it as that of 'Fatehpuri Mahal'. The Daniells' plan [147], however, identifies the western subsidiary tomb *inside* the main complex as hers; and this one is more likely to be the tomb of Satti-un-Nisa Khanum, the chief lady-in-waiting of Mumtaz Mahal. She was an Iranian from Mazandaran, the sister of Taliba Amuli, Jahangir's poet laureate, and herself well educated in Persian literature and an excellent reciter of the Qur'an. After the death of her husband she entered court service and became the close attendant of Mumtaz Mahal and the teacher of Princess Jahanara. When Mumtaz Mahal died Shah Jahan appointed Satti-un-Nisa Khanum to the superintendence of the administration of the female household, and she was one of those chosen to accompany Mumtaz's body from Burhanpur to Agra. The emperor held her in such high esteem that after her death in January 1647 at Lahore he had her body brought to Agra and, as Lahauri tells us, buried in

a tomb (*maqbara*) to the west of the illumined mausoleum (*rauza-i munauwara*) of Her Majesty the Most High Cradle (*Mahd-i ʿUlya*) [a title of Mumtaz], adjoining the square (*chauk*) of the Jilaukhana of the said mausoleum. The building was raised at a cost of 30,000 rupees from the emperor's exalted establishment. And a village with an income of 3,000 rupees was granted for the monthly payment of the keeper and the expenses necessary for the upkeep for the tomb.[157]

The situation indicated by Lahauri leaves room for interpretation: he could also be referring to the western subsidiary tomb inside the Taj complex; but since he clearly says 'to the west of the illumined mausoleum', a phrase that applied also to the entire Taj complex, the tomb outside is more likely. Another clue is that the outer western tomb is built entirely in red sandstone, with no ennobling facing of the dome with white marble. According to the colour

hierarchy of the Taj Mahal, this would indicate the burial of a person not as close to the emperor as one of his wives. The position outside the complex, and the 'colour coding', both point to Satti-un-Nisa Khanum.

The design is a variant of that of the tombs inside the complex, in a more compact form. The inner octagonal body is surrounded not by an arcaded gallery but by eight *pishtaqs*, separated by engaged shafts that terminate in freestanding *guldastas*. The setting too is different: the octagon is placed not in a garden but on a wide and low platform, in conformity with the type of platform tomb established in Jahangir's reign [cf. 59, 108].[158] The platform is surrounded by an arcaded gallery formed of basic Shahjahani columns and multi-cusped arches. The corners are solid and accentuated with *chhatris*, displaying thin elongated colonnettes, a form characteristic of later Shahjahani architecture. The upper surface of the platform, reached through a gate and stairs in the centre of the southern side, is surrounded by a low balustrade filled with *jalis*.

Inside, above a transition zone of eight shallow squinches alternating with eight arches, woven by ornamental netting into the baseline of the smooth dome, the dome itself is built up of curved sandstone slabs in Mughal bond (p. 96), as in the subsidiary tombs within the complex. The doors communicating with the *pishtaqs* are filled with geometrical *jalis* in the usual hexagon pattern. There are two female cenotaphs (characterized by a panel set into a multi-cusped arch topped by a medallion), the larger one in the centre. A staircase leads to the roof.

The outer western tomb, of 'Fatehpuri Begam', probably the tomb of Satti-un-Nisa Khanum

327 *above* View from the south. At the right is the south-western garden tower; in the distance, the mosque. (Photograph taken in 1977)

328 *below* Plan of the octagonal tomb on its plinth.

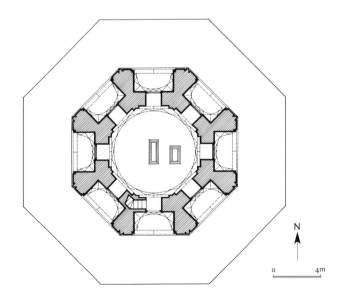

THE 'FATEHPURI MASJID'

The mosque [146:21, 326, 329–332] is situated south of the outer western tomb and is similar in style; but because of its extensive flower decoration in relief it seems to be of a slightly later date, the early 1650s, when the once exclusively imperial organic ornamental motifs had spread to a wider architectural context. No inscription tells us for whom it was built. The association with Fatehpuri Begam is based on tradition, and plausible, because she built a mosque of similar design at Delhi in 1650.[159] The Daniells' plan [147] identifies the western subsidiary tomb inside the main complex [146:13a] as hers, and the position of the mosque just outside would support that attribution.

The mosque stands on a platform which in its present state has on the northern side an extension towards the west. This is not visible in a 19th-century photograph [326], but appears on the Hodgson plan of 1828 [366]. At ground level, in front of its northern wall, is an ornamental sandstone pool which was restored under Curzon in 1904.[160] The platform is fronted by an arcade of Shahjahani columns, with capitals formed of acanthus leaves rather than *muqarnas*, evidence of the wider spread of imperial floral decoration. The oblong structure of the prayer hall, with four elongated *chhatris* on minaret-like towers at its corners, is set back on the platform, so that in front of it a courtyard is created which can be reached by steps on the east side.

The prayer hall represents a creative amalgamation of the two main mosque types of Shahjahani architecture – the formal type composed of bays separated by substantial walls pierced by arches, exemplified by the Taj mosque, and the lighter type with pillars or columns arranged on a grid plan, which was used for Shah Jahan's personal mosques, most magnificently the Moti Masjid in the Agra fort. A solid block with a *pishtaq* in the centre precedes the domed *mihrab* room; this massive element is flanked by open wings, where triple multi-cusped arcades demarcate bays covered with coved ceilings.

A novelty here is that Shahjahani columns replace the more compact pillars hitherto used in prayer halls on a grid plan. Their capitals are formed not of *muqarnas* but of lotus calyxes growing out of a narrow wreath of acanthus leaves, and their bases display small flower vases, reducing the status of what had been inside the mausoleum an élite, prestigious motif [121].

The decoration of the *pishtaq* vault and the main dome [331] transforms plant ornament of the type found in sgraffito technique in the mosque and Mihman Khana [272] into relief and further testifies to the spread of the once exclusive imperial plant ornament. *Qalib kari* was abandoned for plain surfaces or floral decoration. The half-vault of the *pishtaq* is carved with a baluster arcade supporting arches topped by lotus buds from which a trellis of cartouches is built up; all the arches and cartouches contain flowering plants. The main dome has pendentives covered not with netting but with cartouches filled with flowers [331]; its shell, again built up of curved sandstone slabs in Mughal bond, is covered with floral relief. The love of floral ornament is also expressed in the decorative crenellations that form the parapet of the roof of the prayer hall.

The Taj Mahal complex as a whole was built over a span of two decades, and the Fatehpuri Masjid displays the characteristics of the last phase of Shahjahani architecture.

The 'Fatehpuri Masjid'

329 *opposite* The mosque, seen with its courtyard from the south-east. (Photograph taken in 1978)

330 *right* Plan of the main level. It is a hybrid of the two main mosque types of the period: it takes the central configuration of a domed *mihrab* hall preceded by a *pishtaq* from the massive multi-bayed mosque, and combines this with lighter wings taken from the mosque based on multi-pillared halls.

331 *below, left* Detail of the central dome, with interlacing floral scrolls and cartouches carved in relief in the sandstone. (Photograph taken in 1977)

332 Interior of the prayer hall, formed of Shahjahani columns (with the new plant decoration on bases and capitals) and multi-cusped arches. The *mihrab* bay is the second on the left, where the stairs of the pulpit, or *minbar*, are visible. (Photograph taken in 1997)

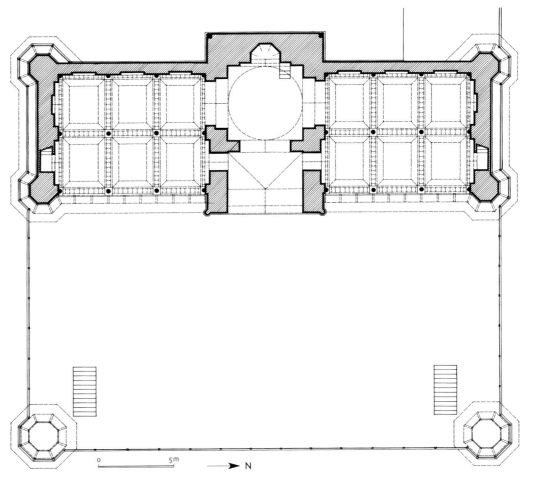

V The paradisiacal house of the queen

. . . the exalted mausoleum which imitates the gardens of Rizwan
[the guardian of Paradise], and gives an impression of the holy abodes . . .

ʿAbd-ul-Hamid Lahauri, *Padshahnama*, 1630s–54¹

For the Mughals the meaning of a building was as important as its form. The Taj Mahal was conceived in post-Platonic terms, which prevailed in the world-view of the Mughal court. The entire potential of Mughal architecture was put into the service of creating a replica here on earth of the paradisiacal house of Mumtaz. As a material expression of an otherworldly building it had to be realized in what Shah Jahan and his builders considered ideal architecture. The abstract planning was, however, clothed in a sensuous garment. The materials used in the facing of the buildings expressed symbolic values, and they also evoked emotions by interacting with the atmosphere; and the aesthetics of a differentiated application of architectural ornament speak directly to the viewer. The mathematical planning provided the correct structure of the ideal concept, accessible to the initiate; the facing of the buildings and their decoration appealed to the senses of the observer. Surface and ornament are our most immediate window into the meaning of the Taj Mahal.

It is this fusion of the intellectual and the sensuous that has made the Taj Mahal so successful over the centuries, thus achieving the project's other object, to be an enduring monument to Shah Jahan as emperor and architect.

THE SYMBOLISM OF WHITE MARBLE AND RED SANDSTONE

The most readily noticed aspect of the buildings of the Taj Mahal complex is the differentiation in their colour [333]. White is reserved for the mausoleum, as the most important structure: the white marble inlaid with *pietra dura* reacts to changes in the light and enhances its mystical and mythical aura. Red is the colour of all the subsidiary structures; their important elements, such as domes and façades, may be ennobled with a facing of white marble and with marble inlay. This hierarchically graded colour dualism is a general feature of imperial Mughal architecture. In this the Mughals elaborated a practice which had already been adopted by the Delhi sultans [334], and which conforms to older Indian concepts, laid down in the *shastras* (theoretical Sanskrit texts about art and building). The *Vishnudharmottara-purana*, an authoritative compilation composed probably in the 8th century, recommended white stones for buildings of Brahmins, the priestly caste, and red ones for those of the *kshatriyas*, the warrior caste:² 'White, it would

seem, is opposed to red as the purity of the Brahmin is opposed to the ruling power of the Kshatriya.'³ The synthesis of the two colours had an auspicious connotation. By using white and red in their buildings the Mughals identified themselves with the two highest levels of the Indian social system. Until Aurangzeb, the emperors were concerned to define themselves as rulers in Hindu terms as well: the orthodox Muslim historian Badauni criticized Akbar for letting himself be addressed as an incarnation, 'like Rama, Krishna and other infidel kings'.⁴

The role of red sandstone (*sang-i surkh*) and white marble (*sang-i marmar*) changed in the course of Mughal architecture. Akbar's builders preferred red sandstone. They valued it not only because it was considered appropriate for the Indian ruling class but also because of its imperial connotation within the Mughal tradition: red was the exclusive colour of imperial tents [126, 127].⁵ Another

333 *opposite* The mausoleum, its platform and the minarets, of white marble, are framed by structures of red sandstone with honorific marble accents. (Photograph taken in 1985)

334 A pre-Mughal application of red sandstone facing highlighted with white marble: the ʿAlaʾi Darwaza of ʿAla-ud-Din Khalji, of 1311, in the complex of the Quwwat-ul Islam Mosque and Qutb Minar at Delhi. (Photograph taken in 1979)

attraction was its integrative faculty: since its overall red hue absorbed stylistic clashes between the various building traditions that were brought together in the great Akbari architectural synthesis, it expressed imperial unification.[6] In residential buildings of Akbar's period white marble was used only as ornament. Funerary architecture made more use of marble accents. The tomb of Humayun [104, 335] demonstrates a purposeful handling of the two colours: marble inlay underlines the role of each structural element in the elevation, and the crowning dome is clad in marble. The tomb of Shaikh Salim Chishti at Fatehpur Sikri is entirely faced with white marble, expressing the spiritual position of Akbar's favourite mystic [336].[7] The colour white had strong associations with purity, goodness and spirituality in the Islamic tradition, too, and a white tomb reflected the spirituality and faith of the person buried in it.[8]

Under Jahangir white marble was employed more frequently. As before, the hierarchic use of colour dualism manifested itself especially in funerary architecture. Akbar's tomb is topped by a marble gallery surrounding the upper cenotaph [106, 107]. The white rooftop court 'floats' over the terraced structure, as if belonging

with the surrounding marble cupolas to a different sphere. The tomb of Iᶜtimad-ud-Daula, Nur Jahan's father and Pillar of the Empire, is entirely faced with marble, further ennobled by inlay of coloured marbles and semi-precious stones [58–60] – in this a direct precursor of the Taj Mahal.

In Shah Jahan's reign, Lahauri tells us, 'the value of the arts has changed, and the divine care has adopted a new method of embellishing the world[:] in place of the old [sandstone buildings], sky-touching mansions of marble were built which reflect like the mirror of Alexander and are pure like the heart of spiritual persons'.[9] Marble became the facing of imperial palace buildings [83, 86, 88] – or if not marble, a coating of white polished plaster which looked like marble (p. 95). The studied use of white marble and red

335 *below* The south-east corner of the tomb of Humayun, Delhi, 1562–71. White marble accentuates the elements of the building clad in red sandstone. (Photograph taken in 1980)

336 *opposite* The white marble tomb of Shaikh Salim Chishti, 1580/81, in the courtyard of the red sandstone Jamiᶜ Masjid at Fatehpur Sikri. (Photograph taken in 1978)

sandstone reached its apogee in the Taj Mahal, where it is handled with unparalleled systematization and sophistication. Throughout the complex, the importance of each building is indicated by the amount of marble used. The pure whiteness of the mausoleum demonstrates its most elevated rank and symbolizes spiritual qualities in the highest terms.

NATURALISTIC ORNAMENT AS AN EXPRESSION OF PARADISE

Paradise in the Qur'an was imagined as gardens (*jannat*, *rauza*) full of trees, flowers and plants and flowing waters. For Shah Jahan and his advisers, one of the means to give the mausoleum paradisiacal qualities was to set it in a real garden with real trees and flowers. However, nature is perishable and impermanent. Lasting paradisiacal qualities could be ensured with artificial plants and flowers. True, they would have no scent, as the poet Kalim conceded (p. 170), but, if realistically done, they would surpass their living counterparts in perfection of form and beautiful colours, and, most important, they would bloom eternally. The flower and plant decoration of the Taj Mahal was meant to invest the buildings with a permanent paradisiacal quality. It was also acceptable to the orthodox, because the depiction of plants was sanctioned by Islamic theologians, in contrast to that of figures (p. 190).

Naturalistic ornament as a paradisiacal property was meted out in a hierarchic progression. It does not appear at all in the subsidiary courts of the Jilaukhana complex and the bazaar and caravanserai complex. (The 'Fatehpuri Masjid' belongs to a later period when this type of ornament had expanded into a wider architectural context.) Within the garden, floral and plant decoration appears only sparingly in the surrounding buildings. It culminates on the riverfront terrace and the buildings there, above all in the mausoleum, the ultimate paradisiacal garden house. There the most precious materials and techniques were used to create the most compelling plant and flower images that would ensure the conditions of Paradise. According to the poet Kalim, even a single painted flower on a wall could stand for spring:

> The painter has drawn such delicate pictures
> That the heart [of the viewer] opens and his [or her] hands
>   become weak [from the emotion of seeing the beautiful
>   image].

> The painting of the flowerbed shows every detail.
> If he draws one flower, its represents spring.[10]

In the arts of the courts of the three great empires of the Islamic world – the Ottomans, the Safavids and the Mughals – the naturalism of Shahjahani flower representation is unique, though by the 17th century 'a predominantly floral decorative vocabulary' had established itself generally as mainstream ornament.[11] Flower and plant decoration took the place of the previously favoured 'typical Islamic' geometrical patterns (*girih bandi*), which were used in less prominent places. In the Taj Mahal complex they were relegated to floors and *jalis*. (The floor patterns are differentiated in complexity and technique to underline the hierarchical importance of the architectural area or building where they occur [337].)

Flowers

The naturalistic plant and flower depictions of the mausoleum bring a long involvement of the Mughals with botanical studies to its monumental apogee. The close observation of the visual world had been a continued interest of the Mughal dynasty. It was first expressed in words, in Babur's descriptions of plants, trees and animals in his autobiography, and was then given visual expression by the painters of Akbar and Jahangir. For models, the Mughals turned to the arts of Europe: they based studies of flowers and plants, including those

native to their own environment, on the illustrations in European scientific herbals.[12] Jahangir's and Shah Jahan's painters knew and used the great herbals of the later 16th and early 17th centuries, such as *Rariorum plantarum historia* . . . by Charles de L'Écluse (Carolus Clusius) (1601), Mathias de L'Obel's *Plantarum seu stirpium historia* . . . (1576), and Rembert Dodoens' *Stirpium historiae pemptades sex* (1583) – all printed in Antwerp – as well as the French florilegium of Pierre Vallet, *Le Jardin du roy très chrestian Henry IV* (1608) [340].[13]

The Mughal artists were led by Ustad Mansur, Jahangir's outstanding painter of natural history subjects, with his famous tulips (c. 1620) [342]. From the herbals' system of depiction they adopted the symmetrical composition, the use of front and side views of blossoms, the progression from bud to full bloom on one plant, and the arrangement of the blossoms to display the botanical details of stamen and carpels [341]. This was combined with a sense of movement in the petals, leaves and stems which was also typical of herbal illustration of the period. A group of such flower studies by artists of Shah Jahan's period appears in the album which Prince Dara Shikoh presented to his wife Nadira Banu Begam in 1641/42 [194].[14]

The flower studies of the painters were transferred by Shah Jahan's craftsmen to marble and sandstone relief and to *pietra dura*. They handled their models quite freely, however, juxtaposing botanical species with imaginary flowering plants or creating hybrids of the two. These were perhaps meant to represent a realistic-looking

337 Geometric patterns (*girih bandi*) of paving as one moves through the Taj Mahal complex (measurements are given in cm; *c.* 80 cm/32 in. = 1 *gaz*):

a platforms in front of the great gate on the garden side and of the southern galleries, and platform of the riverfront terrace, in red and buff sandstone

b all walkways of the garden, in red sandstone

c platforms in front of the garden-wall pavilions, in white marble and red sandstone

d around the platform of the mausoleum, in white marble and red sandstone

e platforms in front of the mosque and Mihman Khana, in red and buff sandstone

f platforms of tanks in front of the mosque and Mihman Khana, in red and buff sandstone

g tomb chamber in the mausoleum and octagonal corner chambers: star and cross pattern of black marble inlaid in white marble

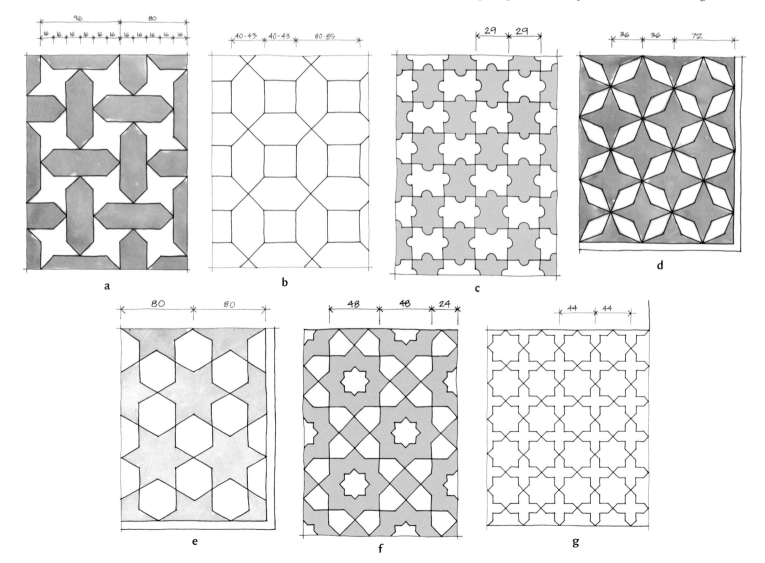

but unworldly paradisiacal species, outside the laws of nature. The flowers also relate to the imperial realm: similar flowers appear at the same time on the dados of several palace buildings in the Agra fort – close to nature in the Shah Burj, freer in the Diwan-i Khass, and in *pietra dura* in the *jharoka* of the Diwan-i ᶜAmm. Particular favourites in all media – painting, relief, and inlay work – are flowers inspired by the martagon lily, crown imperial and tulip [341, 344, 345]. The most spectacular naturalistic plant and flower representation was achieved in *pietra dura*. The aim was to obtain effects similar to painting. Again Kalim tells us of the desired effect:

> Pictures become manifest from every stone.
> In its mirror behold the image of a flower garden.[15]

Flower vases

Vases filled with flowers in marble relief appear as dado decoration of the central tomb chamber [230, 339]. Their placement there tells us

338 *below* Flower vase and butterflies, with an inscription freely after Isaiah 40:6, 8: 'All flesh is grass, oh human being, it does not bring fame/ And your beauty is like a flower': engraving by Claes Jansz. Vischer, Flemish, 1635.

339 *below right* Flower vase that appears in the dados on the eight corners of the tomb chamber. The European model is flattened, and the loose arrangement of its flowers is turned to perfect Shahjahani mirror symmetry on both sides of the central iris. At the same time, the Mughal flowers are much more dynamic, shooting out of the vase. (Photograph taken in 1992)

that they were more highly valued than the single flowers arrayed in 'beds' on the outer dado zones. Like those, their naturalism and shape are inspired by the arts of contemporary Europe, where by the 17th century vases of flowers had become a favourite subject of painting, engraving and decoration [338].[16] Implied in the depiction of flower vases and still-life with flowers was, especially in the Low Countries, a *vanitas* theme – the idea of the transitoriness of human life and of earthly things, which, like the beauty of the flowers, will not last.[17] We do not know whether the Mughals were familiar with this symbolism, but it gives the eschatological meaning of the flower decoration of the Taj Mahal an additional facet.

The shape of the vases of the Taj Mahal and their flower arrangements follows the European form very closely. The Mughals were not worried about borrowing from other traditions: they saw this as deigning to use an offering from a foreign cultural region for their own artistic purposes (p. 68). And the European elements that met with continuous success were those that could give a new expression to artistic or literary concepts already familiar to the Mughals. This is also true of the vases. Vases filled with flowers have a long tradition in Muslim culture, and in an Indian context their attraction was heightened because they related to the pot with overflowing plants, *purna-ghata*, the ancient symbol of prosperity and wellbeing [347].[18] The vases thus had a multiple 'identity' which gave them the universal quality sought by Shah Jahan's artists.

The prestigious vase motif is most spectacularly and most naturalistically expressed in marble in the tomb chamber [230, 339].

340 *above* Martagon lily, from Pierre Vallet, *Le Jardin du roy très chrestian Henry IV*, 1608.

341 *above right* Martagon lily, from the *Small Clive Album*, Mughal, late 17th or 18th century. The artist followed Vallet's model closely, only leaving out the butterfly.

342 *right* Himalayan tulips, painted by Mansur, Mughal, *c*. 1620.

Flowers in the mausoleum

343 Flower type X (with bending stalks supporting pairs of blossoms except at the top, where one of each pair is left out so as to create reverse symmetry) on the dado in one of the cruciform rooms. (Photograph taken in 1997)

344 *below left* Flower type C (with blossoms inspired by tulips) on the north *pishtaq*. (Photograph taken in 1995)

345 *below* Flower type R (double-tiered crown imperial, *Fritillaria imperialis*) on the platform of the upper cenotaph of Shah Jahan. (Photograph taken in 1992)

Vase elements also appear, as an ennobling accent, in the garden-wall pavilions [198] and in the towers, where they are integrated into the brackets of the topping *chhatris*. Monumental flower vases in red sandstone create a spectacular effect on the river frontage of the terrace [208, 209]: here, on the only external façade of the Taj Mahal complex, the élite imagery of the tomb chamber was projected to the outside world.

Plant colonnettes

The flower vases of the tomb chamber are set off by engaged marble colonnettes which grow out of pots, overflowing with fully sculpted acanthus leaves, another reference to the Indian auspicious symbol of the *purna-ghata* or *purna-kalasha*[346, 347]. The bases and capitals of the colonnettes are formed of interlocking acanthus scrolls and leaves. Their shafts, in their shape and naturalistic acanthus decoration, refer to the larger form of the baluster column, which by then had made its exclusive appearance in the ceremonial architecture of Shah Jahan [133].[19] As its Mughal term, *sarw andam*, 'cypress-bodied', indicates, the baluster column was meant to represent a tree or plant. Its actual shape, with acanthus decoration, was again taken from European engravings, probably prints from the circle of Dürer where the column features prominently to frame portraits of kings and holy personages.

In the miniature versions of the colonnettes of the Taj, their plant character is intensified by a unique decoration of flowering creepers, carrying blossoms in the shape of the ever-popular lily with curved-back petals ('martagon lily'), which increases the 'naturalistic' character of the decoration. The combination of cypress-shaped column and creeper evokes in turn an ancient motif of Persian art and poetry, the cypress entangled by a blooming tree [58], symbolizing the lover and the beloved. The poet Kalim, in praising the vegetation of Kashmir, says, 'Wherever a young tree raised its stature, a vine entangled it like a lover.'[20] The symbolically highly charged colonnettes intensify the 'garden room' aspect of the interior of the mausoleum.

Flowers as a symbol of Mughal kingship

The flowers and plants of the Taj Mahal were intended to evoke perfect paradisiacal bloom. At the same time, they have a definite political significance. This is demonstrated by the cenotaphs of Shah Jahan, on which flowers were given preference over inscriptions [233, 243, 246, 349]. Unlike those of Mumtaz, where large individual flowers appear only on the platforms, both of Shah Jahan's memorials are covered with floral motifs and individual flowering plants. They are in keeping with the overall concept of the mausoleum as paradisiacal garden house; but they also conform

346 *far left* Engaged corner colonnette in the tomb chamber of the mausoleum, with plant decoration growing out of a pot with overhanging leaves. (Photograph taken in 1981)

347 *left* A baluster column standing on a pot with overhanging leaves, the Indian symbol of the 'vase of plenty' (*purna-ghata*): part of the frame of a statue of Vishnu from eastern India, 11th–12th century. (Photograph taken in 1979)

348 *opposite* Shah Jahan portrayed among flowers as the Spring of the Empire: detail of a painting by Payag, Mughal, *c.* 1640, from the *Padshahnama*. The complete scene depicts the emperor when still Prince Khurram, being presented by his father Jahangir with a turban ornament, but this is propaganda in retrospect: the setting in this, Shah Jahan's official history, is that of his own time, and the message his own.

to the programme of his court settings, where paradisiacal bloom expressed imperial propaganda. The writers and poets of Shah Jahan eulogized him as the 'the spring of the flower garden of justice and generosity': he was the renewer, the *mujaddid*, under whose rule 'Hindustan has become the rose garden of the earth and his reign which is the cradle of prosperity has become the spring season of the age in which the days and nights are young'.[21]

The image of the garden and its flowers was the main metaphor of Shah Jahan's imperial symbolism: it stood not only for himself and his good government but also for his court and his family. In Shahjahani rhetoric the emperor was an 'erect cypress of the garden of the caliphate';[22] his court was the 'adornment of the meadow of pomp';[23] his marriage to Mumtaz Mahal 'grafted that new flower (*gul*) of the garden of chastity and perfection (*gulshan-i iffat-u-kamal*) [Mumtaz] onto that new plant (*nihal*) of the garden of dignity and splendour (*hadika-i jah-u-jalal*) [Shah Jahan]';[24] his eldest daughter, Jahanara, was 'the noble palm-tree of the orchard of magnificence and excellent fruit of the plant of grandeur';[25] his eldest son, Dara Shikoh, was 'the first flower of this royal garden';[26] and Mumtaz's death turned the world into a garden with thorns:

> Like nightingales we should weep in this garden
> For smiles fade too quickly from the face.[27]

349 Detail of the lower cenotaph of Shah Jahan. Poppies alternate with lily-like flowers; at the left end is the only inscription, the emperor's epitaph, written in Persian, in *nastaʿliq* script. (Photograph taken in 2001)

THE INSCRIPTIONS

The religious prohibition against figural representation in Islam, and the great appreciation of script as the medium in which God's revealed word was materialized in the holy book, the Qur'an, are the reasons why inscriptions became a predominant element of the decoration of religious buildings in the Islamic world. These inscriptions are aesthetically attractive, but not easily readable: some are placed in obscure areas, others are too high and too far away to be read, and most are so intricately composed that the ordinary visitor would not be able to decipher them. However, the mere existence of the Word of God on the walls of a building served as a visible representation of supernatural reality and had a sanctifying and uplifting effect. For literate Muslims who had memorized the entire Qur'an during their elementary education, it often sufficed to decipher a single word or phrase in order to recognize from which *sura* or chapter the passage came.[28]

These inscriptions were not randomly chosen but expressed thematic programmes, a religious iconography of words which represents the Islamic counterpart to figural decoration in Christian churches. For those who understood them, they were the key to the deeper symbolic message of a building.[29] Mausoleums were, in spite of their unorthodoxy, considered as religious buildings, and were often decorated with Qur'anic epigraphy. This was perhaps even meant to counterbalance the unorthodoxy of the structure.

The Taj Mahal displays the largest inscriptional programme in the Islamic world: it has twenty-five Qur'anic inscriptions, of which fourteen are complete *suras*. The inscriptions appear on three of the four major buildings only – the great gate, the mausoleum, and the mosque. In keeping with the overall aesthetic systematization which governs the Taj Mahal, they follow a unified scheme, appearing as elegant bands of black inlaid letters on the rectangular white marble frames that surround the *pishtaqs* and arched niches [224, 230, 351, 352]. In addition, the mosque has an arched inscriptional band around the *mihrab*, and black inlaid inscriptions cover the two cenotaphs of Mumtaz Mahal [246, 350]; the two cenotaphs of Shah Jahan bear only a brief epitaph [244, 349].

All formal Qur'anic inscriptions are in Arabic and written in large and elaborate *sulus* script, the 'mother' of the cursive styles of writing, which was in the 17th century the predominant calligraphic style for architectural epigraphs. The vertical stems of the letters are elongated and produce, with long horizontal lines which may be drawn across several words, the effect of latticework [350]. The epitaphs on the memorials of Mumtaz Mahal and Shah Jahan are in Persian, the official language of the Mughal empire, and styled for Mumtaz in *naskh* (the normal script, simpler than *sulus*) and for Shah Jahan in the elegant *nastaʿliq* script (written with connected 'hanging' letters).[30]

In Persian also are the four historical inscriptions, consisting of dates and dated signatures of the calligrapher, integrated in small letters into the ends of Qur'anic inscriptions on the mausoleum and the great gate [128–131]. They contain the dates 1045 (1635/36), 1046 (1636/37), 1048 (1638/39) and 1057 (1647/48), and two carry the signature of the calligrapher ʿAbd-ul-Haqq from Shiraz, who signed variously as 'son of Qasim as-Shirazi ʿAbd-ul-Haqq, with the title Amanat Khan' (1635/36), and 'Amanat Khan as-Shirazi' (1638/39). He created the inscriptions of Akbar's mausoleum at Sikandra and probably those of the Chini-ka Rauza at Agra (p. 43) and, in 1632,

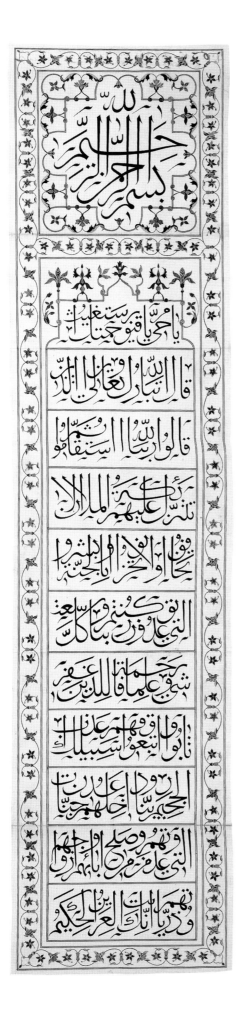

was given the title Amanat Khan ('Lord of Trust') by Shah Jahan. Amanat Khan was the only artist of the Taj Mahal who was allowed to reveal his identity for posterity (pp. 99–100). It demonstrates the high regard the emperor had for the artist, and that the art of writing, which because of its religious connotations was held in highest esteem in the Islamic world, also had a special status at his court.

It has been established that the theme of the inscriptional programme of the Taj Mahal was an eschatological one: all the complete *suras*, or passages from *suras*, speak in one way or another of the Day of Judgment, divine mercy, and Paradise promised to the faithful.[31] It has been argued on this basis that the Taj Mahal was meant to be a symbolic replica of the Throne of God on the Day of Judgment as expressed in a mystical diagram by Ibn al ʿArabi.[32] One of the many points which speak against this hypothesis is that the famous Throne verse (*sura* 2, verse 255) extolling God's majesty[33] is absent from the inscriptional programme.[34]

When all the components of the Taj Mahal are seen together there is no doubt that the inscriptional programme ensures on the intellectual religious level, with God's own words, the overall symbolism of the mausoleum and its setting as the house prepared for Mumtaz in Paradise.[35]

The most programmatic *sura* is 89, *al-Fajr*, 'Daybreak', which is placed on the outer façade of the great gate [351]:

In the Name of God, the Lord of Mercy, the Giver of Mercy [1] By the Daybreak, [2] by the Ten Nights, [3] by the even and the odd, [4] by the passing night – [5] is this oath strong enough for a rational person?

[6] Have you [Prophet] considered how your Lord dealt with the people of 'Ad, [7] of Iram, the city of lofty pillars, [8] whose like has never been built in any land? [9] and the Thamud, who hewed into the rocks in the valley [10] and the mighty and powerful Pharaoh? [11] All of them committed excesses in their lands, [12] and spread corruption there: [13] your Lord let a scourge of punishment loose on them. [14] Your Lord is always watchful.

[15] The nature of man is that, when his Lord tries him through honour and blessings, he says, 'My Lord has honoured me', [16] but when He tries him through the restriction of his provision, he says,'My Lord has humiliated me.' [17] No indeed! You [people] do not honour orphans, [18] you do not urge one another to feed the poor, [19] you consume inheritance greedily, [20] and you love wealth with a passion. [21] No indeed! When the earth is pounded to dust, pounded and pounded, [22] when your Lord comes with the angels, rank upon rank, [23] when Hell is that day brought near – on that day man will take heed,

350 *left* Top of the upper cenotaph of Mumtaz Mahal: Company drawing by an Agra or Delhi artist for Maria, Lady Nugent, *c.* 1812. The Qur'anic inscription, in *sulus* script, includes verse 30 of *sura* 41 and verses 7 and 8 of *sura* 40, which promise Paradise and claim the everlasting gardens for those who follow the right path, 'together with their righteous ancestors, spouses, and offspring'.

overleaf
351 The southern, outward-facing, *pishtaq* of the great gate is framed by *sura* 89 of the Qur'an, which concludes by inviting the believers into Paradise. (Photograph taken in 1992)

352 The south-western arch in the tomb chamber of the mausoleum is surrounded by an inscription band with *sura* 76 of the Qur'an, *al-Insan*, 'Man'. Beginning top right is verse 13, 'They will sit on couches, feeling neither scorching heat nor biting cold.' (Photograph taken in 1981)

but what good will that be to him then? [24] He will say: 'Would that I had provided for this life to come!' [25] On that Day, no-one will punish as He punishes, and no-one will bind as He binds. [27] [But] you, soul at peace: [28] return to your Lord well pleased and well pleasing; [29] go in among My servants, [30] and into My Garden [Paradise].[36]

The special features of Paradise are evoked in the inscriptions of the mausoleum. Around the door within the east *pishtaq* is placed the entire *sura* 98, *al-Bayina*, 'The Clear Evidence', the last two verses of which say

> [7] Those who believe and do good deeds are the best of creation. [8] Their reward is with their Lord: Gardens of everlasting bliss graced with flowing streams. God is well pleased with them and they with Him. All this is for those who stand in awe of their Lord.

The arch of the south-west niche of the central tomb chamber is surrounded by the second half of *sura* 76, *al-Insan*, 'Man' [352], which contains the verses

> [11] So God will save them from the woes of that Day, give them radiance and gladness, [12] and reward them for their steadfastness with a Garden and with silken robes. [13] They will sit on couches, feeling neither scorching heat nor biting cold, [14] with shady [branches] spread above them and clusters of fruit hanging close at hand.

On the upper cenotaph of Mumtaz verse 30 of *sura* 41, *Ha Mim* or *al-Fussilat*, '[Verses] Made Distinct', occurs twice – on the top [350], and on the south end continued on the west side:

> As for those who say, 'Our Lord Is God', and take the straight path towards Him, the angels come down to them and say, 'Have no fear or grief, but rejoice in the good news of Paradise, which you have been promised.'

The appearance of this passage twice indicates that it must have been considered as particularly powerful to ensure divine forgiveness and paradisiacal reward for Mumtaz Mahal.

SOUND AS AN EXPRESSION OF ETERNITY

In the interior of the mausoleum even sound had to evoke eternity. The dome of the tomb chamber holds a tone for almost half a minute, as the musician Paul Horn demonstrated in a night session with his flute on 25 April 1968. He was inspired by the tomb attendant who habitually calls out to demonstrate the remarkable acoustics: 'I never heard anything so beautiful. Each tone hung suspended in space for 28 seconds and the acoustics are so perfect that you couldn't tell when his voice stopped and the echo took over. Also the individual tone didn't spread as in other great halls, but remained pure and round to the very end.'[37] For the Austrian artist Bernhard Leitner (who creates installations with moving sound producing the effect of space), Horn's simple flute melody continuing by itself inside the dome generates the impression of timeless sound: 'The room never ends. Even without sound time is inherent in this space. The silence is tension-filled. The space finds its meaning in an unearthly, infinite silence.'[38]

The acoustics of the Taj Mahal were first described in 1836 by Captain Sleeman, an early British observer of the Taj Mahal (pp. 105, 240):

> of all the complicated music ever heard upon earth, that of a flute blown gently in the vault below, where the remains of the Emperor and his consort repose, as the sound rises to the dome amidst a hundred arched alcoves around, and descends in heavenly reverberation upon those who sit or recline upon the cenotaphs above the vault, is, perhaps the finest to an inartificial ear. We feel as if it were from heaven, and breathed by angels; it is to the ear what the building itself is to the eye; but unhappily, it cannot, like the building live in our recollections. All that we

can, in after life, remember is that it was heavenly, and produced heavenly emotions.[39]

The echo also impressed the American writer Bayard Taylor, who was at Agra in 1853: 'The dome of the Taj contains an echo more sweet, pure and prolonged than that of the Baptistery of Pisa, which is the finest in Europe. A single musical note, uttered by the voice, floats and soars overhead in a long, delicious undulation, fading away so slowly that you hear it after it is silent as you see, or seem to see, a lark you have been watching after it is swallowed up in the blue vault of heaven.'[40]

The echo of the dome still intrigues all visitors, who react to it according to their sensibilities. All sorts of experiments have been undertaken. Florentia Sale (p. 240) complained in 1832–33 that the 'shouting and blowing of horns seem to me to partake of bad taste, although I will allow that Single Notes from a Bugle allowed to die away have a fine effect'. Guidebooks of the 19th century even made recommendations for how to obtain a satisfying result. According to the anonymous mid-century Handbook, 'A very pleasing effect is obtained by fastening a small musical box on a pole and elevating it up the dome'.[41] Keene's Handbook for Visitors to Agra (1899) advised that 'Visitors will be disappointed with the celebrated echo of this dome if they attempt to play or sing any complicated melodies or roulades in it. The echo is so quick that it catches the notes and runs them into one another, so as to produce a most distressing discord, unless the notes chosen be such as form a natural harmony. The chord of seventh produces a very beautiful effect.'[42] The devastating effect which the echo can have has been explored in recent years by Indian visitors through shouting and screaming in the dome.

FUNERARY AND COMMEMORATIVE RITES

When Mumtaz was buried first at Burhanpur, Shah Jahan visited her tomb every Friday, the holy day of the Muslim week, and said the first and briefest sura of the Qur'an, the Fatiha,[43] which is the customary prayer on such occasions, intended to give comfort to the soul of the departed:

[1] In the name of God, the Lord of Mercy, the Giver of Mercy! [2] Praise belongs to God, Lord of the Worlds, [3] the Lord of Mercy, the Giver of Mercy, [4] Master of the Day of Judgement. [5] It is You we worship; it is You we ask for help. [6] Guide us to the straight path: [7] the path of those You have blessed, those who incur no anger and who have not gone astray.

After Mumtaz had been laid to rest in the Taj Mahal, whenever he visited it he would say the Fatiha, and he also appointed Qur'an reciters to sit in the mausoleum day and night, taking turns to read from the holy book to ask divine forgiveness for the departed queen.[44] The reciters and the tomb attendants had their quarters in the Khawasspuras [156–158] and were paid from the endowment that Shah Jahan established for the upkeep of the tomb (p. 100).

The mausoleum was furnished with carpets, chandeliers, 'and other ornaments of that kind'.[45] From the historian Khafi Khan we know that Shah Jahan had a chadar (sheet) made of pearls (p. 232) to be placed on Mumtaz's cenotaph every Friday and on the anniversary of her death, the 'urs, which was celebrated with much funerary pomp, especially in the first years after her death, with

assemblies, prayers, banquets for the family, nobles and religious men, and feeding of the poor and giving alms (pp. 97–99).

The aim of prayer and good deeds was, as the historian Tabataba'i is at pains to point out, 'to secure greater repose and lasting tranquillity for those who have taken up residence in the nearness of divine mercy', 'to obtain divine forgiveness for the departed'.[46] (His explanation was perhaps intended to calm the concerns of the orthodox about prayers at tombs leading to the worship of the dead, which they considered as a form of idolatry.) 'Urs celebrations are still held annually at the Taj Mahal for Shah Jahan and Mumtaz Mahal on the anniversary of the emperor's death, 26 and 27 Rajab, the seventh month of the Muslim calendar.[47]

In India, the tomb of an outstanding personage was and still is treated like the tomb of a Muslim saint. The Mughals developed a ritual of imperial visits of the tombs of their ancestors, in particular that of Humayun, the foundation mausoleum of the dynasty at Delhi [104].[48] According to the English merchant William Finch, who was at Agra in 1610, Akbar's tomb [107] was when still under construction already 'much worshipped both by the Moores [Muslims] and Gentiles [Hindus], holding him for a great saint. . . . Every one approaching neere makes his reverence and puts off his shooes, bringing in his hand some sweete smelling flowers to bestrew the carpets or to adorne the tombe.'[49] The account of a visit to Akbar's tomb by an Iranian delegation in 1621 tells us more about the practices of such a visiting ritual. The envoys removed their shoes at the main gate, and offered their obeisance to the tomb with the ceremonial gestures due to an emperor there and again inside the pishtaq of the mausoleum. They recited the Fatiha, and were presented 'on behalf of the illumined mausoleum' with a robe of honour (khil'at). If the tomb personified the one who was buried in it, the concern of orthodox circles was not without foundation. After the official part was over the Iranians were entertained with a picnic around the pool (in front of the southern pishtaq?), the party sitting on carpets and under tents brought especially from the imperial establishment. The conversation included a discussion of the architecture and Jahangir's involvement in the tomb's design.[50]

The Taj Mahal has long been regarded as a place of pilgrimage by Indian Muslims, and even Hindus include it in their pious visits of sacred sites in the region of Braj, of the cities of Mathura and Vrindavan. When early British observers wrote down their impressions of the architecture of the mausoleum they also noted the behaviour of domestic visitors. Lady Nugent in 1812 mentions in her journal that 'the natives are proud of it, and hold it in great veneration. Many make pilgrimages to it . . .'[51] Lord Hastings, who came to the Taj Mahal as Governor-General of Bengal in 1815, was impressed when the soldiers of his body guard 'on approaching the tombs touched the pavement with their foreheads'. He donated 'a new silver tissue canopy, with proper standard-poles to be raised over the monuments' (i.e. the cenotaphs) to replace the ragged old one, to gratify the sentiments of the attendants.[52]

Visitors take off their shoes before they enter the mausoleum and, until the present railing closed off the screen, would lay the traditional offerings of money and flowers on the cenotaphs [cf. 246]. In the early 21st century I have even seen Westerners praying in the tomb chamber.

V Everybody's Taj Mahal

He [Shah Jahan] purposely made it [the Taj Mahal] near the Tasimacan [Taj Ganj], where all foreigners come, so that the whole world should see and admire its magnificence.

Jean-Baptiste Tavernier, *Six Voyages*, 1676[1]

Shah Jahan wanted the Taj Mahal to become a building acclaimed by the entire world, and he fully succeeded in his intention. The Western eyewitnesses of its construction, the British picturesque travellers and painters who rediscovered it, administrators, scholars, conservationists and tourists, from the 17th century to the present day, were deeply impressed by the monument and voiced their praise in words reminding one of the rhetoric of Shah Jahan. Everyone felt compelled to give his or her comments on the Taj Mahal, and the body of personal emotional and aesthetic responses to it is much larger than that of scholarly investigations. Painters and photographers made the building widely known. Its image was picked up by popular culture and advertising and has become a global metaphor for the excellent and the outstanding, understood by everybody.

THE TAJ MAHAL EMERGES: EARLY TRAVELLERS AND PICTURESQUE DISCOVERY

The last time I saw it was in the company of one of our French merchants, who, like myself, did not tire of looking at it. I did not dare to express my opinion, fearing that my taste might have become corrupted and Indianized; but since he had recently come from France, it was quite a relief for me to hear him say that he had seen nothing in Europe so grandiose and daring.

François Bernier, *Voyages*, 1699[2]

After Shah Jahan's death in 1666 the Taj Mahal faded from Mughal historiography. It features however in the accounts of European travellers who came to Agra during and after his reign. The two most interesting are both French: Jean-Baptiste Tavernier, who financed his travels by dealing in precious stones, and the physician François Bernier. Tavernier was at Agra in 1640–41 and again in 1665. At the latter date he made the claim that Shah Jahan had begun to build his own tomb on the other side of the river but that the project had been abandoned because of the emperor's war with his sons.[3] No other source supports Tavernier's statement, and there is no physical evidence, but the legend has survived with tenacity to the present day (pp. 56, 249). François Bernier was at Agra in 1659, after Shah Jahan's deposition. He gives us the most detailed and best-informed description of the Taj Mahal by any 17th-century

Western observer. He was also the first to venture into an aesthetic appreciation: he felt that the Taj Mahal, despite not being built according to European classical rules, would 'well deserve a place in our books of architecture', and concluded: 'I decidedly think that this monument deserves much more to be numbered among the wonders of the world than the pyramids of Egypt, those unshapen masses which when I had seen them twice yielded me no satisfaction.'[4]

The 18th century

Little is known about the Taj Mahal in the 18th century. The Tyrolean Joseph Tieffenthaler (1710–85), one of the last Jesuits of the Mughal Mission, who arrived in 1743 in India and spent over forty years in the country, wrote a pioneering account in Latin, which was published with maps and views of cities and of individual buildings. He knew Agra well, because after his arrival he had been attached for some time as a teacher to the Jesuit college there, and paints a vivid picture of the city's decay: 'almost all suburban quarters are lying in waste; the houses falling into ruin, either from age or from the recurring rains, and the inhabitants have died of starvation or moved somewhere else. But all ruins testify to the previous splendour and greatness of a magnificent city.' Tieffenthaler devoted only four sentences to the Taj Mahal, which he calls 'the Monument of Shah Jahan', pointing out its main features; he preferred the tomb of I'timad-ud-Daula (pp. 52–53).[5]

The Indian poet Nazir Akbarabadi (b. 1735) loved Agra despite the fact that its glories were departed, and integrated into his Urdu verses unusually realistic observations of the daily life of the common people, the gardens and buildings, the popular sport of swimming in the river (p. 33), and the Rauza-i Taj Ganj – the 'Mausoleum of Taj Ganj', as the Taj Mahal was then known. He describes it as a place where he, like the other citizens of Agra, enjoyed the sight of the buildings and the garden with its fountains, cypress trees, roses and other flowers, and he took pride in the monument which he believed was 'known in every city and country'.[6]

With the waning of Mughal power after the death of Aurangzeb in 1707 the political situation at Agra was highly unsettled. Throughout the century it was occupied intermittently by indigenous and foreign forces trying to wrest territory from the ever-shrinking Mughal empire, most notably the Jats from neighbouring Bharatpur and the Marathas from western India. In 1719, during the power struggles between the successors of Aurangzeb and the Mughal nobility, the Agra fort was plundered by Husain ʿAli Khan, one of the two Sayyid brothers and the 'first noble of the empire'.

353 The Taj Mahal seen from the west, with an Indian visitor, shaded by an umbrella, on the terrace, and a European couple in early Victorian dress on the marble platform: detail of a Company drawing by an Agra or Delhi artist, c. 1840.

He took the imperial treasures away, including the *chadar*, the sheet of pearls which Shah Jahan had had made as a cover for the cenotaph of Mumtaz.[7]

To secure his hold on Agra, as we have seen, the Mughal emperor Muhammad Shah in 1722 appointed the loyal Maharaja Sawai Jai Singh of Jaipur as governor of the Agra province, and Jai Singh in turn made Rai Shivadasa his deputy (p. 76). New city walls were constructed,[8] and maps and plans of prominent buildings were prepared: to the Jaipur surveys we owe the earliest known map of Agra, which enables us to reconstruct the context of the Taj Mahal in the riverfront city [17]. But in 1761 the Jats under Suraj Mal took the fort, vandalized the tomb of Akbar at Sikandra, and are also charged with having carried away, among other things, doors from the Taj Mahal.[9]

During the last quarter of the 18th century the British East India Company extended its hold from Calcutta along the Ganges towards Lucknow, Agra and Delhi. In their progress the British had to deal with the confederacy of Maratha clans which by now controlled the Mughal emperor and much of western and northern India. They established a Resident at the court of Mahadaji Sindhia, who held the Agra fort from 1785 but because of the uncertain situation was based outside the city in camp near Mathura.[10] From 1786 to 1798 the Resident was Major William Palmer; when at Agra, Palmer and his officers stayed in the garden towers of the Taj and his troups were stationed in the Jilaukhana. We learn this from an anonymous 'Major J. H.' (p. 116), who further tells us in his letter of June 1794 that travellers too were put up 'within the walls, that surround the

354 William Hodges, 'The Taj Mahal', drawing, c. 1783: the earliest known view of the mausoleum from the garden.

355 *opposite* William Hodges, 'View of the Fort of Agra on the river Jumna', etching, from *Select Views in India*, 1785–88. The Taj Mahal is visible at the far left. On the right, before the fort, are the remains of the Haveli of Dara Shikoh, serving as a repoussoir; Hodges found its ruins dangerous to explore.

Tauge [Taj], not only for the convenience of seeing, but also as the most safe and secure from thieves'.[11]

Later in the same year, 1794, Thomas Twining, a servant of the East India Company, braved war and marauding bands to satisfy his desire to visit the Taj Mahal, and, on 16 November, approaching Agra from the north in a palanquin carried by four bearers, accompanied by guards, attendants, and his travelling companion, P. F. Juvenal, a Catholic priest stationed at the city, he 'saw, with a delight not to be expressed, the white dome of the Taje rising most beautifully and as if by magic above the distant line which bounded the plain to the west'. After being admitted by the keeper ('derwan') into the complex, he had the Taj all to himself, save for a few gardeners tending to 'thousands of orange trees . . . with their ripe fruit upon them'. Twining took up quarters in the north-west garden tower [299], which he describes as 'an elegant pavilion hanging immediately over the river', and stayed there for a week, also visiting Akbar's tomb, the Agra fort, and Fatehpur Sikri.[12] (Juvenal had to hire guards to escort Twining on to Delhi; see p. 202.)

The first European artists visit the Taj

The increasing consolidation of British power in India made the country more accessible and more attractive to Western travellers. Artists from Britain began to visit India and the Taj Mahal. A pioneer was James Forbes (1749–1819), an amateur whose meticulous renderings of details of the *pietra dura* decoration of the Taj, taken on the spot in 1781, and engraved and coloured by hand, set the direction for the details of the later 'Company drawings' (p. 237).[13]

The internationally renowned painter Johann Zoffany (1733–1810) visited the Taj Mahal in 1786 from Lucknow, but no pictorial records survive from his expedition. On seeing the Taj he is said to have exclaimed, 'Where is the case to cover so many beauties? For this is too fine to be exposed to the impression of the air'[14] – the earliest record of what was to become a popular reaction to the monument. A friend of Zoffany who had come with him to India, the painter Thomas Longcroft (d. 1811), prepared the earliest known topographical watercolour of the mausoleum, reportedly in 1786 [357].[15]

The first overall views of the Taj Mahal were taken by the landscape artists William Hodges and Thomas and William Daniell, who came to India in search of 'the sublime, picturesque and exotic', in the new romantic spirit which had begun to inform attitudes to landscape and architecture. India became part of the 'Picturesque Voyage'.

William Hodges (1744–97) had sailed with Captain Cook to the Cape of Good Hope, Antarctica, New Zealand and the South Pacific, and afterwards visited India between 1780 and 1783. His travels in northern India took him towards the end of February 1783 to Agra, where he prepared pioneering views of the city and the Taj Mahal [354], of some of which he later exhibited versions in oil in 1794 at the Royal Academy of Arts in London.[16] Two views of Agra, one with the Taj Mahal in the background [355], were published between 1785 and 1788 as aquatints in his *Select Views in India, Drawn on the Spot in the years 1780, 1781, 1782, and 1783*. He described the Taj in his *Travels in India* (1793) as a 'most perfect pearl on an azure ground.

356 *left* The earliest known depiction of the Taj Mahal, combining Europeanizing perspective with the Mughal painting tradition, by a Lucknow artist, 1780s. It contrasts with the early Western views.

357 *opposite* The earliest known European depiction of the Taj, by Thomas Longcroft, *c.* 1786.

358 *below* Thomas and William Daniell, 'The Taje Mahel, Agra', aquatint, from *Views of the Taje Mahel*, 1801. The monument is seen across the river, with the eastern tower of the Mahtab Bagh in the right foreground [cf. 66].

359 An English blue-and-white Staffordshire plate decorated with a view of the Taj Mahal seen across the river. Produced by John Hall and Sons *c.* 1825, the pattern is called 'Oriental Scenery: Tomb of the Emperor Shah Jahan'.

360 Thomas and William Daniell, 'The Taje Mahel, Agra. Taken in the Garden,' aquatint, from *Views of the Taje Mahel*, 1801.

The effect is such as, I confess, I never experienced from any work of art. The fine materials, the beautiful forms, and the symmetry of the whole, with the judicious choice of the situation, far surpasses [sic] any thing I ever beheld.'[17] Hodges found the bazaar and caravanserai complex ruined, but the fountains in the garden still playing.

Thomas Daniell (1749–1840) and his nephew William (1769–1837) followed in the footsteps of Hodges across northern India from 1789 to the end of 1791, using a camera obscura as a drawing aid to produce their topographical views. On 20 January 1789 they arrived at Agra and, as they write in their journal, pitched their tents 'immediately opposite the Tage Mahl'. The following day they 'breakfasted with Major Palmer in one of the Mosques in the Tage' – meaning the Mihman Khana.[18] The Daniells worked for three days in the Taj and prepared several sketches of it. Two of these views, one from the river and one from the garden, were published in 1801 as aquatints, separate from their famous *Oriental Scenery* series, with the title *Views of the Taje Mahel at the City of Agra in Hindoostan taken in 1789* [358, 360], accompanied by a booklet with a description and a plan of the entire complex, engraved by James

Newton, with references to the various parts of the building [147]. The Daniells' depictions were the earliest and largest views published of the Taj Mahal.[19]

The Daniells' aquatints and paintings had a deep influence on the 'Oriental' taste for Indian architecture which then became fashionable in Britain. It found its expression in Mughalizing buildings like Sezincote, a country house in Gloucestershire built by S. P. Cockerell about 1805, and the schemes of Humphry Repton and John Nash for the Royal Pavilion at Brighton (1805 and 1812–15). Views of the Taj Mahal even made their way into domestic interiors in the forms of wallpaper and Staffordshire pottery [359].[20]

IN BRITISH HANDS

The encounter between the British and the Taj Mahal is one of the most captivating chapters in the history of architectural reception.[21] In the end, the British East India Company was most instrumental in carrying out Shah Jahan's intention that his creation should become known to the entire world.

In 1803 Agra came into British hands when Lord Lake took the city in the Second Maratha War. The myth of the Great Mogul, his splendid court and fabled buildings, had fascinated Europe from the days of the Jesuit missions and the establishment of the East India Companies, and had drawn early travellers and artists to India. Now the Taj Mahal was seen and recorded by an increasing number of British officials and private visitors, as well as by professional and amateur artists. They expressed their admiration of the monument in writing, and recorded it visually, or commissioned images from Indian artists [e.g. 361–364].[22] The building and its *pietra dura* decoration became a favourite subject of 'Company drawings' and 'Company paintings', a late 18th- and 19th-century genre in which Indian artists produced watercolours for British patrons, and adjusted their styles and love of detail to British taste and to subjects of British interest, combining in their representation of buildings, as J. P. Losty put it, 'a secure grasp of European perspective . . . with an Indian painterly passion for precise and meticulous detail'.[23] In order further to satisfy British curiosity, manuscripts were composed in Persian by local writers which contained largely fictional data about the construction, the materials and the supposed architect of the Taj Mahal.[24] This is where the legend of 'Ustad Isa' as the architect had its origin (p. 89). More reliable information was put together at the behest of British administrators (p. 34).

The first official visitors and pictorial records

In November 1812 Sir George Nugent, Commander-in-Chief of the Bengal Army, visited the garrison of Agra. His wife, Maria (d. 1834), was the first of a number of British women who left in their journals comments on the mausoleum and the city. When the party approached Agra, she wrote, 'immense piles of ruins presented themselves on every side, and we passed through decayed gardens, ruinous mosques, temples and palaces, which strike the mind with the deepest melancholy, to reflect upon the fate of all human grandeur'.[25] On the 18th she and her husband mounted elephants, 'to see the famous Taaje. In spite of my high expectations, it greatly exceeded them – it is quite impossible to describe it!' Three days later, 'we took three hours to examine it in the minutest manner. I could look at it for as many months,

without being tired – it is really like the most beautiful Sevres china, and deserves to have a glass case made for it – What a pity it should be exposed to decay!'[26] As we have seen, Lady Nugent inscribed her name on the top of one of the minarets; she had a wooden model made of one 3 ft (90 cm) tall, commenting on 'the native workmen, who are famed for their patience in executing everything of the kind, as well as for their minute attention to the most trifling circumstance'.[27] She also composed a long poem on the Taj as a monument of 'wedded love', which ends with the verses

> And ye, blest pair! So fond, so true of heart,
> Who underneath this marble mouldering lie,
> Ye who have known the agony to part,
> Are now rewarded with eternal joy;
> So may fond love and truth for ever rest,
> And like Jehan and Taaje eternally blest.[28]

Lady Nugent had drawings made 'of everything – the beautiful Taaje in particular' by an anonymous artist from Agra.[29] They show views of the mausoleum and the great gate and spectacular details

of the *pietra dura* work, with almost full-size copies of the cenotaphs [240–243, 350, 361, 362]. The Nugent drawings stand at the beginning of the early Company drawings of the Taj and the monuments of Agra, made in the first quarter of the 19th century, which it has been argued are the most artistic, combining a lovely sense of volume and the atmospheric aura of the monuments with a high sensibility in the minute rendering of their details.[30]

In February 1815 Lord Hastings, Governor-General of Bengal, undertook a formal inspection of the monuments of Agra on the occasion of his great tour through northern India and found the Taj Mahal not wanting: 'Many monuments of human skill and labour exist more vast and more sublime than this; but it may be doubted whether genius ever conceived and executed another fabric of equal taste or elegance.' He even went to see the mausoleum by moonlight; and his only complaint was that mango trees intercepted the full view from the great gate.[31] To record the monuments he visited, Hastings employed the highly gifted Bengali artist Sita Ram, who introduced a poetic note with atmospheric effects into his topographical views [45, 364].[32] The Hastings collections also contain two albums with works by other Indian

361, 362 *above and left* The upper cenotaph of Shah Jahan, seen from the side, and a detail of the top of its platform: Company drawings by an Agra or Delhi artist for Maria, Lady Nugent, *c.* 1812.

opposite
363 *above* The Taj Mahal seen from the garden: Company drawing from an album of Lady Hastings, *c.* 1815.

364 *below* Sita Ram, view of the Taj Mahal from the Mihman Khana, painted for Lord Hastings, *c.* 1815.

artists, one in a small format put together by Lady Hastings [205, 363]. Both albums contain a strictly composed frontal view of the Taj from the garden along the central canal [363]. It was to become a classic image, adopted by the later photographers, and was very popular for the postcard-size paintings with which the artists of Agra met an increasing demand for pictures of the Mughal buildings of the city.[33]

These small-scale standardized views were also used to illustrate journals or accounts of Agra. Florentia, Lady Sale (1790–1853), who stayed at Agra in 1832–33 while her husband, Major-General Sir Robert Henry Sale, was in command of the 13th Foot, had a keen eye for architecture and illustrated her witty and perceptive *Notebook* with views commissioned from Agra artists [77, 96, 150, 154]. Several show buildings that are not depicted anywhere else. The husband of Fanny Parks (1794–1875), Charles, was Collector of Customs at Allahabad, but that did not keep her from travelling through India on her own; in 1835 she bought drawings executed in the 1820s by Latif, one of the few named Agra artists of the period, and used two of them as illustrations to her insightful *Wanderings of a Pilgrim in Search of the Picturesque* (1850).

The Taj as meeting ground

For the British and the Indians the Taj Mahal presented an opportunity to observe each other at close range. It functioned as a guest house for visitors, who would pitch their tents in the garden or stay in the buildings, and put up their servants in the Jilaukhana. The great gate as well as several of the structures of the right or eastern side – the towers, the garden-wall pavilion, and the wings flanking the Mihman Khana – were fitted up for this purpose.[34] Lieutenant Taylor, who was appointed in 1810 to repair the Taj Mahal (p. 251), resided for some years in the wing north of the Mihman Khana.[35] The rooms were considered 'in the cold weather . . . pleasant enough, but in the hot season quite insufferable from the heat and glare'.[36] The Mihman Khana itself was 'occasionally used as a banqueting hall by native potentates, when on visits to Agra they desire, as sometimes happens, to entertain the [British] ladies and gentlemen of the station'.[37]

The Taj Mahal and its garden remained the favourite recreational area of the city. It was open to the public and well kept. The garden was full of fruit trees, which, continuing an earlier practice, were let out by the British Government to local gardeners who derived a thriving trade during the season from harvesting and selling the fruit (p. 139). There were flowers and shrubs, the smell of roses and lemon blossom, and the song of birds.[38] The fountains played almost every evening – a time when, as Captain William Sleeman (a British official engaged in suppressing the Thugs, or religious assassins; cf. p. 105) observed in 1836, the garden was 'much frequented by the European gentlemen and ladies of the station, and by natives of all religions and sects'.[39] On Sundays and holidays and festivals (*mela*), stalls with Indian sweetmeats were put up in the Jilaukhana and huge numbers of people filled the garden. For Fanny Parks, the

> crowds of gaily dressed and most picturesque natives . . . added great beauty to the scene, whilst the eye of taste turned away pained and annoyed by the vile round hats and stiff attire of the

European gentlemen, and the equally ugly bonnets and stiff and graceless dresses of the English ladies.[40]

A vivid picture, though from a somewhat condescending colonial viewpoint, is painted of the 'natives' in one of the earliest guides to the Taj Mahal, an anonymous *Handbook* of 1854 (new edition 1862) based on older sources:

> Sunday is a great day at the Taj with the inhabitants of Agra; crowds attend from the city and from the country around, and every hue and fanciful color [sic] dress may be seen; first and foremost precocious young Agra, youths from the college, with their white garments and small pugrees, imitating what they fancy a European swagger, and profaning the sanctity of the place with the most unoriental whistling, which dreadfully disturbs the devout contemplation of that Moolah who is counting his beads and looking as if the Taj belonged to him alone. Then the clean-dressed Mahomedans from the Government offices, and the *kâit* [*kayasth*] or Hindoo writer; now a group of country people staring with open eyes headed by some loquacious old granddame, who takes care to inform everyone that 'the Feringees' [Europeans] stole all the precious stones out of the inlaid flowers in the Taj walls. When Agra was taken by Lord Lake the 22nd Dragoons may have done a little pilfering in this line; but the example had been set then by the Jats when they looted Agra . . . Then parties of Bunniahs [Hindi *baniya*, shopkeeper, tradesman] . . . that foremost man has had the whole of his pleasure trip spoilt by the idea that he has left his shop for the day in the hands of his nephew . . . he sees not beauty in the Taj; he does not enjoy the fragrance of the flowers; true it is he utters the words 'Ram, Ram' of astonishment, meaning 'wonderful, wonderful, God bless me'; but he does not mean it for the Taj; he is repenting of his rashness in leaving his shop . . . The . . . Affghan [sic] may also be seen, who declares that the tomb of Mahmood of Guznee [Ghazni] is a much grander affair than the Taj; it is as well those Agra Mahomedans, just before him, do not understand what he is saying, or there would be a war of words . . . Some times a clean dressed Persian may be seen with his black lamb skin cap and shining waist dagger; he generally shows off his superior knowledge by reading to himself the Persian inscriptions, which the crowd knows as much the meaning of, as the crowd in London do of the Latin written upon our tombs and monuments; some Moulvie will stop, and the Persian will expatiate upon the beauties of Hafiz or Sadi, from the latter poet he declares himself to be a direct descendant. . . . The clever native youths make a lime or orange remain as it were suspended into midair; by the force of the water [of the fountains] the lime is sometimes, when the water is at full power, carried up into the air to the height of 15 or 20 feet [4.5–6 m] and gradually descends as the column of water diminishes in power; to a person, who may never happen to have seen this before, the effect is most curious and striking. Young Agra is in the habit of making bets as to whose orange or lime will keep up longest, and great excitement is caused . . . by such puerile and innocent amusement.[41]

The Taj Mahal was recognized as a unifying power, a utopian space; in the words of Keene's *Handbook* of 1899, 'As much admired by the Natives as by Europeans, the Taj and its garden furnish a proof that, like a touch of nature, an appeal of true art also can make the whole world kin.'[42] There was however occasion for friction. Both the 'natives' and sensitive British visitors like Fanny Parks took offence that the Europeans had 'the [military] band to play on the marble terrace, and dance quadrilles in front of the tomb', flirted 'beneath the shade of the cypresses', arranged entertainments in the Mihman Khana, and behaved in all sorts of undignified ways.[43] One of these events, on 23 December 1832, took a bad turn, when one of two ladies who had raced on the marble platform of the mausoleum became dizzy and fell to her death while her brother-in-law watched helplessly from one of the minarets.[44] At British picnic parties the gentlemen might work at the mausoleum with hammer and chisel and present agates and cornelians to the ladies of their acquaintance.[45] And, as Florentia Sale's sharp tongue put it, 'with that propensity to scribbling so commonly evinced by the English and which must be considered as a National propensity of considerable bad taste much nonsense has been scribbled on the walls of one of these apartments'. She speaks of poems on the walls in one of the side rooms of the mausoleum, and copied those she thought most interesting into her *Notebook*.

> O Thou whose great Imperial mind could raise
> This splendid Trophy to a woman's praise,
> If love or grief inspired the bold design
> No mental joy or sorrow equalled thine –
> Sleep on Serene, this Monument shall stand
> When desolation's wing sweeps o'er the Land
> By time or death in one wide ruin hurl'd
> The last triumphant wonder of the world.[46]

Today these scribblings appear as a curious literary evidence of how the British of those days reacted to the Taj. They have been obliterated, but graffiti of 19th-century visitors can still be made out, scratched into the panes of glass fitted into the *jalis* of the arches in the central hall of the mausoleum [365].

On the other hand, Keene's guidebook felt that 'as long as the natives hold constant fairs in the enclosure and throw orange-peel and other debris about the whole place, it is perhaps somewhat hypercritical [sic] to object to a few Englishmen refreshing themselves, within the limits of becoming mirth, in a remote corner used for no other purpose'.[47]

The relationship between the British and the Taj became strained under Lord William Cavendish Bentinck. When Governor-General he was famous for his drive for economy, and during his great northern Indian tour of 1830 he was said to have entertained the idea of demolishing the Taj Mahal in order to sell its marbles. The rumour had its origin in the fact that Bentinck did indeed auction off the marble facing and perhaps even pillars of Shah Jahan's *hammam* in the Agra fort, for the benefit of the British Government (p. 69).

India's great uprising against British rule in 1857–58 – previously designated the Mutiny, now called by Indian scholars the First War of Independence – had a dampening effect on the

365 Visitors' names scratched on the glass of a *jali* of the upper floor of the tomb chamber of the mausoleum, opposite the entrance: they read 'Miss Jones 1849' and 'Miss King from Cawnpore 1849'. (Photograph taken in 1999)

idyllic intercultural gatherings at the Taj Mahal. The headquarters of the North-Western Provinces Government were removed to Allahabad, and Agra dwindled to the position of a more provincial town.

Aesthetic reception and documentation

The British were also instrumental in the aesthetic reception, conservation, and scientific documentation of the Taj Mahal. From the beginning every observer felt compelled to come up with a judgment of form and style which was generally enthusiastic. Europeans were drawn to the monument, finding that although it had unusual features and was 'Oriental' it had qualities they could easily relate to. Already the perceptive Bernier had reflected along these lines and had noted the Italian connotations of the fine workmanship of the *pietra dura* (p. 92).[48] Tavernier found the dome 'scarcely less magnificent than that of the Val-de-Grâce in Paris' (completed in 1667).[49] As the fame of the Taj Mahal spread, all those who saw it were invariably astonished at how well it lived up to its reputation.[50] The dialectics of the Shahjahani aesthetics expressed in the monument had something for everyone, for the Classical as well as for the Picturesque taste. The perfect 'symmetry of the whole' praised by Hodges[51] paralleled the complexes of

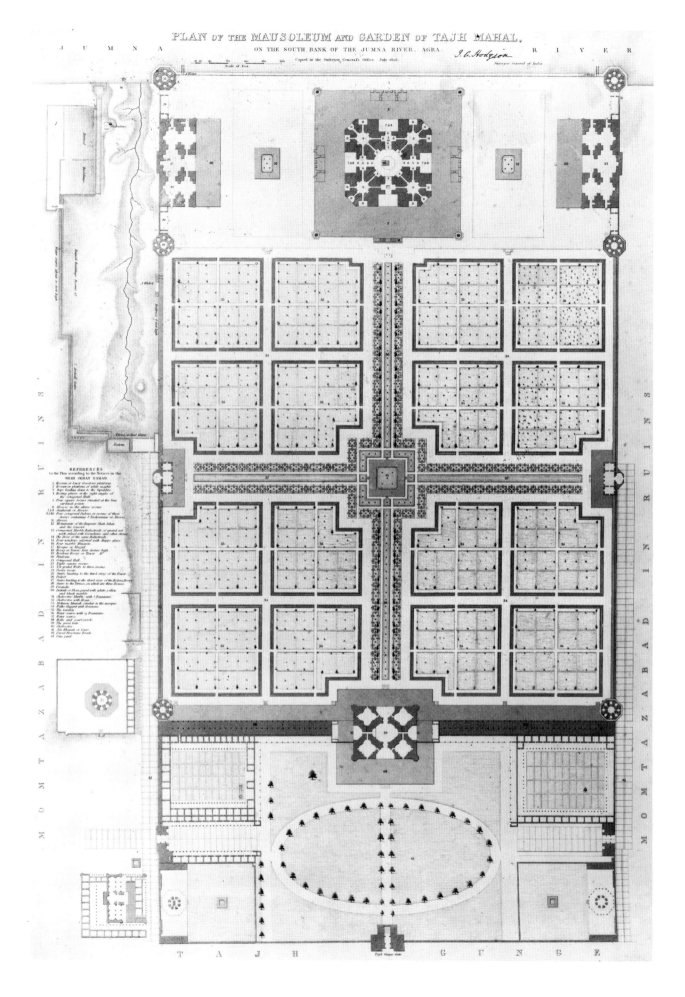

366 'Plan of the Mausoleum and Garden of Tajh Mahal, on the south bank of the Jumna River, Agra, copied in the Surveyor-General's Office, July 1828'. The plan – signed by J. A. Hodgson – was surveyed by M. Burke, Assistant, and W. N. James and E. Winston, Sub-Assistants, and drawn by Peeareelaul and J. Biswass; engraved in London by James Basire, it was published in the *Journal of the Royal Asiatic Society* in 1843. A key on the left gives 'References to the Plan according to the Notices in the Shah Jehan Namah', i.e. Lahauri's *Padshahnama*, beginning with the mausoleum and moving south to the Jilaukhana. Some of the arcaded ranges of the Jilaukhana and bazaar streets in the south and south-east had already disappeared [cp. 147], and the rooms of the Khawasspuras are not accurately rendered. The bazaar and caravanserai complex is excluded.

absolutist Europe. The pointed arches were seen as relating to Gothic, a style favoured by the Picturesque movement.[52] The riverfront situation of the monu-ment among the ruins of Agra, and the garden which, though ordered in its planning, was by then filled with exuberant growth, appealed to the British feeling for Picturesque landscape. And romantic sentiment was gratified through the love story of Shah Jahan and Mumtaz Mahal. The few who wanted to find fault complained that the aesthetics of the Taj Mahal expressed womanish and thus lesser qualities; in this they conflated the burial with the buried, and also conformed to a general opinion that the Orient was feminine.[53]

From the beginning it was felt that the architectural excellence of the Taj Mahal could only have been created with European involvement. In 1640–41 the Augustinian friar Sebastian Manrique came up with the claim that the architect of the Taj Mahal was an Italian goldsmith named 'Geronimo [Jerónimo] Veroneo', which gave rise to an enduring controversy between British and Indian scholars (p. 249).[54] As we have seen, textual research has made it clear that the monument was conceived by a team of architects working under Shah Jahan's supervision, and formal analysis shows that it is entirely within Mughal architectural traditions (pp. 84, 104–5). To Ida Pfeiffer (1797–1858), a world-travelling lady from Vienna [368], this was evident already in the mid-19th century: 'Many ascribe it to Italian masters; but when it is seen that there are so many other admirable works of Mahomedan architecture, either the whole must be considered foreign or this must be admitted to be native.'[55]

The first British plan of the Taj was that made by the Daniells in 1789 and published in 1801, which included the bazaar and caravanserai complex [147]. This was followed in 1828 by a more exact plan drawn up on the order of the Surveyor-General of India, Colonel J. A. Hodgson [366]. That plan did not, however, include the by then ruined bazaar and caravanserai complex: published in 1843 in the *Journal of the Royal Asiatic Society*, it served as the basis of all later plans, and was thus instrumental in creating the incomplete concept of the monument which persists today.

In 1860 the Archaeological Survey of India was founded, with the initial agenda to survey and record the historical monuments of India. In 1873 conservation was delegated to the local governments (p. 251). In 1895 regional Survey Circles were created and equipped with surveyors and draughtsmen. However, even in 1914 there existed 'as yet no complete series of detailed drawings of the Taj Mahal'.[56] In the following decades new survey plans and measured drawings were prepared of the Taj Mahal complex and of its individual buildings but only a few of these were published.[57] While

the Archaeological Survey brought out in its 'New Imperial Series' monumental monographs documenting other Mughal complexes such as Fatehpur Sikri (1894–98) and Akbar's tomb at Sikandra (1909), no publication was ever devoted to the Taj Mahal: not even a guidebook was issued. This reserve did not change after India's independence, when the office of the Archaeological Survey was continued by the new Indian Government.[58]

The first photographers

The advent of photography in Europe in 1839 soon affected India, where it was enthusiastically received by British and Indians alike, as a new medium to document the immensity of the country and the variety of its people. Photography was recognized as both a means of artistic expression and a documentary tool, and was welcomed for being more accurate than painting to record architecture and archaeology. The early photographers in India came from diverse backgrounds and were not always professionals, but they did not let the complex techniques and bulky equipment of early photography dampen their enthusiasm.[59]

The earliest known photographs of Agra and the Taj Mahal were made by Dr John Murray (1809–98), who was appointed civil surgeon at Agra in 1848 [38, 40, 70]. He took up the new medium in the late 1840s, and is considered as the finest exponent of photography based on paper negatives in India of his time. The technique produces prints with a broad and subtle tonal range, evoking engravings. Murray started photographing at Agra in the early 1850s: his favourite subject was the Taj Mahal, of which he made a series of large-format studies, from inside the overgrown garden as well as from the river and the adjoining ruined garden buildings, including a spectacular three-part panorama [367].[60] The contrast between the perfect marble building and the luxuriant nature or ruins around it emphasized the picturesque and romantic qualities which the earlier travellers had so appreciated. In 1858 a portfolio of thirty of his topographical and architectural views, of which five depict the Taj Mahal, was published under the title *Agra and Its Vicinity*. Murray also took a keen personal interest in the Taj Mahal and the monuments of Agra (p. 251), and set up initiatives to revive the craft of *pietra dura*, which had almost died out by then.[61]

Better known than Murray's views of the Taj are those of Samuel Bourne (1834–1912), a professional photographer who in 1865 formed a partnership with Charles Shepherd. Bourne & Shepherd established studios in Simla, Calcutta and Bombay and became the leading suppliers of photographic views of India. (Because of the difficult technique, most travellers did not take pictures themselves, but ordered them from professionals.) Though Bourne's main interest was the landscapes of Kashmir and the Himalayas, he also came to Agra in 1865 and 1866 and photographed the Taj Mahal and other buildings.[62]

Other early photographers who documented the Taj were Harriet (1827–1907) and Robert (1818–72) Tytler; Felice Beato (1825–1907), who took views of Agra in the late 1850s in connection with his recording of the Indian Mutiny; John Edward Saché (in India 1865–82), who photographed the Taj in the late 1860s; and the Indian photographer Lala Deen Dayal (1844–1905). In the later 19th century, Johnston & Hoffman, a British company based at Calcutta,

367 Three-photograph view of the Taj in its garden: albumen prints by Dr John Murray, dated 30 January 1854. The view extends out to the garden-wall pavilions on either side, and gives the fullest impression of the wilderness of the garden in the 19th century.

prepared views which document changes in the planting of the garden.[63]

VISITORS AND COMMENTS

After the British 'discovered' it in the late 18th century the Taj Mahal became a must on the itinerary of every traveller to India, and the visitors and their comments have made cultural history in themselves. Edward, Prince of Wales, who visited India in 1875–76, observed that it was a commonplace for every writer 'to set out with the admission that it is indescribable, and then proceed to give some idea of it.'[64] Here is Thomas Bacon, who visited the Taj Mahal on 28 December 1835:

> So much I had heard, on all sides, of this extraordinary edifice, that I had fully prepared myself for a disappointment; but when I stood in presence of the noble pile, I could not help feeling that, had fifty times as much been said in its praise, and had it been but one-half as exquisite, I should have allowed that all these rhapsodies had fallen short of its real magnificence. It appears absurd to attempt a description of such a structure. I am fully sensible of my own utter inability to the task, but I fear this would be deemed an insufficient apology for passing over it.[65]

Reginald Heber (1783–1826), the Anglican Bishop of Calcutta, saw the Taj on 13 January 1825, and, 'after hearing its praises ever since I had been in India', felt that 'its beauty rather exceeded than fell short of my expectations'. The central hall of the mausoleum seemed to him 'about as large as the interior of the Ratcliffe [sic] library' at Oxford where he had studied. He did not, however, like the dome and the minarets: 'the bulbous swell of the former I think clumsy, and the minarets have nothing to recommend them but their height and the beauty of their materials'.[66]

The most famous statement is perhaps that of the wife of Captain Sleeman: when after their visit to the Taj in January 1836 her husband asked what she thought of it, she answered, 'I cannot tell you what I think, for I know not how to criticize such a building, but I can tell you what I feel. I would die tomorrow to have such another over me.'[67] In the previous year Fanny Parks had expressed a similar sentiment: 'And now adieu! – beautiful Taj – adieu! In the far, far West I shall rejoice that I have gazed upon your beauty; nor will the memory depart until the lowly tomb of an English gentlewoman closes on my remains.'[68]

Another female traveller, the perceptive Ida Pfeiffer [368], who came to Agra from Vienna in January 1848, was the first modern observer to voice the idea that the mausoleum was meant not only to be a magnificent burial for Mumtaz Mahal but was also to testify to the glory of Shah Jahan: 'Properly speaking the Sultan's memory is more perpetuated by this building than that of his favourite, for everyone who saw it would involuntarily ask who created it.'[69]

Lord Curzon (1859–1925) saw the Taj first in 1887 and found it a 'snow-white emanation starting from a bed of cypresses, and backed by a turquoise sky, pure, perfect and unutterably lovely'.[70] After he became Governor-General and Viceroy of India in 1898 he made 'the Taj his obsession' and visited Agra annually to supervise its restoration (pp. 251–52). The lamp of Egyptian 'Saracenic' design that he commissioned for the tomb chamber [233] (p. 166) was to hang there as his 'last tribute to the glories of Agra which float like a vision of eternal beauty in my memory'.[71]

One of the most enduring responses to the Taj was the perception of its otherworldliness and immateriality. The Western viewers recognized spontaneously, despite coming from different cultures and without having read the contemporary Mughal texts, the intention that it should represent an edifice not of this world.

The building itself conveyed its message, speaking directly through its forms and materials. The German Captain Leopold von Orlich (1804–60), who had arrived in India in 1842 to join the British Afghan war, found it had ended, and instead went round the country and wrote an account of his journeys, was at Agra on 21 February 1843: 'We perceived at a considerable distance this diamond of the buildings of the world, which from the dazzling whiteness of the marble, of which this magnificent sepulchre is built, looks like an enchanted castle of burnished silver.'[72]

Samuel Bourne, the photographer, first visited the Taj in spring 1863, and described it for the readers of the *British Journal of Photography*. For him it was a dream taking material form, a fantasy, a caprice of imagination transformed into marble, and he summed up his impression in verse:

368 The Viennese traveller Ida Pfeiffer visiting the Taj Mahal, from her book *A Woman's Journey round the World*, 1851.

A palace lifting to eternal summer
Its marble halls from out a glassy bower
Of coolest foliage, musical with birds.[73]

Even specific associations made by Shah Jahan's poets, like the comparison of the Taj to an insubstantial cloud (p. 105), were echoed unknowingly by later visitors. Bayard Taylor (1825–78), an American novelist and journalist writing for the *New York Tribune*, visited Agra in 1853 and felt that 'If there were nothing else in India, this alone would repay the journey.' He remarked, like so many others, on the immateriality of the mausoleum:

> Did you ever build a Castle in the Air? Here is one, brought down to earth, and fixed for the wonder of ages; yet so light it seems, so airy, and, when seen from a distance, so like a fabric of mist and sunbeams, with its great dome soaring up, a silvery bubble, about to burst in the sun, that even after you have touched it, and climbed to its summit, you almost doubt its reality.[74]

The German philosopher Count Hermann Keyserling (1860–1946) commented similarly on the Taj when he saw it during his stay in India in 1911–12: 'A massive marble structure, without weight, as if formed of ether, perfectly rational and at the same time entirely decorative . . . it is perhaps the greatest art work which the forming spirit of mankind has ever brought forth.' For Keyserling the Taj was the perfect work of art because it had no meaning: it was art for art's sake. He did however grasp some of the Platonic concept of Shah Jahan and his advisers (p. 215): 'In this way the primordial image of the Taj may have ornamented the world of ideas since eternity.'[75] And no less an art-historical luminary than the Swiss Heinrich Wölfflin (1864–1945) envisaged the building as 'On a white marble terrace an immaterial light shell like the apartments of the blessed, whose foot does not touch ordinary ground.' He saw in 'the feminine shy grace of the Taj the true spirit of India'.[76] In the same vein, E. B. Havell (1861–1934), principal of the Calcutta art school in the early 20th century and a promoter of Indian nationalism, declared the Taj to be the personification of 'Mumtaz Mahal herself radiant in her youthful beauty . . . India's noble tribute to the grace of Indian womanhood – the Venus de Milo of the East.'[77]

Indian authors too reacted to their most famous building. Yusuf Khan Kambalposh travelled in England and France in 1837 and wrote an account in Persian, which he translated into Urdu. There he used the Taj, which he calls 'Rauza-i Taj Bibi' (Mausoleum of the Taj Lady), as a standard against which to measure the buildings he admired. Of St Paul's Cathedral in London he says, 'When I saw the building, I was deeply amazed and wondered if I should compare it to the Rauza-i Taj Bibi or consider it even better than that.' And later in France he writes of the palace of Versailles, 'Truly, that place (*makan*) was a *lakh* [100,000] times better than Rauza-i Taj Bibi. It was better than all the buildings in Hindustan and London.'[78] The celebrated Bengali writer Rabindranath Tagore (1861–1941) devoted two poems to Shah Jahan and the Taj Mahal. For him it was, famously, a teardrop on the cheek of time.

> You knew, Emperor of India, Shah-Jahan,
> That life, youth, wealth, renown
> All float away down the stream of time.

Your only dream
Was to preserve forever your heart's pain.
The harsh thunder of imperial power
Would fade into sleep
Like a sunset's crimson splendour,
But it was your hope
That at least a single, eternally heaved sigh would stay
To grieve the sky.
Though emeralds, rubies, pearls are all
But as the glitter of a rainbow tricking out empty air
And must pass away,
Yet still one solitary tear
Would hang on the cheek of time
In the form
Of this white and gleaming Taj Mahal.
. . .
You could not maintain
Your grief forever, and so you enmeshed
Your restless weeping
In bonds of silent perpetuity.
The names you softly
Whispered to your love
On moonlit nights in secret chambers live on
Here
As whispers in the ear of eternity.
The poignant gentleness of love
Flowered into the beauty of serene stone.[79]

The 20th century also brought more critical voices. In the 1920s Aldous Huxley (1894–1963) disliked the Taj because everyone else admired it and he did not want to join in the chorus of eulogizers. 'The world admires; but I cannot. I wish I could.' Looking to find fault, he criticized the Taj's 'expensiveness and picturesqueness', judged the architecture poor, dry and negative, 'the product of a deficiency of fancy, a poverty of imagination', considered the *pietra dura* decorations uninteresting, and dismissed the minarets as 'among the ugliest structures ever erected by human hands'.[80]

Today one may meet with a less pronounced but similarly guarded attitude to the Taj Mahal on the part of the traveller. He or she has seen the building reproduced so often, especially in its classic frontal view, that the encounter with the real structure can produce an effect of déja vu and the feeling that there is nothing left to discover. The perfection of the Taj has to be accepted in a rather passive way, which irritates adventurous spirits.

The most critical responses come from the inhabitants of Agra, who have even coined the saying 'Taj hatao – Agra bachao', or 'Remove the Taj – save Agra', because they feel left out of the profits the government makes from its most popular sightseeing attraction.

A visit to the Taj Mahal is part of the programme of every visiting head of state. This has dire consequences for the ordinary tourist (as well as for the investigating scholar!), because on such occasions the entire complex will be closed at short notice for hours – if not for the entire day, as it was for President Clinton on 22 March 2000.

THE TAJ MAHAL IN POPULAR CULTURE

The image of the Taj Mahal has been reproduced more often than that of any other building. It has become a symbol of India, despite India's uneasiness with its Islamic past and despite being a tomb, which has no place in the Hindu tradition (p. 85).

Models of the Taj Mahal are one of the most popular souvenirs of India, and one can find hundreds of them in all sizes [369]. Already in 1812, as we have seen, Lady Nugent had a replica of one of the minarets made, and from the mid-19th century onwards large models of the Taj Mahal, in wood or alabaster, were shipped to Europe and the United States where they survive in various collections and private homes.[81] The largest reproduction is a model on a scale of 1:25 erected in 1975 as one of the famous buildings of the world in the architectural theme park Minimundus at Klagenfurt in Austria (incidentally, my home town) [370]. It is based on the designs of the architect Jakob Strauss, who travelled to India to obtain measured drawings from the Archaeological Survey of India.[82]

Marble plates, boxes and table tops with the characteristic *pietra dura* inlay feed a thriving tourist market, and one can observe craftsmen at work in front of the shops in Taj Ganj [115]. The Taj Mahal appears on souvenir items like T-shirts, bags, and even women's underwear. Its image is widely used by travel agencies and airlines to attract tourists to India.

369 Souvenir Taj Mahals in the Taj Gift Center, 2/16 South Gate. (Photograph taken in 2002)

370 Model of the Taj Mahal at a scale of 1:25 in the architectural theme park Minimundus, Klagenfurt, Austria, made between 1973 and 1975. (Photograph taken in 2003)

In popular culture the Taj has become a metaphor for excellence, the superlative, abstracted from its original context. It is used in advertisements to sell all sorts of products which have nothing at all to do with its being a tomb – jewelry, teabags, Scotch whisky, liqueur and beer [371].[83] To promote the sale of alcohol with the image of the Taj Mahal is particularly ironic, because Shah Jahan as an orthodox Muslim was averse to drinking and touched wine only upon his father's insistence (p. 19).

In the United States the Taj Mahal is a byword for prestigious architecture. If you have constructed a particularly grand house, your friends will say: 'You have built yourself a real Taj Mahal!' The property 'mogul' Donald Trump literally did so in 1990 with the Trump Taj Mahal, his casino resort in Atlantic City, New Jersey. Inside its garish shell it houses surprisingly well observed adaptations of elements of Shah Jahan's palace and garden architecture, if not of the Taj Mahal. The Tata Group in India named three of its hotels 'Taj Mahal' (one in Bombay and two in Delhi). Indian restaurants all over the world carry its name and entice clients with replicas of the Taj in their windows.

Even popular musicians like to associate themselves with the Taj Mahal. Henry St Clair Fredericks, a rock-blues singer from Massachusetts, adopted 'Taj Mahal' as his stage name.[84] Paul Horn's flute session recorded in 1968, 'Inside the Taj Mahal', sold more than a million copies and became a key work of 'new age' music (p. 228). In 1997 the Greek singer Yanni succeeded, despite fierce opposition, in giving a concert below the mausoleum on one of the islands that form during the dry season, requiring the construction of a special pontoon bridge.

The widest popularization of the Taj Mahal comes through tourists. They take photographs or have their pictures taken by

371 An advertisement for Godiva Liqueur, 1995.

372 A tourist 'holding' The Taj Mahal. (Photograph taken in 2002)

professional photographers who linger around the great gate and specialize in optical illusions where the Taj seems to be hanging from the hand of the person photographed [372]. Thus it becomes everybody's Taj Mahal.

The myths of the Taj Mahal

Like many a great building the Taj Mahal has its myths and legends, the Taj perhaps more than others because the monument's singularity stimulated extravagant responses. It seems that there is more fiction on the Taj than serious scholarly research. Several of the stories belong solely to oral tradition and are told by the guides, some are so established that they form a popular history of the monument and have made their way into guidebooks,[85] and some have been taken up by scholars, or even created by them, and thus become part of the scholarly debate.

To the last category belong the oldest tales of the Taj. Here the most widely known is the story of the second Taj , the 'Black Taj' which Shah Jahan intended to build in black marble opposite the present mausoleum, on the site of the Mahtab Bagh (p. 56) [374]. It goes back to Jean-Baptiste Tavernier who, when at Agra in 1665, reported that 'Shahjahan began to built his own tomb on the other side of the river, but the war with his sons interrupted his plan, and Aurangzeb, who reigns at present, is not disposed to complete it.'[86] Though there is no other historical evidence to support this claim, it became the most enduring of the legends of the Taj, and even led to excavations in the Mahtab Bagh in the early 1990s. These showed no foundations of a mausoleum.

Another story that came up in the 16th century and survived through much of the 20th century was, not surprisingly, also reported by a European, namely that the Taj was built by a European architect. The source is Sebastian Manrique, a Spanish friar of the Augustinian order, who visited Agra in 1640–41 and reported:

> The architect of these works was a Venetian, by name Geronimo Veroneo [373], who had come to this part in a Portuguese ship and died at the City of Laor just before I reached it . . . the Emperor summoned him and informed him that he desired to erect a great and sumptuous tomb to his dead wife, and he was

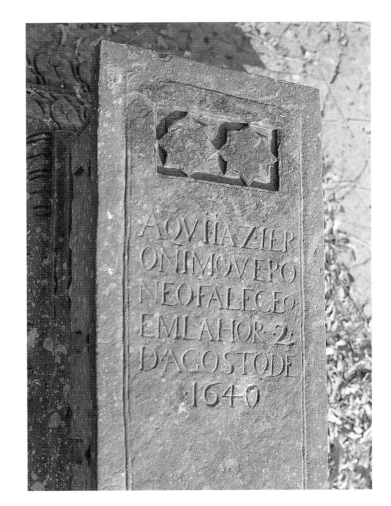

required to draw up some designs for this, for the Emperor's inspection. The architect Veroneo carried out this order . . . [and] pleased this Ruler in respect of the designs, but, in his barbaric pride and arrogance, His Majesty was displeased with him owing to his low estimates, and it is said that, becoming angry, he told Veroneo to spend three crores of rupees, that is three hundred lakhs [30 million rupees] and to inform him when it was expended.[87]

373 Inscription on the tomb of Geronimo Veroneo in the old Catholic cemetery at Agra. It says 'Here lies Zieronimo Veroneo, who died at Lahore on 2 August 1640'. (Photograph taken in 2005)

374 Percy Brown's reconstruction of Tavernier's report of the 'Black Taj', entitled 'Conjectural Realization of the Emperor Shah Jahan's scheme for the Royal Tombs at Agra', from *Indian Architecture (Islamic Period)*, 1956.

Since the early 19th century it was also said that an architect from Ottoman Turkey, 'Ustad Isa', might have been the builder of the Taj (p. 89).

Recent Western scholars came up with extravagant theories of their own which have a somewhat sexist tint. Wayne Begley was convinced that the Taj Mahal could not just be a tomb for Mumtaz, but that it was meant to represent the Throne of God (p. 225). Henri Stierlin felt that, given the inferior position of women in Muslim societies, the Taj could not have been built for Mumtaz (ignoring other tombs for women in the Islamic world), and that Shah Jahan had begun to build it for himself before the death of Mumtaz (ignoring the data of the construction history provided by the contemporary historians as well as the fact that previous Mughal imperial mausoleums were built by sons for their fathers).[88]

Present-day India is more interested in the story that the Taj was originally a Hindu temple, dedicated to Shiva. A direct attempt to realize this idea had been made in the 18th century, after Suraj Mal's conquest of Agra in 1761, when a court priest is said to have suggested to convert the Taj Mahal into a temple.[89] That the Taj was founded as a Hindu temple is now the firm belief of many a visitor, who is at pains to put his foreign fellow visitors right about the origin of the building. The hottest propagator of this idea is P. N. Oak (b. 1917 in Indore), who has many followers. Oak founded the Institute for Rewriting Indian History in 1964 and published an enormous body of writing to show, among other things, that 'All historic structures in India (and even abroad) currently ascribed to Muslim sultans and courtiers (including so-called tombs and mosques, gardens, forts, canals, townships, castles, towers and bridges) are pre-Muslim constructions.'[90] The Taj Mahal is really 'Tejo-Mahalaya', a Shiva temple.

Then there are the guides' tales. The most popular is the story that Shah Jahan killed the architect and the workers after completion of the building, so that they would not be able to build another like it. There are variants – that the emperor had their hands chopped off, or their eyes put out, or had them thrown into the dungeons of the Agra fort to which they were brought through a tunnel leading off from the Tahkhana, the underground chambers in the terrace of the Taj. The Muslim guides have a toned-down version: that Shah Jahan made the workers sign a contract so that they would not build another building of the kind.

This story is not peculiar to the Taj: it belongs to a well established group of folk motifs which can be found in many cultures. In Stith Thompson's classic compilation these motifs are listed as 'King kills architect after completion of great building, so that he may never again build one so great', 'Artisan who has built palace blinded so that he cannot build another like it', and 'Masons who build mausoleum of princess lose their right hands so they may never again construct so fine a building'.[91] Versions of these motifs are reported from various parts of Europe – Great Britain, Ireland, Russia – and Asia.[92] In a Muslim context, the legend appears earlier in the context of the Sasanian castle of Khwarnaq, some 200 km (125 mi.) south of Baghdad near Najaf, which was considered one of the thirty wonders of the world in the early Arabic Middle Ages: according to Arab historians and geographers, the patron had the architect thrown from its battlements after its completion.[93]

For the Taj these stories are presented as historical facts. Even journalists of renowned newspapers may garnish their reports with additions like 'The chief architect is known to have been Ustad – or Master – Ahmad Lahori. Shah Jahan is said to have had his eyes put out on the Taj's completion so nothing could ever be built to rival it.'[94]

Muslim guides like to recount that the saints whose *dargahs* (shrines) are situated around the Taj helped in the construction: Sayyid Jalal-ud-Din Bukhari, whose *dargah* is to the west, and Sayyid Ahmad Bukhari, to the east, brought stones and mortar and blessed them. Other tales hold that once a year in August, in the rainy season, a drop of water falls on the cenotaphs, obviously to signify a blessing from heaven. And another story goes that if the silhouette of the Taj finial inlaid into the platform in front of the Mihman Khana [263] is beaten, water will come forth. The staff of the Taj say they often find pieces of broken bangles of women who tried this out.

CONSERVATION AND FUTURE

The first repairs to the mausoleum were already necessary soon after its completion. On 4 December 1652 Aurangzeb wrote to his father that he had visited Agra and inspected the condition of the Taj Mahal: he reported that the building was on the whole in a satisfactory condition, but that the dome of the mausoleum leaked in two places on the north side, that water was also coming in elsewhere – the four large *pishtaqs*, several of the arched niches (*shah nashin*) of the second storey, the four small domes (presumably the roof *chhatris*), the four northern arched niches (*suffa*) [of the ground floor?], and the Tahkhana in the platform – and that the domes of the mosque and Mihman Khana had leaked during the rainy season. He consulted with the builders (*bannayan*) and they suggested taking up the paving of the flat surface of the roof (*farsh-i pusht-i bam*) and treating it with concrete (*rekhta*) and mortar (*tahkari*); the work was put in hand.[95] After that no more repairs are mentioned in the Mughal sources: we learn only that in 1691 Aurangzeb ordered the governor of every province to make it a practice of sending 2,000 rupees (yearly?) to Khwaja Khidmat Khan, whom he had established as caretaker (*wali*) for the maintenance of the Taj Mahal.[96]

Not much is known about the condition of the Taj Mahal until the end of the 18th century. Then the mausoleum does not seem to have suffered any major damage and the fountains of the garden were at least partly in working order, but the buildings of the outer courts were falling into ruin. On 22 January 1794 Colonel Sir John Murray, Commissary-General at Calcutta and then Military Auditor-General, wrote to General de Boigne, in the army of Mahadaji Sindhia (p. 232), that on the occasion of a visit to Agra a few years ago he had 'had the Mortification to observe that, that Masterpiece of elegant Taste and exquisite Workmanship, was much neglected', and suggested measures to preserve the monument 'for admiration in future ages'. De Boigne replied that he had tried to convince Sindhia to finance the upkeep and that some payment of 'the few Mahavers or Priests [obviously the tomb attendants and Qur'an reciters] about it as keep the building and the Garden in repair' was under discussion but that he feared his efforts would meet with little success'.[97] In June of that same year another British observer, Major J. H. (p. 232), noted the decay of the institution of the *khadim*:

'On either side [of the great gate] are apartments formerly occupied by fackeers who lived on Shah Jehann's bounty; these are now going fast to ruin.'[98]

After Lord Lake took Agra in 1803, the mausoleum became the focus of selective preservation of Indian monuments by the British. The Court of Directors of the East India Company had a guarded attitude towards such expenses: only a few buildings were to be conserved, which were regarded 'as models of perfection in their several stiles' – the Moti Masjid in the fort, the tomb of Akbar at Sikandra, and the great gate, the Buland Darwaza, of the mosque of Fatehpur Sikri.[99] These are also the buildings that feature most frequently in Company drawings.

In 1808 a local Committee was formed, comprising the Magistrate, the Collector and the Commanding Officer at Agra, which was directed to report on the arrangements proposed for the maintenance of the Taj Mahal, the rules for visiting it, the establishment to be employed for the buildings and gardens, and the repairs required, which were to be carried out by the Engineer Officer stationed at Agra. In November Lieutenant-Colonel Alexander Kyd, the first to assess what works were necessary, voiced the early enthusiasm for

> this splendid monument which for magnificence and taste and costliness of materials far exceeds anything of the same kind that is probably in the universe, the repairing and keeping in order of which will reflect such credit on the British Government through every part of Indoostan.

He found the mausoleum in fairly good repair, with only minor surface damage to be mended, such as removing plants and trees from marble joints.[100] The main problem was missing stones: visitors, the Jats, and Lord Lake's soldiers had pilfered some of the inlay work.[101] In 1810 Lieutenant Joseph Taylor was appointed, under the guidance of Colonel Hyde, the acting Chief Engineer, to repair and clean the entire outer surface of the mausoleum, and to renew the inlay work by replacing missing stones. Taylor's use of coloured stucco in place of the original inlaid stones proved a failure, as the work was badly damaged during heavy rains.[102] (When the pinnacle of the dome was regilded in 1874 an inscription was found on the crescent, cut in the copper: 'Joseph Taylor 1811'. The first restorer of the Taj had immortalized himself in this way.[103])

The British efforts were duly acknowledged by Bayard Taylor, the American journalist, in 1853: 'Too much praise cannot be awarded to the British rulers in India, for the care with which they have restored and protected all of these monuments of the past, expending large sums to prevent the mosques, palaces and tombs of the former rulers from falling into decay.'[104]

A new initiative was undertaken in 1864 by Dr John Murray, the first photographer of the Taj (p. 243), to organize the repair of the inlay of the cenotaphs, screen, and interior wall of the mausoleum, which had been damaged particularly during the Uprising of 1857–58. The work was continued under Colonel Rowlatt, 'Local Agent in charge of the Taj Buildings', who replaced all the corners of the platforms of the upper cenotaphs, with their inlaid flowers and scrollwork, because cracks had developed. He was fully aware that his efforts were under close scrutiny, the Taj being the showpiece of British conservation in India, and was proud to report in April 1867:

except on very close inspection, it is not possible to discover that pieces have been let in, or that any injury had taken place to these tombs . . . [which are] in a more perfect state of preservation than they ever were before, and may now be examined and admired by the numberless tourists of all nations who visit the Taj, without any fear of disparaging remarks being made on the government for want of proper care being taken of them.

Rowlatt also devised a stage suspended on ropes, passed around the finials of the domes, which enabled their repair without costly scaffolding, and submitted a plan for the restoration of the water system of the garden, to renew the broken 'old earthenware pipes 6 feet [1.8 m] underground . . . embedded in solid masonry' in the stretch from the great gate to the foot of the mausoleum, to put the fountains back in working order.[105]

A few years earlier, in 1860, the Archaeological Survey of India had been founded under the Governor-General and Viceroy Lord Canning, and in 1862 General Cunningham was officially appointed as the first Archaeological Surveyor to the Government (he had actually begun work at the end of 1861).[106] The main agenda of the Survey was to record the monuments. In 1873 the duty to care for 'all buildings and monuments of historical or architectural interest' was assigned by the Public Works Department to the local governments.[107] This led to the foundation of the Agra Archaeological Society at the end of the same year, with the personal involvement of Sir John Strachey, Lieutenant-Governor of the North-Western Provinces. The Society advised on the repairs to the Taj Mahal and other monuments, and reported about it in its *Transactions* which were published between 1874 and 1878. J. W. Alexander, Executive Engineer, Agra, was put in charge of the restoration work at the Taj. In 1874 he replaced broken marble in the walls and vaults of the mausoleum, restored the inlay work, and made the dome watertight and regilded its pinnacle.[108]

After several years it was felt that the local governments were not always 'alive to the importance of such a duty', and in 1880 Major Henry Hardy Cole was appointed Curator of Ancient Monuments, a post he held from 1881 to 1883. His reports formulated a new overall programme of conservation work. In 1885 the functions of conservation were amalgamated with those of survey and research, and five survey areas were mapped out and a surveyor appointed to each. Agra belonged to the North-Western Provinces and Oudh, which with Central India and the Central Provinces formed a unit of the Northern Provinces, later the Northern Circle.[109]

Under Lord Curzon, Governor-General and Viceroy (1898–1905), who took the keenest interest in the monuments of India, the Archaeological Survey was reorganized and the centralizing office of the Director-General was revived. The priorities were defined as principally conservation, secondly exploration and research, and lastly epigraphy. Also the funds for the restoration of monuments were considerably increased. The Ancient Monuments Preservation Act of 1904 provided the legal framework to unify the archaeological and conservation work and control it nationwide.[110]

It was also under Curzon that the most comprehensive restoration campaign of the Taj Mahal was undertaken. While the conservation endeavours of the 19th century had focused on the mausoleum, Curzon's efforts were directed to the entire complex and included the restoration of the garden and the reconstruction of the outer courts.[111] He began on the occasion of his first official visit to the Taj, in December 1899, with ordering the replanting of the cypresses of the garden 'in a single row on either side [of the main walkway], the trees being placed in the middle of the beds'.[112] Between 1900 and 1908 the south-east garden tower was rebuilt, the complexes of the subsidiary tombs and of the Khawasspuras were restored, and the southern ranges and eastern bazaar street of the Jilaukhana complex were reconstructed (where only the foundations and the back walls remained, they were built anew on the model of what survived [cp. 152 and 366 with 163]).[113] The bazaar and caravanserai complex was ignored, however, and was even robbed of its bricks to rebuilt the ranges of the Jilaukhana.[114] On 18 March 1904 Curzon was able to report proudly to the Legislative Council at Calcutta that the Taj

> is no longer approached through dusty wastes and a squalid bazaar. A beautiful park takes their place; and the group of mosques and tombs, the streets and grassy courts, that precede the main building, are once more as nearly possible what they were when completed by the masons of Shah Jehan. Every building in the garden enclosure of the Taj has been scrupulously repaired, and the discovery of old plans [cf. 193] has enabled us to restore the water channels and flower beds of the garden more exactly to their original state.

Curzon also pointed out that before his arrival in India the total annual expenditure on archaeology was £7,000 per annum, while he spent on Agra alone some £40,000–50,000. 'Every rupee has been an offering of reverence to the past and a gift of recovered beauty to the future . . . It will take some three or four years more to complete the task, and then Agra will be given back to the world, a pearl of great price.'[115] For Curzon the Taj and the Agra monuments were 'the best and most beautiful body of architectural remains in the world'. He visited Agra annually, and personally supervised every detail of the restoration.[116] He even concerned himself with the outfits for the hereditary guardians of the tomb, the *khadims*, who were made to wear what he and his advisors conceived as 'the traditional garb of Mughal days' – white suits with a green scarf and a badge.[117] One of Curzon's special concerns was lamps for the Taj Mahal [233] and the great gate [182]. He wanted the one for the Taj to be of 'Saracenic design', and turned to Lord Cromer, British Agent in Egypt, to obtain a copy of a Mamluk lamp of the early 14th century.[118]

In the first quarter of the 20th century the reconstruction of the outer courts was completed. Particular attention was also given to the garden. Trees were thinned and removed, to improve the view of the mausoleum and its flanking buildings, and it was decided to keep the cypresses no higher than 25–30 ft (7.6–9 m). The 'character' of the planting was also considered: 'It would appear that conifers, and trees and shrubs of restful and compact foliage, are perhaps more suited for the "tout ensemble" of the Taj than palms of various varieties, some of which produce rather a restless effect.'[119]

In 1947 the Archaeological Survey was taken over by the new Indian Government, and the restoration work continued on more or less the same lines.[120] It consists in stabilizing structural damage, replacing elements, cleaning the buildings, and replanting the garden.

The structure of the Taj Mahal is remarkably sound and has survived earthquakes, lightning and floods for over four hundred years. The main problem is the deterioration of the marble and sandstone facing, with discoloration and corrosion, cracking and breaking of slabs, and in the case of sandstone flaking of the surface [121].

The conservation of the Taj Mahal became a matter of worldwide concern in the 1970s, in connection with the construction of an oil refinery at Mathura, only some 40 km (25 mi.) north of Agra, which was commissioned in 1972 (and has been operating at full capacity since 1983).[121] In 1982 UNESCO recognized the Taj Mahal as a World Heritage Site. Concern about the possible effects on the marble of the sulphur dioxide and fine iron-oxide powder emissions of the refinery sharpened awareness of sources of damage in the more immediate surroundings of the Taj Mahal, and, also in 1982, the Government of India declared the 'Taj Trapezium', an area of about 50 km (30 mi.) radius around Agra, as a controlled development zone, thus mandating that no major polluting industry would be permitted. In 1984 the 'Green' advocate M. C. Mehta filed a Public Interest Litigation against the Government because the initial measures for the Taj Trapezium proved inadequate; as a result, a 2-km (1.2 mi.) radius emission-free zone was established as a green belt around the Taj. In 1996 Supreme Court judgments decreed a series of measures to control the pollution at Agra. A major step was the banning of small-scale polluting industries (iron foundries). It was also ruled that no polluting vehicles of visitors should be allowed within 500 m (1,640 ft) of the monument, that all emporia and shops within the Taj premises should be closed, that no new constructions should be erected within 200 m (656 ft) of its boundaries, and that all those occupying land within should be removed.[122] If applied to the letter, this would affect the entire Taj Ganj, because it was originally part of the Taj Mahal complex!

The concern about the conservation of the Taj Mahal engendered a worldwide debate about how to protect the marble from the effects of emissions and acid rain.[123] The condition of the sandstone got less attention, though it was in a more precarious condition due to its porosity [121]. Conservationists and producers of chemicals from various countries made a number of suggestions about sealing the surface of the marble to make it watertight and consolidating the stone by coating it with substances like oxalate acid or acrylic resin. The Archaeological Survey of India has largely refrained from these methods because their long-term effects in the real environment are hard to predict, and discoloration does happen in practice. The treatment of the marble and sandstone is the subject of ongoing debate. In the last decades the Chemical Conservation Branch of the Science Department of the Archaeological Survey has been cleaning the surfaces with brushes and water containing ammonium and non-ionic detergents (with the brand name Teepol), hydrogen peroxide and triethanolamine;[124] with absorbent clay packs containing magnesium trisilicate, aluminium silicate with a little Teepol, ammonium hydroxide and hydrogen peroxide; and with solvents like ethylene dichloride, benzene and triethanolamine. The cleaned surface is washed with distilled water.[125] More recently, packs with Bentonite clay or Fuller's earth have been used – on the screen with *pietra dura* work around the cenotaphs as well.[126] In the 1990s the chemically cleaned surfaces of the façade of the riverfront

terrace, the western garden-wall pavilion (Taj Museum), and the east and west walls were treated with coats of 2 per cent polymethyl methacrylate acetate.[127]

Another type of pressure on the monuments comes from the increasing number of visitors – up to 10,000 may enter the Taj on a weekday, and on Sundays and holidays more than 13,000. The action of their feet wears out the paving of the walkways of the garden and of the floors of the terraces and buildings. Inside the tomb chamber the crowds create a high level of humidity, and many succeed in writing their names on the walls with felt pens or the like, necessitating the use of aggressive cleaning substances.

In 2001 a new initiative was started for 'the conservation and restoration . . . of the Taj Mahal and surrounding areas and a new site visitor management' in a partnership between the Indian Government (represented by the Archaeological Survey of India) and the private sector (the Indian Hotels Company Ltd, that is the Tata Group of Hotels). The project is monitored by the Taj Mahal Conservation Collaborative, directed by the architect Rahul

Mehrotra and heritage management expert Amita Baig, and advised by a body of specialists – on preservation issues Sir Bernard Feilden and François LeBlanc, on gardens James Wescoat Jr, and on architecture myself.[128] As part of the initiative, a new Site Management Plan for the Taj Mahal complex and its precincts, sympathetic to tourism, has been worked out, and as I write a new Visitor Centre is being established in the courts of the Khawasspuras. It will eventually house a model of the entire complex, which will enable visitors to understand the full scope of the design.[129]

POSTSCRIPT: VISITING THE TAJ MAHAL

The Taj Mahal is seen every year by over 2 million visitors, of whom about 200,000 come from abroad. The tourist season begins when the temperatures are going down, in October, and lasts through the cool winter season until March. Most visitors come in October, November and February. October and late February–early March are best for taking photographs: in winter the air may not be clear because of pollution. If one is prepared to face the heat and humidity of the monsoon season from July to September, one can take spectacular views of the Taj against a cloudy sky.

Agra has a population of 1.2 million. It is situated 193 km (some 120 mi.) south of Delhi, and can be reached from there by train, bus, rented car or plane. Your hotel in Delhi will help to make the arrangements. The trains are very convenient, especially for a one-day trip. Two trains leave Delhi early in the morning – the Shatabdi from the New Delhi Railway Station, and the Taj Express from the Nizamuddin Railway Station. Both return to Delhi in the evening. The journey takes about two hours.

Since polluting traffic is not allowed near the monument, the visitor with a car has to use one of the parking lots, either the 'Parking' west of the Taj or the 'Shilpgram Ground Parking' to the east. From there you can walk or take a battery-operated bus, a horse-drawn *tonga*, or a cycle rickshaw to the respective gate – the 'Fatehpuri Darwaza' on the west side, or the 'Fatehabadi Darwaza' on the east. The approach from the west through the Shah Jahan Park is green, shady and quite pleasant. The approach from the east is congested, and lined by souvenir and refreshment stalls; it has, however, the advantage of a booth with a cash machine opposite the gate, where one experiences the contrast of drawing money with one's plastic card while looking at buffaloes walking by.

The west and east gates are open from 6:00 a.m. to 7:00 p.m. The gate from Taj Ganj to the south ('Sirhi Darwaza') is open from 8:00 a.m. to 5:00 p.m. The Taj is closed on Fridays, except for Muslims who want to pray in the mosque. It may be closed at short notice on any day for a VIP's visit (p. 246). The ticket prices keep changing, and are differentiated: international tourists pay considerably more than domestic tourists, which leads to arguments when the booking clerk thinks a 'Non-Resident-Indian' is trying to pass as an Indian national. The use of a still camera is free; a charge is levied for a video camera. There are security checks for possibly dangerous objects, food, mobile phones, etc., which are not allowed on the premises. Since 1 May 2002 the entire site has been guarded by the Central Industrial Security Force.

Licensed guides operate through a union, and their services have to be booked through the Tourist Office. Unlicensed guides, who offer their services in the forecourt (the Jilaukhana), make up for their ignorance of historical facts by telling fictional stories, of which the most gruesome is that Shah Jahan had the hands of the workmen of the Taj chopped off so they could not build another (p. 250).

Visitors usually walk straight up to the mausoleum, but an exploration of the entire complex is highly rewarding. Just before the flight of steps leading up to the mausoleum one has to take off one's footwear, or rent 'overshoes' from the attendants.

A longer stay will enable the visitor to see the Taj Mahal at different times of day, with changing effects of light. An exploration of the surviving riverfront sites will add an adventurous touch and will create an understanding of the original context of the Taj Mahal, in the garden city of the Mughals. Though the Yamuna is usually very low and highly polluted, taking a boat on the river – across to the Mahtab Bagh (pp. 56–57) if the water level is high enough – provides a view of the Taj from the water and evokes the way the Mughals moved around at Agra [377; cf. 25, 358]. The boat leaves from Dassehra Ghat, on the eastern side of the Taj. Other monuments of riverfront Agra can be reached with a rented car or a rickshaw. The splendid fort is nearby. For the Nur Afshan garden/Ram Bagh, the Chini-ka Rauza and the tomb of Iᶜtimad-ud-Daula, it is necessary to cross the river by the bridge of the bypass of National Highway No. 2, or the Iron Bridge north of the fort. The old Catholic Cemetery with the tomb of Geronimo Veroneo is in the northern part of the city; further northwest is Akbar's tomb at Sikandra.

377 The Taj Mahal seen from a boat on the river. On this side of the Taj is Dassehra Ghat – site of one of the riverfront gardens of Agra. The boatsman, Vijay, is – at the passengers' request – singing a popular song from a Bollywood film. (Photograph taken in 2001)

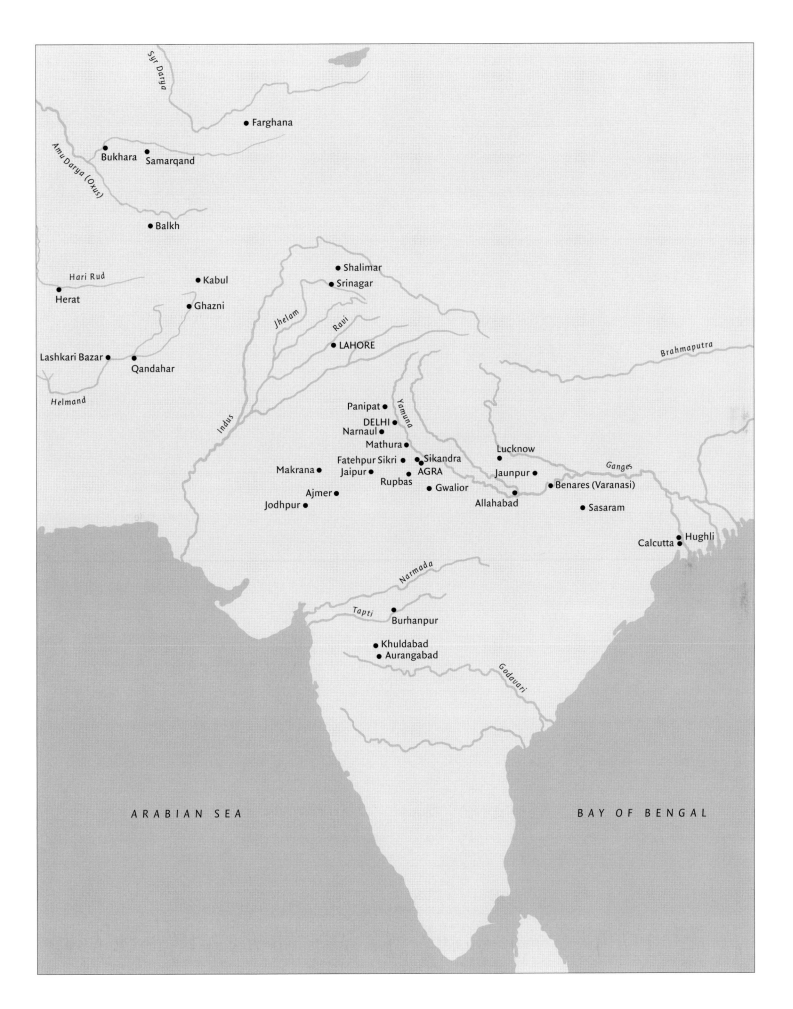

Farghana

Bukhara ● ●Samarqand

Amu Darya (Oxus)

Syr Darya

●Balkh

Hari Rud

Herat ●

●Kabul

Ghazni ●

Lashkari Bazar ●

●Qandahar

Helmand

Jhelam

Ravi

●Shalimar

●Srinagar

●LAHORE

Brahmaputra

Indus

Yamuna

Panipat ●

DELHI ●

Narnaul ●

Mathura ●

Makrana ●

Fatehpur Sikri ● ●Sikandra

Jaipur ● ●AGRA

Rupbas ●

Ajmer ●

●Gwalior

Jodhpur ●

●Lucknow

Jaunpur ●

Allahabad ●

Ganges

●Benares (Varanasi)

●Sasaram

Calcutta ●●Hughli

Narmada

Tapti

●Burhanpur

●Khuldabad

●Aurangabad

Godavari

ARABIAN SEA

BAY OF BENGAL

Lahauri's account of the complex of the Taj Mahal on the occasion of its formal completion, on the twelfth anniversary of Mumtaz Mahal's death

Lahauri's description was written on the order of Shah Jahan, as part of the official history of the emperor, who supervised and edited in personal meetings what his historian wrote (pp. 19–20). It is an extraordinary document which describes precisely every architectural element of the large complex of the Taj Mahal. The emperor wanted to have his architecture – the monument of his reign (pp. 83–84) – recorded in exact terms for posterity; the scientific approach to the visual world which he inherited from his predecessors (pp. 10, 12) is here directed towards his own artifacts. Lahauri employs a consistent architectural terminology which represents a characteristic and unique contribution of this period and which enables us to assess Mughal architecture in its own terms.[1]

[p. 322] On the night of the 17th [Zi'l-Qaʿda 1052/6 February 1643], the gathering on the anniversary of the death (ʿurs) of Her Majesty the Most High Cradle (Mahd-i Ulya),[2] the Chosen One of the Age (Mumtaz az-Zamani)[3] was held at the Illumined Tomb (rauza-i munauwara) of that [person] enveloped in divine forgiveness and favour, which had been finished around this time, and of which a detailed description will be given. And the pious men who were in attendance – scholars, holy individuals, those who had committed the Qur'an to memory (huffaz =pl. of hafiz) – and the needy and deserving recited the Qur'an and the Fatiha. And having honoured this blessed place with his presence, the ruler as generous as the ocean distributed half of the allotted sum of 50,000 rupees; the next morning he returned, and distributed the remaining half among the assembled women.

Explanation of the building of the Pure Tomb (rauza-i mutahhara)[4]

At the start of the fifth year after the exalted accession [January 1632], excavation began for the foundation (bunyan) of this sublime structure [p. 323] which overlooks the Jaun (Yamuna) river that flows past it to the north. And when the diggers (beldar-an) with stout arms and hands as strong as steel had with ceaseless labour excavated down to the water table, the inventive builders (banna-yan-i badiʿ kar) and architects of remarkable accomplishment (miʿmar-an-i shigarf asar) constructed the foundation (asas) very firmly of stone (sang) and mortar [or cement: saruj] up to the level of the ground (sath-i-zamin). And on top of this foundation the platform (kursi) of the exalted mausoleum – which imitates the gardens of Rizwan [the guardian of Paradise] and gives an impression (nishan) of the holy abodes – was raised of brick (ajir) and mortar (ahak) like a terrace (chabutra asa) in one solid block (yak lakht), 374 ziraʿ long[5] and 140 wide and 16 high, to serve as the plinth (kursi).

And from all sides and parts of the imperial territories were assembled troop after troop of [skilled] men, stonecutters (sangtarash) of smooth work, inlayers (parchinkar), and those who do carving in relief (munabbatkar), each one an expert in his craft, who began work together with the other labourers. The exterior (ru-yi kar) of this [terrace] was decorated by facing it with dressed slabs of red stone (sang-i surkh-i-tarashida) in the wonderful artistic techniques of relief (munabbat kari) and inlay work (parchin kari) so smoothly joined, that even on close inspection one cannot see any cracks between them; and the floor of that [terrace] was paved with red stone in geometrical patterns (girih bandi).

In the centre of this terrace of the rank of the Throne of God (kursi-yi ʿArsh-martaba) another platform (kursi) was raised, solid and square, with a length and width of 120 ziraʿ and 7 high, faced with white marble (sang-i marmar). In the centre of [this] the second platform, the building (ʿimarat) of the mausoleum, as high as heaven and resembling Paradise, was constructed on the plan of a Baghdadi octagon (musamman baghdadi) 70 ziraʿ in diameter (qutr) on a plinth (kursi) 1 gaz in height.

Precisely in the centre of this building is the dome[d hall] (gunbad) over the tomb (marqad) of the one who receives divine grace, and it is clad in white marble from top to bottom and inside and out. From the floor (sath) to the springing (zih) of the dome [p. 324], the hall is octagonal, with a diameter of 22 ziraʿ. The springing is ornamented with muqarnas, and from the cornice to the inner

summit of the dome, 32 gaz above the floor of the building, there are arranged marble slabs, carved in net pattern (qalib kari).

And above this inner dome, which glows like the hearts of angels, there is another dome, heaven-touching and guava-shaped (amrudi shakl): to calculate its precise mathematical degrees (darajat-i daqaiq) would defeat even the celestial geometer (muhandis-i falak) [i.e., Saturn]. Crowning this heavenly dome, whose outer circumference is 110 gaz, there is a golden finial (kalas) 11 gaz high that glitters like the sun, and rises to a total height of 107 gaz above the ground.

Below the dome, on the eight sides, there are eight niches (nashiman; lit., 'seat') on both storeys, each 5½ ziraʿ long and 3 wide. In the four cardinal directions, there are four square rooms (khana-i murabbaʿ) on two storeys (martaba), each of them 6 ziraʿ long and wide, with four niches (nashiman) 4½ ziraʿ wide and 3 deep. In front of each of the square rooms is a pishtaq 16 ziraʿ wide, 9 deep and 25 tall. In the four corners there are four octagonal rooms (khana-i musamman) on each of three storeys; each is 10 ziraʿ in diameter and has eight niches (nashiman). The third level of these rooms [i.e., freestanding on the roof] has an octagonal verandah (iwan) and a domed roof (gunbad-i saqf). On the three outer faces of these octagonal rooms there are three niches (pishtaq) [the 'sub-pishtaqs' flanking the large ones], each 7 ziraʿ wide, 4 deep[6] and 10 tall.

In the centre of the domed hall (gunbad) is the divinely blessed grave (mazjaʿ) of that leader of holy women and model of the pious, who reclines on the couch of the topmost heaven and occupies the chief seat in the highest mansions (manazil-i ʿilliyin) [of Paradise] and is hedged about with divine mercy and pardon and wrapped in divine absolution and pleasure. [Directly] above the actual grave (turbat) of that dweller in Paradise is a platform (chabutra) of marble on which a cenotaph (surat-i qabr, lit. 'the likeness of a tomb') stands. And round this is an octagonal latticed screen (mahjar-i musamman-i [p. 325] mushabbak) which is highly polished and pure, made completely of this stone [marble] of which the splendid inlay (parchin) work will be described, with an entrance of jasper (sang-i yashm) [which can also mean agate] in the Turkish style (tarhbandi-yi rumi) closed with gilded iron fasteners, which cost 10,000 rupees. In this Throne of God (ʿArsh)-like structure, orbs (kaukaba) and hanging lamps (qanadil, pl. of qindil) of enamelled gold (tala'i minakar) shine out. And the four arches (taq) of this heavenly dome [i.e., the tomb hall] are set with Aleppo glass (maraya-yi halabi); in one of them a doorway is left to come in and go out.

At each corner of the white marble platform (kursi- yi sang-i marmar), 23 gaz above ground level, is an elegant minaret (minar), also of the above-mentioned stone, 7 ziraʿ in diameter [at the base] and 52 ziraʿ tall from the pavement of the platform to the finial (kalas), [and they all look like] ladders to the foot of the sky. And on the top [of each minaret] is a pavilion (chartaq) of the same stone.

The pavement of the platform (kursi) of this paradisiacal mausoleum is of white marble. The floor [inside] the mausoleum is paved most beautifully and delicately with geometric patterns (girih bandi) of white marble and black stones, which lend colour to day and night.[7] All over the interior and exterior of the building of this mausoleum, artisans (sannaʿ) creating wonders and magic designs have inlaid (parchin namuda) carnelian (ʿaqiq) and other kinds of coloured stones (sangha-yi rangin) and precious stones (ahjar-i samin) – jewels which narrative cannot describe and pearls whose praises the tongue cannot weigh, whose lustre causes the sun to be resplendent[8] and whose splendour causes the dawn, that illuminates the world, to blush – in such a manner that the sharpest eye cannot comprehend its subtleties and the keenest mental perception fails to comprehend its wonders.

And a description of both the quality and quantity of the craftsmanship employed in the inlay work (parchin kari) of the platform of the resting place (chabutra-i marqad) and the screen (mahjar) around it, the reflection of whose wonderful designs causes the eye of the sun to be beautified and the skirt of the sky to blossom like spring, and [p. 326] the miracle which the magic-working carvers (naqqar) and artisans (sannaʿ), producing work akin to that of Mani, have accomplished, could never be finished and brought to a close even with trees for pens and oceans of ink.

Previously in this position there had been a screen of enamelled gold, which weighed 40,000 tolas and cost 6 lakhs [600,000] of rupees, as recorded among the events of the sixth regnal year of the first cycle [1633]. The ruler who considers the end of everything and reflects on consequences through his foresight and prudence had ordered the overseers (*mutasaddiyan*) of the affairs of the building of the Illumined Tomb to prepare a screen of white marble as described above. It was completed in ten years at a cost of 50,000 rupees, and according to the most holy order it has now been set up in place of the screen of pure gold.[9]

The inscriptions on the inside and outside of the Holy Tomb (*rauza-i muqaddas*),[10] which consist of Qur'anic *suras* and verses promising forgiveness (*ayat-i rahmani*) and [of] the [Ninety-Nine] Beautiful Names of Allah, and traditional prayers, have been executed in inlay work in a way that baffles the dwellers of the earth, and even the dwellers in the holy places of the heavens. And to give an account of the relief work (*munabbat*) on this building of firm foundation and solid base and its terrace (*kursi*)[11] would require a separate volume.

West of the Illumined Tomb, on a platform (*kursi*) of red stone, there is a mosque (*masjid*) of three arched bays (*chashma*) of the same stone, 70 *zira'* long and 30 wide, with three domes (*gunbad*), all three of which are of red stone inside and white marble outside. The central dome is 14 *zira'* in diameter, and each of the other two is 11 *zira'* in diameter. The central dome has a *pishtaq*, 14 *zira'* wide, 10 deep and 21 tall. In front of each of the two lateral domes, there is a chamber (*khana*) 11 *gaz* long and 9 wide. The border (*hashiya*) of the dado (*izara*) of the mosque, both inside and out, is inlaid with white marble and yellow and black stone in a wave pattern (*ba-tarh-i mauj*) [**p. 327**]. The floor (*farsh*) of the mosque is paved with red stone, inlaid with yellow and black stone to form the shapes of prayer mats (*ja-yi-namaz*). And in front of that [mosque] is a platform (*chabutra*), 70 *zira'* long and 20 wide. Before the platform is a tank (*hauz*) 14 *zira'* long and 10 wide. Its soul-refreshing court (*sahn*) serves as the place of prayer of the Autad,[12] and its heart-lifting expanse serves for the faithful to prostrate themselves.

To the east of the Pure Tomb (*rauza-i mutahhara*) stands the Mihman Khana, which is the counter image (*qarina*) of the mosque in every detail, except that its wall [at the back] has no *mihrab* and its floor does not have the prayer-mat pattern.

At the four corners of the red stone terrace (*kursi*) there are four three-storeyed octagonal towers (*burj*), of which the third storey is topped by a domed roof (*gunbadi saqf*). The cap of the dome (*kulah-i gunbad*) is inside of red stone, and outside of white marble. And beside each tower is a verandah (*iwan*), 12 *gaz* long and 6 deep, which has a room (*hujra*) on either end.

Below the red stone terrace is the Paradise-like garden (*bagh-i firdaus-a'in*), 368 *gaz* square, full of all sorts of aromatic herbs (*riyahin*) and various kinds of trees (*ashjar*).[13] Within the four walkways (*khiyaban*) in the middle of the garden, which are 40 *zira'* wide, there runs a canal (*nahr*), 6 *gaz* wide, in which fountains (*farwara*) send up spouts of water from the river Jaun (Yamuna). Where the canals meet, there is a platform (*chabutra*), 28 *gaz* square, around which the said canal runs. In the middle of the platform is a pool (*hauz*), 16 *gaz* square, containing five fountains. And the floor of the walkways of this replica of Paradise (*namudar-i jannat*) is of red stone, arranged entirely in a geometrical pattern (*girih bandi*).[14]

On the east side and again on the west side of the garden is [a building[15] with] a verandah (*iwan*) 11 *gaz* wide and 7 deep, with two flanking rooms (*hujra*); and at the back of the verandah is a room (*tanabi khana*) [**p. 328**] 9 *zira'* wide and 5 deep, and in front a platform (*chabutra*), 46 by 10 *zira'*. The southern side (*zal'*) of the garden from one end to the other is formed of double verandahs (*iwan dar iwan*, lit. 'pillared hall within pillared hall') facing north, which are 12 *gaz* deep. At the two corners of this side are two towers (*burj*), counter images (*qarina*) of those of the red stone terrace.

In the centre of the above-mentioned side, the [great] gate of the mausoleum (*darwaza-i rauza*) raises its head to the sky. The diameter of the plan of the domed hall (*sath-i gunbad*) of the gateway, which [has the shape of] a Baghdadi octagon, is 16 *zira'*; and to the east and west of this domed hall there are two half-octagonal niches (*nashiman*), each 7 by 4 *gaz*,[16] with half-domed ceilings. In the four corners of the building (*'imarat*) of the gateway there are four square chambers (*khana-i murabba'*) on two storeys, each measuring 6 *zira'* and with four half-octagonal niches.

On the north and south faces of this building there are two *pishtaqs*, each 16 *gaz* wide, 9 deep and 25 tall; on the east and west sides there are two *pishtaqs*, each 12 *gaz* wide, 7 deep and 19 tall. At the top of the outer and inner faces of the gateway there are seven [in fact eleven] cupolas (*chaukhandi*), topped by white

marble domes (*kulah*). At the four corners of this building are four minarets (*minar*) [rather, engaged corner towers], richly crafted and of great beauty.

And the walls (*judran*) of the garden and the buildings (*'imarat*), and the inside and outside of the houses (*duran*), the floors of the buildings, the crenellations (*shurfat*) of the walls (*hitan*) of the garden, which reach to the circle of the heavens, are [all] finished with red stone, inlaid with white marble and black stone.

In front of the gateway, there is a platform (*chabutra*) 80 *zira'* long and 34 wide, and a large forecourt (*jilaukhana*) 204 *zira'* long and 150 wide. And round the four sides of the forecourt there are 128 rooms (*hujra*). Next to the garden wall there are two quarters for servants (*khawass* [**p. 329**] *pura*), one to the east of the forecourt and the other to the west, each 76 *zira'* long and 64 wide and containing 32 rooms (*hujra*), and each with a verandah (*iwan*) in front, which were built for the attendants (*khadim*)[17] of the one who is enshrined in divine mercy. East and west of the forecourt there are shops (*bazar-ha*), the verandahs (*iwan-ha*) of which are of red stone and the rooms (*hujra-ha*) of brick (*khisht*) and mortar (*ahak*); and the distance between these bazaars is 20 *gaz*.

On the south side of the forecourt there is a cross-axial market (*charsu bazar*), and the width of its east–west bazaar street is 90 *gaz* and that of the north–south street 30 *gaz*. Around this market there are four caravanserais (*sarai*). Two of these were built of baked brick (*khisht-i pukhta*) and *chuna* by the imperial establishment (*sarkar-i padshahi*); each is 160 *zira'* square, with a courtyard (*sahn*) on the plan of a Baghdadi octagon, containing 136 rooms (*hujra*) in front of each of which is a verandah (*iwan*). At the three corners of each of these two caravanserais, there are three squares (*chauk*), of which the court (*sahn*) measures 14 by 14 *zira'*. And at the fourth corner of each of the two caravanserais there is a gateway (*darwaza*) through which men come and go. And [the gates form four] sides of an octagonal court (*chauk*), 150 *zira'* long and 100 wide, which has been arranged in the middle of the market.[18] The other two caravanserais are mirror images (*qarina*) of these.

And in these *sarais* they buy and sell merchandise of divers sorts from every land, varied goods from every country, all kinds of luxuries of the day, and things that are essential to a civilized and comfortable life, brought from all quarters of the world. Behind the imperial caravanserais, merchants have built many substantial houses (*manazil-i pukhta*) and caravanserais. And this thriving dwelling-place founded for all eternity, which has become a large city, is called Mumtazabad.[19]

The cost of all the buildings [**p. 330**] described in detail here, which were completed in the space of about twelve years, under the supervision (*ba-sarkari*) of Makramat Khan and Mir 'Abd-ul Karim, is 50 *lakhs* [5,000,000] of rupees. And an endowment (*waqf*) for the Illumined Tomb has been set up, which includes the annual revenues from thirty villages in the dependencies of the district (*pargana*) of the territory of the Seat of the Caliphate (*Dar-al-Khilafat*) Akbarabad [Agra] and Nagarchain,[20] amounting to 40 *lakhs* [4,000,000] of *dams*.[21]

. . .

And together with this annual income (which is equivalent to 1 *lakh* of rupees, though in good years and months it may be more, because of increase in the yield), the endowment also draws on the revenue from the shops in the bazaars and the flourishing caravanserais mentioned above, which amounts to 2 *lakhs* of rupees a year. Should repairs be needed, money from this endowment may be used for maintenance. The remainder may be used for the normal expenditure on annual wages and monthly salaries, and also food and drink, for the keepers (*sadanat*), inmates (*'aukaf*), administration (*khidmat*), and attendants (*khadim*) of this elevated and solemn place, and for other indigent and poor people. And should there be a surplus, the *khalifa* of the time [Shah Jahan], who has the trusteeship (*tauliyat*) of this house of fragrant bounty, will act as he sees fit.

		Factfile by Richard André Barraud	length/ width/ diameter	breadth/ depth/ side	height	length/ width/ diameter	breadth/ depth/ side	height	length/ width/ diameter	breadth/ depth/ side	height
			metric measure			our gaz measure			Lahauri gaz		
1		**OVERALL COMPLEX**	896.1	300.84*		1112.5	374*			374	
2		**OVERALL PRESERVED COMPLEX**	561.2	300.84*		696	374*				
3	3a	**BAZAAR and CARAVANSERAI COMPLEX** overall	334.9	300.84*		416.5	374*				
	3b	north–south street	25.3			c. 31.5			30		
	3c	east–west street				76.5			90		
	3d	chauk				153	110.5		150	100	
	3e	typical caravanserai		137.77 #1		170	170		160	160	
	3f	corner courtyard in typical caravanserai							14	14	
4	4a	**JILAUKHANA ZONE** court, overall	165.1/ 165.23**	123.51***		204	153		204	150	
	4b	east gate		7.2	11		9	c. 13.5			
	4c	south gate	12.2	10.87	16.74	15	c. 13.5	20.75			
	4d	bazaar street	61.85/ 62.5**	16.18/ 16.3**	6.1	77–78	20	7.5		20	
	4e	Khawasspura court, internal	49.65	35.08, 35.22**		61.5	43.5				
	4f	court, external	61.85	53.66	6.1	76.5	66.5	c.7.5	76	64	
	4g	inner subsidiary tomb complex, overall	67.8	58.92		85	73.5				
	4h	octagonal tomb, overall	16.25			20					
	4i	**GREAT GATE** overall	41.2	34	23.07	51	42	28.5			
	4j	platform in front of great gate, to south	64.36	26.2		80	32.5		80	34	
	4k	to north	74.18			92					
	4l	pishtaq: north / south	12.9	7.08	17.25	16	8.75	c. 21.33	16	9	25
	4m	east / west	9.75	5.55	12.91	12	6.875	16	12	7	19
	4n	central hall, ground floor	12.9		17.01	16		21	16		
	4o	semi-octagonal niche (average)	5.65	3.36	5.98	7	4.125	c. 7.33	7	4	
	4p	corner room: central square (average)	5.25	5.25	6.2	6.5	6.5	7.66	6	6	
	4q	semi-octagonal niche (average)	4.05	2.22	4.97	5	2.75	6.17			
	4r	southern gallery		8.98			11			12	
	4s	terrace in front of the southern gallery		9.77			12				
5	5a	**GARDEN**	296.31	296.31		368	368		368	368	
	5b	width of main walkway (average)	30.85			c. 38			40		
	5c	width of central canal	4.96			c. 6			6		
	5d	central platform	22.75		1.22	28		1.50	28		
	5e	pool in central platform	13.16			16			16		
	5f	garden-wall pavilion	20.81	8.5	20.87	26	10.5	26			
	5g	verandah	8.9	5.5	4.5	11	6.75	c. 5.5	11	7	
	5h	back room	7.53	4.05		c. 9.25	5		9	5	
	5i	lower platform	37.13	8.05	1.24	46	10	1.5	46	10	
	5j	garden wall: walkway		5.68			7				
	5k	height (west side)		2	9.47		2.5	11.5			
	5l	first burial enclosure	4.97	4.16	1.9	c. 6	c. 5.1	c. 2.33			
6	6a	**RIVERFRONT TERRACE**	300*	111.89	8.7 #2	373*	138	#3, #4	374	140	16
	6b	Tahkhana		7.90 #5			c. 8				
	6c	white marble platform of the mausoleum	95.69	95.69	5.6	118	118	7	120	120	7
	6d	rooms on west face: central room	8.7	4.98	4.03	c. 11	c. 6.1	5			
	6e	side rooms	5.09	4.97	4.05	c. 6.25	c. 6.1	5			
7		**MAUSOLEUM** exterior									
	7a	overall height including finial			67.97			84			
	7b	with terrace, marble platform, and finial			#3			107 #4			107
	7c	height of finial									11
	7d	height of terrace and platform			#3			23 #4			23
	7e	plinth	56.9	56.9	0.84	70	70	1	70	70	1
	7f	main body	56.76	56.76	23.04	70	70	28.5	70	70	70
	7g	pishtaqs (average)	12.91	7.68	19.18	16	c. 9.5	c. 23.75	16	9	25
	7h	dado			1.9			c. 2.375			
	7i	ground floor semi-octagonal corner niche (average)	5.65	3.26	7.96	7	4	c. 10	7	4	10
	7j	lateral rectangular niche (average)	5.65	3.24	7.95	7	4	c. 10	7	4	10
	7k	upper floor semi-octagonal corner niche (average)	5.65	3.25	7.9	7	4	c. 9.75			
	7l	lateral rectangular niche (average)	5.65	3.25	7.9	7	4	c. 9.75			
8		**MAUSOLEUM** ground floor									
	8a	main tomb chamber	17.72	17.72	24.74	22	22	30.5	22	22	32
	8b	side of octagon (average)		7.34125							
	8c	niches (average)	4.5563	2.4225	6.4763	5.66	3	8	5.5	3	
	8d	dado			1.75						
	8e	screen, exterior (average)	3.695		2.7						
	8f	interior (average)	3.59		1.93						
	8g	cenotaph of Mumtaz, base (top)	3.23	2.01	0.53	4	2.5				
	8h	top	1.6	0.37	1.14	2	0.5				

			metric measure			our gaz measure			Lahauri gaz		
			length/ width/ diameter	breadth/ depth/ side	height	length/ width/ diameter	breadth/ depth/ side	height	length/ width/ diameter	breadth/ depth/ side	height
	8i	cenotaph of Shah Jahan, base (top)	3.56	2.2	0.725	c. 4.4	2.75				
	8j	top	1.81	0.49	1.495	2.25	0.625				
	8k	cruciform room: central square (average)	4.8450	4.85	8.0612	6	6	10	6	6	
	8l	niches (average)									
	8m	leading to central chamber	3.7675	2.235	6.0363	c. 4.66	2.75	c. 7.5	4.5	3	
	8n	leading to pishtaq	3.7675	1.86	6.045	c. 4.66		c. 7.5			
	8o	leading to passages	3.7775	2.4238	6.03	c. 4.66	3	c. 7.5			
	8p	central axis (average)		3.75			4.66				
	8q	ambulatory axis (average)	9.66	3.75		12	4.66				
	8r	octagonal corner room (average)	8.0688	3.33	9.2925	10	c. 4.125	11.5	10		
	8s	rectangular niche (average)	2.3169	1.3228	3.8566	c. 2.875	c. 1.6	4.75			
9		MAUSOLEUM lower tomb chamber	8.1	6.9	4.77	10	c. 8.5	c. 5.8			
	9a	cenotaph of Mumtaz, base (bottom)	2.76	1.54	0.3			c. 0.375			
	9b	top	1.59	0.37	0.9	2	0.5	1.1			
	9c	cenotaph of Shah Jahan, base (bottom)	3.15	1.8	0.42		2.25	0.5			
	9d	top	1.84	0.49	1.22	2.25	c. 0.625	1.5			
10		MAUSOLEUM upper floor									
	10a	cruciform room: central square (average)	4.895		7.885	6		c. 9.75	6	6	
	10b	niches (average)									
	10c	leading to central chamber	3.78	2.395	5.8175	c. 4.66	c. 3	c. 7.25	4.5	3	
	10d	leading to pishtaq	3.76	1.76	5.8033	c. 4.66		c. 7.25			
	10e	leading to passages	3.755	2.3888	5.8025	c. 4.66	c. 3	c. 7.25			
	10f	central axis (average)	9.05	3.7667			c. 4.66				
	10g	ambulatory axis (average)	9.6875	3.7667		12?	c. 4.66				
	10h	octagonal corner room (average)	8.7175		10.4388	11		c. 13	10		
	10i	rectangular niche (average)	2.51	1.4375	3.6775	c. 3	c. 1.75	c. 4.5			
11		MAUSOLEUM roof level									
	11a	chhatri	8.49	3.52		10.5			10		
	11b	upper dome, interior	18.55		29.61	23		36.75			
	11c	exterior	26.65 #6	83.72 #4	43.78	33	104	c. 54	35	110	
12	12a	MINARET (south-east, average), with plinth			43.02			53.5	7		52
	12b	without plinth	5.65		42.15	7		52.5			
13	13a	MOSQUE/ MIHMAN KHANA overall	56.6	23.38	20.3	70	29	25/29	70	30	
	13b	pishtaq	11.34	7.28	15.35	14	9	19	14	10	21
	13c	lateral room at front	8.85	7.25	7.65	11	9	9.5	11	9	
	13d	central hall	11.34	11.34	18.67	14	14	23	14	14	
	13e	lateral hall at rear	8.88	8.88	15.38	11	11	19	11	11	
	13f	platform in front of mosque	56.6	16.7		70	20		70	20	
	13g	octagonal corner tower	12.72			16					
	13h	verandah in side wing between mosque and tower	11.28	4.42		14	5.5		12	6	
	13i	sunken court in front of mosque	95.52	46.15		118	57.5				
	13j	platform for ablution tank	19.65	17.19	0.4			0.5			
	13k	ablution tank	11.53	9.09		c. 14.3	11.5		14	10	
14		BUILDINGS OUTSIDE THE WALL									
	14a	'SANDLI MASJID' overall	60.4	40.97		c. 75	c. 51				
	14b	'FATEHPURI MASJID' overall	40.6	30.08		c. 50	37				
	14c	TOMB OF 'FATEHPURI BEGAM'									
	14d	octagonal plinth of tomb	21.65	8.96		c. 27	c. 11.1				
	14e	octagonal tomb (exterior)	13.6	5.65		c. 17	7				
	14f	(interior)	7.05	2.91		c. 8.75					

LEGEND and NOTES:

· All measurements are taken on site unless otherwise stated.
· Individual figures totalled up may not tally, because of discrepancies in workmanship.
· All dimensions are given in metres. For larger dimensions they may be rounded off to the nearest metre.
· Measurements in plan are taken from the face of buildings.
· Heights in elevation are taken from the plinth of buildings as far as possible, unless otherwise stated. Most heights are taken to the top of rooftop parapet walls.
· *Gaz* figures are what they should be, rather than precise conversions of metric dimensions.
· Lahauri's measurements have been used because his texts (pp. 256–57) were officially approved.
  Kanbo gives fewer measurements, but when he does they tally with those of Lahauri.

* The overall width is 300.84 m (374 *gaz*) at the Jilaukhana, but at the north end of the complex it is 300 m (373 *gaz*).
  The figure of 373 *gaz* is the result of adding to the clear width of the garden, 368 gaz, the thickness of the outer walls, 2.5 gaz on each side.
  The ideal planning concept is based on 374 *gaz*; 373 *gaz* represents a deviation in the execution.
** Note the variation in measurements in these areas, indicating slipshod workmanship.
*** The width of the Jilaukhana varies from 123.51 to123.96. We took 123.51 since that is the width along the central N–S axis of the complex/ Jilaukhana.

#1 This figure has been worked out as follows: 300.84−25.3, divided by 2 = 137.77.
#2 For the height of the riverfront terrace we have 8.7 m. This does not match any *gaz* figure in the texts, because the level of the river has changed.
#3 These overall heights cannot be given, because we do not know the height of the original terrain.
#4 Significantly, though, if we take the terrace height as 16, we get 16+7+84=107 *gaz*.
#5 This figure is the depth of the Tahkhana, up to the outer face of the platform.
#6 Diameter and circumference of the dome.

Glossary

Persian – the administrative and cultural language of the Mughal empire – and Urdu use, for all but a few letters, the Arabic script, for which, contrary to Sanskrit and Hindi, no uniform transliteration system exists. I have largely followed the system of the dictionary of Steingass (see the Bibliography, p. 274), which is widely employed in India. I have, however, diverged from Steingass when transliterating word combinations and compounds, and have put a hyphen (-) between the first word and the letter 'i' that indicates its combination with the second word; and I have also put hyphens between the first word and the assimilated Arabic definite article and the following word. Thus I have written 'sang-i marmar' and I'timad-ud-Daula', while Steingass would have 'sangi marmar' and 'I'timadu'd-Daula'.

abshar (*ābshār*) Waterfall.

abshar-i chadari (*ābshār-i chādarī*) Waterfall in the form of a thin sheet of water.

amir (*amīr*) Commander; high-ranking person in the Mughal administrative system.

–an Persian plural.

ayina bandi, *ayina kari* (*āyīna bandī*, *āyīna kārī*) 'Mirror work': mosaic of pieces of mirror glass set in *chuna* (q.v.).

bagh (*bāgh*) Garden.

bait 'House': modular unit of rooms to create residential wings around a courtyard. The Shahjahani *bait* is a tripartite module, consisting of an oblong pillared verandah flanked by rectangular or square rooms, *hujras* (q.v.) [165].

bakhshi (*bakhshī*), also *mir bakhshi* High-ranking Mughal official in charge of military administration and intelligence.

baluster column Column with shaft tapering up from a bulb at its foot, and base and capital formed of leaves [133, 134]. The Mughals called it *sarw-andam sutun*, 'cypress-bodied column'. First used exclusively in Shah Jahan's architecture of appearances, it became the most widely used Indian column form.

bangla Roof with curved-up eaves derived from the Bengali hut, whence the name [87, 88]. There are two types of *bangla*: the *do-chala* with a pronounced oblong plan and eaves curved on the longer sides, and the *char-chala* or *chau-chala* with eaves curved on both axes. The term is also applied to vaults of similar shape, and pavilions with a *bangla* roof.

bangla-i darshan Pavilion on the outer front of a palace, where the emperor makes his formal appearances.

baoli (*bāolī*) Underground step-well [64, 301–303]. In a step-well a vertical well-shaft is connected with a stepped corridor or staircase which leads, often through several storeys, from ground level down to the water. The well-shaft may also be used to haul up water from the top.

baradari (*bāradārī*) 'Twelve-doored': rectangular or square pavilion with a tripartite arcade or colonnade on each of its sides; more generally, a summerhouse.

burj Tower, usually in a defensive context; also tower in the wall of a garden. Its upper storeys may be given the shape of an open pillared pavilion [e.g. 82, 300].

caravanserai (*karwānsarā'ī*) Inn for travellers and merchants and their beasts of burden. In Mughal India, usually a four-sided enclosure with fortified corners and one or two gates; the courtyard may contain a mosque, wells, and an open bazaar street connecting the gates.

cenotaph 'Empty tomb': the Mughal *surat-marqad* or *surat-i qabr* ('shape of a tomb') is a stone block shaped like a sarcophagus and set on a plinth [e.g. 61, 233].

chabutra (*chabūtra*) Raised platform.

chadar (*chādar*) Veil, sheet; also a waterfall.

chahar bagh, *charbagh* (*chahār bāgh*, *chārbāgh*) Walled garden divided into several compartments. In its canonical Mughal form it has a square plan subdivided into four quarters by paved walkways (*khiyaban* [q.v.]) and canals (*nahr* [q.v.]) [146:B].

chahar taq (*chahār ṭāq*) Four-arched pavilion.

charbagh See *chahar bagh*.

charsu (*chārsū*) Crossing in a bazaar: an open square with four arched doorways or gates, at the intersection of two bazaar streets [146:17] or inserted in a single bazaar street; also, as *charsu bazar*, a cross-axial bazaar.

chashma Arched bay; room unit defined by arches.

chauk Open court, square.

chaukhandi (*chaukhandī*) A Hindi term which Shah Jahan's authors use to mean a domed pavilion supported by four arches [186]; a *chahar taq* (q.v.).

chevron Zig-zag pattern, the Mughal *tarh-i mauj*.

chhajja Sloping or horizontal projection from the top of a wall, supported by brackets, to protect from rain or sun [e.g. 153, 186].

chhatri (*chhatrī*, *chhattrī*) Small, typically domed, kiosk, usually an open pillared construction [e.g. 254, 299]; a baldachin. Also a Hindu commemorative structure [99].

chihil sutun (*chihil sutūn*) 'Forty-pillared hall': a hall with many pillars; in Shah Jahan's time, another name for the *diwan-i 'amm* (q.v.).

chini khana (*chīnī khāna*) 'China room': wall decoration consisting of small niches in which were placed bottles, vases and the like; the motif also appears in relief or inlay work [e.g. 41, 69, 165]. See also *taqcha*.

chuna, popularly *chunam* (*chūna*, *chūnam*) Quicklime; highly polished plaster made of powdered marble or shells or of a calciferous white stone.

columns See baluster column, Shahjahani column.

coved ceiling Ceiling joined to the wall by a large concave moulding.

dado The lower part of a wall, set off by decoration.

darbar, *durbar* (*darbār*) Reception, audience, court assembly.

dargah (*dargāh*) In India, a place or complex where the shrine of a Muslim (Sufi) saint is situated. The Mughals also used the term to designate the imperial court.

darshan 'Beholding': in the Mughal context the viewing of the emperor at the *jharoka* (q.v.); the practice was inspired by the Hindu custom of beholding a deity, and coincided with the ancient Persian light-cult of the ruler.

darwaza (*darwāza*) Gate, gatehouse, door.

dasa (*dāsā*) Moulding with pendant leaves [209 bottom, 222] (a Hindi term, not found in Mughal sources).

daulat khana (*daulat khāna*) Imperial palace; a less common term is *daulat sara*.

daulat khana-i khass (*daulat khāna-i khāṣṣ*) 'Palace building for the special ones'. See *diwan-i khass*.

daulat khana-i khass-u-'amm (*daulat khāna-i khāṣṣ-u-'āmm*) 'Palace building for the special ones and for the wider public'. See *diwan-i 'amm*.

diwan (*dīwān*) Term with several meanings, for which see *diwan-i 'amm*, *diwan-i khass*, *wazir*. Also used for the collected works of a poet.

diwan-i 'amm (*dīwān-i 'āmm*) Hall of public audience.

diwan-i khass (*dīwān-i khāṣṣ*) Hall of private audience.

faqir (*faqīr*) A poor man, a religious mendicant.

farman (*farmān*) Order.

farwara (*farwāra*) Fountain.

Fatiha (*Fātiḥa*) First and shortest *sura* of the Qur'an; prayer for the dead, recited when visiting tombs.

faujdar (*faujdār*) Officer commanding a military force stationed in one of the administrative divisions of a province of the Mughal empire, in charge of law and order.

gaz The Mughal linear yard (also called *zira'*). The prevailing *gaz* for architecture was the *gaz-i Ilahi*, introduced under Akbar. In Shah Jahan's time its length was 80–82 cm.

ghat (*ghāt*) Flight of steps giving access to water [206].

girih bandi (*girih bandī*) Geometrical ornament [337].

gul Rose, flower.

guldasta 'Bunch of flowers': ornamental pinnacle usually terminating in a flower motif, hence the name [e.g. 257].

gunbad Dome, domed mausoleum.

–ha Persian plural.

hafiz (*ḥāfiz*) One who knows the whole Qur'an by heart; a Qur'an reciter.

hadis (*ḥadīs*) Recorded sayings and actions of the prophet Muhammad, which with the Qur'an form the basis of Islamic law.

hammam (*ḥammām*) Bath, bath-house. Usually a group of rooms for the various stages of bathing. A Mughal *hammam* has three main units: the *rakht kan* (dressing room), *sard khana* (cold room) and *garam khana* (hot room).

haram (ḥaram) 'Forbidden', 'unlawful', 'sacred': a sanctuary, the women's apartments, harem; for the latter see also *zanana*.

hasht bihisht 'Eight paradises': building on a ninefold plan [22, 23, 220]. A square or rectangle, often with chamfered corners so as to form an irregular octagon, is divided by four intersecting construction lines into nine parts: a central domed chamber, rectangular open halls in the middle of the sides (in the form of either a *pishtaq* [q.v.] or a pillared verandah), and double-storey vaulted corner rooms. The 'eight paradises' are the rooms surrounding the central hall. There is no hard evidence that this term, coined for Iranian and Timurid architecture, was current in Mughal India.

hauz (ḥauẓ) Pool, tank.

haveli (ḥavēlī, ḥawīlī) Residential building complex with one or more open courts, often multi-storeyed. The term is used to designate non-imperial residences.

hazira (ḥazīra) Enclosure; tomb platform surrounded by a balustraded or latticed screen [228].

hujra (ḥujra) 'Room', 'closet', 'cell': a small windowless self-contained cell. Also an element of the Shahjahani *bait* (q.v.): there it is a side room flanking a verandah to which it is connected, and it may have windows or doors to the outside [e.g. 157, 165].

-i The Persian genitive, 'of'.

imam (imām) Leader of the Muslim community. The Shiʿa demand that the *imam* belong to the family of the Prophet, and be a descendant of his daughter Fatima and her husband ʿAli.

ʿimarat (ʿimārat) Building; garden pavilion.

iwan (īwān) A term with various applications. Art historians and archaeologists generally use it to refer to a single vaulted hall walled on three sides and opening directly to the outside on the fourth. In the Mughal context, the term denotes a pillared construction of any dimension and plan.

jali (jālī) Perforated stone screen with ornamental design [e.g. 166, 233].

jharoka (jharōka) Architectural frame for official appearances of the Mughal emperor. Its conventional pre-Shahjahani shape is that of an oriel window supported by brackets. Shah Jahan used two types: the *jharoka-i darshan*, a *bangla* (q.v.) pavilion on the outer face of the palace (also known as *bangla-i darshan*) [87]; and the *jharoka-i khass-u-ʿamm*, in the diwan-i ʿamm or hall of public audience, first at Agra a loggia [84], then at Delhi a throne construction with a *bangla* roof.

jilaukhana (jilaukhāna) 'In front of the house': forecourt, assembly place in front of a palace, mausoleum or mosque.

kalasha (kalaśa) In Sanskrit, a water pot [347]; also the crowning emblem of a Hindu temple. In Mughal Persian spelt *kalas* and used for the pot-like finial of a dome [232, 254, 263].

kangura Crenellation [191].

kankar Hindi word for a nodular limestone found in many parts of India, used for mortar.

khadim (khādim) A domestic servant or slave; a servant who has charge of a tomb or mosque.

khan (khān) A Turkish title with several applications. In Mughal India, initially restricted to the principal nobles; eventually it became a common affix to the names of Muslims of all classes, and is often regarded as a surname.

khan-i khanan (khān-i khānān) 'Lord of lords': commander-in-chief.

khan saman (khān sāmān), also *mir saman* Imperial steward.

khana (khāna) Room, house.

khawasspura (khawaṣṣpūra) Quarters for attendants.

khisht Brick.

khiyaban (khiyābān) Avenue, paved raised walkway in a garden [189].

kursi (kursī) Throne, chair. In architecture, a platform or plinth.

lakh 100,000.

lakhauri (lakhaurī) Popular term for a brick format (see p. 94).

lala (lālā) Red flower with a dark centre; generally, tulip; in 17th-century India, both poppy and tulip.

mahal (maḥal) A palace; more specifically, a palace for women.

mahi pusht (māhī pusht) Stone relief in a fish-scale pattern on water chutes, to create ripples [35].

mahdi (mahdī) Eschatological leader expected to appear at the end of time in order to restore religion and justice.

mansab (manṣab) Rank in the Mughal bureaucratic system represented by numbers, determining status, pay, and size of military contingent required of the holder. Since about 1595 the mansab was divided into two ranks: the *zat*, which came to determine the personal pay of the holder, and his comparative status; and the *sawar*, which determined the size of the contingent of soldiers and horses he had to provide, and the amount of pay sanctioned to cover the cost of their maintenance.

mansabdar (manṣabdār) Holder of a *mansab* (q.v.).

manzil Mansion of a noble; in later Mughal times replaced by the term *haveli* (q.v.).

maqbara Burial-place, graveyard, sepulchre.

maqsura (maqṣūra) Term with various meanings. In architecture, most commonly a box or compartment for the ruler in a mosque [273].

masjid Mosque.

masnawi (maṣnawī) Heroic, romantic or didactic poem composed of distichs corresponding in measure, each consisting of a pair of rhymes.

mihman khana (mihmān khāna) Guest house.

mihrab (miḥrāb) Arched niche in the *qibla* (q.v.) wall of a mosque [272, 276].

miʿmar (miʿmār) Architect.

minar (mīnār) Minaret, tower.

minbar Raised structure or pulpit in a mosque from which sermons are preached, placed next to the *mihrab* (q.v.).

mir bakhshi (mīr bakhshī) See *bakhshi*.

mir saman (mīr sāmān), also *khan saman* Imperial steward.

mujaddid A renewer.

munabbatkar (munabbatkār) Stonecarver, stone sculptor.

munabbat kari (munabbat kārī) Stone sculpture, stone relief.

munshi (munshī) Secretary, writer, language teacher.

muqarnas Concave element or group of elements in vaults, usually arched [229, 271]. In a dwarf form, may also appear in other architectural contexts, e.g. on capitals of columns [e.g. 157].

musamman baghdadi (muṣamman baghdādī) 'Baghdadi octagon': a favourite Mughal plan configuration, in the shape of a square or rectangle with corners chamfered so as to form an irregular octagon [220].

nahr Canal; the main canal of a garden (its branches may be designated *jadwal* or *juy*).

nama (nāma) History.

naqqar khana (naqqar khāna) See *naubat khana*.

nashiman (nashīman) Seat, niche, alcove; also a pavilion. Cf. *shah nishin* (q.v.).

naskh (naskh) A form of Perso-Arabic script in cursive style [233].

nastaʿliq (nastaʿlīq) A form of Perso-Arabic script written with connected 'hanging' letters [244].

naubat khana (naubat khāna), also *naqqar khana* 'Drum house': structure for the orchestra which accompanied the ceremonial proceedings of the court.

padshah, badshah (pādshāh, bādshāh) Ruler, emperor.

padshahnama, badshahnama (pādshāhnāma, bādshāhnāma) Imperial history.

parchin kari (parchīn kārī) Stone inlay. See also *pietra dura*.

parchinkar (parchīnkār) Inlayer.

pargana Territory delimited by the Mughal administration for revenue and administrative purposes.

pari (parī, perī) A good genius or fairy, often represented with wings [37, 101].

pietra dura In Italian, 'hard stone': a highly specialized form of stone intarsia developed in Florence (*commesso di pietre dure*, 'placing together of hard stones'). Thin slices of stones of extreme hardness (e.g. jasper, chalcedony, agate) are fitted together and fixed in hollowed-out depressions usually in a marble ground so that their colours and natural markings form the desired image [e.g. 117]. Ideally, after the composition has been polished the joints are not visible. The Mughals called this *parchin kari*.

pishtaq (pīshṭāq) High portal, associated with the *iwan* (q.v.). In its developed Mughal form it consists of a monumental arched niche (usually covered by a half-dome) enclosed by a rectangular frame [224]. Its vertical sides are accentuated by engaged polygonal shafts terminating above the parapet in freestanding ornamental pinnacles or *guldastas* (q.v.).

purna-ghata, purna-kalasha (*pūrna ghaṭa, pūrna kalaśa*) Auspicious symbol in Hindu and Buddhist architecture, in the form of a pot with overflowing foliage [347].

qalib kari (*qalib kārī*) 'Mould-work': decorative network applied to the facing of vaults or the curved part of coved ceilings (q.v.) [183, 268]. The term indicates that in its original form the pattern was applied by means of moulds, presumably of wood.

qarina (*qarīna*) 'Female friend', 'companion': counter-image. Favourite compositional scheme of Shah Jahan's architecture and art, consisting of two equal features arranged symmetrically on either side of a central axis.

qibla Direction of Mecca.

rauza (*rauza*) 'Garden'; in India, used for tombs of persons of standing or of Sufi mystics.

Rizwan (*Rizwān*) Gatekeeper of Paradise.

sadr (*ṣadr*) Official entrusted with supervising and recommending revenue and cash grants, as well as the appointment of judges.

Sahib-i Qiran (*Ṣāḥib-i Qirān*) 'Lord of the auspicious conjunction' (of the planets Jupiter and Venus). Title assumed by Timur, and after his death by other rulers, in particular Shah Jahan, who styled himself *Sahib-i Qiran-i Sani* or Second Lord of the Auspicious Conjunction.

sahn (*ṣaḥn*) Courtyard.

sang Stone.

sang-i marmar Marble.

sang-i surkh (*sang-i surkh*) Red sandstone.

sangtarash Stonemason, stonecutter, stonecarver.

sara'i (*sarā'ī*) See caravanserai.

saruj (*sārūj*) Waterproof plaster.

sawar (*sawār*) Part of the *mansab* (q. v.).

sgraffito Technique of producing a design by scratching through a layer of paint or other material to reveal a ground of a different colour [271–274].

shah burj (*shāh burj*) 'Royal tower': ceremonial building type in Shah Jahan's palaces, reserved for the emperor, his sons, and the highest courtiers.

Shahjahani column Column with a multi-faceted shaft, multi-faceted or *muqarnas* (q. v.) capital, and base formed of four flat faces with a multi-cusped outline [84, 157, 296]. The most widely used form in Shah Jahan's time.

Shahnama (*Shāhnāma*) History of the mythical and historical kings of Iran written by Firdausi around AD 1000.

shah nishin, shah nashin (*shāh nishin, shāh nashin*) 'Royal seat': an arched niche with a half dome, or an alcove of similar shape. Also called *nashiman* (q.v.)

shastras Ancient Indian texts on art and science. The *shilpa shastras* formed the primary teachings on the fine arts or sacred sciences, such as architecture, dance, painting, jewelry-making, pottery, weaving, basketry, garland-making, metalworking, acting, cooking and horsemanship. The *vastu shastras* deal specifically with architecture.

Shi'a General name for a large group of Muslim sects who recognize 'Ali as the legitimate caliph after the death of the Prophet Muhammad.

shish mahal (*shīsh maḥal*) Room decorated with mirror mosaic (see *ayina bandi*).

simurgh (*sīmurgh*) Mythical bird with a royal connotation.

silsila A chain, succession, an unbroken tradition.

suba (*ṣūba*) Province.

subadar (*ṣubadār*) Governor of a province.

Sufi (*Ṣūfī*) Islamic mystic.

sulus (*ṣuluṣ*) The most formal of the cursive styles of writing, with elongated vertical stems to the letters

and long horizontal lines [351], which may be drawn across several words, producing lattice effects [128]; the predominant calligraphic style for architecture in the 17th century.

sura (*sūra*) A chapter of the Qur'an.

tahkhana (*tahkhāna*) Underground chamber.

takhtgah (*takhtgāh*) Platform, podium.

talar (*tālār*) Term with several meanings. In Safavid Iran, a hypostyle wooden hall with tall columns, open on three sides, preceding the vaulted masonry part of a building.

tanabi khana (*tanabī khāna*) Hall or room of oblong plan in a building, combined with a verandah.

taq (*tāq*) Arch.

taq-i marghul, taq-i marghuldar (*tāq-i marghūl, tāq-i marghūldār*) 'Curled arch': multi-cusped arch.

taqcha (*tāqcha*) Cluster of small decorative wall niches. See also *chini khana*.

tarh (*tarḥ*) Design, ground-plan, layout.

tawaf (*tawāf*) Ritual circumambulation.

'urs 'Marriage': anniversary of the death of a saintly person, referring to the union of the soul with God.

ustad (*ustād*) A master in any art or profession.

verandah Porch or balcony with flat roof supported by pillars on the outside of a building; called by the Mughals *iwan*.

wakil (*wakīl*) The highest minister at the Mughal court, not in charge of a department.

waqf Trust for religious purposes.

wazir (*wazīr*) Minister in charge of imperial finance and revenue collection. Also called *diwan* or *diwan-i kul*.

zanana (*zanāna*) Quarters or palace for women.

zat (*zāt*) Part of the *mansab* (q.v.).

zira' (*zirā'*) See *gaz*.

ziyarat (*ziyārat*) Visit paid to a holy tomb, pilgrimage.

Notes

APR	Annual Progress Report (see Hingorani 1978)
APRASI	Annual Progress Report of the Archaeological Survey of India (see Hingorani 1978)
ASINIS	Archaeological Survey of India New Imperial Series
ASI	Archaeological Survey of India
ASIAR	Archaeological Survey of India Annual Report
ASIR	Archaeological Survey of India Report
Enc. of Islam	Encyclopaedia of Islam, 2nd edn (Leiden 1979–2004)
IAR	Indian Archaeology – A Review
V&A	Victoria & Albert Museum, London

Unless otherwise indicated, references are always to the latest edition cited.

Preface (pp. 6–7)
1 Qazwini, fol. 234b (librarian's refoliation 235b); cf. trans. in Begley and Desai 1989, p. 42.
2 Lahauri 1866–72, vol. 1, pt 1, p. 403; cf. trans. in Begley and Desai 1989, p. 43.

Introduction (pp. 8–21)
1 Reported, for instance, by the Jesuit father Antonio Monserrate, the chronicler of the first Jesuit mission to the court of Akbar, in his *Mongolicae Legationis Commentarius*: see the translation in Monserrate 1922/1993, Appendix, p. xvi.
2 Bert G. Fragner, *Die 'Persephonie': Regionalität, Identität und Sprachkontakt in der Geschichte Asiens* (Berlin 1999) has drawn attention to the role which Persian played as second language, after Arabic, in Asia, and the cultural links established by it.
3 Jonaraja 1898/1986, p. 411 *et passim*.
4 Babur 1996, pp. 112–13, 334–38 *et passim*.
5 Lahauri 1866–72, vol. 1, pt 1, p. 153; trans. Nur Bakhsh 1903–4, p. 193.
6 In areas far from Delhi, such as Bengal and Kashmir, the sultans had presented themselves in Indian terms as rulers and had interacted with the local societies and cultures. For Bengal see R. M. Eaton, *The Rise of Islam and the Bengal Frontier, 1204–1760* (Berkeley/Los Angeles/London 1993), pp. 66–70 *et passim*. For Kashmir see Jonaraja 1898/1986, pp. 147, 166.
7 Badauni 1898/1973, vol. 1, p. 573.
8 V. Minorsky, 'A Civil and Military Review in Fars in 881/1476', *Bulletin of the School of Oriental and African Studies*, 10 (1940–42): 150–51.
9 Khwandamir 1940, pp. 80–81; cf. G. Necipoğlu, 'Framing the Gaze in Ottoman, Safavid, and Mughal Palaces', in Necipoğlu 1993, pp. 313–14.
10 Khwandamir 1940, pp. 37–40.
11 It has been known as the *Houghton Shahnama*, but is now more fittingly referred to as the *Shah Tahmasp Shahnama*. Many art historians consider it the greatest masterpiece of Persian painting.
12 Koch 2002a, pp. 43–69.

13 Abu'l Fazl, *Akbar Nama*, 1902–39/1979, vol. 3, p. 1011.
14 Roe 1926/1990.
15 E. Koch, 'Netherlandish Naturalism in Imperial Mughal Painting', *Apollo*, vol. 152, no. 465 (2000): 31.
16 Alvi and Rahman 1968, pp. 15, 67–77.
17 Koch 2002a, pp. 70–92.
18 Khafi Khan 1869–1925, pt 1, pp. 739–40, 757–58.
19 Losensky 1998, pp. 3–7, 40–42, 198–202.
20 After Akbar, Aurangzeb is the Mughal emperor who has received the largest amount of attention: see W. Irvine (Mohammad Habib), 'Awrangzib', *Enc. of Islam*, vol. 1, pp. 768–69 with further literature.
21 Keyserling 1923, pp. 233–35; my trans. from the German. Keyserling saw in Akbar the embodiment of the Mughal genius.
22 Alam and Subrahmanyam 2000, p. 138.
23 Saksena 1976, p. 2.
24 Kanbo 1967–72, vol. 1, pp. 196–97. The passage reads: 'And sometimes with the people of the Hindi race whose horse of understanding cannot run in the racing ground of Persian he speaks the Indian idiom (*muhawarat-i Hindi*)'.
25 Saksena 1976, pp. 2–5.
26 Beach, Koch and Thackston 1997, cat. nos 30, 33, 46; for Shah Jahan's hunts and Khassban see also E. Koch, 'The Copies of the Qutb Minar', *Iran* 29 (1991): 102, and E. Koch, *Dara-Shikoh shooting Nilgais: Hunt and Landscape in Mughal Painting* (Washington, D.C. 1998).
27 Beach, Koch and Thackston 1997, cat. no. 30.
28 Kanbo 1967–72, vol. 1, p. 36; cf. Andrews 1999, vol. 2, pp. 944, 982–83 *et passim*.
29 Saksena 1976, pp. 8–9.
30 Beach, Koch and Thackston 1997, cat. nos 12–13.
31 Qazwini, fol. 43a (refol. 44a), my trans.; cf. trans. in Begley and Desai 1989, pp. 1–2; Saksena 1976, p. 9. For an assessment of Mumtaz and Shah Jahan based on Persian sources see also Chowdhuri 1937.
32 Begley and Desai 1989, pp. 2–3; Saksena 1976, p. 11.
33 Begley and Desai 1989, pp. 4–6; Saksena 1976, pp. 13–14.
34 Qazwini, fol. 48b (refol. 49b), my trans.; cf. trans. in Begley and Desai 1989, p. 6.
35 ibid., fol. 233a (refol. 234a), my trans.; cf. trans. in Begley and Desai 1989, p. 14.
36 Saksena 1976, p. 15.
37 ʿInayat Khan 1990, p. 7.
38 See the detailed description of the circumstances of Shah Jahan's accession in Aziz 1927, pp. 237–57; also Saksena 1976, pp. 56–65.
39 Kanbo 1967–72, vol. 1, p. 133; Saksena 1976, pp. 34–35.
40 Kanbo 1967–72, vol. 1, pp. 186–93; cf. Koch in Beach, Koch and Thackston 1997, p. 160.
41 Kanbo 1967–72, vol. 1, pp. 163–69, who states that a woman in power can only lead to the ruin of a country.
42 Qazwini, fols. 9b–10b (refol. 11a–12a); Kanbo 1967–72, vol. 1, pp. 1–3, 187–93; on p. 177 Shah

Jahan is likened to the 'best rider in the battle of the last day', the Mahdi. For Mumtaz as Bilqis see p. 41.
43 Manucci 1907/1965–67, vol. 1, p. 176; Saksena 1976, p. 106 *et passim*.
44 For a depiction and discussion of the event see Beach, Koch, and Thackston 1997, cat. nos 19 and 20.
45 Kanbo 1967–72, vol. 1, p. 113; Saksena 1976, p. 18.
46 On the project of Shah Jahan's official history and his historians see Conermann 2002, pp. 101–9, 125, 418–19 *et passim*.
47 See e.g. *Handbook* 1862, p. 3; Anderson 1873, p. 234; Khan 1929, pp. 94–95; Necipoğlu 1992, pp. 343–44.
48 For this and what follows see Qazwini's description of the death of Mumtaz and Shah Jahan's mourning, fols. 231a–234b (refol. 232a–235b); Lahauri 1866–72, vol. 1, pt 1, pp. 384–90; Kanbo 1967–72, vol. 1, pp. 370–76; ʿInayat Khan 1990, pp. 70–71, Saksena 1976, pp. 309–10; Begley and Desai 1989, pp. 11–39.
49 Qazwini, fol. 232b (refol. 233b); Begley and Desai 1989, p.13.
50 Koch in Beach, Koch and Thackston 1997, p. 181.
51 ibid., p. 185.
52 The letter was discovered by Dr Yunus Jaffery, bound into Munshi Lal Chand, *Nigarnama*, a collection of letters of the Mughal period, dated '28 Ramazan 24th year of accession' of Akbar Shah II (?), in the National Museum, New Delhi, Persian ms. no. 55.73/2154. The manuscript is from the collection of Mir Khan, Nawab of Tonk. The collection of Tonk was purchased by Maulana Azad and given to the National Museum in 1955. I thank Dr Jaffery for providing me with the reference and the translation. On Qasim Khan Juwaini nicknamed 'Manija' see Shah Nawaz Khan 1911–64, vol. 2, pp. 497–500.
53 Kalim, *Padshahnama*, f. 163b, trans. in Begley and Desai 1989, p. 34.
54 G. Necipoğlu, 'Dynastic Imprints on the Cityscape: The Collective Message of Imperial Funerary Mosque Complexes in Istanbul', in *Islam Dünyasinda Mezarliklar ve Defin Gelenekleri' inden ayribasim (Cimetières et traditions funéraires dans le monde islamique)*, ed. J. L. Bacqué-Grammont and Aksel Tibet (Ankara 1996), p. 26.

I Mughal Agra, a riverfront garden city (pp. 22–81)
1 Kalim 1957, p. 341, verse 24.
2 There are only a few works on pre-Mughal and Mughal Agra: see Latif 1896/1981; Nevill 1921; Aziz 1928, pp. 128–47; I. P. Gupta 1986. An early mention is by the Ghaznavid court poet Masʿud Saʿd Salman of Lahore (d. 1121), who extolls his patron Prince Mahmud's conquest of the city and its fort: Sharma 2000, pp. 44–45; Latif 1896/1981, pp. 1–4; Aziz 1928, pp. 130–31; Hasan 1979; I. P. Gupta 1986, ch. 1. On Sikander Lodi, see Husain 1942, and Aziz 1928, p. 133, where the foundation of the city as recorded by Ni'matullah, *Makhzan-i Afghani*, is given in translation.
3 Zain Khan 1982, pp. 16off.; Babur 1996,

pp. 359–60.

4 Hegewald 2002, p. 14.

5 Aziz 1928, p. 129.

6 Mandelslo 1669, p. 35.

7 Aziz 1928, p. 138; I. P. Gupta 1986, p. 31.

8 The riverfront scheme of Agra has not yet been studied in its entirety; it was only partly recognized by I. P. Gupta 1986, pp. 15, 19–20, 69, and his map 2 should be used with caution.

9 For the translation of all the verses see S. C. Welch, A. Schimmel, M. L. Swietochowski and W. M. Thackston, *The Emperor's Album: Images of Mughal India* (New York 1987), pp. 36, 198–201.

10 Wescoat 1989, p. 76.

11 For a fuller discussion of this and the following see Koch 1997b and Koch 1997c with further literature.

12 See above, Introduction, n. 4.

13 See e. g. Stronach 1990: there the innermost garden of the palace area is reconstructed as a four-part garden on the basis of a postulated visual axis from the throne of the king.

14 Ruggles 2000.

15 Senake Bandaranayake, 'Among Asia's Earliest Surviving Gardens: The Royal and the Monastic Gardens at Sigiriya and Anuradhapura', *Historic Gardens and Sites / Jardins et Sites Historiques*, Sri Lanka, National Committee of ICOMOS (1993), pp. 1–36; idem, *Sigiriya: City Palace and Royal Gardens* (Colombo 2000); Hegewald 2002, pp. 181–82.

16 'For insightful persons it is clear that the gestures of the *padshahs* of pure spirits, who are like water to the *chahar bagh* of the world, and the acts of the *shahinshahs* of bright hearts, who are like the sun in the sky of world-rulership, are not at all devoid of wisdom.' Kanbo 1967–72, vol. 1, p. 270.

17 Koch 1997b (repr. in Koch 2001a).

18 ibid.

19 One of these nobles was Jaꞌfar Khan, who also had a riverfront *haveli* and tomb at Agra (see pp. 75, 77–79). His Delhi house was visited by Aurangzeb in 1665: Saqi Mustꞌad Khan 1947/1986, p. 33.

20 Koch 2002a, pp. 45–50.

21 Jairazbhoy 1961 traces the migrations of the plan.

22 Schinz 1996, esp. pp. 71–73.

23 ibid., pp. 282–96; A. Schimmel, *The Mystery of Numbers* (New York 1993), pp. 169–71.

24 Schinz 1996, pp. 294–95.

25 J. Sesiano, 'Wafk', in *Enc. of Islam*, vol. 11, pp. 28–31.

26 A. Northedge et al., *Studies on Roman and Islamic ꞌAmman, vol. 1: History, Site and Architecture* (Oxford 1992), pp. 75–82, 88, figs. 37–43.

27 Ettinghausen 1972, figs. A, B, L.

28 D. Schlumberger, *Lashkari Bazar: Une résidence royale ghaznévide et ghoride* (Paris 1978), pp. 80–84, pl. 31; Hillenbrand 1994, p. 413, fig. 7.100.

29 Ettinghausen 1972, pp. 49–58. Machiel Kiel, 'The Quatrefoil Plan in Ottoman Architecture: The "Fethiye Mosque" of Athens', *Muqarnas* 19 (2002): 109–22, tries to establish the origins of this plan within the context of Ottoman architecture, disregarding non-Ottoman examples.

30 Munajjim-bashi, *Sahaiful-akhbar*, cited by Browne 1902–24/1997, vol. 3, p. 414; cf. Jairazbhoy 1961, p. 76.

31 'The Travels of a Merchant in Persia', in *A Narrative of Italian Travels in Persia, in the Fifteenth and Sixteenth Centuries*, trans. and ed. by C. Grey, vol. 2 (London 1873), pp. 173–75, cf. Jairazbhoy 1961, pp. 75–76.

32 Qazwini, in the text used as the motto of this book (p. 4), speaks of the 'nine vaults' of the sky; cf. trans. in Begley and Desai 1989, p. 42.

33 L. Gardet, 'Djanna', in *Enc. of Islam*, vol. 2, pp. 447–52, esp. p. 450.

34 A. Schimmel, 'The Celestial Garden in Islam', in *The Islamic Garden* (Washington, D.C., 1976), p. 20–21; Daneshvari 1986, pp. 27–30.

35 Jairazbhoy 1961; Golombek 1981.

36 Babur 1996, p. 234; cf. Babur 1993, p. 396, for the Persian and Turkish text. Thackston translates *hujra* as alcove, but the Mughals used the term for a rectangular enclosed room.

37 Subtelny 1997.

38 Koch 2002a, pp. 45–46.

39 For a discussion of these Indian building principles see Michell 1977, pp. 89–93.

40 The Mughal and Western ninefold plan merged in the bungalow of the British, where it was expressed in a new, often Palladian, vocabulary. Lady Wilson, the wife of a British administrator who began her life as a memsahib in Shahpur, Panjab, in 1889, described her residence as 'a square one-storeyed flat-roofed house with a pillared verandah at each side; indoors nine rooms, three in a row, without an entrance hall or any passage, each room opening into the other': *Letters from India* (1921, repr. London 1984), p. 7. During my ten-year stay in India from 1976 to 1986 I lived with my husband and our two sons in such a bungalow in New Delhi, 42 Amrita Shergill Marg, dating from the 1920s.

41 Athar Ali 1985, pp. xi–xxiv; J. F. Richards, 'Mansab and Mansabdar', in *Enc. of Islam*, vol. 6, pp. 422–23.

42 Thackston in Jahangir 1999, p. xx.

43 See above, n. 41.

44 Jahangir 1909–14/1994, p. 8, ordered after his accession that 'if anyone, whether unbeliever or Musalman, should die, his property and effects should be left for his heirs, and no one should interfere with them'. This ruling obviously did not apply to the land property of the Muslim nobles. Sarkar 1952, pp. 146–60; Day 1970, pp. 193–200; Islam 1987; Islam 1988; Firdos Anwar, 'Implementation of Escheat under Shahjahan: Some Implications', *Proceedings of the Indian History Congress*, 52nd Session (1991–92) (New Delhi 1992), pp. 266–73. Guha 1963/1996, in his famous study of the debate preceding the proclamation of the so-called Permanent Settlement of 1793 by Lord Cornwallis regulating the holding of property in Bengal, shows how various schools of thought interpreted land ownership under the Mughals differently (esp. pp. 32–36, pp. 100–106). None, however,

considers the way buildings and gardens were handled. A telling example is that of Asaf Khan, the father of Mumtaz Mahal. Before his death in 1641 he was visited by Shah Jahan, and had to lay open his estate. Besides a fabled residence at Lahore and other houses and gardens in Delhi, Kashmir and Agra, including a waterfront garden at Agra (p. 74), it included 2 krors 50,000 rupees (20,050,000) in jewels, coins, gold and silver. The emperor gave 20 *lakhs* (2,000,000) – the value of the palace at Lahore – to the sons and daughters of Asaf Khan, and the Lahore palace to his favourite son, Dara Shikoh. Everything else went to the state or crown. Shah Nawaz Khan 1911–64/1979, vol. 1, p. 293. Habib 1996, p. 134, notes that by Aurangzeb's time 'smaller gardens that also displayed the essential features of Mughal gardens' could be 'owned by medium or lower nobles and other private individuals'.

45 Roe 1926/1990, p. 105. The lack of private property as reported by European travellers played a crucial role in the debate over Oriental despotism in 17th-century Europe. See Rubiés 2005 with further literature.

46 Pelsaert 1925/1972, p. 5; cf. Tavernier 1925/1977, vol. 1, p. 89. See also Habib 1996, p. 135, who adduces evidence that tomb gardens were exempt from the garden tax.

47 I. P. Gupta 1986, p. 57, does not understand the differentiations in the right to own land when he claims that 'Right to hold private property and ownership of land in the city [Agra] was recognized'.

48 T. W. Lentz, 'Memory and Ideology in the Timurid Garden', and A. Welch, 'Gardens that Babur did not like: Landscape, Water, and Architecture for the Sultans of Delhi', both in Wescoat and Wolschke-Bulmahn 1996, pp. 31–58 and 59–93. Welch traces the Sultanate gardens only up to the 14th century and does not include the gardens of the Lodis, the immediate precursors of Babur.

49 Babur 1921/1970, pp. 531–32; cf. Babur 1996, pp. 359–60.

50 For this and what follows see Koch 1997b (repr. in Koch 2001a).

51 Abu'l Fazl, *Akbar Nama*, 1902–39/1979, vol. 2, pp. 117–18, 187–88; cf. Abu'l Fazl, *Aꞌin-i Akbari*, 1927–49/1978, vol. 2, pp. 190–91.

52 Jahangir 1909–14/1994, vol. 1, pp. 3–7.

53 Pelsaert 1925/1972, pp. 2ff. See also Finch in Foster 1921/1985, p. 182.

54 Mundy, vol. 2, 1914/1967/1991, p. 214.

55 Lahauri 1966–72, vol. 1, pt 1, pp. 155–58, gives the circumference (*daur*) as 10 *karoh padshahi*. Elsewhere (vol. 1, pt 2, p. 15) he tells us that the *karoh* (also known as a *kos* or *mil*) is equal to 200 *jarib*; 1 *jarib* is 25 *zira*ꞌ, 1 *zira*ꞌ is 40 *angusht*. The Shahjahani *zira*ꞌ or *gaz* is *c.* 80–82 cm or *c.* 32 in., so 1 *karoh* is *c.* 4,064 m.

56 This description of Agra is based on Qazwini, fols. 142a–143a (refol. 143a–144a); Lahauri 1866–72, vol. 1, pt 1, pp. 154–58; Chandar Bhan Brahman 2004, pp. 89–90; Aziz 1928, p. 136. Chandar Bhan calls the residences of the princes *manzil*

and those of the nobles *haveli*. For a discussion of *havelis* but solely in a Rajput context see Jain 2004, esp. pp. 20–36.

57 Kanbo, *Bahar-i sukhan*, fols. 248a and 248b, as trans. in Koch 1997b, p.143 (repr. in Koch 2001a, pp. 194–95).

58 Bernier 1891/1972, p. 285.

59 Thévenot 1687, p. 34.

60 I. P. Gupta 1986, pp. 19, 24, 69. For the attempt to reconstruct the riverfront of Mughal Agra under Jahangir see Nath 1994, pp. 244–50.

61 Kanbo 1967–72, vol. 2, p. 193.

62 Lahauri 1866–72, vol. 1, pt 2, pp. 251–52; ʿInayat Khan 1990, pp. 205–6.

63 Kanbo 1967–72, vol. 2, pp. 192–93. A brief overview of the area west of the fort is provided by J. Hasan 1990.

64 Selected verses from Kalim, *Padshahnama*, fols. 115a–b.

65 Koch 1993a, p. 11 (repr. in Koch 2001a, p. 171).

66 *Khulasat-ut-tawarikh*, completed 1695/96: Sujan Rai 1918, p. 40. I thank Sunil Sharma for this reference.

67 The Agra event reflected the bathing festival of Pairaki at nearby Mathura, the holy city of the Krishna cult, for which see Growse 1882/1979, p. 181. For the religious meaning of bathing at Mathura see Sinha and Ruggles 2004.

68 Sil Chand 1836–37, fols. 97b–98a.

69 Nazir Akbarabadi 1951, pp. 448–51, trans. Dr Yunus Jaffery and E. Koch. The complete poem is entitled 'The Art of Swimming [*tairaki*] at Agra' and has twelve stanzas.

70 *Taj Mahal, Agra: Site Management Plan*, p. 19.

71 Sil Chand 1836–37, fol. 97b; Bhatnagar 1974, pp. 162–63; Singh 1986, pp. 190, 192; Gole 1989, pp. 200–201.

72 Bhatnagar 1974, p. 331; Singh 1986, pp. 190–92; Bahura and Singh 1990, p. 11; Sachdev and Tillotson 2002.

73 Maharajah Sawai Man Singh II Museum, Jaipur, cat. no. 126. I have studied the map since the mid-1980s and discussed it in several publications: see Koch 1986b; Koch 1997b (repr. in Koch 2001a); Beach, Koch and Thackston 1997, cat. no. 29, pp. 185–87, cat. no. 45, pp. 209–10, fig. 132. Since then, J. Hasan 1990 has also looked at the whole plan – very sketchily, though. I thank Dr B. M. Jawalia, Keeper of Manuscripts, for assisting me in reading the inscriptions on the map in July 1985 and February 1986, and Dr Aśok Kumar Das, then Director of the Museum, for permission to study and to publish it. I also thank Maharaj Narindra Singh for renewing this permission in March 2005, and Director Himmat Singh and Mr Pankaj Sharma for making the map accessible to my studies.

74 BL, ms. Or. 6371; see Titley 1977, p. 117, no. 253.

75 BL, ms. I.O.L. 2450; see Archer 1972, p. 192, no. 157 i–v.

76 The text was put into English in 1928 by S. Abu Muhammad, who undertook the task, he comments, although the 'style was unsuited to a work of historical research', because it provided

'a useful catalogue of some of the notable names and places which will afford an opportunity for further research'. Raja Ram 1928, p. 12, n. 1.

77 I thank J. P. Losty for drawing my attention to this map.

78 Nevill 1921, p. 220, refers to it as 'Yatni-ki-kothi', and says that by his time it had become the property of Messrs John, a company which had mills and factories, as well as bungalows for its employees to the north in the quarter of Rajwara (p. 80). The map in Newell 1934 shows the 'Yatni ka bagh' on the same site as the Johns Flower Mill and Ice Factory.

79 Athar Ali 1985, p. 323 S7367.

80 Shah Nawaz Khan 1911–64, vol. 2, pp. 767–71; Beach, Koch and Thackston 1997, cat. no. 45.

81 On the garden see Sil Chand 1836–37, fol. 105b; Raja Ram 1928, p. 23.

82 Raja Ram 1928, p. 18; Carlleyle 1871–72/1966, p. 203; Führer 1891/1969, p. 53; Latif 1896/1981, p. 190.

83 Size of complex c. 50 x 180 m; brick format 21.5 x 12.5 x 3 cm.

84 *Complete Set of Site Plans of the Major Gardens of the United Provinces*, 1924, pl. vi.

85 Size of garden c. 253 x 340 m; size of raised terrace area 144.5 x 99.20 m; size of platform of pavilions 40 x 28 m; north pavilion 27.3 x 5.6 m; south pavilion 31.2 x 5.6 m; brick format 19–20 x 12.5 x 3.5 cm (Jahangiri), and larger.

86 Sil Chand 1836–37, fols. 119b–29b; Raja Ram 1928, p. 17, who attributes the buildings wrongly to Raja Jawahir Singh of Bharatpur; Carlleyle 1871–72/1966, p. 199; Führer 1891/1969, p. 53. For this and what follows see Koch 1986a.

87 Latif 1896/1981, p. 188, believes that the name 'Nur Afshan' goes back to a garden of Babur's time.

88 Jahangir 1909–14/1994, vol. 1, pp. 269–70; vol. 2, pp. 75–76, 151, 192, 226.

89 ibid., vol. 2, pp. 197–99, 202, 205–6.

90 In addition to the one in the Freer Gallery [5] (Koch 1986a, pp. 60–61), there is one in the Chester Beatty Library, Dublin, showing Jahangir and his ladies celebrating Holi, the Indian spring festival: Leach 1995, vol. 1, cat. no. 3.14, col. pl. 59.

91 *Complete Set of Site Plans of the Major Gardens of the United Provinces* 1924, pl. vi.

92 I have surveyed the garden since 1978; for the plan of the pavilions see Koch 1986a. My overall plan [34] is based on our survey of 2001 and 2002; the subsequent ASI restoration, still under way in 2005, has introduced some changes in the walkways and levels.

93 Koch 1983 (repr. in Koch 2001a).

94 Hastings 1858, p. 31.

95 Keene 1899, p. 39; Latif 1896/1981, p. 189. Murray's photograph was published in the catalogue *India after the Mutiny* [2005], p. 19, no. 33. I thank Christoph Tauber for presenting me with a copy of this catalogue.

96 Taylor 1855, p. 131.

97 ASIAR (1924–25): 3, pl. I.

98 IAR (1958–59): 83; (1975–76): 135; (1976–77):

140; and following issues.

99 Size of garden c. 386 x 334 m; brick format taken in *hammam* 17.7 x 11–12 x 2.5 cm (Shahjahani: see p. 94).

100 Koch 1986b; Koch 2002a, p. 117. Lahauri 1866–72, vol. 2, p. 99, says that it was founded by Shah Jahan when a prince and given to Mumtaz after his accession; but since Kalim was writing closer to the time, his statement is likely to be more correct.

101 Kalim 1957, p. 346, line 8; p. 350, lines 6, 8, 9, 12, 20–23; p. 351, lines 1, 2; trans. E. Koch.

102 ibid., pp. 346–51; trans. E. Koch. If not otherwise indicated, the translation of the plant names follows Steingass 1892/1973 and Platts 1884/1977. I list the plants not in order of their appearance in the poem but in the sequence flowers–bushes–trees. On this passage and a discussion of the plants see also Thackston 1996, pp. 239–41.

103 In India *lala* denotes tulips as well as the red poppy: Fallon 1879/1989, p. 1035; Platts 1884/1977, p. 947. See also the paintings of poppies in the *Small Clive Album*, V&A, I.S. 48-1956, dating from the 17th and 18th centuries, which are inscribed as *lala*: fol. 20b (*gul-i lala*) [195], fol. 23a (*lala-i rasmi*) (see also p. 139).

104 Fallon 1879/1989, p. 1002.

105 ibid.

106 Jahangir 1909–14/1994, pp. 5–6; Jahangir 1999, pp. 24–25.

107 Lahauri 1866–72, vol. 2, p. 99.

108 I have surveyed the garden repeatedly since 1978, and with R. A. Barraud took measurements of the remaining structures in February 2001 and March 2003.

109 Sil Chand 1836–37, fol. 119b.

110 Parks 1850/1975, vol. 1, p. 374; cf. Führer 1891/1969, p. 53, who says that the Zahara Bagh was 'also called Said-ka-Bagh from the tomb of a Musalman saint that stands in it'. See also Smith 1901, p. 3.

111 Size of tomb 24 x 24 m.

112 Athar Ali 1985, p. 167 S2326; Shah Nawaz Khan 1911–64/1979, vol. 1, pp. 149–53.

113 The architecture of the tomb is described by Smith 1901, pp. 3–17, with special emphasis on its decoration, which was to inspire contemporary design.

114 Tieffenthaler 1785, p. 117.

115 Losty 1995.

116 Parks 1850/1975, p. 373.

117 Curzon Papers, pp. 110, 117. See also Smith 1901, p. 6, who deplores that 'The crypt . . . has been used for years as a cattle-shed by the *zamindar* or farmer ploughing the fields round the tomb, and the result is that very little vestige is left of the dadoes, which were of coloured tiling.'

118 Length of riverfront 148 m; brick format Shahjahani (see p. 94).

119 Raja Ram 1928, p. 16.

120 Athar Ali 1985, p. 45 J126.

121 So does does I. P. Gupta 1986, on his maps 1 and 2.

122 Athar Ali 1985, p. 97 S67, p. 105 S325, p. 117 S698,

p. 175 S2599, p. 177 S2653.

123 At Chiniot in the Panjab he erected many civic buildings, roads, shops, mosques, rest houses, a school, a hospital and wells; Shah Nawaz Khan 1911–64, vol. 2, pp. 981–83, comments that he did more for his home town than any other *amir* in Hindustan.

124 Asher 1992, pp. 225–26.

125 Beach, Koch and Thackston 1997, cat. nos 5, 10, 32, 38, 44.

126 Sil Chand 1836–37, fols. 111b–112a.

127 Carlleyle 1871–72/1966, p. 160.

128 I have not yet been able to check whether the features mentioned still exist.

129 Size of platform 27.6 x 27.6 m; size of tomb 12.60 x 12.60 m; brick format 17.7 x 11–12 x 2.5 cm (Shahjahani).

130 Pelsaert 1925/1972, p. 5; *Dutch Chronicle* 1927/1978, p. 53; cf. Raja Ram 1928, p. 16.

131 Athar Ali 1985, p. 87 J1471. He gives the death date erroneously as 1624/25.

132 Prasad 1922, p. 428.

133 Beach, Koch and Thackston 1997, cat. nos 21–22, 23–24.

134 Sil Chand 1836–37, fol. 109b; Raja Ram 1928, p. 16.

135 Size of garden 154 m (along the river) x 160 m.

136 Jahangir 1999, p. 373; Shah Nawaz Khan 1911–64, vol. 2, pp. 1072–79, who includes with the account of the life of Ghiyas Beg that of his daughter Nur Jahan; Athar Ali 1985, p. 52 J352, p. 78 J1194, and references in between.

137 *Dutch Chronicle* 1927/1978, p. 53.

138 Asher 1992, pp. 130–33; For a new detailed photographic survey, unfortunately with an incorrect plan (which shows the tomb of Maryam az-Zamani at Sikandra), see Amina Okada (text) and Jean-Louis Nou (photographs), *Un Joyau de l'Inde moghole: Le mausolée d'Itimad ud-Daulah* (Milan 2003).

139 Koch 2002a, pp. 72–75.

140 Smith 1901, pp. 18–19; with his characteristic approach, he saw the tomb mainly as a carrier of ornamental design.

141 Undertaken by the ASI from October 1999 to February 2000.

142 Tieffenthaler 1785, p. 117; my trans.

143 Hastings 1858, p. 32.

144 Cole 1882, p. 5.

145 Carlleyle 1871–72/1966, p. 141.

146 Curzon Papers, pp. 110, 117; on the criticized repair carried out by the Public Works Department in 1881–82, which included a survey of the tomb and the removal of British additions to the riverfront pavilion, see Cole 1882, pp. xxxi and ccx.

147 Shah Nawaz Khan 1911–64, vol. 2, pp. 326–27; Athar Ali 1985, p. 138 S1362.

148 Beach, Koch and Thackston 1997, cat. nos 5, 9, 10, 17, 23, 32, 38, 43, 44.

149 Raja Ram 1928, p. 15. Sil Chand 1836–37, fol. 104b, mentions no mosque.

150 Pelsaert 1925/1972, p. 5.

151 Mundy, vol. 2, 1914/1967/1991, pp. 214–15.

152 Beach, Koch and Thackston 1997, cat. no. 29.

153 Koch 1997b, pp. 140–41 (repr. in Koch 2001a, p. 184).

154 Babur 1993, pt 3, pp. 642–43, with my own adjustments from the Persian text. Thackston, like Beveridge, translates 'gul wa nastaran' as 'roses and narcissus', but *gul* also means flower, and *nastaran* is the white musk rose: see below, Chapter III, n. 80.

155 *Syzygium cumini*: Sahni 2000, pp. 109–10; Menon 2000, p. 114

156 Persian term for this fruit: Fallon 1879/1989, p. 866.

157 Hindi term for a variety of the plantain: Fallon 1879/1989, p. 137.

158 Sil Chand 1836–37, fol. 100b. For the garden's condition in the later 19th century see Carlleyle 1871–72/1966, pp. 102–3.

159 Size of garden 300 m (along the river) x 310 m; brick format Shahjahani (see p. 94).

160 Moynihan 2000; for the reflected image of the Taj see pp. 31, 40.

161 Moynihan 2000, p. 28.

162 Since no contemporary description of these features of the Mahtab Bagh exists, I have used the terms of Waris's description (fol.388/403a) of similar elements of the pavilions of the Hayat Bakhsh garden in the Red Fort at Delhi, which was completed in 1648.

163 Sil Chand 1836–37, fol. 100b.

164 Athar Ali 1985, p. 199 S3412 and previous references.

165 The event is strikingly depicted in the Windsor Castle *Padshahnama*: Beach, Koch and Thackston 1997, cat. no. 31. For other depictions of Khan-i Dauran see cat. nos 10, 18, 19, 32, 35, 36, 40, 43.

166 Beach, Koch and Thackston 1997, cat. nos 35, 36.

167 ʿInayat Khan 1990, p. 325; Shah Nawaz Khan 1911–64/1979, vol. 1, pp. 778–83; Moin-ud-din 1905, pp. 102–6 (the Gwalior mosque is mentioned on pp. 105–6).

168 Sil Chand 1836–37, fol. 53b; see also Raja Ram 1928, p. 22; Latif 1896/1981, p. 192.

169 Taj Museum, Acc. nos. 20 [72] and 21 (11.6 x 97.6 cm).

170 Athar Ali 1985, p. 302 S6646 and previous references; Raja Ram 1928, p. 21; Begley and Desai 1989, pp. xlix, 136.

171 See above, n. 169.

172 She seems to have thought that both *havelis*, nos. 18 and 19, were built or owned by a person named 'Dowlat Khan' or 'Doulah Khan'.

173 According to an inscription on the temple's board.

174 Nevill 1921, pp. 212–13; Latif 1896/1981, p. 100.

175 APRASI, *North-Western Provinces and Oudh Circle* (1900–1901): Introduction by W. H. Nightingale, pp. 2–3. The park was named after Sir Anthony MacDonnell, Lieutenant-Governor of the North-Western Provinces and Chief Commissioner of Oudh. See also Sanwal 1968, pp. 15–16.

176 *APR of the Superintendent, Muhammadan and British Monuments, Northern Circle* (1913–14), p. 28.

177 Size of garden 128 x 136 m; brick format of pavilion 19 x 12 x 3 cm; brick format of *tahkhana* in eastern extension 20–21 x 13.5 x 3.5 cm.

178 Pelsaert 1925/1972, p. 4; Sil Chand 1836–37, fol. 77b; Raja Ram 1928, p. 21, who calls the noble 'Jan-i Alam'.

179 Shah Nawaz Khan 1911–64/1979, vol. 1, pp. 389–92; Athar Ali 1985, p. 117 S702 and previous references.

180 Beach, Koch and Thackston 1997, cat. nos 5, 10.

181 See above, n. 169.

182 Shah Nawaz Khan 1911–64/1979, vol. 1, pp. 295–99; Athar Ali 1985, p. 210 S3763 and previous references. Asalat Khan features several times in the Windsor Castle *Padshahnama*: Beach, Koch and Thackston 1997, cat. nos 32, 33, 44, figs. 112, 113.

183 Shah Nawaz Khan 1911–64, vol. 2, pp. 9–28; Athar Ali 1985, p. 126 S976; Athar Ali, 'Mahabat Khan', in *Enc. of Islam*, vol. 5, p. 1214. Mahabat Khan is shown with such a necklace in one of several appearances in the Windsor Castle *Padshahnama*: Beach, Koch and Thackston 1997, cat. no. 37; for other depictions of him see cat. nos 5, 9, 10, 31, 38.

184 Begley and Desai 1989, p. 175.

185 Pelsaert 1925/1972, p. 4; Sil Chand 1836–37, fol. 79a; Raja Ram 1928, p. 21; Führer 1891/1969, p. 62; Mundy, vol. 2, 1914/1967/1991, p. 206, n. 2.

186 Shah Nawaz Khan 1911–64/1979, vol. 1, p. 628.

187 The taking of Dharur is depicted in the Windsor Castle *Padshahnama*: Beach, Koch and Thackston 1997, cat. no. 15. For portraits of Aʿzam Khan see also cat. nos 5, 10, 37.

188 Shah Nawaz Khan 1911–64/1979, vol. 1, pp. 315–19; Athar Ali 1985, p. 236 S4559 and previous references.

189 Beach, Koch and Thackston 1997, cat. no. 29.

190 I am grateful to J. P. Losty for informing me about Thomas Daniell's drawing. Its present whereabouts are unknown. It was exhibited at Walker's Galleries, London, in February 1961, no. 119, as 'Palace near the Fort of Agra'; its measurements were given as 13⅜ x 21⅛ in. [34 x 53.6 cm].

191 A stone tablet in the fort there documents his appointment in June 1636: Khwaja Muhammad Ahmad, 'Inscriptions from Udgir, Bidar District', *Epigraphia Indo-Moslemica* (1929–30): 18–31, esp. 22–23; Beach, Koch and Thackston 1997, cat. no. 40.

192 Shah Nawaz Khan 1911–64, vol. 2, pp. 107–9; Athar Ali 1985, p. 269 S5641 and previous and following references.

193 Shah Nawaz Khan 1911–64/1979, vol. 1, pp. 698–701; Sil Chand 1836–37, fols. 79b–80a; Führer 1891/1969, p. 62; Nevill 1921, p. 213.

194 Shah Nawaz Khan 1911–64/1979, vol. 1, pp. 694–96; Raja Ram 1928, p. 22; Athar Ali 1985, p. 126 S969, p. 128 S1024, p. 228 S4306 and previous references.

195 Lahauri 1866–72, vol. 1, pt 2, p. 87.

196 Personal communication from J. P. Losty, 16 January 2002: the painting was shown by the Daniells together with other views at the Royal

Academy, London, in 1799, with the title 'View of the fort at Agra taken from the ruins of Islaum Khan Rumi'. Its present whereabouts are unknown.

197 Acc. no. 26 (11.8 x 100.6 cm). The much ruined drawing shows the Agra fort from the river and a building to its left which could be the *haveli*.

198 Carlleyle 1871–72/1966, p. 200. Führer 1891/1969, p. 62, also mentions the *haveli*.

199 On the fort see Maulvi Muhammad Ashraf Husain, *An Historical Guide to the Agra Fort Based on Contemporary Records* (Delhi 1937); Koch 2002a, pp. 53–55, 106–9, 125; Asher 1992, pp. 49–51, 111–13, 182–89.

200 Monserrate 1922/1993, pp. 34–35.

201 Curzon Papers, pp. 109–88.

202 ASIAR (1923–24): 8.

203 Between 1976 and 1986 I carried out a survey of all its Mughal buildings as part of my projected documentation and analysis of the palaces and gardens of Shah Jahan (see Chapter II, n. 10). The plan [81], published *inter alia* in Koch 2002a (p. 53, fig. 36), is a result of this documentation.

204 Kanbo, *Bahar-i sukhan*, fol. 251b.

205 Size of Diwan-i ʿAmm courtyard 153.1 x 116.1 m; size of hall 61.48 x 20.72 m.; height of pillars 4.24 m. The courtyard measurement in *gaz* is 190 x 142.5; 190 is precisely 2.5 times 76 – the length of the hall as given in contemporary texts.

206 Koch 1994 (repr. in Koch 2001a).

207 Kalim 1957, p. 345, lines 19–21; he speaks here of the *chini khana* of the Shah Burj.

208 Size of 'Machchhi Bhavan' courtyard 56.95 x 45.35 m – in *gaz*, 70 x 56.

209 Lahauri refers to it as 'sahn-i ru-yi zamin' and 'sahn-i pa'in': Lahauri 1866–72, vol. 1, pt 2, p. 238; trans. Nur Bakhsh 1903–4, p. 179.

210 Spear 1949; Losty 1989, pp. 45–46. Of the pillars, two are in the Taj Museum (p. 143) and some are built into the porch of the Circuit House of Agra; the greatest number went to the V&A. See Koch 1982b (repr. in Koch 2001a).

211 Lahauri 1866–72, vol. 1, pt 2, p. 240; trans. Nur Bakhsh 1903–4, pp. 180–81.

212 Lahauri 1866–72, vol. 1, pt 1, pp. 144–45; vol. 1, pt 2, pp. 240–41; trans. Nur Bakhsh 1903–4, pp. 188, 180; cf. Koch 1994, p. 155 (repr. in Koch 2001a, p. 253).

213 The *chahar bagh* measures 64.1 x 53.6 m.

214 ʿInayat Khan 1990, pp. 309–10.

215 Lahauri 1866–72, vol. 1, pt 2, p. 238; trans. Nur Bakhsh 1903–4, p. 179.

216 Lady Nugent in 1812 called them 'Siche Mahal' (Nugent 1839, p. 361), Florentia Sale in 1832–33 'Shees Mahil'.

217 Information kindly provided by Mr Naveen Chand, the present owner of Mubarak Manzil, on 12 March 2004.

218 Pelsaert 1925/1972, p. 3. Jahangir 1909–14/1994, vol. 1, p. 48, mentions that the garden had belonged to Shah Quli Khan Mahram, who had no heirs, so the emperor after his accession in 1605 gave it to Ruqaiya Sultan Begam, 'the honoured wife of my father', who had brought

up Khurram/Shah Jahan.

219 Athar Ali 1985, p. 322 S7348 and previous references.

220 Hasrat 1982.

221 Koch 2002a, p. 117.

222 The three visits are mentioned by Kanbo: Kanbo 1967–72, vol. 2, pp. 320, 324, 338.

223 Waris, fol. 475a; cf. Begley and Desai 1989, p. 135.

224 Kanbo 1967–72, vol. 3, pp. 202–3; cf. ʿInayat Khan 1990, p. 544.

225 Muhammad Kazim 1865–68, vol. 1, p. 119.

226 The drawing is related in style and unrealistic form of representation to those done by Indian artists for the French officer Jean-Baptiste Gentil (1726–99), collected in an album entitled *Palais indiens recueillis par M. le Gentil*, kept in the Département des Estampes et de la Photographie, Bibliothèque Nationale, Paris. See Lafont 2001, pls 46–50.

227 Hodges 1794/1999, p. 117.

228 Sil Chand 1836–37, fols. 83b–84a.

229 Raja Ram 1928, p. 18.

230 A.F. no. 236. Agra office, ASI.

231 Nevill 1921, p. 198. This later building is still standing, some 250 m north of the fort, set back from the Yamuna Kinara Road: it bears a tablet on its west façade in English and Persian giving its name, 'Municipal Hall', and the date 1882. Another inscription states that in 1903 it was converted into the Shri Baburam Higher Secondary School. Later it became the Baikunti Devi College.

232 Athar Ali 1985, p. 110 S496.

233 Beach, Koch and Thackston 1997, cat. no. 16.

234 Shah Nawaz Khan 1911–64/1979, vol. 1, p. 800; De Laet 1928/1975, p. 39. De Laet follows Pelsaert (1925/1972, pp. 2–5), who was at Agra between 1621 and 1627, in his listing of the riverfront estates but inserts two more palaces to the north of the fort between the palace of Iʿtimad-ud-Daula and that of Khwaja Abdul Hasan, namely that of Khurram and that of Khan-i Jahan Lodi.

235 Athar Ali 1985, p. 181 S2802 and previous references.

236 Shah Nawaz Khan 1911–64/1979, vol. 1, pp. 287–95.

237 Lahauri 1866–72, vol. 1, pt 1, p. 224.

238 Koch 2002a, pp. 96, 116. There I indicated twelve terraces as given in the entire secondary literature, but when one consults the historians of Shah Jahan they all mention that the garden had nine terraces (*martaba*) 'like heaven'. See e.g. Lahauri 1866–72, vol. 1, pt 2, p. 28.

239 ibid., p. 103.

240 Jahangir 1999, pp. 309, 360, 366.

241 Sil Chand 1836–37, fol. 88b.

242 Carlleyle 1871–72/1966, p. 201; cf. Mundy, vol. 2, 1914/1967/1991, p. 207, n. 2; Nevill 1921, p. 213. Raja Ram, however, writing shortly before 1857, saw only a tower remaining: Raja Ram 1928, p. 19.

243 Athar Ali 1985, p. 322 S7350 and previous references.

244 Abu'l Fazl, *Akbar Nama*, 1902–39/1979, vol. 2,

pp. 187–88; Ram Kishore Pandey, *Life and Achievements of Muhammad Bairam Khan Turkoman* (Bareilly 1978), p. 260.

245 Jahangir 1909–14/1994, vol. 1, p. 12.

246 De Laet 1928/1975, pp. 38–39. See also n. 234 above.

247 Qazwini, fol. 121a (refol. 122a); Lahauri 1866–72, vol. 1, pt 1, pp. 86–87; Kanbo 1967–72, vol. 1, pp. 186–87; ʿInayat Khan 1990, p. 15.

248 Lahauri 1866–72, vol. 1, pt 1, p. 463.

249 Kanbo 1967–72, vol. 1, p. 460.

250 The fight started in front of the princely palace and moved down the Yamuna to the fort. Beach, Koch and Thackston 1997, cat. no. 29, esp. Koch, pp. 185–87.

251 Lahauri, writing about Aurangzeb's wedding in May 1637, says that the property had been granted to the prince by Shah Jahan 'after his accession': Lahauri 1866–72, vol. 1, pt 2, p. 268; Beach, Koch and Thackston 1997, esp. Koch, p. 187, n. 10.

252 It was sold on 28 June 1878 at public auction for 17,000 gold *mohurs* to Seth Hira Lal, from a family known as the Seths of Mathura. I identified the Mubarak Manzil on 12 March 2004 with the help of its present owner, Mr Naveen Chand, a direct descendant of Seth Hira Lal, who kindly provided details of the acquisition of the building and its history and allowed a brief survey of the architecture.

253 Curzon Papers, pp. 170–71. On the Mubarak Manzil see also Sil Chand 1836–37, fols. 92b–93a; Raja Ram 1928, p. 20; Nevill 1921, p. 198. Latif 1896/1981, pp. 200–202, speaks of a mosque of Aurangzeb which was used as the Collector's Office.

254 Permission for the tablet was given by the owner, Seth Chuni Lal, son of Seth Hira Lal. *APR of the Archaeological Surveyor of the United Provinces and Punjab Circle* (1903–4), p. 23; see also I. P. Gupta 1986, p. 19. The tablet erroneously gave the date of the battle as June 1659, whereas it was on 29 May 1658.

255 Carlleyle 1871–72/1966, pp. 195–96.

256 The whole structure measures *c.* 23.5 x 52 m.

257 Sil Chand 1836–37, fol. 93b.

258 Athar Ali 1985, p. 322 S7343 and previous references.

259 Shah Nawaz Khan 1911–64, vol. 2, pp. 825–36.

260 Tieffenthaler 1785, p. 114.

261 Lahauri 1866–72, vol. 1, pt 2, p. 279; Kanbo 1967–72, vol. 2, p. 210.

262 Sil Chand 1836–37, fol. 93b.

263 ibid., fol. 94a.

264 A marble tablet at the gate gives its name as 'Rai Bahadur Seth Suraj Bhan ki Haveli'. The building still belongs to a branch of the Seths of Mathura, descended from Suraj Bhan. Personal communication of Mr Naveen Chand, owner of the surviving part of the Haveli of Aurangzeb called Mubarak Manzil (no. 35), on 12 March 2004.

265 Shah Nawaz Khan 1911–64, vol. 2, p. 925.

266 ibid., p. 989; Athar Ali 1985, p. 44 J119.

267 Sil Chand 1836–37, fol. 94a; Raja Ram 1928, p. 20.

268 Shah Nawaz Khan 1911–64/1979, vol. 1, pp. 767–70; Athar Ali 1985, p. 323 S7369 and previous references.

269 Sil Chand 1836–37, fol. 97a; Raja Ram 1928, p. 22.

270 Nazir Akbarabadi 1951, p. 448.

271 Sil Chand 1836–37, fol. 97b.

272 Führer 1891/1969, p. 67; Nevill 1921, p. 221; Singh 1986, p. 190–92.

273 Nazir Akbarabadi 1951, p. 449.

274 Sil Chand 1836–37, fol. 97b. This seems to have been an ancestor of the owner of the John company: see n. 78 above; cf. Nevill 1921, p. 221.

275 There are other references which contain the element 'Hakim' or 'Qasim' (similar to Kazim), but it cannot be ascertained whether they mean the same garden. Führer 1891/1969, p. 67, speaks of the 'Haqimji-ka-Bagh or the garden of Haqim Karim ʿAli Khan'. Raja Ram 1928, p. 20, names only a 'Haveli of Qasim Khan' – a *mansabdar* of 5,000 under Shah Jahan – which Sil Chand (1836–37, fol. 94a) lists as the 'Haveli of Nawwab Qasim Khan (Munija)' (Manija was married to the sister of Nur Jahan: p. 19), separate from the Bagh Hakim Kazim ʿAli Khan.

276 Size of garden *c.* 180 x 180 m.

277 Beach in Beach, Koch and Thackston 1997, pp. 183–84.

278 Athar Ali 1985, p. 204 S3561, p. 212 S3799, p. 239 S4667, p. 258 S5341, p. 261 S5406, p. 321 S7309, p. 322 S7368.

279 Beach, Koch and Thackston 1997, cat. nos 10, 13, 23, 25, 32, 33, 43–45.

280 He was visited there by Aurangzeb in 1665. Saqi Mustʿad Khan 1947/1986, p. 33.

281 Shah Nawaz Khan 1911–64/1979, vol. 1, p. 722–23.

282 Raja Ram 1928, p. 23.

283 Führer 1891/1969, p. 67.

284 Koch 2002a, pp. 75–77.

285 Shah Nawaz Khan 1911–64/1979, vol. 1, p. 754; Athar Ali 1985, p. 163 S2201, p. 278 S5917, p. 322 S7342.

286 Sil Chand 1836–37, fol. 99a; Führer 1891/1969, p. 67; Raja Ram 1928, p. 23.

287 Sil Chand 1836–37, fols. 98b–99a; see also I. P. Gupta 1986, p. 19.

II The Construction of the Taj Mahal (pp. 82–101)

1 fol. 163b, trans. E. Koch; cf. trans. in Begley and Desai 1989, p. 82.

2 Kanbo 1967–72, vol. 3, p. 18, as trans. in Koch 1982a, p. 259 (repr. in Koch 2001a, p. 56), with some modifications.

3 Lahauri 1866–72, vol. 1, pt 1, pp. 144–54; trans. Nur Bakhsh 1903–4, pp. 188–93.

4 Ibn Khaldun 1967, pp. 216, 263–66, 314–17, 319–21, 327–32 *et passim*; cf. Behrens-Abouseif 1999, pp. 159–85.

5 For Louis XIV's interest in the self-representation and rituals of 'Oriental rulers', see Necipoğlu 1993, p. 317.

6 Cf. Koch 2002a, pp. 13–14.

7 Qazwini, fol. 139a (refol. 140a), as trans. by E. Koch in Beach, Koch and Thackston 1997, pp. 131–32, with slight modifications.

8 Lahauri 1866–72, vol. 1, pt 1, p. 149, trans. E. Koch; cf. trans. Nur Bakhsh 1903–4, pp.190–91.

9 Kanbo 1967–72, vol. 1, p. 108.

10 I have surveyed and documented the entire palace and garden architecture of Shah Jahan, in a project initiated in 1976 (see also Chapter I, n. 203). The results will be published in three volumes – on the hunting palaces, the garden palaces and country residences, and the large fortress-palaces.

11 Koch 2002a, pp. 93–124.

12 ibid., p. 96, with references to the sources.

13 Lahauri 1866–72, vol. 2, pp. 322–31.

14 Kanbo 1967–72, vol. 2, pp. 315–20.

15 Kalim, *Padshahnama*, fols. 163b–164b; see also Begley and Desai 1989, pp. 82–86.

16 All contemporary descriptions and poetic appraisals of the Taj Mahal are translated in Begley and Desai 1989, pp. 65–86.

17 Jahangir 1909–14/1994, vol. 1, p. 436. On this point see also Fairchild-Ruggles 1997. Laura Parodi has, albeit with some speculation, expanded the notion of Humayun's and Akbar's mausoleums as 'symbols for the presence of the deceased'. See Parodi 2000, p. 87; Parodi 2001; and Parodi, 'Humayun's Tomb in Mughal Imagery: Some Possible Levels of Interpretation' (forthcoming).

18 Daneshvari 1986, pp. 1–2; article 'Makbara', in *Enc. of Islam*, vol. 6, pp. 122–28; Leisten 1990; Baker 2004, pp. 115–38.

19 Daneshvari 1986, pp. 9–31, 36–41.

20 The problem has been addressed by Brand 1993, though his interpretation of the shapes of the tombs differs significantly from mine.

21 Kanbo 1967–72, vol. 1, p. 12; ibid., vol. 2, p. 317; Lahauri 1866–72, vol. 2, p. 324.

22 Bogdanov 1923–24; Shepard Parpagliolo 1972; Zajadacz-Hastenrath 1997.

23 Golombek 1969, pp. 100–124, discusses this tomb type in the Timurid context.

24 Misra and Misra 2003, with further literature.

25 C. B. Asher, 'The Mausoleum of Sher Shah Suri', *Artibus Asiae* xxxix (1977): 273–98.

26 Golombek and Wilber 1988, pp. 80–81.

27 Koch 1993a, pp. 12–14 (repr. in Koch 2001a, pp. 174–76).

28 The only monograph is still Smith 1909; see also Asher 1992, pp. 105–10; Parodi 2001.

29 Jahangir 1909–14/1994, vol. 1, p. 152. That this was well known in his time is evident from the discussion of an Iranian delegation with Mughal officials in 1621: cf. Desai 1999, p. 195; also below, Chapter IV (p. 229).

30 Nath 1976a, pp. 86–91, pls. 51–54, where past voices about this conjecture are discussed. See also Nath 1994, pp. 394–95.

31 Koch 2002a, pp. 72–75.

32 Kanbo 1967–72, vol. 1, p. 11; cf. Koch 2002a, pp. 97–98.

33 Sarkar 1928/1972, p. 58; cf. Asher 1992, p. 260.

Both refer to ʿInayat Allah Khan Kashmiri, *Kalimat-i taiyabat* – Asher to the published version, ed. and trans. by S. M. A. Husain (Delhi 1982), pp. 38–39, 47. Aurangzeb felt, like Firuz Shah Tughluq three centuries before him, that the visits of women to shrines would lead to immoral behaviour: see N. B. Roy, 'The Victories of Sultan Firuz Shah of Tughluq Dynasty (English Translation of Futuhat-i Firuz Shahi)', *Islamic Culture* 15 (1941): 456.

34 Koch 2002a, p. 127; Asher 1992, pp. 263–65; L. E. Parodi, 'The Bibi-ka Maqbara in Aurangabad: A Landmark of Mughal Power in the Deccan?', *East and West* 48, 3–4 (1998): 349–83.

35 Z. Hasan 1922, p. 16.

36 Growse 1882/1979, pp. 306–7, pl. opp. p. 308.

37 Lahauri 1866–72, vol. 1, pt 1, p. 149; trans. E. Koch, cf. trans. Nur Bakhsh 1903–4, pp. 190–91.

38 Qazwini, fol. 139a (refol. 140a); Lahauri as in preceding note; Kanbo 1967–72, vol. 1, p. 206.

39 Losensky 2003, p. 16.

40 'Mihmar-i karkhana-i daulat-u-din', Qazwini, fol. 385a (refol. 389a).

41 Statue 'F', Paris, Louvre, AO2. See F. Johansen, *Statues of Gudea Ancient and Modern, Mesopotamia,* Copenhagen Studies in Assyriology, vol. 6 (1978): 10, pls 19–22; C. E. Suter, *Gudea's Temple Building: The Representation of an Early Mesopotamian Ruler in Text and Image* (Groningen 2000), pp. 58, 69, fig. 4.

42 See e.g. Koch in Beach, Koch and Thackston 1997, p. 141. I discussed the validity of such cross-cultural comparisons between the Mughals and ancient Near Eastern kings with Irene Winter at Harvard in November 2002; see also I. J. Winter, 'Opening the Eyes and Opening the Mouth: The Utility of Comparing Images in Worship in India and the Ancient Near East', *Ethnography & Personhood: Notes from the Field,* ed. M. W. Meister (Jaipur/New Delhi 2000), pp. 129–62.

43 Begley and Desai 1989, pp. xli–xlix.

44 An article reporting the use of mason's marks as a possible lead to the builders of the Taj, Kounteya Sinha, 'Shirazi, Afridi, Hanif built Taj 350 yrs ago', *The Asian Age,* 6 July 2004, was widely picked up in Western papers.

45 Lahauri 1866–72, vol. 2, p. 322, trans. E. Koch; cf. trans. in Begley and Desai 1989, p. 66.

46 Tavernier 1925/1977, vol. 1, p. 91.

47 Manrique 1927, vol. 2, p. 172.

48 Qaisar 1988, pp. 12, 24–25, 28 *et passim*.

49 Nath 1985, Appendix III; Koch 2002b, p. 60; and the unpublished paper by S. Ali Nadeem Rezavi of Aligarh Muslim University, 'Stone-Cutters' Marks in Mughal Monuments with Special Reference to Fatehpur-Sikri'. For the dangers of their interpretation, see n. 44 above.

50 Abu'l Fazl, *A'in-i Akbari,* vol. 1, 1927/1977, p. 235.

51 See also Qaisar 1988, pp. 24–25.

52 Koch 1988a, esp. pp. 16–22, and n. 24 (repr. in Koch 2001a, esp. pp. 76–104); see also Andrews 1995.

53 Giusti 1992, pp. 273–93 *et passim.* Koch 1988a, esp. p. 39 (repr. in Koch 2001a, pp. 61–129,

esp. pp. 76–77).

54 Koch 1988a, pp. 17–22 (repr. in Koch 2001, pp. 81–104).

55 Bernier 1891/1972, p. 298.

56 Outcome of a discussion with Rudolf Distelberger in 2003 while visiting his outstanding exhibition on the lapidary arts in the Kunsthistorisches Museum, Vienna: *Die Kunst des Steinschnitts: Prunkgefässe, Kameen und Commessi aus der Kunstkammer*, 2002–3.

57 Voysey 1825, p. 434.

58 Kalim, *Padshahnama*, fol. 164a, trans. E. Koch.

59 Schimmel 1992, pp. 156–57.

60 Voysey 1825, pp. 430–35. For a more detailed description of the hardstones and their occurrence see Coggin Brown 1936, pp. 298–308; also Andrews 1995.

61 ASIAR (1903–4): 15.

62 Based on measurements taken since 1976 in my survey of Shahjahani buildings.

63 Coggin Brown 1936, p. 158–59.

64 Abu'l Fazl, *A'in-i Akbari*, vol. 1, 1927/1977, p. 233.

65 Coggin Brown 1936, pp. 168–69; *Marble in India* 1983, pp. 20–22.

66 Begley and Desai 1989, p. 165.

67 Manrique 1927, vol. 2, p. 172; cf. Begley and Desai 1989, p. 293.

68 Personal communication from Mr S. K. Sharma, ASI office at the Agra fort, 28 February 1981. The plaster applied by Madan Singh Mistri in March 1999 to the galleries at the backs of the *pishtaqs* on the roof of the mausoleum was a coarser formula, containing concrete.

69 Waris, fol. 387b; Lahauri 1866–72, vol. 1, pt 2, p. 236; cf. Koch 2002a, p. 138. On historical Mughal plasters see Qaisar 1988, pp. 18–22; the author gathers evidence from the texts but does not connect it with built architecture.

70 Lahauri 1866–72, vol. 1, pt 2, p. 236; trans. Nur Bakhsh 1903–4, p. 176, who translates 'chuna-az sang-i marmar' as 'shell plaster'.

71 Pelsaert 1925/1972, pp. 66–67. Later, the artist William Hodges admired Indian *chuna* and its affinity to marble: Hodges 1794/1999, pp. 2, 9.

72 Kanbo 1967–72, vol. 3, p. 21; see also Qaisar 1988, p. 23.

73 Kalim, *Padshahnama*, fol. 116a.

74 The excavations were carried out by the ASI. IAR (1957–58,): 83, pl. CII; (1958–59): 95, pl. XCII.

75 Lahauri 1866–72, vol. 2, p. 323; cf. Begley and Desai 1989, pp. 66, 78. *Saruj* was a special mortar for waterproof construction; see Qaisar 1988, p. 21.

76 I identified this technique in my field studies of Mughal buildings.

77 Coggin Brown 1936, pp. 166–68.

78 Vats 1946.

79 Tavernier 1925/1977, vol. 1, p. 91.

80 Qazwini, fol. 234a (refol. 235a), trans. E. Koch; cf. Lahauri 1866–72, vol. 1, pt 1, p. 402–3; Kanbo 1967–72, vol. 1, pp. 375–76; trans. in Begley and Desai 1989, pp. 41–44.

81 From Shah Jahan's *farman* of transfer of possession, it is evident that these properties

formerly belonged to Hindu rajas, but there is no indication how, when and why they became crown property. In this document all properties under discussion are termed *haveli*. The translation of the *farman* is given in full in Begley and Desai 1989, pp. 168–71.

82 Kanbo 1967–72, vol. 1, p. 376; Begley and Desai 1989, pp. 41–44. For Kanbo's use of the term see Steingass 1892/1973, p. 1185–86, 1378.

83 Lahauri 1866–72, vol. 2, pp. 233–34. He mentions various kinds of fruit trees, cypresses (*sarw*), planes (*chenar*), different kinds of flowering plants or trees (*nihal asnaf gul*), and scented plants (*riyahin*).

84 Mundy, vol. 2, 1914/1967/1991, pp. 213–14.

85 For this and the following see Tabataba'i, fols. 8b–9a; cf. trans. in Begley and Desai 1989, pp. 47–48; cf. Begley and Desai 1989, pp. 48–50 for the reports of Qazwini and Lahauri.

86 Mundy, vol. 2, 1914/1967/1991, p. 213.

87 Tabataba'i, fols. 43a–43b; cf. trans. in Begley and Desai 1989, pp. 51–52. For Qazwini and Lahauri see their pp. 52–54.

88 Begley and Desai 1989, pp. 55–65.

89 The main Arabic and Persian scripts are briefly explained in Schimmel 1970, pp. 5–10; see also Thackston 1994, p. 47. All inscriptions of the Taj are published and translated in Begley and Desai 1989. For the dates see pp. 188–91.

90 Lahauri 1866–72, vol. 2, p. 8; cf. Begley and Desai 1989, p. 62.

91 Manrique 1927, pp. 171–74.

92 Lahauri 1866–72, vol. 2, pp. 322–31; Kanbo 1967–72, vol. 2, pp. 315–20.

93 Qazwini, fol. 234b (refol. 235b); Lahauri 1866–72, vol. 1, pt 1, p. 403, Kanbo 1967–72, vol. 1, p. 376; cf. Begley and Desai 1989, pp. 41–44.

94 Moreland 1923, pp. 148–49; Moosvi 1986, p. 296. Moosvi states that an unskilled workman earned 3 rupees a month, and refers to Moreland – who gives this figure, however, for the Indian servants of the Dutch. The information on wages and cost of living for Shah Jahan's time is very scanty. The two main sources are the *A'in-i Akbari* of Abu'l Fazl, of 1595, and the records of the Dutch factory at Agra for 1637–39. In the *A'in-i Akbari* (vol. 1, 1927/1977, p. 235) the daily wages of a skilled labourer (plasterer) are given as 7 *dams* a day (40 *dams* equalled 1 rupee), which would come to about 4.8 rupees a month. Habib 1982/1987, p. 378, claims that by 1637–38 wages showed an increase of 67–100 per cent above the rates in the *A'in-i Akbari*. From the chronicles of the Dutch factory we know that in 1637 1 *man-i Shahjahani* of wheat flour (33.56 kg) came to 1.09 rupees, and 1 *man* of *ghee* or clarified butter came to 8.53 rupees. See Aziza Hazan, 'The Silver Currency Output of the Mughal Empire and Pieces in India during the Sixteenth and Seventeenth Centuries' [1969] in Subrahmanyam 1994, pp. 156–85, esp. p. 175. See also Neelam Chaudhary, *Labour in Mughal India* (New Delhi 1998), esp. pp. 73, 82.

95 Lahauri 1866–72, vol. 2, pp. 330–31; Begley and Desai 1989, pp. 75, 77, 81–82.

96 Saqi Must'ad Khan 1947/1986, p. 203.

97 The duties of the *khadims* have been best studied for the attendants of Sufi shrines. See P. M. Currie, *The Shrine and Cult of Mu'in al-din Chishti at Ajmer* (New Delhi 1989), pp. 141–47.

98 See also Tavernier 1925/1977, vol. 1, p. 91.

99 On 13 July 2005 the Uttar Pradesh Sunni Central Waqf Board claimed the Taj Mahal as *waqf* property, on the grounds that it was a graveyard, and thus part of the Muslim mosques and graveyards managed by the Board throughout India. The decision was contested by the ASI. See *Hindustan Times*, 14 July 2005, and *Times of India*, 15 July 2005.

100 Cole 1882, p. 5, entries 20 and 23.

101 APR of the Archaeological Surveyor, Northern Circle (1905–6), p. 20. In 1999, the monument was looked after by 75 guards, 4 clerks, 25 craftsmen and 25 sweepers, all employed by the ASI.

102 Lahauri 1866–72, vol. 2, pp. 351–52, 404; Begley and Desai 1989, pp. 123–24.

103 Waris, fol. 475a; Kanbo 1967–72, vol. 3, p. 150; trans. in Begley and Desai 1989, p. 135.

104 Saksena 1976, p. 334–36; 'Inayat Khan 1990, pp. 563–65.

105 For this and the following see the reports of Kanbo, Kazim and Saqi Must'ad Khan, trans. in Begley and Desai 1989, pp. 141–60.

106 The intended funeral is illustrated in an early 19th-century copy of his work: Kanbo, *'Amal-i Salih*, BL, ms. Add. 20735, fols 609–610.

107 All Mughal emperors got new titles after their death. See Translator's Preface in Jahangir 1999, pp. xi–xiii.

III More than a Tomb: the Parts of the Taj Mahal (pp. 102–213)

1 Lahauri 1866–72, vol. 1, pt 1, p. 403, trans. E. Koch; cf. trans. Begley and Desai 1989, p. 43.

2 Tavernier 1925/1977, vol. 1, p. 90.

3 Koch 2002a, p. 46.

4 Acc. no. 22. The plan is drawn and painted on paper and pasted on cloth; it is in poor condition, and mounted behind sliding sheets of glass.

5 With the ASI; see BL, ASI photos 3566 and 3567. I have not seen the original, and was told that it is in poor condition.

6 See e. g. Lahauri 1866–72, vol. 2, p. 327 with regard to the Taj Mahal, namely the placement of the Mihman Khana and mosque on either side of the mausoleum.

7 E. E. Rosenthal, *The Palace of Charles V in Granada* (Princeton 1985), pp. 249–50, speaking of the palace that Charles V built into the Muslim Alhambra in 1526 as a statement of the Christian Reconquista of Spain.

8 Koch 2002a, p. 93.

9 See Waris's description of the buildings of the palace of Shahjahanabad: Diwan-i Khass, fol. 389b (refol. 404b); Imtiyaz or Rang Mahal, fol. 390a (405a); Diwan-i 'Amm, fol. 390b (405b).

10 Kalim, *Padshahnama*, fol. 164a, margin, trans. E. Koch; cf. trans. Begley and Desai 1989, p. 82.

11 Kanbo 1967–72, vol. 3, p. 268, trans. E. Koch;

12 Sleeman 1915/1980, pp. 312–13.

13 Begley 1996; Begley and Desai 1989, figs. 13–15

14 This is indeed true of all Mughal buildings. Among the examples we studied in the context of modular planning are the Red Fort at Delhi and the Diwan-i-ᶜAmms at Agra, Delhi and Lahore.

15 The 9 and 12 module grid would follow from the Mughal system of tripartite subdivisions.

16 *Vastu purusha mandalas*, a set of principles for the division of any space, describe a sequence of *mandalas* or grids of increasing complexity. These include a 3 × 3 or 9-square grid and a 16 × 16 or 256-square grid.

17 Hodgson 1843. For Hodgson's plan see below, p. 242.

18 For example, the metric equivalents we found for the 16-*gaz* module are: 1,290 cm (diameter of the central hall of the great gate), 1,291 cm (southern *pishtaq* of the mausoleum), 1,300 cm (projection behind each 'Naubat Khana'), and 1,315 cm (tank in the centre of the garden).

19 This means, for instance, that if one divides 1,300 cm by 16 and obtains 81.25 cm, while 1,290 divided by 16 gives a *gaz* of 80.625 cm, it is safe to assume that both overall figures are meant to be 16 *gaz*.

20 The sexagesimal was a base-60 system of numeration which was used in the Islamic world since the 'Abbasid period: see Kennedy 1986. In contrast, today we use the base-10 system of numeration.

21 In the Red Fort at Delhi the *burjs* (tower-bastions) on the south wall are spaced at 92 *gaz*, or 23 × 4.

22 Hodgson 1843, p. 54, had measured this as 313 ft 7.91 in., and found it resulted in a *gaz* figure smaller than his final *gaz* equivalent.

23 Calculation rather than drawing is preferred, since a reduced scale sometimes results in errors not visible to the naked eye, causing incorrect inferences.

24 According to the plan figure, the width of the complex should be 374 *gaz*, but according to our measurements it is 373 *gaz* on the riverfront and 374 on the Jilaukhana side. This discrepancy is a flaw in the design, but when details are designed it is not necessary for all dimensions to fit perfectly into the overall scheme. See also the annotations to these measurements in the Factfile (pp. 258–59).

25 Even Hodgson found the 150 *gaz* for the width of the Jilaukhana courtyard incongruous, and ignored it in his calculations for the *gaz*.

26 The overall width of the gateway is 17 × 3 = 51 *gaz*, and its depth is 17 × 2.5 = 42.5 *gaz*. It is, however, beyond the scope of this section to go into the details of how grids of individual buildings were arrived at.

27 For instance, the rear wall of the 'Sandli Masjid' is 11.5 *gaz* from the grid line of the garden – half the 23-*gaz* module.

28 For the term, derived from P. Hamon, *Expositions: Literature and Architecture in Nineteenth-Century France* (Berkeley 1992), and its application to a Safavid

29 See Lahauri 1866–72, vol. 2, pp. 322–31; and Kanbo 1967–72, vol. 2, pp. 315–20; both trans. in Begley and Desai 1989, pp. 65–82.

poetic architectural description, see Losensky 2003, p. 9.

30 Lane Smith 1998. The author's convincing hypothesis is marred by wild and speculative overinterpretation: each architectural feature is said to symbolize a stage in the life of Shah Jahan and Mumtaz Mahal. I thank George Michell for drawing my attention to this publication.

31 For the present designations of these buildings see *Taj Mahal, Agra: Site Management Plan*, figs. 4 and 10. For a photograph of 1858–62 by Murray, which confirms the appearance of the gate in the *Notebook* of Florentia Sale [150], see *India after the Mutiny*, p. 40, no. 90.

32 After a judgment by the Supreme Court of India this practice was stopped and the shops evicted. IAR (1997–98): 262.

33 Lahauri 1866–72, vol. 2, pp. 328–29; Kanbo 1967–72, vol. 2, p. 319.

34 Kanbo 1967–72, vol. 3, p. 20.

35 Lahauri 1866–72, vol. 2, p. 257; here he describes it more fully as *chauk-i jilaukhana*, 'courtyard in front of the house'. For a plan see Cole 1884, pl. 1, and, more recently, Naeem Mir, Hussain and Wescoat 1996, pp. 11–12. The jilaukhana of Jahangir's tomb is now wrongly called 'Akbari Serai'.

36 Major J. H. 1803, p. 75: Letter II (Agra, 18 June 1794).

37 APRASI, *United Provinces of Agra and Oudh Circle* (1901–2): Report by A. C. Polwhele, p. 15.

38 Letter of 5 August 1900. Curzon Papers, pp. 120, 124.

39 Curzon Papers, pp. 120, 124, 140, 163; *APR of the Archaeological Surveyor of the United Provinces and Punjab Circle* (1903–4), pp. 15–17; (1904–5), pp. 21–22, 37; (1905–6), p. 19: beginning of the reconstruction of the western range of the Jilaukhana (east of the western inner subsidiary tomb), dismantling of flanking building of the western subsidiary tomb; *APR of the Archaeological Surveyor, Northern Circle* (1906–7), p. 9: reconstruction of the southern wing of the eastern bazaar street and the eastern wing of the Jilaukhana (west of the eastern subsidiary tomb); (1907–8), p. 8: reconstruction of the northern wing of the eastern bazaar street. The southern range was restored on the occasion of the visit of the Prince of Wales on 13 February 1922, see ASIAR (1921–22): 2. Newell 1934, p. 65, claims that the bricks used in the reconstruction came from the bazaar and caravanserai complex, now called Taj Ganj.

40 For the *bait* system see Hillenbrand 1994, pp. 395, 397, 405, 413. The author does not include India within the scope of his investigations, which deprives him of the opportunity of noting how forms of early 'mainstream' Islamic architecture were explored, further developed, surpassed, or revived there.

41 After excavation to secure any evidence of the

Mughal latrines, these spaces will be adapted as toilets for the Visitor Centre. *Taj Mahal, Agra: Site Management Plan*, fig. 12.

42 APRASI, *North-Western Provinces and Oudh Circle, from 1 July 1899 to 31 March 1900*: Report by G. J. Joseph, Executive Engineer, Agra Provincial Division, on the Conservation of Archaeological Buildings in the Agra District During the Year 1899–1900, p. 3: he describes the restoration of the 'very dilapidated' Gaushala courtyard.

43 Parks 1850/1975, vol. 1, pp. 354–55.

44 ᶜInayat Khan 1990, pp. 447–48.

45 Sale 1832–33.

46 ᶜInayat Khan 1990, pp. 451, 513.

47 Curzon Papers, pp.140, 149; *APR of the Archaeological Surveyor of the United Provinces and Punjab Circle* (1903–4), pp. 15–17, with a plan, 'B', of 'Saheli Burj No. 1' (western tomb); (1904–5), pp. 21–22, 37; (1905–6), p. 19: dismantling of the ruined flanking building of the western 'Saheli Burj', recorded in measured drawings before it was taken down, pl. 4; *APR of the Archaeological Surveyor, Northern Circle* (1906–7), p. 9.

48 See the preceding note.

49 In the Islamic context it had an effect similar to that of its counterpart at Jerusalem, the Holy Sepulchre (340–50, restored 628), in the Christian context. The descendants of the Holy Sepulchre were identified by Krautheimer in his seminal article on the nature of medieval copying; see R. Krautheimer, 'Introduction to an "Iconography of Medieval Architecture,"' *Journal of the Warburg and Courtauld Institutes* 5 (1942): 1–33. See also Koch 1993b.

50 Ill. Hillenbrand 1994, pp. 194–95, 255, 295–97, 327, 329.

51 E. Koch, 'Look it up in India: Subcontinental Solutions to Problems of Early Islamic Architecture', lecture presented at the *Majlis* of HIA (Symposium of Historians of Islamic Art) sponsored by the Metropolitan Museum of Art on 25 February 2002 on the occasion of the 2000 CAA (College Art Association) Meeting in New York.

52 Welch and Crane 1983.

53 For illustrations see Tadgel 1990, pp. 162, 170–71, 243.

54 Koch 2002a, pp. 42, 101–2.

55 For the description of the gate see Lahauri 1866–72, vol. 2, p. 328; see also the present book, p. 257.

56 Koch 2002a, p. 71.

57 *Chaukhandi* is a Hindi term, which for the Mughals meant a four-arched pavilion (as Kanbo 1967–72, vol. 2, p. 33, explains in the context of Jahanara's garden in Kashmir). Kanbo also mentions that another Hindi word for it was *ra'oti*. At the gateway of the Taj the four arches of each *chaukhandi* are fused into a continuous gallery.

58 Lahauri 1866–72, vol. 2, p. 328. See also Koch 1993b.

59 Lahauri 1866–72, vol. 2, p. 324; see also the present book, p. 256.

60 *APR of the Archaeological Surveyor, Northern Circle*

(1908–9), p. 8; cf. Curzon Papers, p. 149.

61 The upper storeys and domes of these two landward towers were rebuilt in 1881–82. See Cole 1882, p. ccix. Hastings had declined to repair them in 1815. See Gurner 1924, p. 152.

62 Bernier 1891/1972, p. 295, who calls the emperor 'Chah Chehan'.

63 Lahauri 1866–72, vol. 2, p. 328 (see also the present book, p. 257); Kanbo 1967–72, vol. 2, p. 319; cf. Begley and Desai 1989, p. 81, where it is not quite correctly translated as 'multiple porticoes'.

64 Koch 1997c, p. 158 (repr. in Koch 2001a, p. 227).

65 Lahauri 1866–72, vol. 2, p. 327 (see also the present book, p. 257); Kanbo 1967–72, vol. 2, p. 318.

66 Kanbo 1967–72, vol. 3, p. 268; the phrase occurs in sura 3, verse 15, and sura 98, verse 8. See also below, p. 228, where it is translated as 'Gardens . . . with flowing streams'.

67 APR of the Archaeological Surveyor, Northern Circle (1907–8), p. 8. Curzon passed the order in December 1903: see Curzon Papers, p. 142.

68 Bernier 1891/1972, p. 295.

69 APR of the Archaeological Surveyor, Northern Circle (1908–9), p. 8; (1909–10), p. 11.

70 APRASI, United Provinces Circle (1902–3): Report by A. C. Polwhele, p. 15.

71 Curzon 1906, p. 199; Curzon Papers, pp. 109, 112, 116, 120, 122, 124, 125, 129, 130–31, 138–39, 141, 148

72 Begley and Desai 1989 p. 85.

73 Bernier 1891/1972, p. 296. Sir Anthony MacDonnell, who did research for Curzon on the garden and read Bernier, wished 'he had told us what flowers were grown'. Curzon Papers, p. 124.

74 Moin-ud-Din 1905, p. 34. On the plan of the Taj in Khan 1929, opposite p. 92, it is indicated as 'old tree' south of the Mihman Khana near the north-eastern corner of the garden.

75 Menon 2000, p. 125; Sahni 2000, pp. 119–20.

76 Mundy, vol. 2, 1914/1967/1991, pp. 214–15. Footnotes omitted.

77 Desai 1999, p. 196. He translates it as tulip.

78 Villiers Stuart 1913/1979, pp. 72–75, sought out these flowers in the Murree Hills and Kashmir.

79 Mundy, vol. 2, 1914/1967/1991, fig. 14 between pp. 210 and 211.

80 The poet uses three names – Persian nastaran and nasrin, and Hindi sewati (which can also be transliterated as sewti or seoti) – for what according to 19th-century dictionaries would be similar types of rose. (Nastaran is also the term used by Babur for flowers that grew in his garden in Agra: see p. 54.) See Forbes 1859/2002, pp. 495, 739, 740; cf. Fallon 1879/1989, p. 1161; Steingass 1892/1973, p. 1400. According to Ivan Louette, these would be varieties of Rosa moschata Herrm., an ancient rose of Persia (where it was called nasrin or gul-i nasrin, see Fouchécour 1969, p. 85), described by Johannes Herrmann in 1762 and rediscovered in the 20th century, growing as a large bush with matt green leaves and panicles of small to medium-sized white flowers, with a pronounced musk smell. Close relatives were Rosa brunoni, a wild rose of India, called 'the musk rose of the Himalayas', and Rosa moschata var. nastarana. Another Indian relative was Rosa glandulifera (sewati). See Ivan Louette, 'Les Origines botaniques et géographiques de Rosa moschata Herrm.', lecture presented at the 8th International Conference of Ancient Roses, Lyon, 29 May 1999, for which see <home.tiscali.be/ivan.louette/botarosa/roses/lyon-99.htm> (15.5.2005). Fouchécour 1969, pp. 84–85, identifies nastaran as eglantine ('l'églantier') and nasrin as 'the small white rose with a hundred petals' ('la petite rose blanche à cent pétales'). The Irshad az- zira'a by Qasim b. Yusuf Abu Nasri Haravi (ed. Muhammad Musiri [Teheran 1977], nasrin p. 205, nastaran pp. 206–7) also makes a distinction between gul-i nastaran and gul-i nasrin. I thank Rüdiger Lohlker for refering me to Fouchécour and the Irshad and checking out the references to the latter.

81 Gul-nar, gul-i anar, pomegranate flower, gulnari rang, carnation; Fallon 1879/1989, p. 1004.

82 Nazir Akbarabadi 1951, p. 462, trans. Dr Yunus Jaffery and E. Koch.

83 Major J. H. 1803, p. 75: Letter II (Agra, 18 June 1794).

84 For this plan see n. 4 above. Desai and Kaul 1982, pp. 17–18; Curzon Papers, p. 131.

85 Handbook 1862, p. 14.

86 An order of General Perron, in command of Sindhia's army, registers acceptance of an auction bid of 3,200 rupees made by one Ahmad Zaman for 'the fruits of the garden of the mausoleum of Tajganj' for the period 9 September 1800–31 August 1801 (Taj Museum, Acc. no. 1); Desai and Kaul 1982, p. 23.

87 Schimmel 1992, p. 164.

88 Melikoff 1967, pp. 356–60; Schimmel 1992, pp. 169–76.

89 Fallon 1879/1989, pp. 1002, 1035.

90 Small Clive Album, V&A, I.S. 48-1956, fols. 20b [195] and 23a. Jahangir 1909–14/1994, vol. 2, p. 144, 153; translated there as black tulip, but obviously it was a species with red blossoms.

91 Melikoff 1967; Losensky 1998, pp. 94–95, 129–32, 150–51. I thank Paul Losensky and Sunil Sharma for their help in establishing the meaning of lala. Poppies appear on the cenotaphs of Shah Jahan [242, 349] and on the surrounding screen [239].

92 Lahauri 1866–72, vol. 2, p. 327 (see also the present book, p. 257); Kanbo 1967–72, vol. 2, p. 318.

93 Literally, 'tent-rope room'. Steingass 1892/1973, p. 820. The Mughals used it to denote a room or hall of oblong plan inside a building, preceded by a verandah.

94 Desai and Kaul 1982. The museum was first installed in the great gate, in 1881, when M. Lawrence, the Collector of Agra, moved the collection, hitherto kept in the Agra fort, to the Taj: see Cole 1881–82, pp. ccvii–ccviii.

95 Taj Mahal: Acc. nos. 20 [72], 21, 24, 25; riverfront: Acc. no. 27 [73]; Agra fort: Acc. no. 26.

96 Lahauri 1866–72, vol. 2, p. 323.

97 Kanbo 1967–72, vol. 2, p. 316, trans. E. Koch; see also Lahauri 1866–72, vol. 2, p. 323 (trans. in the present book, p. 256).

98 Aurangzeb's term should be translated as 'terrace tahkhana of seven arches' or 'seven-arched sub-chamber of the terrace' – not 'subchambers of the seven-arched plinth', as given by Begley and Desai 1989, p. 175.

99 It had been filled in by Lieutenant Taylor (see p. 251) 'in consequence of a dangerous crack in its length caused by settlement of the river'; Alexander thought the crack would render it necessary to close the passage again, and had the plan prepared to record its existence. Transactions of the Archaeological Society of Agra (June–December 1874), p. 29; cf. Kanwar 1974, who is however unaware of Alexander's report and drawing.

100 Kalim, Padshahnama, fol. 38a; trans. in Koch 1993a, p. 12 (repr. in Koch 2001a, p. 174), where I erroneously gave fol. 37a.

101 Tabataba'i, fol. 67b; cf. trans. in Begley and Desai 1989, p. 51.

102 Lahauri 1866–72, vol. 2, p. 323 (trans. in the present book, pp. 256–57); Kanbo 1967–72, vol. 2, p. 316.

103 Tabataba'i, fol. 43a et passim; Lahauri 1866–72, vol. 2, pp. 322–31 et passim; Kanbo 1967–72, vol. 2, pp. 315–20; cf. Begley and Desai 1989, pp. 51, 65–81 et passim.

104 Lahauri 1866–72, vol. 2, p. 324 (trans. in the present book, p. 256); Kanbo 1967–72, vol. 2, p. 317.

105 Skelton 1972; Rich 1981; Rich 1987.

106 I thank Professor Friedrich Ehrendorfer, of the Botanical Institute of Vienna University, as well as Henry J. Noltie, of the Royal Botanic Garden, Edinburgh, for kindly giving me their opinion on the flowers of the Taj Mahal.

107 Cenotaph of ʿUmar bin Ahmad al-Kazaruni, adjacent to the Jamiʿ Masjid of Cambay (1333). See Koch 1988b/2003, ill. p. 185.

108 This was A. C. T. E. Prisse d'Avennes, L'Art arabe d'après les monuments du Kaire depuis le VIIe siècle jusqu'à la fin du XVIIIe (Paris 1877), trans. J. I. Erythraspis, Arab Art as seen through the Monuments of Cairo from the 7th Century to the 18th (Paris/London 1983), pl. 158: 'Lamp, Tomb of Sultan Baibars II, 14th century [AD 1309–1310]'. The same illustration is found in Stanley Lane-Poole's Art of the Saracens in Egypt (London 1886), fig. 76. Cf. Curzon Papers, pp. 171–78; the quote is on p. 176. The lamp was only put up after Curzon had left India, on 16 February 1909: APR of the Archaeological Surveyor, Northern Circle (1908–9), p. 8; Metcalf 1998. The Egyptian model is discussed in D. Behrens-Abouseif, Mamluk and Post-Mamluk Metal Lamps (Cairo 1995), pp. 26–27, pl. 14.

109 Lahauri 1866–72, vol. 2, p. 325 (trans. in the present book, p. 256); Kanbo 1967–72, vol. 2, p. 317.

110 Stainton 1990, p. 67. I have also seen it on graves in Iran and Turkey.

111 On the adoption of the *purna-ghata* or *purna-kalasha* in Mughal architecture see Nath 1976b, pp. 6–10.

112 *IAR* (1994–95): 106.

113 For the Indian *jali* see Dhaky 2004.

114 For Muslim burial practices in general see A. S. Tritton, 'Djanaza', in *Enc. of Islam*, vol. 2, pp. 441–42; for India in particular, Meer Hassan Ali, *Observations on the Mussulmauns of India Descriptive of their Manners, Customs, Habits and Religious Opinions Made During a Twelve Years' Residence in Their Immediate Society* (London 1832), vol. 1, pp. 129–35; Asad 1988, pp. 77–84.

115 Founder of the sect of the Manicheans.

116 Lahauri 1866–72, vol. 2, pp. 325–26; trans. E. Koch; cf. trans. in Begley and Desai 1989, pp. 72–73, 79.

117 Kalim, *Padshahnama*, fol. 164a and its margin; trans. E. Koch. My translation differs somewhat from that of Begley and Desai 1989, p. 83.

118 Parks 1850/1975, p. 349; see also p. 358.

119 Begley and Desai 1989; pp. 235, 187.

120 Polunin and Stainton 1984/1990, pp. 422; Stainton 1990, pl. 560.

121 Rendered into English by E. Koch after Melikoff 1967, p. 353.

122 Koch 1988a, pl. 13 (repr. in Koch 2001a, fig. 4.13).

123 cf. Begley and Desai 1989, p. 193; they add 'Ghazi' after 'Padshah', which does not appear in the original.

124 The pious Muslim repeats them and meditates on them, usually with the help of the beads of the rosary (*tasbih*, *subha*). L. Gardet, 'al-Asma' al Husna' ('The most Beautiful Names'), in *Enc. of Islam*, vol. 1, pp. 714–17.

125 Koch 2002a, p. 97.

126 Begley and Desai 1989, p. 187.

127 ibid., p. 193.

128 Andrews 1985, with overview of previous literature.

129 Lahauri 1866–72, vol. 2, p. 325 (see also the present book, p. 256); Kanbo 1967–72, vol. 2, p. 317.

130 A. B. M. Husain, *The Manara in Indo-Muslim Architecture* (Dacca 1970), pp. 185–90, figs. 84–89.

131 Bloom 1989. Bloom does not include Mughal minarets in his investigation.

132 Lahauri 1866–72, vol. 2, p. 325 (see also the present book, p. 256), calls the *chhatri* a *chartaq*, i.e. a *chahar taq*, a term used for four-arched pavilions, though it is octagonal.

133 Nugent 1839, pp. 369, 378.

134 All the minarets were found to be 'quite stable up to 1976–77, since 1941' – the period of observation. Unpublished *Report on the Verticality of Four Minars of Taj Mahal, Agra, Including Evidence on Structural Disturbance of the Building* (1984).

135 e.g. Saurab Sinha, 'Monumental Apathy: Taj Tilting for Years', *Hindustan Times*, 27 October 2004.

136 Lahauri 1866–72, vol. 2, pp. 326–27 (trans. in the present book, pp. 256–57); not so by Kanbo 1967–72, vol. 2, pp. 317–18.

137 Curzon Papers, pp. 155–56.

138 Lahauri 1866–72, vol. 2, p. 326 (trans. in the

139 ibid., p. 326.

140 The original decoration has been restored with painted plaster, see *IAR* (1995–96): 151.

141 See e.g. Rudi Paret, 'Das islamische Bilderverbot,' in J. Iten-Maritz, *Das Orientteppich-Seminar*, 8 (1975). He refers to the classical *hadis* collections of the 9th and 10th centuries, of al-Muslim and al-Bukhari.

142 Lahauri 1866–72, vol. 2, p. 327, trans. E. Koch; cf. Kanbo 1967–72, vol. 2, p. 318.

143 Hegewald 2002, pp. 149–77.

144 Lahauri 1866–72, vol. 2, p. 329 (see also the present book, p. 257); Kanbo 1967–72, vol. 2, p. 319.

145 Losensky 2003, p. 5; cf. p. 23. See also Sunil Sharma, 'The City of Beauties in the Indo-Persian Poetic Landscape' in *Comparative Studies of South Asia, Africa and the Middle East*, 24, no. 2 (2004), where he includes in his discussion parts of the *shahr-ashub* passage of Kalim's *masnawi*. On *shahr-ashub* (also called *shahr-angiz*) in general see J. T. P. Bruijn, Talat Sat Halman and Munibur Rahman, 'Sharangiz', in *Enc. of Islam*, vol. 9, pp. 212–14. I also thank Robert Skelton for personal communications about *shahr-ashub* on 24 January 2004.

146 Kalim 1957, selected verses from pp. 341–43; trans. Dr Yunus Jaffery and E. Koch. I also thank Sunil Sharma for improving the translation.

147 Mundy, vol. 2, 1914/1967/1991, p. 214.

148 Foster 1914, p. 220; Foster 1921, p. 70.

149 Twining 1893, p. 206.

150 Endensor 1998, p. 168.

151 Rahul Mehrotra has called these the Static (*pukka*) and Kinetic (*kutcha*) City: Mehrotra, 'Die Basarstadt-Metapher südasiatischer Urbanität / Bazaar City – A Metaphor for South Asian Urbanism', in *Kapital & Karma: Aktuelle Positionen indischer Kunst / Recent Positions in Indian Art*, exh. cat., Kunsthalle (Vienna 2002), pp. 95–108.

152 Lahauri 1866–72, vol. 2, p. 329 (see also the present book, p. 257); Kanbo 1967–72, vol. 2, p. 319; trans. in Begley and Desai 1989, pp. 75, 81.

153 The temple has gradually been extended over the inlet. Both the inlet and its channel can still be seen next to the temple, labelled 'Mahadave' (Mahadev, a name of Shiva), on the Hodgson plan [366]. See also a plan entitled 'Khanialams Govt. Nursery Survey Plan 1923', in *Complete Set of Site Plans of the Major Gardens of the United Provinces*, 1924, pl. II. The waterworks also feature in the early 19th-century plan in the Taj Museum (see p. 103), where they are identified in Persian as 'diwar az an ab az Jumna darun bagh-i rauza' (wall by which the water [gets] from the Jamna into the garden of the mausoleum), and in the Company drawings showing the Taj and its flanking buildings from the river, also in the Taj Museum, Acc. nos 20 [72] and 21.

154 On the working of the pipe system see Nath 1996, pp. 24–28.

155 *APRASI, United Provinces Circle* (1902–3): Report by A. C. Polwhele, p. 15.

156 Parks 1850/1975, vol. 1, p. 358.

157 Lahauri 1866–72, vol. 2, pp. 628–29; trans. E. Koch; cf. Begley and Desai 1989, pp. 125–26.

158 Koch 2002a, pp. 72–74 *et passim*.

159 ibid., p. 123.

160 *APR of the Archaeological Surveyor of the United Provinces and Punjab Circle* (1904–5), p. 21.

IV The Paradisiacal House of the Queen (pp. 214–29)

1 Lahauri 1866–72, vol. 2, p. 323 (see also the present book, p. 256); cf. Begley and Desai 1989, p. 66.

2 *Vishnudharmottara* 1990, pp. 268, 271.

3 Beck 1969, p. 559. Beck investigates the use of the two colours red and white in South Indian ritual; her findings tally with the recommendations of the *Vishnudharmottara-purana*.

4 Koch 2002c, pp. 21–22 with further references.

5 Andrews 1999, vol. 2, pp. 914, 938, 944, 952, 982–83 *et passim*.

6 Koch 2002a, p. 43; 2002b, pp. 28–29.

7 Koch 2002a, pp. 56–58.

8 Daneshvari 1986, pp. 79–81.

9 Lahauri 1866–72, vol. 1, pt 1, pp. 154–55, cf. trans. Nur Bakhsh 1903–4, p.175.

10 Kalim, *Diwan*, 'Tarikh-i Sara'i', BL MS Add. 24002, fol. 53b, lines 11 and 12.

11 Necipoğlu 1995, pp. 217–23.

12 This was first shown by Robert Skelton: Skelton 1972. Subsequently, Vivian A. Rich carried out a study of the impact of European herbals on Mughal floral representation in her dissertation for the School of Oriental and African Studies, London (unpublished): see Rich 1981; cf. Rich 1987.

13 Blunt 1950/1994, pp. 63–65, 88–91.

14 Falk and Archer 1981, cat. no. 68.

15 Kalim, *Padshahnama*, fol. 164a, margin, trans. E. Koch.

16 W. Oechslin, *Die Vase* (Zurich 1982); for another engraving close to the Taj vases see cat. no. 34: Anna M. Vaiani, flower vase, from J. B. Ferrari, *De Florum Cultura Libri IV* (Rome 1633), p. 421.

17 *Das flämische Stillleben*, exh. cat., Vienna, 2002, pp. 140–45.

18 On the adoption of the *purna-ghata* in Mughal architecture see Nath 1976b, pp. 6–10

19 Koch 1982a (repr. in Koch 2001a).

20 Kalim 1957, p. 376, line 8; Koch 1988a, p. 26 and p. 43, n. 80 (repr. in Koch 2001a, p. 109). The entwined flowery creepers are expressed in *pietra dura* on the baluster columns of Shah Jahan's throne in the Red Fort of Delhi: ibid., fig. 4.4.

21 Koch 1997c, p. 159 (repr. in Koch 2001a, pp. 227–28).

22 Kanbo, *'Amal-i Salih*, trans. in Begley and Desai 1989, p. 147.

23 Qazwini, fol. 231a (refol. 232a); cf. trans. in Begley and Desai 1989, p. 11.

24 Qazwini, fol. 42b (refol. 43b); cf. trans. in Begley and Desai 1989, p. 2.

25 Muhammad Kazim, *'Alamgirnama*, trans. in Begley and Desai 1989, p. 157.

26 'Inayat Khan 1990, p. 6.

27 Kanbo, 'Amal-i Salih, trans. in Begley and Desai 1989, p. 24.

28 See e.g. Thackston 1994, pp. 43–53; also Blair 1998.

29 Erica Cruikshank Dodd was the first to show this: Dodd 1969, Dodd and Khairallah 1981.

30 For the scripts see Schimmel and Thackston (above, Chapter II, n. 89).

31 The eschatological nature of the theme was established by Wayne Begley and Z. A. Desai. All inscriptions are translated in Begley and Desai 1989.

32 Begley 1979.

33 Dodd 1969, p. 59; Blair 1998, pp. 69, 198, 214.

34 Personal communication from Maria Eva Subtelny at Toronto on 5 December 2002.

35 For Parodi 2000, p. 539, who prefers Begley's more far-fetched hypothesis, my interpretation 'appears reductive'. Both overlook the fact that the themes of Shahjahani art and architecture were conventional, a fact one tends to ignore because of their spectacular realization. My interpretation is supported by Maria Subtelny 2002, especially pp. 122–25, where she discusses a similar concept, that 'the Persian garden was often seen as a microcosm of the celestial garden of the Muslim afterlife'.

36 This and the following Qur'anic passages are rendered according to Haleem 2004.

37 From the text on a CD by Paul Horn, Inside the Taj Mahal and Inside II, 1969 and 1972, CBS Records Inc. Released under license from Inside Music, Inc. 11062–2.

38 B. Leitner and U. Conrads, 'Der hörbare Raum: Erfahrungen und Mutmassungen / The Acoustic Space: Experiences and Conjectures', Daidalus 17 (1985): 28–46, quoted passage p. 31.

39 Sleeman 1915/1980, pp. 320–21.

40 Taylor 1855, p. 137.

41 Handbook 1862, p. 11.

42 Keene 1899, p. 33.

43 Lahauri 1866–72, vol. 1, p. 386; trans. in Begley and Desai 1989, p. 18.

44 Tavernier 1925/1977, vol. 1, p. 91, refers to these as 'Mollahs'. (The term hafiz is used for the Qur'an reciters at Akbar's tomb in 1621: Desai 1999, p. 192.)

45 ibid., pp. 90–91.

46 Tabataba'i, fol. 8b; cf. trans. in Begley and Desai 1989, p. 47

47 Endensor 1998, p. 140.

48 Koch 1993a (repr. in Koch 2001a).

49 Finch in Foster 1921/1985, pp. 186–87.

50 Desai 1999.

51 Nugent 1839, pp. 377–78.

52 Hastings 1858, p. 26.

V Everybody's Taj Mahal (pp. 230–54)

1 Tavernier 1925/1977, vol. 1, p. 90.

2 Trans. E. Koch, from the French edn of 1699; cf. Bernier 1891/1972, pp. 294–95.

3 Tavernier 1925/1977, vol. 1, p. 91.

4 Bernier 1891/1972, pp. 293–99, quotes on pp. 294 and 299.

5 Tieffenthaler was a polymath in being a geographer, historian, mathematician and astronomer. He left a sizeable legacy of writing. His Descriptio Indiae, composed originally in Latin, was brought out in German and French translations by Jean Bernouilli, as Historisch-geographische Beschreibung von Hindustan (Berlin/Gotha 1785–87) and Description historique et géographique de l'Inde (Berlin/Paris/London 1786–89 and 1791). It was considered a classic in its time – an 18th-century Baedeker guide to India, invaluable to both traders and military commanders. Tieffenthaler died in 1785 in Lucknow and was buried at Agra, in the Catholic cemetery. See S. Noti, S. J., 'Joseph Tieffentaller [sic]: A Forgotten Geographer of India', East and West, vol. V, pt I (1906), pp. 142–52, 269–77, 400–413; Maclagan 1932/1990, pp. 137–43. I have used the German edition: Tieffenthaler 1785, pp. 116–17.

6 Nazir Akbarabadi 1951. On Agra see pp. 445–46, 'The city of Akbarabad [Agra]'; pp. 448–50, 'The art of swimming (tairaki) in Agra'; pp. 461–62, 'The Mausoleum (Rauza) of Taj Ganj'; pp. 889–90, 'The city of Agra'.

7 Khafi Khan, vol. 2, 1869–74, p. 837.

8 Tieffenthaler 1785, p. 114; Hodges 1794/1999, p. 116; see also Gole 1989, p. 201.

9 Latif 1896/1981, p. 59.

10 Personal communication from J. P. Losty; see also Losty 2006.

11 Major J. H. 1803, pp. 73, 75: Letter I (Agra, 17 June 1794), and Letter II (Agra, 18 June 1794).

12 Twining 1893, pp. 190–207.

13 Pal 1989, p. 203.

14 Archer 1979, p. 157.

15 See also Bautze 1998, p. 209. I thank J. P. Losty for drawing my attention to this painting.

16 Combs Stuebe 1979, in particular pp. 44–46, figs. 125–34; Tillotson 2000.

17 Hodges 1794/1999, p. 124.

18 Losty 2006, pp. 201–2; see also Archer 1980, p. 43 and nos 28, 29.

19 Bautze 1998, pp. 209–11.

20 Archer 1980, pp. 225–33; Pal 1989, pp. 200–203.

21 I am extremely grateful to J. P. Losty, former Head of the Prints, Drawings and Photographs Section of the Asia, Pacific & Africa Collections of the BL, for most generously providing information and advice on the British reception of the Taj, and for reading Chapter V.

22 Several of these reactions are collected in Alexander 1987, pp. 191–206.

23 Losty 1989, p. 41; cf. Losty 1998.

24 One manuscript, written by a certain 'Mughal Baig' and dated 24 August 1878, is kept in the Taj Museum. Desai and Kaul 1982, p. 20. Another manuscript of this type, entitled Ahwal-i shahr-i Akbarabad (BL, ms. Or. 2030), was partially translated and published by Anderson 1873; see also Rieu 1888, vol. 3, p. 958. Hodgson 1843, p. 50, already observed that the measurements given in one of these manuscripts did not tally with the actual architecture, and described the

work as the 'fabrication of an impostor'. On the problem of these manuscripts see also Begley and Desai 1989, p. xxxii.

25 Nugent 1839, p. 357.

26 ibid., pp. 363, 369. The idea of a glass case over the Taj Mahal had first been expressed by the painter Zoffany (see p. 233). The Taj showed no signs of decay, but a monument exposed to ruin was part of the Picturesque conception.

27 ibid., pp. 369, 378.

28 ibid., p. 367.

29 ibid., p. 364.

30 Personal communication from J. P. Losty on 16 January 2002. The drawings made for Lady Nugent are in the BL, which has the largest holdings of Company drawings and paintings.

31 Hastings 1858, pp. 10, 11, 29.

32 Sita Ram was first studied by Losty 1995.

33 The large view is illustrated in Visions of India including the Paul F. Walter Collection, sale cat., Christies, London, 25 May 1995, no. 5.

34 Parks 1850/1975, vol. 1, pp. 352, 354.

35 Sale 1832–33 gives his rank as colonel.

36 Handbook 1862, p. 11.

37 J. Murray, civil surgeon at Agra, Photographic Views in Agra, and its Vicinity, with Letter-Press Descriptions by J. Middleton, principal of the Honourable East India Company's College at Agra (London 1858), p. 7.

38 Taylor 1855, p. 133.

39 Sleeman 1915/1980, p. 317.

40 Parks 1850/1975, vol. 1, p. 353.

41 Handbook 1862, pp. 12–13.

42 Keene 1899, p. 35. Keene's Handbook for Visitors to Agra was based on the Handbook of 1854 and its subsequent editions (1862, 1869); first published in 1873, with several revised editions, it became a standard guide until the 20th century.

43 Parks 1850/1975, p. 355; Handbook 1862, pp.16–17; Keene 1899, pp. 33–34.

44 Sale 1832–33; Parks 1850/1975, p. 355–56, says it was the husband, who had just ascended the minaret.

45 Sir John Strachey, Lieutenant-Governor, North-Western Provinces, minute of 25 August 1875, in Transactions of the Archaeological Society of Agra, January–June 1876, p. 6: he quotes 'a distinguished member of the Civil service . . . [who] assured me that 'perhaps 40 years ago, this was a common practice'. Cf. Raleigh 1906, p. 190.

46 Sale 1832–33; cf. Gen. Godfrey Charles Mundy on 8 January 1828 in his Journal of a Tour in India, quoted by Bautze 1998, p. 208; see also Alexander 1987, p. 202.

47 Keene 1899, p. 34.

48 Bernier 1891/1972, pp. 295–99.

49 Tavernier 1925/1977, vol. 1, p. 90.

50 Pal 1989, p. 206.

51 Hodges 1794/1999, p. 124.

52 Major J. H. 1803, p. 74, Letter II (Agra, 18 June 1794). William Hodges deliberately falsified details of Mughal architecture to impress on Europe the similarity between Indian and Gothic architecture, and in his Dissertation on the Prototypes

of Architecture, Hindoo, Moorish, and Gothic (London 1787) pleaded that these styles be recognized, and not judged by the standards of classical Greek and Roman architecture. See also Tillotson 2000, pp. 76, 80.

53 Keene 1899, p. 29.

54 Manrique 1927, pp. 173–74. The Italian form of the name is 'Girolamo', but the Portuguese (and Spanish) sources of the period had a tendency to alter Italian names to sound Portuguese: see Gauvin Alexander Bailey, Counter-Reformation, Symbolism and Allegory in Mughal Painting, PhD thesis, Harvard, 1996, p. 103, n. 64. For the controversy see Havell 1903; Hosten 1910; Chughtai 1940; Dixon 1987; G. H. R. Tillotson, 'Politics and the Taj Mahal', Oriental Art, n.s. (1986): 266–69; T. R. Metcalf, An Imperial Vision: Indian Architecture and Britain's Raj (London/Boston 1989), pp. 46–48. For Geronimo Veroneo's tomb at Agra see Maclagan 1932/1990, p. 332.

55 Pfeiffer 1851, p. 179.

56 APR of the Superintendent, Muhammadan and British Monuments, Northern Circle (1913–14), p. 2.

57 They are kept at the Agra office of the ASI.

58 The only publication brought out by the ASI is a booklet on the Taj Museum: see Desai and Kaul 1982. On the lack of scientific studies on the Taj see also Bautze 1998, p. 212.

59 Pal 1989, pp. 219–23; Falconer 2001, esp. pp. 8–10, 15–16.

60 Pal 1989, pp. 219–21; Early Photographs of India: The Archives of Dr. John Murray, Sotheby's, London, 18 June 1999; Falconer in Dehejia 2000, pp. 34, 39, 75–76, pls. 15, 16, 17, 21; S. Gordon, checklist of the exhibition, in Johnson 2004, cat. nos. 118, 119 on pp. 177–78; Sotheby's, London, 25 May 2005.

61 Birdwood 1880, p. 209.

62 Pal 1989, p. 221; Pohlmann 2001, pp. 14–16, 158, 160, 161, 258; Falconer 2001, pp. 26–29.

63 See the following in Dehejia 2000: Falconer, pp. 39; Harris, p. 122; Sampson, pp. 259–71. Falconer 2001, pp. 29 and 137–41. Besides the BL, the Alkazi Collection of Photography has particularly rich holdings of views of the Taj by Murray, Bourne and Saché. On Lala Deen Dayal see Luther 2003. The Photographic Collection of the Aga Khan Program at Harvard has inter alia Johnston & Hoffman photographs of the Taj.

64 Pal 1989, p. 206. Pratapaditya Pal assembled and analysed reactions to the Taj.

65 Thomas Bacon, First Impressions and Studies from nature in Hindostan, embracing an Outline of the Voyage to Calcutta and Five Years' Residence in Bengal and the Do'ab, from MDCCXXXI to MDCCCXXXVI (London 1837), vol. 2, pp. 371–75, p. 382, quoted after Bautze 1998, p. 208.

66 Heber 1827/1993, vol. 2, pp. 340–42.

67 Sleeman 1915/1980, p. 317.

68 Parks 1850/1975, vol. 1, p. 359.

69 Pfeiffer 1851, p. 179. She anticipated Begley 1979, pp. 7–11 et passim.

70 Linstrum 1995, p. 3.

71 Curzon Papers, pp. 109–88; Metcalf 1998, p. 24, for Curzon's comment on the lamp.

72 Capt. Leopold von Orlich, Travels in India including Sinde and the Punjab, trans. from the German by H. Evans Lloyd (Leipzig 1845; repr. New Delhi 1985), vol. 2, p. 45. The original German edition, Reise in Ostindien in Briefen an Alexander von Humboldt und Carl Ritter (Leipzig 1845), is illustrated with prints after Company drawings of the Taj Mahal and other monuments of Agra.

73 Pohlmann 2001, p. 15.

74 Taylor 1855, pp. 132, 137–38.

75 Keyserling 1923, vol. 1, pp. 250–53.

76 In his introduction to Emanuel LaRoche, Indische Baukunst (Munich 1921–22), p. xiii.

77 Havell 1924/70, p. 78.

78 Yusuf Khan Kambalposh, ʿAjaʾib-i Firang, ed. by Tahsin Firaqi (Lahore 1983). I thank Sunil Sharma for this reference and the translation.

79 Lines 1–15 and 49–58 of the 145 verses of the poem 'Shah-Jahan', which came out in the collection entitled Balaka ('Wild Geese') in 1916. See Rabindranath Tagore, Selected Poems, trans. W. Radice (London 1985, repr. 1994), pp. 78–81, also notes on pp. 145–46; also the earlier translation by Aurobindo Bose, A Flight of Swans: Poems from Balaka by Rabindranath Tagore (London 1955), pp. 15–24, where the same poem is entitled 'Taj-Mahal 1' and followed by a second poem, 'Taj-Mahal 2'.

80 Huxley 1926/1969, pp. 57ff.

81 Pal 1989, pp. 238–39.

82 Information from his daughter, my schoolfriend, the photographer Britta Elsner, on 11 September 2003 when she took the photograph [370]. The model was built by the School of Engineering, Villach, Carinthia. See Minimundus: Die kleine Welt am Wörthersee (Klagenfurt 1990), pp. 4–5.

83 Pal 1989, pp. 9–13.

84 ibid., p. 11.

85 India, Lonely Planet Travel Guide, 8th edn (Melbourne/Oakland/London/Paris 1999), p. 392.

86 Tavernier 1925/1977, vol. 1, p. 91.

87 Manrique 1927, vol. 2, p. 173.

88 Henri Stierlin, Islamic Art and Architecture (London 2004), pp. 180–81.

89 Natwar-Singh 1981, pp. 95–96.

90 Oak 1974.

91 S. Thompson, Motif-Index of Folk Literature, 6 vols (Copenhagen 1955–58), vol. 5, 1957: in order of listing: p. 497, Motif W181.2; p. 312, Motif S165.7; p. 311, Motif S161.0.1.

92 A. Wesselski, Versuch einer Theorie des Maerchens (Reichenberg 1931), p. 15. See also recent reports in Folklore Society News which Emily Lane kindly forwarded to me from Jacqueline Simpson: T. B. Edwards, 'Mutilated Architects', and J. Simpson, 'Architect murdered by Patron', both 38 (November 2002): 5–6; G. Whittaker, M. Ross and B. Hooper, 'Architect and Patron', 39 (February 2003): 2–3; J. Simpson, 'Architect, Wife and Patron', 41 (November 2003): 16.

93 R. Basset, 'Les Alixares de Grenade et le Château de Khaouaraq [sic]', Revue Africaine, 50ème Année, no. 260 (1er Trimestre, 1906): 22–36; R. Würsch,

'Das Schloss Hawarnaq nach arabischen und persischen Quellen', Wiener Zeitschrift für die Kunde des Morgenlandes, Bd 88 (1998): 261–79; I thank Markus Ritter for referring me to this publication.

94 J. Huggler, 'Craftsmen who built Taj Mahal preserved their names in stone', Independent, London, 7 July 2004.

95 Begley and Desai 1989, pp. 175-77.

96 Saqi Mustʿad Khan 1947/1986, p. 203; Asher 1992, p. 261.

97 Cotton 1927, pp. 14–18.

98 Major J. H. 1803, p. 75, Letter II (Agra, 18 June 1794).

99 Lord Hastings in Gurner 1924, p. 152.

100 Gurner 1924, pp. 149–50; see also Kyd's letter to the 'Committee for the Care of the Taaj Mehal, Agra', dated 24 November 1808 (BL), the content of which was kindly sent to me by J. P. Losty on 29 January 2004.

101 Handbook 1862, p. 12.

102 Cole 1882, p. 4; Vats 1946, p. 5. Taylor's rank is given as captain, though at that time he was a lieutenant: he became captain in 1818. I thank J. P. Losty for this information.

103 Transactions of the Archaeological Society of Agra, January–June 1874, p. 11.

104 Taylor 1855, p. 131.

105 Rowlatt 1867, pp. 70–74.

106 Curzon Papers, pp. 77–81; Curzon 1906, p. 192; APRASI, North-Western Provinces and Oudh Circle, from 1 July 1899 to 31 March 1900, with 'A short history of the Archaeological Department, and its connection with, and the work done by the Public Works Department in the North-Western Provinces and Oudh', by W. G. Wood.

107 Strachey (above, n. 45), p. 1.

108 Transactions of the Archaeological Society of Agra, January–June 1876, pp. 3–4; Vats 1946, p. 6.

109 Report by W. G. Wood (above, n. 106). In 1899 the Survey areas were reorganized into five Survey Circles: (1) Bombay, including Sind and Berar, (2) Madras and Coorg, (3) Panjab, Beluchistan, and Ajmer, (4) North-Western Provinces and Central Provinces, (5) Bengal and Assam. J. H. Marshall in the introduction to the new ASIAR (1902–3): 1–13, gives an overview of Indian conservation. The Annual Report was the new chief periodical of the ASI, which had been reorganized by Curzon with Marshall as its new director-general. The Survey staff was defined as essentially an active, not a contemplative, corps, and its duty would therefore be to place before European scholars material for elucidation rather than to attempt elucidation on its own account.

110 Marshall (see the preceding note), p. 12; Curzon Papers, pp. 83–89; cf. Curzon 1906, pp. 195–203.

111 Curzon Papers, 'Agra', pp. 109–88.

112 ibid., p. 109. This was criticized by the art historian E. B. Havell, who in a letter of 5 November 1903 drew attention to the fact that the cypresses were originally planted outside the geometrical flowerbeds: ibid., p. 138.

113 APRASI, North-Western Provinces and Oudh Circle, from

1 July 1899 to 31 March 1900: Report by G. J. Joseph, Executive Engineer, Agra Provincial Division, on the Conservation of Archaeological Buildings in the Agra District during the year 1899–1900, pp. 2–4; (1900–1901): Report by G. J. Joseph, pp. 15–16; *APRASI, United Provinces of Agra and Oudh Circle* (1901–2): Report by A. C. Polwhele, Executive Engineer, Agra Provincial Division, on the Conservation of Ancient Buildings in the Agra Division for the year 1901–2, pp. 14–15; *APRASI, United Provinces Circle* (1902–3): Report by A. C. Polwhele, pp. 14–15, with statement of expenditure; *APR of the Archaeological Surveyor of the United Provinces and Punjab Circle* (1903–4): Report by A. C. Polwhele, pp. 15–17; (1904–5): Report by A. C. Polwhele, pp. 21–22, 'Notes on the Conservation of Ancient Muhammadan Buildings during the year ending 31st March 1905', by W. H. Nicholls, pp. 36–38; *APR of the Archaeological Surveyor, Northern Circle* (1905–6): 'Conservation of Muhammadan Buildings in the United Provinces and Panjab [sic] and at Ajmer', by W. H. Nicholls, p. 17: beginning of reconstruction of Jilaukhana wings on the east side of the western Subsidiary Tomb (Saheli Burj), dismantling of flanking building of western Subsidiary Tomb; (1906–7): Notes on Conservation in the United Provinces, and Punjab and Ajmer, by W. H. Nicholls, p. 9: reconstruction of wings to the north and west sides of eastern Subsidiary Tomb; (1907–8): Notes on Conservation in the United Provinces, Punjab and Ajmer, by R. Froude Tucker, p. 8: northern wing of eastern Bazaar Street. The remaining south wing of the Jilaukhana was restored only in 1922, on the occasion of the visit of the Prince of Wales on 13 February 1922: see *ASIAR* (1921–22), p. 2.

114 Newell 1934, p. 65, who refers to these ranges as *dalans*.

115 Curzon Papers, pp. 83–89; Curzon 1906, pp. 197–99.

116 Curzon Papers, 'Agra', p. 136; see also Linstrum 1995.

117 Curzon Papers, 'Agra', pp. 145–46.

118 ibid., pp. 171–78; Metcalf 1998.

119 G. Sanderson, 'Notes on the conservation of the Muhammadan and British Monuments in the United Provinces, in the Punjab, and at Ajmer', *APR of the Superintendent, Muhammadan and British Monuments, Northern Circle* (1911–12), p. 29.

120 The work has been reported in the yearly issues of the *ASIAR*, and in its successor journal, *IAR*.

121 See *inter alia* 'Monumental Neglect', *The State of India's Environment: The Second Citizen's Report 1984–85* (New Delhi 1985), p. 127.

122 The judgment, dated 30 December 1996, was published in *The Times of India* on 7 February 1997. See also *IAR* (1997–98): 262.

123 Agrawal 1995 reviews earlier studies on atmospheric pollutants damaging the Taj and points out the effect of physical, chemical and biological factors.

124 See e. g. *IAR* (1983–84): 246–47; (1984–85): 270; (1988–89): 181; (1989–90): 207; (1990–91): 159; (1994–95): 150; (1993–94): 201; (1995–96): 201.

125 See e.g. *IAR* (1983–84): 246–47; (1984–85): 270; (1985–86): 201; (1987–88): 219; (1988–89): 181; (1989–90): 207; (1990–91): 159; (1992–93): 199; (1993–94): 201; (1995–96): 201.

126 *IAR* (1993–94): 201; (1996–97): 319.

127 *IAR* (1994–95): 150; (1995–96): 201; (1997–98): 352; (1998–99): 363.

128 The aims of the venture were set out in the *Taj Mahal, Agra: Site Management Plan*; for my Mission Statement, delivered at the end of the first Advisors' meeting on the conservation of the Taj, held 25–28 September 2001, see pp. 5–6. See also D. Gupta 2002, pp. 12–13, who gives an overview of the initiatives dedicated to the Taj since 1971.

129 *Taj Mahal, Agra: Site Management Plan*, pp. 66–67, 70, fig. 12. See also Koch 2001b.

Lahauri's account of the complex of the Taj Mahal
(pp. 256–57)

1 Lahauri 1866–72, vol. 2, pp. 322–31, trans. E. Koch (cf. Begley and Desai, pp. 65–77).

2 A title of Mumtaz Mahal.

3 Another title of Mumtaz.

4 'Rauza-i mutahhara' is also used to designate the tomb of the prophet Muhammad: see p. 152.

5 Lahauri uses *zira*ꞌ and *gaz* interchangeably to denote the same measurement, c. 80–82 cm.

6 Begley and Desai 1989, p. 67, give a depth of 6 *zira*ꞌ, but the Persian text has 'chahar', 4.

7 It means that the white marble makes day brighter and the black stone makes night darker.

8 Lahauri means either that the pearls are more luminous than the sun and that their shining thus reflects on it, or else that the sun feels compelled to shine brighter in order not to be outshone by the pearls.

9 Shah Jahan was obviously concerned that the precious gold screen would attract robbers.

10 Here the tomb is called holy because the Qur'anic inscriptions, which represent its most religious aspect, are addressed.

11 Lahauri seems to speak here of the riverfront terrace and its relief work, because the white marble platform has hardly any carving, and he uses the term *kursi* for both. Begley and Desai do not realize that Shah Jahan's authors use '*munnabat*' consistently for the technique of relief, and translate it as 'engraved work'.

12 The four holy persons charged with the surveillance of the four cardinal points, in the centre of which they have their dwelling-place. See I. Goldziher, 'Awtad', *Enc. of Islam*, vol. 1 (1979), p. 772.

13 Kanbo 1967–72, vol. 2, p. 318 tells us slightly more, that the garden had 'various kinds of fruit-bearing trees (*ashjar mewadar*) and rare aromatic herbs (*riyahin badi*ꞌ*a'in*)'; see p. 138.

14 When Begley and Desai translated this (1989, p. 74), they were not aware that *girih bandi* has the specific meaning of geometrical ornament. This was discussed by Necipoğlu 1995, 9, 92–93, 132, *et passim*.

15 This describes the east and west garden-wall pavilions.

16 Again, Begley and Desai 1989, p. 74, give 6 *gaz*, but the Persian text has '*chahar*', 4.

17 Lahauri spells this *khwadim*.

18 Begley and Desai 1989, p. 75, misunderstood the passage when they translated that 'the market square (*charsu-bazar*)' had been laid out in the centre of the octagonal *chauk*.

18 By 'Mumtazabad' Lahauri means the quarters and caravanserais surrounding the bazaar and caravanserai complex known as Taj Ganj.

20 The Persian text has '*nagarchand*', which might be a misprint for Nagarchain, as was tacitly assumed by Begley and Desai 1989, p. 75. Nagarchain was a place south of Agra; it is known because Akbar had a hunting palace there, which does not seem to have survived. For the list of villages and the amount of revenue given by Lahauri see Begley and Desai 1989, p.75.

21 The *dam* was the Mughal copper coin, used for revenue accounts and small transactions, officially rated in the 16th century at one-fortieth of the rupee: see Habib 1982/87.

Select bibliography

ASINIS   Archaeological Survey of India New
          Imperial Series
ASIR   Archaeological Survey of India Report
BL   British Library, London

1. Persian, Urdu, Turkish, Arabic and Sanskrit Sources

*Translated works are given with the spelling used by
the translator; untranslated works are given in my
transliteration system.*

Abu'l Fazl ᶜAllami *The A'in-i Akbari by Abu'l-Fazl
ᶜAllami*, trans. in 3 vols: vol. 1 by H. Blochmann,
2nd edn rev. and ed. by D. C. Phillot (Calcutta
1927); vols 2 and 3 by H. S. Jarrett, 2nd edn
corrected and further annotated by J. Sarkar
(Calcutta 1948–49) (all 3 vols repr. New Delhi
1977–78)
— *The Akbar Nama of Abu-l-Fazl*, trans. by H.
Beveridge, 3 vols (Calcutta 1902–39, 2nd repr.
Delhi 1979)
Akbarabadi, Nazir *Kulliyat-i Nazir Akbarabadi*, ed. by
Maulana ᶜAbdul Bari Sahib Asi and Maulawi
Ashraf 'Ali Lakhnawi, 3rd edn (Lakhnau
[Lucknow] 1951)
Babur, Zahir-ud-Din Muhammad *Babur-Nama
(Memoirs of Babur)*, trans. by A. S. Beveridge (1921,
repr. New Delhi 1970)
— *Baburnama, Chaghatay Turkish Text with Abdul-
Rahim Khankhanan's Persian Translation, Turkish
Transcription, Persian Edition and English Translation
by W. M. Thackston*, 3 vols (Cambridge 1993)
— *The Baburnama: Memoirs of Babur, Prince and Emperor*,
trans., ed. and annotated by W. M. Thackston
(Washington, D.C./New York 1996)
Badauni, ᶜAbd al-Qadir *Muntakhabu-t-Tawarikh by
ᶜAbdu-l-Qadir-ibn-i Muluk Shah known as Al-Badaoni*,
3 vols, trans. by: vol. 1, G. S. A. Ranking (Calcutta
1898); vol. 2, W. H. Lowe (2nd edn Calcutta 1924);
vol. 3, T. W. Haig (Calcutta 1925) (all 3 vols repr.
Delhi 1973)
Brahman, Chandar Bhan *Chahar Chaman*, bound in
BL, ms. Add. 16863
— *Chahar Chaman*, ed. by Sayyid Muhammad Jaffery
(New Delhi 1383 sh/2004)
Dawani, Jalal-ud-Din 'Arznama, ed. Iraj Afshar, 'Arz-i
sipah-i Uzun Hassan', in *Majalla-i Danishkada-i
Adabiyyat*, 3, 3 (Tehran 1335sh/1957): 26–66
Jahangir *Tuzuk-i Jahangiri or Memoirs of Jahangir*,
trans. by A. Rogers, ed. by H. Beveridge, 2 vols
(1909–14, repr. Delhi 1994)
— *The Jahangirnama: Memoirs of Jahangir, Emperor of
India*, trans., ed. and annotated by W. M.
Thackston (New York 1999)
Jonaraja *The Rajatarangini of Jonaraja*, trans. by
Jogesh Chunder Dutt (1898, repr. Delhi 1986)
Kalim, Abu Talib *Diwan*, ed. by Partau Bayza'i
(Tehran 1336 sh/1957)
— *Diwan*, BL, ms. Add. 24002
— *Padshahnama*, BL, ms. Ethé 1570

Kambalposh, Yusuf Khan ᶜAja'ib-i Firang, ed. by
Tahsin Firaqi (Lahore 1983)
Kanbo, Muhammad Salih ᶜAmal-i Salih or Shah
Jahannama, rev. and ed. by Wahid Quraishi, based
on the Calcutta edn of 1912–46 by Ghulam
Yazdani, 2nd edn, 3 vols (Lahore 1967–72)
— *Bahar-i sukhan*, BL, ms. Or. 178
Kashi, Mir Muhammad Yahya Padshahnama, BL, ms.
Or. 1852
Kazim, Muhammad ᶜAlamgirnama, ed. by Khadim
Husain and ᶜAbd al-Hayy (Calcutta 1865–68)
Khafi Khan, Muhammad Hashim Muntakhab al-
lubab, pts 1 and 2, ed. Kabir-ud-Din Ahmad
(Calcutta 1869, 1874). The portions relating to
Aurangzeb's reign have been trans. as *History of
ᶜAlamgir* by S. Moinul Haq (Karachi 1975)
Khaldun, Ibn *The Muqaddimah, An Introduction to
History*, trans. by F. Rosenthal, ed. and abridged
by N. J. Dawood (London 1967)
Khan, ᶜInayat *The Shah Jahan Nama of ᶜInayat Khan*,
trans. by A. R. Fuller, rev. and ed. by W. E. Begley
and Z. A. Desai (New Delhi 1990)
Khan, Muhammad Bakhtawar Mir'at al-ᶜAlam
(*History of Aurangzeb: 1658–68*), with introduction
and notes by Sajida S. ᶜAlvi, 2 vols (Lahore 1979)
Khan, Muhammad Sadiq Tawarikh-i Shahjahani, BL,
ms. Or. 174
Khan, Saqi Mustᶜad *Maasir-i-Alamgiri: A History of the
Emperor Aurangzib-ᶜAlamgir (Reign 1658–1707 AD)*,
trans. and annotated by J. Sarkar (Calcutta 1947,
repr. New Delhi 1986)
Khan, Shah Nawaz *Ma'athir-ul-Umara: Being
Biographies of the Muhammadan and Hindu Officers of
the Timurid Sovereigns of India from 1500 to about
1780 A.D. by Nawwab Samsam-ud-Daula Shah Nawaz
Khan and his Son ᶜAbdul Hayy*, trans. by H.
Beveridge, 3 vols (Calcutta 1911–64, repr. Patna
1979 [for vol. 1, I refer to the 1979 repr.])
Khan, Zain *Zain Khan's Tabaqat-i Baburi*, trans. by
Sayed Hasan Askari, annotated by B. P. Ambastha
(Delhi 1982)
Khwandamir, Ghiyas ud-Din *Qanun-i Humayuni (Also
Known as Humayun Nama) of Khwandamir*, trans.
and annotated by B. Prasad (Calcutta 1940)
Lahauri, ᶜAbd-ul-Hamid Padshahnama, ed. by M.
Kabir-ud-Din Ahmad and M. ᶜAbd al-Rahim
(Calcutta 1866–72)
Qazwini, Muhammad Amin, or Amina-i Qazwini
Padshahnama, BL, ms. Or. 173
Qudsi, Haji Muhammad Jan Zafarnama-i Shah Jahan,
BL, ms. Ethé 1552
Sil Chand, L. Tafrih al-ᶜimarat, copied 1836–37 for
James Davidson, BL, ms. I.O.L. 2450
Sujan Rai, Bhandari of Batala Khulasat-ut-tawarikh,
ed. by M. Zafar Hasan (Delhi 1918)
Tabataba'i, Jalal ud-Din Padshahnama, or
Shahjahannama, BL, ms. Or. 1676
*Vishnudharmottara Shri Vishnudharmottara: A Text on
Ancient Indian Arts*, trans. by Priyabala Shah
(Ahmedabad, n.d. [1990])
Waris, Muhammad Padshahnama, BL, ms. Add. 6556
Yadgar, Ahmad Tarikh-i Shahi, Persian text ed. by
M. Hidayat Husain (Calcutta 1939)
Yazdi, Sharaf-ud-Din ᶜAli Zafarnama, extracts trans.

by H.M. Elliot and J. Dowsen in *The History of India
as Told by Its Own Historians: The Muhammadan
Period*, 3 (1867–77, repr. Lahore 1976)

2. European Sources of the 16th and 17th Centuries

Bernier, F. *Travels in the Mogul Empire: A.D.
1656–1668*, trans. by A. Constable (1891, repr.
New Delhi 1972)
Bordeaux, A. 'Four Letters by Austin de Bordeaux',
Journal of the Punjab Historical Society, 4, 1 (1916):
3–17
De Laet, J. *The Empire of the Great Mogol: A translation of
De Laet's 'Description of India and Fragment of Indian
History' by J. S. Hoyland* (Delhi 1928, repr. 1975)
A Dutch Chronicle of Mughal India ed. and trans. by
B. Narain and S. R. Sharma (1927, repr. Lahore
1978)
Foster, W., ed. *Early Travels in India: 1583–1619*
(London 1921, repr. New Delhi 1985)
— *The English Factories in India 1646–1650* (Oxford
1914), *1651–1654* (Oxford 1915), *1655–1660*
(Oxford 1921)
Mandelslo, J. *Des HochEdelgeborenen Johan Albrechts von
Mandelslo Morgenländische Reyse-Beschreibung . . .*,
ed. A. Olearius (Schleswig 1658)
— *The Voyages and Travels of J. Albrecht Mandelslo in
the East Indies*, trans. by John Davies of Kidwelly
(London 1669)
Manrique, S. *Travels of Fray Sebastien Manrique,
1629–1643*, trans. by C. E. Luard and H. Hosten,
2 vols (Oxford 1927)
Manucci, N. *Storia do Mogor or Mogul India:
1653–1708*, trans. with intro. and notes by W.
Irving, 4 vols (London 1907, repr. Calcutta
1965–67)
Monserrate, A. *Mongolicae Legationis Commentarius or
The First Jesuit Mission to Akbar*, Latin text ed. by H.
Hosten, in *Memoirs of the Asiatic Society of Bengal* 3,
no.9 (1914): 513–704
— *Commentary of Father Monserrate*, trans. by J. S.
Hoyland and annotated by S. N. Banerjee
(Nagpur 1922, repr. Jalandhar 1993)
Mundy, P. *The Travels of Peter Mundy in Europe and Asia,
1608–1667*, ed. by R. C. Temple, 3 vols (London
1911–19; vol. 2 1914, repr. Nendeln,
Liechtenstein, 1967, new repr. 1991)
Pelsaert, F. *Remonstrantie*, publ. as *Jahangir's India*,
trans. by W. H. Moreland and P. Geyl (1925, repr.
Delhi 1972)
Roe, Sir T. *The Embassy of Sir Thomas Roe to India,
1615–19*, ed. by W. Foster (1899, repr. Nendeln,
Liechtenstein, 1967, 2nd edn 1926, repr. New
Delhi 1990)
Tavernier, J.-B. *Travels in India*, 2 vols, trans. by
V. Ball, 2nd edn by William Crooke (1925, repr.
New Delhi 1977)
Thévenot, J. de *Indian Travels of Thévenot and Careri*,
trans. of pt 3 of his *Voyages: Relation de l'Indoustan,
des nouveaux Mogols et des autres peuples et pays des
Indes* (Paris 1684), in *India in the Seventeenth Century*,
ed. by J. P. Guha (New Delhi 1984)
— *The Travels of Monsieur de Thevenot. The Third Part.
Containing the Relation of Indostan, the New Moghuls*

and of other People and Countries of the Indies (London 1687)

3. Later Sources and Secondary Literature

Agrawal, O. P. 'Conservation of Taj Mahal: The Real Problem', in *Conservation, Preservation and Restoration: Traditions, Trends and Techniques*, ed. by G. Kamalakar and V. Pandit Rao (Hyderabad 1995), pp. 1–14

Alam, S., and S. Subrahmanyam 'Witnessing Transition: Views on the End of the Akbari Dispensation', in *The Making of History: Essays Presented to Irfan Habib*, ed. K. N. Panikkar, Terence J. Byres and Utsa Patnaik (Delhi 2000), pp. 104–41

Alexander, M. *Delhi and Agra: a Travellers' Companion*, texts selected and intro. by M. Alexander (London 1987)

Alfieri, B. M. *Islamic Architecture of the Indian Subcontinent* (London 2000)

Alvi, M. A., and A. Rahman *Jahangir the Naturalist* (New Delhi 1968), pp. 15, 67–77

Anderson, R. P. 'The Taj: A Translation from the Persian', *Calcutta Review*, 57 (1873): 233–37

Andrews, P. A. 'Trellis Tent and Bulbous Dome', in *Geschichte des Konstruierens I/History of Structural Design I*, Konzepte SFB CCXXX/5 (1985): 63–97

— 'Parcîn-Kari', *Encyclopaedia of Islam*, vol. 8 (1995), pp. 267–70

— *Felt Tents and Pavilions, The Nomadic Tradition and its Interaction with Princely Tentage*, 2 vols (London 1999)

Archer, M. *Company Drawings in the India Office Library* (London 1972)

— *India and British Portraiture 1770–1825* (London/New York/Delhi/Karachi 1979)

— *Early Views of India: The Picturesque Journeys of Thomas and William Daniell 1786–1794* (London 1980)

Asad, M. *Indian Muslim Festivals and Customs*, trans. by M. R. Sharma (New Delhi 1988)

Asher, C. B. *Architecture of Mughal India*, New Cambridge History of India, 1, 4 (Cambridge/New York/Oakleigh 1992)

Athar Ali, M. *The Apparatus of Empire: Award of Ranks, Offices and Titles to the Mughal Nobility (1574–1658)* (Delhi 1985)

Aziz, A. 'History of the Reign of Shah Jahan', *Journal of Indian History* 6 (1927): 235–57; 7 (1928): 127–47, 327–44; 9 (1930): 132–72, 279–305; 11 (1932): 86–113, 356–65; 12 (1933) 47–78

Bahura, G. N., and C. Singh *Catalogue of Historical Documents in Kapad Dwara, Jaipur*, pt 2, Maps and Plans (Jaipur 1990)

Baker, P. L. *Islam and the Religious Arts* (London 2004)

Bautze, J. K. *Interaction of Cultures: Indian and Western Painting 1780–1910, The Ehrenfeld Collection* (Alexandria 1998)

Beach, M. C., E. Koch and W. Thackston *King of the World: The Padshahnama: An Imperial Mughal Manuscript from the Royal Library, Windsor Castle* (London/Washington, D.C., 1997)

Beale, T. W. *An Oriental Biographical Dictionary* (London 1894, repr. 1971)

Beck, B. E. F. 'Colour and Heat in South Indian Ritual', *Man – Journal of the Royal Anthropological Institute*, n.s., 4, 4 (1969), pp. 553–72

Begley, W. E. 'Amanat Khan and the Calligraphy on the Taj Mahal', *Kunst des Orients* 12 (1978–79): 5–39

— 'The Myth of the Taj Mahal and a New Theory of its Symbolic Meaning,' *Art Bulletin* 61 (1979): 7–37

— 'Ustad Ahmad', *Macmillan Encyclopedia of Architects* (London 1982), 1, pp. 39–42

— 'The Garden of the Taj Mahal: A Case Study of Mughal Architectural Planning and Symbolism', in Wescoat and Wolschke-Bulmahn 1996

— and Z. A. Desai *Taj Mahal: The Illumined Tomb: An Anthology of Seventeenth-Century Mughal and European Documentary Sources* (Cambridge 1989)

Behrens-Abouseif, D. *Beauty in Arabic Culture* (Princeton 1999)

Bhatnagar, V. S. *Life and Times of Sawai Jai Singh, 1688–1743* (Delhi 1974)

Birdwood, G. C. M. *The Industrial Arts of India* (London 1880)

Blair, S. S. *Islamic Inscriptions* (New York 1998)

Bloom, J. *Minaret: Symbol of Islam*, Oxford Studies in Islamic Art 7 (1989): 188–90

Blunt, W. *The Art of Botanical Illustration: An Illustrated History* (London 1950, repr. New York 1994)

Bogdanov, L. 'The Tomb of the Emperor Babur near Kabul', *Epigraphia Indo-Moslemica* (1923–24): 1–12

Brand, Michael, 'Orthodoxy, Innovation, and Revival: Considerations of the Past in Imperial Mughal Tomb Architecture', *Muqarnas*, 10 (1993): 323–34

Brandenburg, D. *Der Taj Mahal in Agra* (Berlin 1969)

Brown, P. *Indian Architecture (Islamic Period)*, 1956, repr. Bombay 1975

Browne, E. G. *Literary History of Persia, From the Earliest Time until Firdawsi*, 4 vols (1902–24, repr. New Delhi 1997)

Carlleyle, A. C. L. 'Agra', *ASIR*, IV (1871–72, repr. Varanasi [Benares] 1966): 93–247

Chaghtai, M. A. *Le Tadj Mahal d'Agra* (Brussels 1938)

Chowdhuri, J. N. 'Mumtaz Mahall', *Islamic Culture* 11 (1937): 373–81

Chughtai [Chaghtai], M. A. 'Is there a European Element in the Construction of the Taj Mahal, Agra?', *Islamic Culture* 14 (1940): 196–206

Coggin Brown, J. *India's Mineral Wealth, A Guide to the Occurrences and Economics of the Useful Minerals of the Indian Empire* (London 1936)

Cole, H. H. *Preservation of National Monuments: First Report of the Curator of Ancient Monuments in India for the Year 1881–82* (Simla 1882)

— *Preservation of National Monuments in India: Tomb of Jahangir at Shahdara near Lahore*, published by Order of the Governor-General in the Council for the Office of Curator of Ancient Monuments in India (1884)

Combs Stuebe, I. *The Life and Works of William Hodges* (New York 1979)

A Complete Set of Site Plans of the Major Gardens of the United Provinces, Supplement to the Report on the Working and Administration of the United Provinces Government Gardens for the Year 1923–24 (Allahabad 1924)

Conermann, S. *Historiographie als Sinnstiftung, Indo-persische Geschichtsschreibung während der Mogulzeit (932–1118/1516–1707)* (Wiesbaden 2002)

Cotton, J. J. 'General De Boigne and the Taj', *Bengal Past and Present* 33, nos 65–66 (1927): 12–24

Crane, H. 'Babur 1483–1530: Mogul Ruler and Garden Designer', in *Encyclopedia of Gardens*, vol. 1, pp. 98–101

Curzon, Nathaniel, Lord Curzon Papers, BL, ms. Eur. F/111/621: Indian Archaeology (1899–1905)

— *Lord Curzon in India being a Selection from his Speeches as Viceroy and Governor-General of India 1898–1905 with a Portrait, Explanatory Notes and an Index and with an Introduction by Sir Thomas Raleigh* (London 1906)

Dale, S. *The Garden of the Eight Paradises: Babur and the Culture of Empire in Central Asia, Afghanistan and India (1483–1530)* (Leiden/Boston 2004)

Daneshvari, A. *Medieval Tomb Towers of Iran, An Iconographical Study* (Lexington, Ky., 1986)

Das, J. 'Mogul Gardens', in *Encyclopedia of Gardens*, vol. 2 , pp. 899–901

Day, U. N. *The Mughal Government A.D. 1556–1707* (New Delhi 1970)

Dehejia, V., ed. *India through the Lens, Photography 1840–1911* (Washington, D.C., 2000)

Desai, Z. A. 'A Foreign Dignitary's Visit to Akbar's Tomb: A First-Hand Account', in I. A. Khan 1999

— and H. K. Kaul *Taj Museum* (New Delhi 1982)

Dhaky, M. A. *The Indian Temple Traceries* (New Delhi 2004)

Dixon, J. S. 'The Veroneo Controversy', *Journal of Imperial and Commonwealth History* 15 (Jan. 1987): 170–78

Dodd, E. C. 'The Image of the Word: Notes on the Religious Iconography of Islam', *Berytus* 18 (1969): 35–79

— and S. Khairallah *The Image of the Word: A Study of Quranic Verses in Islamic Architecture* (Beirut 1981)

Encyclopedia of Gardens: History and Design, ed. by C. A. Shoemaker, 3 vols (Chicago/London 2001)

Encyclopaedia of Islam, 2nd edn prepared by a number of leading orientalists, ed. by a committee consisting initially of H. A. Gibb, J. H. Kramers, E. Lévi-Provençal, J. Schacht, B. Lewis and C. Pellat, and later by others, vols. 11 and 12 (Supplement) with various supplementary fascicles (Leiden 1979–2004)

Endensor, T. *Tourists at the Taj, Performance and Meaning at a Symbolic Site* (London/New York 1998)

Ettinghausen, R. *From Byzantium to Sasanian Iran and the Islamic World* (Leiden 1972)

Fairchild-Ruggles, D. 'Humayun's Tomb and Garden: Typologies and Visual Order', in Petruccioli 1997, pp. 173–79

Falconer, J. *India: Pioneering Photographers 1850–1900* (London 2001)

Falk, T., and M. Archer *Indian Miniatures in the India Office Library* (London/Delhi/Karachi 1981)

Fallon, S. W. *A New Hindustani-English Dictionary, with Illustrations from Hindustani Literature and Folk-Lore* (Benares 1879, repr. New Delhi 1989)

Fouchécour, C.-H. de, *La Description de la nature dans la poésie lyrique persane du XIᵉ siècle. Inventaire et analyse* des thèmes (Paris 1969)

Führer, A. *The Monumental Antiquities and Inscriptions in the North-Western Provinces and Oudh, ASINIS*, 12 (Allahabad 1891, repr. Varanasi [Benares]/Delhi 1969)

Giusti, A. M. *Pietre Dure: Hardstone in Furniture and Decorations*, trans. by J. Condie and M. Roberts, foreword by A. G. Palacios (London 1992)

Gole, S. *Indian Maps and Plans: From Earliest Times to the Advent of European Surveys* (New Delhi 1989)

Golombek, L. *The Timurid Shrine at Gazur Gah* (Toronto 1969)

— 'From Tamerlane to the Taj Mahal', in *Essays in Islamic Art and Architecture in Honor of Katharina Otto-Dorn*, ed. by A. Daneshvari (Malibu 1981), pp. 43–45

— and D. Wilber *The Timurid Architecture of Iran and Turan*, 2 vols (Princeton 1988)

Growse, F. S. *Mathura: District Memoir* (?Benares 1882, repr. New Delhi 1979)

Guha, R. *A Rule of Property for Bengal* (Paris 1963, 2nd edn New Delhi 1982, new edn Durham/London 1986

Gupta, D. 'Romancing the Taj', *Journal of Landscape Architecture* 2, 1 (2002): 12–13

Gupta, I. P. *Urban Glimpses of Mughal India: Agra: The Imperial Capital (16th & 17th Centuries)* (Delhi 1986)

Gurner, C. W. 'Lord Hastings and the Monuments of Agra', *Bengal Past and Present* XXVII (1924): 148–53

Habib, I. 'Monetary System and Prices', in Raychaudhuri and Habib 1982/1987, pp. 360–81

— 'Notes on the Economic and Social Aspects of Mughal Gardens', in Wescoat and Wolschke-Bulmahn 1996, pp. 127–37

— ed. *Akbar and his India* (Calcutta 1997)

Haleem, M. A. S. Abdel *The Qur'an: A New Translation* (Oxford 2004)

Handbook of the Taj at Agra; Fort of Agra; Akbar's tomb at Secundra, and Ruins of Futtehpore Sikree [anonymous] Translation from a Persian ms. with an English version of the poetry inscribed on the walls, tombs, etc.; Description of the Taj, and extracts from several authors on the subject (1854, Lahore 1862)

Hasan, J. 'Mapping the Mughal City of Agra', *Proceedings of the Indian History Congress*, 51st session, Calcutta University (Calcutta 1990), pp. 241–45

Hasan, N. 'Agra', in *Encyclopaedia of Islam*, vol. 1 (1979), pp. 252–54

Hasan, Z. *A Guide to Nizam-ud Din, Memoirs of the Archaeological Survey of India* 10 (Calcutta 1922)

Hasrat, B. J. *Dara Shikuh: Life and Works* (Delhi 1982)

Hastings, C. W. G. *The Private Journal of the Marquess of Hastings*, ed. by the Marchioness of Bute (London 1858)

Havell, E. B. 'The Taj and its Designers', *The Nineteenth Century and After* 53 (1903): 1039–49 (repr. in *Essays on Indian Art, Industry and Education*, Madras 1910), pp. 1–23

— *A Handbook to Agra, the Taj, Sikandra, Fatehpur Sikri and the Neighbourhood* (Calcutta 1924, repr. New Delhi 1970)

Heber, R. *Narrative of a Journey through the Upper Provinces of India from Calcutta to Bombay: 1824–25*, 3 vols (London 1827, repr. Delhi 1993)

Hegewald, J. A. B. *Water Architecture in South Asia* (Leiden/Boston/Cologne 2002)

Hillenbrand, R. *Islamic Architecture* (Edinburgh 1994)

Hingorani, R. P. *Site Index to A[rchaeological] S[urvey of] I[ndia] Circle Reports . . . (1881–1912)* (New Delhi 1978)

Hodges, W. *Travels in India during the Years 1780, 1781, 1782 and 1783* (London 1794, repr. New Delhi 1999)

Hodgson, A. 'Memoir on the Length of the Illahee Guz, or Imperial Land Measure of Hindostan', *Journal of the Royal Asiatic Society* 7 (1843): 42–63

Horn, P. *Inside the Taj Mahal and Inside II* (CD, CBS Records 1969 and 1972)

Hosten, H. 'Who Planned the Taj Mahal', *Journal of the Royal Asiatic Society* 6 (1910): 281–88

Husain, M. 'Agra before the Mughals,' *Journal of the United Provinces Historical Society* 15, 2 (1942): 80–87

Hussain, M., A. Rehman and J. L. Wescoat, Jr *The Mughal Garden: Interpretation, Conservation and Implications* (Lahore 1996)

Huxley, A. *Jesting Pilate* (London 1926, repr. Geneva 1969)

India after the Mutiny: Travel Photography from India and Sri Lanka 1857–1900 exh. cat., Shapero Gallery (London n. d.[2005])

Islam, Z. 'Nature of Landed Property in Mughal India: Views of Two Contemporary Scholars', *Islamic Culture* 61, 4 (Oct. 1987): 46–62

— 'The Mughal System of Escheat and the Islamic Law of Inheritance', *Islamic Culture* 62, 4 (Oct. 1988): 22–36

J. H., Major 'Four Letters containing a minute Description of the celebrated City Fortress of Agra, of the Tauge Mukal, or Mausoleum of Shah Jehaun, and the Tomb of Akbar, at Secundra', *Asiatic Annual Register* V (1803): 71–79

Jain, S. *Havelis: A Living Tradition of Rajasthan* (Gurgaon 2004)

Jairazbhoy, R. A. 'Early Gardens of the Mughals', *Oriental Art*, n.s., 4 (1958): 68–75

— 'The Taj Mahal in the Context of East and West: A Study in Comparative Method', *Journal of the Warburg and Courtauld Institutes* 24 (1961): 59–88

— *An Outline of Islamic Architecture* (London 1961, repr. Bombay 1972)

Johnson, R. F. *Reverie and Reality: Nineteenth-Century Photographs of India from the Ehrenfeld Collection* (San Francisco 2004)

Keene, H. G. *A Handbook for Visitors to Agra and its Neighborhood* (1873, 6th edn Calcutta 1899)

Kennedy, E. S. 'The Exact Sciences in Timurid Iran', *Cambridge History of Iran* 6 (Cambridge 1986), pp. 568–81

Keyserling, Graf H. 'Der Taj Mahal', *Kunst und Kuenstler* 12 (1914): 521–22

— *Das Reisetagebuch eines Philosophen* (Darmstadt 1923), 1, pp. 250–53

Khan, A. N. *Islamic Architecture in South Asia: Pakistan–India–Bangladesh* (Karachi 2003)

Khan, I. A., ed. *Akbar and his Age*, Indian Council of Historical Research Monograph series 5 (New Delhi 1999)

Khan, M. K., & Son *Guide and History of Moghal Buildings, Agra*. Map and Plan, Description of Arabic and Persian Poems with Translation in English (Agra 1929)

Koch, E. Koch 1982a: 'The Baluster Column – a European Motif in Mughal Architecture and its Meaning', *Journal of the Warburg and Courtauld Institutes*, 45 (1982): 251–62 (repr. in Koch 2001a, pp. 38–60)

— Koch 1982b: 'The Lost Colonnade of Shah Jahan's Bath in the Red Fort of Agra', *Burlington Magazine*, 124/951 (1982): 331–39 (repr. in Koch 2001a, pp. 255–68)

— Koch 1983: 'Jahangir and the Angels: Recently Discovered Wall Paintings under European Influence in the Fort of Lahore', in *India and the West*, ed. by J. Deppert (New Delhi 1983), pp. 173–95 (repr. in Koch 2001a, pp. 12–37)

— Koch 1986a: 'Notes on the Painted and Sculptured Decoration of Nur Jahan's Pavilions in the Ram Bagh (Bagh-i Nur Afshan) at Agra', *Facets of Indian Art*, symposium held at the Victoria & Albert Museum on 26, 27, 28 April and 1 May 1982, ed. by R. Skelton, A. Topsfield, S. Strong, R. Crill and G. Parlett (London 1986), pp. 51–65

— Koch 1986b: 'The Zahara Bagh (Bagh-i Jahanara) at Agra', *Environmental Design* (1986): 30–37

— Koch 1987: 'Pietre Dure and Other Artistic Contacts between the Court of the Mughals and that of the Medici', *A Mirror of Princes: The Mughals and the Medici*, ed. by D. Jones (Bombay 1987), pp. 29–56

— Koch 1988a: *Shah Jahan and Orpheus: The Pietre Dure Decoration and the Programme of the Throne in the Hall of Public Audiences at the Red Fort of Delhi* (Graz 1988) (repr. without intro. in Koch 2001a, pp.38–129)

— Koch 1988b: '[The] Influence[of Gujarat] on Mughal Architecture', in *Ahmadabad*, ed. by G. Michell and S. Shah (Bombay 1988, repr. 2003), pp. 168–85

— Koch 1993a: 'The Delhi of the Mughals prior to Shahjahanabad as Reflected in the Patterns of Imperial Visits', in *Art and Culture: Felicitation Volume in Honour of Professor S. Nurul Hasan*, ed. by A. J. Qaisar and S. P. Verma (Jaipur 1993), pp. 2–20 (repr. with tables of imperial visits in Koch 2001a, pp. 163–82)

— Koch 1993b: 'Muthamman', in *Encyclopaedia of Islam*, vol. 7 (1993), pp. 795–96

— Koch 1994: 'Diwan-i 'Amm and Chihil Sutun: The Audience Halls of Shah Jahan', *Muqarnas* 11 (1994): 143–65 (repr. in Koch 2001a, pp. 229–54)

— Koch 1997a: 'The Hierarchical Principles of Shah-Jahani Painting', in Beach, Koch and Thackston 1997, pp. 131–43 (repr. in Koch 2001a, pp. 130–62)

— Koch 1997b: 'The Mughal Waterfront Garden', in Petruccioli 1997, pp. 140–60 (repr. in Koch 2001a, pp. 183–202)

— Koch 1997c: 'Mughal Palace Gardens from Babur to Shah Jahan (1526–1648)', *Muqarnas* 14 (1997): 143–65 (repr. in Koch 2001a, pp. 203–28)

— Koch 2000: 'Tadj Mahall', in *Encyclopaedia of Islam*, vol. 10 (2000), pp. 58–60

— Koch 2001a: *Mughal Art and Imperial Ideology: Collected Studies* (New Delhi 2001)

— Koch 2001b: 'The Reconstruction of the Taj Mahal (Taj Ganj) and the Gardens of Agra', *LA: Journal of Landscape Architecture* 2, 1 (2001): 19–20

— Koch 2001c: 'Taj Mahal, Agra, Uttar Pradesh', in *Encyclopedia of Gardens* (2001), vol. 3, pp. 1287–91

— Koch 2002a: *Mughal Architecture: An Outline of Its History and Development (1526–1858)* (Munich 1991, 2nd edn New Delhi 2002)

— Koch 2002b: 'Taj Mahal', in *The Seventy Architectural Wonders of Our World*, ed. N. Parkyn (London 2002), pp. 57–61

— Koch 2002c: 'The Intellectual and Artistic Climate at Akbar's Court', in J. Seyller, *The Adventures of Hamza: Painting and Storytelling in Mughal India*, exh. cat. (Washington, D.C./London 2002)

— Koch 2003: 'Mission Statement', in *Taj Mahal, Agra, Site Management Plan*, prepared by the Taj Mahal Conservation Collaborative on behalf of the Indian Hotels Company Ltd, for the Archaeological Survey of India, compiled by A. Lopez (March 2003)

— Koch 2005: 'The Taj Mahal: Architecture, Symbolism, and Urban Significance', *Muqarnas* 23 (2005): 128–49

Lafont, J.-M. *Chitra: Cities and Monuments of Eighteenth-Century India from French Archives* (New Delhi 2001)

Lall, J., and D. N. Dube *Taj Mahal and the Glory of Mughal Agra* (New Delhi 1982, repr. 1985, 1987, 1991)

Lane-Smith, R. *The Taj-Mahal of Agra: Shah Jahan's Vision of Heaven on Earth: An Analysis of its Architectural Design Basis* (New Delhi 1999)

Latif, S. M. *Agra, Historical and Descriptive, with an Account of Akbar and his Court and of the Modern City of Agra* (Calcutta 1896, repr. Lahore 1981)

Leach, L. Y. *Mughal and Other Indian Paintings from the Chester Beatty Library*, 2 vols (London 1995)

Leisten, T. 'Between Orthodoxy and Exegis: Some Aspects of Attitudes in the Shari'a towards Funerary Architecture', *Muqarnas* 7 (1990): 12–22

Lentz, T. W. ' Memory and Ideology in the Timurid Garden', in Wescoat and Wolschke-Bulmahn 1996, pp. 31–58

Linstrum, D. 'The Sacred Past: Lord Curzon and the Indian Monuments', *South Asian Studies* 11 (1995): 19–26

Losensky, P. E. *Welcoming Fighani* (Costa Mesa, Calif., 1998)

— 'The Palace of Praise and the Melons of Time: Descriptive Patterns in ʿAbdi Bayk Sirazi's Garden of Eden', *Eurasian Studies* 2, 1 (2003): 1–29

Losty, J. P. 'The Great Gun at Agra', *British Library Journal* 14, 1 (London 1989): 35–58

— 'The Governor-General's Draughtsman: Sita Ram and the Marquess of Hastings' Album', *Marg* 47, 2 (1995)

— 'The Place of Company Painting in Indian Art', in Bautze 1998, pp. 21–27

— *A Picturesque Voyage? William Daniell's Journal and the Daniells' Vision of India* (London 2006)

Luther, N. *Raja Deen Dayal: Prince of Photography* (Hyderabad 2003)

Maclagan, E. *The Jesuits and the Great Mogul* (1932, repr. Gurgaon 1990)

Mahrarvi, S. A. *Muraqqa'-i Akbarabad* (1930)

Marble in India 2/1983, Technical Consultancy, Mining Research & Publication Division, Indian Bureau of Mines, Ministry of Steel and Mines, Bulletin no. 12 (Nagpur 1983)

Melikoff, I. 'La Fleur de la souffrance: recherche sur le sens symbolique de lale dans la poésie mystique turco-iranienne', *Journal Asiatique* 255 (1967): 341–60

Menon, S. *Trees of India* (New Delhi 2000)

Metcalf, T. R. 'Past and Present: Towards an Aesthetics of Colonialism', in *Paradigms of Indian Architecture: Space and Time in Representation and Design*, ed. by G. H. R. Tillotson (London 1998), pp. 12–25

Michell, G. *The Hindu Temple: An Introduction to its Meaning and Forms* (London 1977)

Misra, N., and T. Misra *The Garden Tomb of Humayun: An Abode of Paradise* (New Delhi 2003)

Moin-ud-din, M. *The History of the Taj and the Buildings in Its Vicinity* (Agra 1905)

Moosvi, S. 'Expenditure on Buildings under Shahjahan – A Chapter of Imperial Financial History', in *Indian History Congress: Proceedings of the forty-Sixth Session, Guru Nanak University Amritsar 1985* (Amritsar 1986), pp. 285–99

Moreland, W. H. 'Some Side-Lights on the Life in Agra, 1637–39', *Journal of the United Provinces Historical Society*, ed. by S. A. Khan, 3, pt 1 (1923): 146–61

Moynihan, E. B. *The Moonlight Garden, New Discoveries at the Taj Mahal* (Washington, D.C., 2000)

Mukhia, H. *The Mughals of India* (Oxford/Carlton 2004; 1st Indian repr. 2005)

Murray, J. *Photographic Views in Agra and its Vicinity by J. Murray with Letter-Press Descriptions by J. Middleton* (London 1858)

[—] *Early Photographs of India: the Archives of Dr. John Murray*, Sotheby's, London, 18 June 1999

Naeem Mir, M., M. Hussain and J. L. Wescoat Jr *Mughal Gardens in Lahore: History and Documentation* (Lahore 1996)

Nath, R. *The Immortal Taj Mahal, The Evolution of the Tomb in Mughal Architecture* (Bombay 1972)

— 'Plan of Akbar's Tomb at Sikandra (Agra) and a Proposed Dome over it', in *Some Aspects of Mughal Architecture* (New Delhi 1976[a]), pp. 86–91

— *History of Decorative Art in Mughal Architecture* (Delhi/Varanasi [Benares]/Patna 1976[b])

— *Agra and its Monumental History* (Bombay 1977)

— *History of Mughal Architecture*, 4 vols: vol. 1, Formative Period [Babur to Humayun] (New Delhi 1982); vol. 2, Akbar (1556–1605): The Age of Personality Architecture (New Delhi 1985); vol. 3, The Transitional Phase of Colour and Design: Jehangir, 1605–1627 A.D. (New Delhi 1994); vol. 4, pt 1, The Age of Architectural Aestheticism, Shah Jehan, 1628–1658 A. D. (New Delhi 2005)

— *The Taj Mahal and its Incarnation* (Jaipur 1985)

— *Art and Architecture of the Taj Mahal* (Agra 1996)

Natwar-Singh, K. *Maharaja Suraj Mal 1707–1763: His Life and Times* (New Delhi 1981)

Necipoğlu, G. Review of Begley and Desai 1989, in *Journal of the Society of Architectural Historians*, 60, 3 (1992): 341–44

— *The Topkapi Scroll – Geometry and Ornament in Islamic Architecture* (Santa Monica, Calif., 1995)

— 'The Suburban Landscape of Sixteenth Century Istanbul as a Mirror of Classical Ottoman Garden Culture', in Petruccioli 1997, pp. 32–71

— ed. *Pre-modern Islamic Palaces*, special issue of *Ars Orientalis* 23 (1993)

Nevill, H. R. *Agra: A Gazetteer* (Allahabad 1921)

Newell, H. A. *Three Days at Agra* (Bombay 1934)

Nugent, Maria, Lady *A Journal from the Year 1811 till the Year 1815, including a Voyage to and Residence in India with a Tour to the North-Western Parts of the British Possessions in that Country, under the Bengal Government*, 2 vols (London 1839)

Nur Bakhsh 'The Agra Fort and Its Buildings', *ASIAR* (1903–4): 164–93

Oak, P. N. *The Taj Mahal is a Temple Palace* (New Delhi 1974)

Okada, A. *Taj Mahal*, photography by Jean Nou, text by A. Okada and M. C. Joshi (New York/London/Paris 1993)

Pal, P., J. Leoshko, J. M. Dye 3rd and S. Markel *Romance of the Taj Mahal* (Los Angeles/ London 1989)

Paret, R. 'Das islamische Bilderverbot', *Das Orientteppichseminar* 8 (1975)

Parks, F. *Wanderings of a Pilgrim in Search of the Picturesque*, 2 vols (London 1850, repr. 1975)

Parodi, L. E. 'A Creative Dialogue: The Timurid and Indo-Muslim Heritage in Akbar's Tomb', *Rivista degli Studi Orientali* 74 (2000): 75–91

— 'Solomon, the Messenger and the Throne: Themes from a Mughal Tomb', *East and West* 51, 1–2 (2001): 127–42

Petruccioli, A., ed. *Gardens in the Time of the Great Muslim Empires: Theory and Design*, Muqarnas Supplements, vol. 7 (Leiden/New York/Cologne 1997)

Pfeiffer, I. *A Woman's Journey Round The World from Vienna to Brazil, Chili, Tahiti, China, Hindostan, Persia and Asia Minor, An unabridged translation from the German . . .* (London 1851)

Platts, J. T. *A Dictionary of Urdu, Classical Hindi and English* (Oxford 1884, repr.New Delhi 1977)

Pohlmann, U., D. Siegert and E. Ruelfs, eds *Samuel Bourne, Sieben Jahre Indien: Photographien und Reiseberichte 1863–70*, exh. cat. (Munich 2001)

Polunin, O., and A. Stainton *Flowers of the Himalaya* (New Delhi 1984, repr. New Delhi 1990)

Prasad, B. *History of Jahangir* (Madras 1922)

Qaisar, A. J. *Building Construction in Mughal India, The Evidence from Painting* (Delhi 1988)

Quilley, G., and J. Bonehill, eds *William Hodges 1744–1797, The Art of Exploration* (New Haven/London 2004)

Rai, R. *Taj Mahal* (Singapore 1986, 2nd edn 1987, repr. New Delhi 1997)

Raja Ram 'Tamirat Agra', written 'a few years before the mutiny' and trans. by S. Abu Muhammad under the title 'The Gardens of Agra', *Journal of the United Provinces Historical Society* 4, 1 (1928): 12–27

Raleigh, Sir T., ed. *Lord Curzon in India: Being a Selection from his Speeches as Viceroy & Governor-*

General of India 1898–1905 (London 1906)

Raychaudhuri, T., and I. Habib, eds *Cambridge Economic History of India*, vol. 1: *c. 1200–c. 1750* (Cambridge 1982, repr. 1987)

Rehman, A. *Earthly Paradise: The Gardens in the Times of Great Muslim Empires* (Lahore 2001)

Rich, V. *The Origins of Mughal Painting and its Development with particular Reference to the 17th and 18th Centuries*, submitted for a PhD degree, School of Oriental and African Studies, London (1981)

— 'Mughal Floral Painting and its European Sources', *Oriental Art* XXXIII (1987)

Rieu, C. *Catalogue of the Persian Manuscripts in the British Museum*, 3 vols: 1 (1879); 2 (1881); 3 (1888)

Rowlett, Colonel 'Report on the Taj at Agra No. 5 Dated Agra 25th April 1867 to H. W. Dashwood, Collector of Agra', from the *Records of Government North Western Provinces*, 2nd ser., vol. 1 (Allahabad 1869), BL, IOR mf. 1/2805

Rubiés, Joan-Pau 'Oriental Despotism and European Orientalism: Botero to Montesquieu', *Journal of Early Modern History*, vol. 9, nos 1–2 (2005): 109–80

— *Gardens, Landscape, and Vision in the Palaces of Islamic Spain* (University Park, Pa., 2000) esp. chapters 4 and 5

Sachdev, V., and G. Tillotson *Building Jaipur, The Making of an Indian City* (London/New Delhi 2002)

Sahni, K. C. *The Book of Indian Trees* (New Delhi 1998, 2nd edn 2000)

Saksena, B. P. *History of Shahjahan of Dihli* (Allahabad 1976)

Sale, Florentia, Lady *Notebook, 1832–33*, BL, mss. Eur. 360a and 360b

Sanwal, B. D. *Agra and its Monuments* (New Delhi 1968)

Sarkar, J. *History of Aurangzib* (Calcutta 1928, repr. New Delhi 1972)

— *Mughal Administration*, 4th edn (Calcutta 1952)

Schimmel, A. *A Two-Colored Brocade: The Imagery of Persian Poetry* (Chapel Hill/London 1992)

— *Islamic Calligraphy* (Leiden 1970)

— *The Empire of the Great Mughals, History, Art and Culture* (London 2004, Indian edn New Delhi 2005) [*Im Reich der Grossmoghuln: Geschichte, Kunst, Kultur* (Munich 2000), trans. by S. Attwood]

Schinz, A. *The Magic Square: Cities in Ancient China* (Stuttgart/London 1996)

Sharma, S. *Persian Poetry at the Indian Frontier: Masʿud Saʿd Salman of Lahore* (Delhi 2000)

Shepard Parpagliolo, M. T. *Kabul: The Bagh-i Baburi* (Rome 1972)

Singh, C. 'Early 18th-Century Painted City Maps on Cloth', in *Facets of Indian Art* (London 1986), pp. 185–192

Sinha, A., and D. Fairchild-Ruggles 'The Yamuna Riverfront, India: A Comparative Study of Islamic and Hindu Traditions in Cultural Landscapes', *Landscape Journal* 23, 2 (2004): 141–52

Skelton, R. 'A Decorative Motif in Mughal Art', in *Aspects of Indian Art: Papers presented in a symposium of the Los Angeles County Museum of Art, October 1970*, ed. P. Pal (Leiden 1972): 147–52

— 'Imperial Symbolism in Mughal Painting', in *Content and Context of Visual Arts in the Islamic World*, papers from a colloquium in memory of Richard Ettinghausen, Institute of Fine Arts, New York University, ed. by P. Soucek (University Park/London 1988)

Sleeman, W. H. *Rambles and Recollections of an Indian Official* (1844, new edn 1915, repr. Karachi 1973, 2nd impr. 1980)

Smith, E. W. *Moghul Colour Decoration of Agra*, ASINIS 30 (Allahabad 1901)

— *Akbar's Tomb, Sikandra near Agra, Described and Illustrated*, ASINIS 35 (1909)

Spear, P. 'Bentinck and the Taj', *Journal of the Royal Asiatic Society* (1949): 180–87

Stainton, A. *Flowers of the Himalaya: A Supplement* (New Delhi 1988, 2nd impr. 1990)

Steingass, F. *A Comprehensive Persian-English Dictionary including the Arabic Words and Phrases to be met with in Persian Literature being Johnson and Richardson's Persian, Arabic and English Dictionary revised, enlarged and entirely reconstructed* (London 1892, repr. 1973)

Stronach, D. 'The Garden as a Political Statement: Some Case Studies from the Near East in the First Millennium B.C.', *Bulletin of the Asia Institute*, n.s., 4 (1990): 171–80

Subrahmanyam, S. *Money and the Market in India 1100–1700* (Delhi 1994)

Subtelny, M. E. 'Agriculture and the Timurid Chaharbagh: The Evidence from a Medieval Persian Agricultural Manual', in Petruccioli 1997, pp. 110–28

— 'Le Monde est un jardin: aspects de l'histoire culturelle de l'Iran médiéval', *Cahiers de Studia Iranica* 28 (2002)

Tadgel, C. *The History of Architecture in India* (London 1990)

Taj Mahal, Agra, Site Management Plan, prepared by the Taj Mahal Conservation Collaborative on behalf of the Indian Hotels Company Ltd, for the Archaeological Survey of India, compiled by A. Lopez (March 2003)

Taylor, B. *A Visit to India, China and Japan* (New York 1855)

Thackston, W. M. 'The Role of Calligraphy', in *The Mosque*, ed. by M. Frishman and H.-U. Khan (London 1994), pp. 43–53

— 'Mughal Gardens in Persian Poetry', in Wescoat and Wolschke-Bulmahn 1996, pp. 233–58

Tieffenthaler, J. *Des Pater Joseph Tieffenthaler's d. G. J. und apostolischen Missionarius in Indien historisch-geographische Beschreibung von Hindustan*, German trans. by Johann Bernoulli (Berlin 1785)

Tillotson, G. H. R. *The Artificial Empire: The Indian Landscapes of William Hodges* (Richmond, Surrey, 2000)

Titley, N. M. *Miniatures from Persian Manuscripts: Catalogue and Subject Index of Paintings in the British Library and the British Museum* (London 1977)

Transactions of the Archaeological Society of Agra (1874–1878 available at BL)

Twining, T. *Travels in India a Hundred Years ago with a Visit to the United States* (London 1893)

Vats, M. S. 'Repairs to the Taj Mahal', *Ancient India* I (1946): 4–7

Villiers Stuart, C. M. *Gardens of the Great Mughals* (1913, repr. Allahabad 1979)

Voysey, H. 'On the Building Stones and Mosaic of Akberabad or Agra', *Asiatic Researches* 15 (1825): 429–35

Welch, A., and H. Crane 'The Tughluqs: Master Builders of Delhi Sultanate', *Muqarnas* 1 (1983): 123–66

Wescoat, J. L., Jr 'Picturing an Early Mughal Garden', *Asian Art* 11, 4 (1989): 59–79

— and J. Wolschke-Bulmahn *Mughal Gardens: Sources, Places, Representations, and Prospects* (Washington, D.C., 1996)

Zajadacz-Hastenrath, S. 'A Note on Babur's Lost Funerary Enclosure at Kabul', *Muqarnas* 14 (1997): 135–42

Sources of illustrations

BL   British Library, London
BM   British Museum, London
EK   Ebba Koch
RAB   Richard André Barraud
V&A   Victoria & Albert Museum,
           London

frontispiece Photo EK
1 Photo akg-images, London/Jean-Louis Nou
2 *Padshahnama*, fol. 50b. Royal Library, Windsor Castle, OMS 1612. Photo The Royal Collection © 2006, Her Majesty Queen Elizabeth II
4 The Nasser D. Khalili Collection of Islamic Art, ms. 874. Photo Nour Foundation, London
5 Freer Gallery of Art, Washington, D.C., 07.258
6 Freer Gallery of Art, Washington, DC, 39.49
7 Rijksprintenkabinet, Amsterdam
8 Musée Guimet, Paris, NA 1909
9 Grünes Gewölbe, Dresden (photo EK)
10 Schönbrunn, Vienna (photo EK)
11 *Padshahnama*, fol. 135b. Royal Library, Windsor Castle, OMS 1632. Photo The Royal Collection © 2006, Her Majesty Queen Elizabeth II
12 Chester Beatty Library, Dublin, 7B.34. Photo The Trustees of the Chester Beatty Library, Dublin
13 BM, 1948-10-9-069
14 V&A, I.S. 90-1965
15 Photo EK
16 BL, ms. Or. 12208, fol. 165v.
17 Maharaja Sawai Man Singh II Museum, Jaipur, cat. no. 126; painted on cloth, 294 x 272 cm (photo EK)
18 Metropolitan Museum of Art, New York, 55.121.10.241
19 Drawing by RAB
20 V&A, I.M. 276-1913
21 Photo EK
22–24 Drawing by RAB
25 Collection of Howard Hodgkin, London
26, 27 Drawings by RAB
28 BL, Map X/1381/1–15
29 Drawing by RAB
30 Maharaja Sawai Man Singh II Museum, Jaipur, no. 126 (photo EK)
31–33 Photo EK
34 Drawing by RAB
35–37 Photo EK
38 Photo courtesy Shapero Gallery, London
39 Drawing by RAB
40 BL, OIOC 35/(106)
41 Photo EK
42 Drawing by RAB
43 Photo EK
44 BL, ms. Add. Or. 2662
45 BL, ms. Add. Or. 4863
46 Photo EK
47 Collection of Ludwig Habighorst
48 Drawing by RAB
49 Photo EK
50 V&A, I.M. 9-1925/Photo V&A Images

51 Photo EK
52 Drawing by RAB
53 Photo EK
54 *Padshahnama*, fol. 43b. Royal Library, Windsor Castle, OMS 1607. Photo The Royal Collection © 2006, Her Majesty Queen Elizabeth II
55 Photo EK
56 Maharaja Sawai Man Singh II Museum, Jaipur, Map no. 128
57 Drawing by RAB
58, 59 Photo EK
60 BL, ms. Stowe Or. 17a, fol. 19
61 Photo EK
62 BL, ms. Add. Or. 1780
63, 64 Photo EK
65 *Padshahnama*, fol. 134a. Royal Library, Windsor Castle, OMS 1631. Photo The Royal Collection © 2006, Her Majesty Queen Elizabeth II
66 Photo EK
67 Drawing by RAB
68, 69 Photo EK
70 The Alkazi Collection of Photography, New York, 99.17.0045
71 Photo EK
72 Taj Museum, Acc. no. 20; watercolour on paper, 19.6 x 112 cm (photo EK)
73 Taj Museum, Acc. no. 27; watercolour on paper pasted on cloth mounted on cardboard, 11.2 x 106 cm (photo EK)
74, 75 Photo EK
76 BL, ASI photo 1007/11 (1974)
77 BL, ms. Eur. B360b, ill. 23
78 Drawing by RAB
79 Photo EK
80 Photo Witt Library, Courtauld Institute, London
81 Drawing by RAB
82–84 Photo EK
85 Drawing by RAB
86–89 Photo EK
90 *Padshahnama*, fol. 72b. Royal Library, Windsor Castle, OMS 1616. Photo The Royal Collection © 2006, Her Majesty Queen Elizabeth II
91 V&A, AL 1761/Photo V&A Images
92 Photo EK
93 Maharaja Sawai Man Singh II Museum, Jaipur, Map no. 128
94, 95 Photo EK
96 BL, ms. Eur. B360a, ill. 43
97 Photo EK
98 Drawing by RAB
99, 100 Photo EK
101 V&A, I.S. 2-1896, fol. 46
102–109 Photo EK
110 *Padshahnama*, fol. 72b. Royal Library, Windsor Castle, OMS 1616. Photo The Royal Collection © 2006, Her Majesty Queen Elizabeth II
111, 112 Drawing by RAB
113 Photo EK
114 *Padshahnama*, fol. 116b. Royal Library, Windsor Castle, OMS 1621. Photo The Royal Collection © 2006, Her Majesty Queen Elizabeth II
115, 116 Photo EK
117 Photo akg-images, London/Jean-Louis Nou
118–122 Photo EK

123, 124 Drawing by RAB
125 Photo EK
125, 127 Drawing by RAB
128–131 Photo EK
132 Museum für Indische Kunst, Staatliche Museen zu Berlin; watercolour on cloth, 80 x 280 cm. Photo BPK, Berlin 2006/Jürgen Liepe
133–140 Photo EK
141–146 Drawing by RAB
147 From Thomas and William Daniell, *Views of the Taje Mahel*, 1801
148 Space Imaging Inc.
149 Drawing by RAB
150 BL, ms. Eur. B360b, ill. 26
151 Photo EK
152 BL, ASI photo 1007/9 (D-961)
153 Photo EK
154 BL, ms. Eur. B360b, ill. 1
155–160 Photo EK
161, 162 Drawing by RAB
164–171 Photo EK
172–180 Drawing by RAB
181, 182 Photo EK
183 Drawing by RAB
184–191 Photo EK
192 BL, R.A.S. Loan 3, fol. 22
193 Taj Museum. Photo Neil Greentree
194 BL, ms. Add. Or. 3129, fol. 63v
195 V&A, I.S. 48-1956, fol. 20b
196–198 Photo EK
199–204 Drawing by RAB
205 BL, ms. WD 4403, fol. 44
206 Archaeological Survey of India, Agra
207–210 Photo EK
211 Drawing by RAB
212, 213 Photo EK
214 Drawing by RAB
215–217 Photo EK
218–221 Drawing by RAB
222, 223 Photo EK
224 Photo akg-images, London/Jean-Louis Nou
225–227 Photo EK
228 V&A, I.S. 249-1961/Photo V&A Images
229 Photo EK
230 Photo akg-images, London/Jean-Louis Nou
231 Drawing by RAB
232 BL, ms. Add. Or. 923
233 Photo akg-images, London/Jean-Louis Nou
234, 235 Photo © Bharath Ramamrutham
236, 237 Photo EK
238 Photo © Bharath Ramamrutham
239 Photo EK
240 BL, ms. Stowe Or. 17a, fol. 11
241 BL, ms. Stowe Or. 17a, fol. 4
242 Photo akg-images, London/Jean-Louis Nou
243 BL, ms. Stowe Or. 17a, fol. 5
244–246 Photo EK
247 Drawing by RAB
248–251 Photo EK
252, 253 Drawing by RAB
254 Photo akg-images, London/Jean-Louis Nou
255–263 Photo EK
264–267 Drawing by RAB
268–274 Photo EK

275 Drawing by RAB
276, 277 Photo EK
278 Drawing by RAB
279–296 Photo EK
297, 298 Drawing by RAB
299–301 Photo EK
302–306 Drawing by RAB
307 Photo EK
308 BL, ms. Add. 27255, fol. 267b
309, 310 Photo EK
311 Drawing by RAB
312–316 Photo EK
317 Drawing by RAB
318–320 Photo EK
321 Drawing by RAB
322, 323 Photo EK
324 Drawing by RAB
325 Photo EK
326 The Alkazi Collection of Photography, New York, 96.39.001.3
327 Photo EK
328 Drawing by RAB
329 Photo EK

330 Drawing by RAB
331–336 Photo EK
337 Drawing by RAB
339 Photo akg-images, London/Jean-Louis Nou
340 Photo Robert Skelton
341 V&A, I.S. 48-1956, fol. 1
342 Alighar Muslim University, Maulana Azad Library (photo EK)
343, 344 Photo EK
345 Photo akg-images, London/Jean-Louis Nou
346 Photo EK
347 BM
348 *Padshahnama*, fol.195a. Royal Library, Windsor Castle, OMS 1641. Photo The Royal Collection © 2006, Her Majesty Queen Elizabeth II
349 Photo EK
350 BL, ms. Stowe Or. 17a, fol. 6
351 Photo akg-images, London/Jean-Louis Nou
352 Photo EK
353 V&A, I.M. 38-1919
354 Yale Center for British Art, New Haven, Paul Mellon Collection, B 1978.43.1735
355 Photo EK

356 Museum für Indische Kunst, Staatliche Museen zu Berlin
357 V&A, Dept of Prints and Drawings, Seawright Collection/Photo V&A Images
358 BL, P. 395
359 Private collection
360 BL, P. 396
361 BL, ms. Stowe Or. 17a, fol. 3
362 BL, ms. Stowe Or. 17a, fol. 8
363 BL, ms. WD 4403, fol. 42
364 Collection of EK. Photo Gudrun Vogler
365 Photo EK
366 BL, Map X/1384
367 By courtesy of Sotheby's Picture Library, London
369 Photo EK
370 Photo Britta Elsner
371 Photo EK
372 Anonymous Agra photographer
373 Photo EK
375–377 Photo EK

Index

Page numbers in *bold italic type* refer to illustrations and related captions.

Author's acknowledgments

This book would not have been possible without the generous permission of the Archaeological Survey of India (ASI) to take measurements and photographs of the Taj Mahal and the monuments of Agra during the years 1995–2005. I thank here especially the Director Generals M. C. Joshi, Ajai Shankar, Komal Anand, Kasturi Gupta Menon, and C. Babu Rajeev, and Joint Director General Dr R. K. Sharma, as well as Directors R. C. Agarwal, Dr K. P. Poonacha, and Superintending Archaeologist A. K. Sinha. In the Agra office special thanks are due to the Superintending Archaeologists D. V. Sharma and K. K. Muhammad, as well as to K. Sherwani. I am also very grateful to the staff of the ASI at the Taj who, throughout the years, have facilitated my survey and study of the monument in every way. I would like to mention in particular the Senior Conservation Assistants 'Panditjis' S. K. Sharma and R. K. Dixit, and Conservation Assistant P. N. Kulshrestra. An outstanding support has been Foreman A. K. Raizada, ever ready to provide staff and keys to investigate the remotest corners of the monument. Dilip Mathur of the air pollution station kindly allowed me to measure his office: the north-east tower. The monument attendants Lal Singh, Uma Shankar, Muhammad Mustaqim, Om Prakash and G. Ram were the ever present good spirits of my work, and Sajjad Ali also helped. Draftsman S. K. Kulshrestha in the ASI office, and Assistant Archaeologist Atul Bhargava and Marksman Ashraf Ali in the Taj Museum assisted me in the study of plans. At Agra, Mr. Naveen Chand, owner of the Mubarak Manzil, and Mr S. K. Dwivedi of Taj Ganj kindly allowed me to investigate their dwellings. At Jaipur, in the Maharaja Sawai Man Singh II Museum, Maharaj Narindra Singh, Director Himmat Singh and Pankaj Sharma made it possible to renew my study of the large map of Agra, the primary document for any study of the city.

Still in India, I would like, once again, to express my gratitude to the two pillars of my work: Dr Yunus Jaffery, for his assistance in reading Mughal textual sources, and architect Richard A. Barraud, for surveying the Taj with me and for his attention and care in preparing the measured drawings which illustrate this book.

In London in the British Library I am enormously indebted to J. P. ('Jerry') Losty, former head of the Department of Prints, Drawings and Photographs of the Oriental and India Collections for his help in the study of the British reception of the Taj; Chapter V profited greatly from his generosity and from our discussions. I thank here also Jennifer Howes and Helen George. In the Victoria and Albert Museum I am grateful to Deborah Swallow (now Director of the Courtauld Institute), Susan Stronge, Rosemary Crill, Graham Parlett, Divia Patel, Nicholas Barnard and Michael Snodin for access to paintings, drawings and photographs. I also appreciate the help of the staff of the libraries of the Royal Institute of British Architects (RIBA) and the School of African and Oriental Studies (SOAS) of London University. Esa Epstein in New York and Sophie Gordon in London assisted me in my research at the Alkazi Collection of Photography. In the Metropolitan Museum, New York, I thank Stefano Carboni and Navina Haider. At Harvard, András Riedlmayer and Jeffery Spurr, of the Aga Khan Program for Islamic Architecture, facilitated library and photographic research; and at Yale, I thank Phillip Basner, of the Department of Prints and Drawings, Yale Center for British Art.

A visiting fellowship of the Aga Khan Program for Islamic Architecture at Harvard in autumn 2002 enabled me to work on the manuscript of this book. I appreciate Gülru Necipoglu's and David Roxburgh's interest in my research.

Friedrich Ehrendorfer, Professor Emeritus of Botany and former Director of the Botanical Gardens, Vienna University, and Henry J. Noltie of the Royal Botanic Garden, Edinburgh, kindly gave me their opinion on the real and imaginary flowers of the Taj and the plants of the gardens of Agra.

I am also happy to acknowledge my debt to a number of friends and colleagues who have given assistance, information, support and advice in the preparation of this book. I am especially grateful, as always, to Robert Skelton for his generosity, then to Shahid Amin, Jeremy Currie, Deborah Dunham, John Fritz, Narayani Gupta, Ludwig Habighorst, Sunil Kumar (for reading and commenting on the Introduction), Rüdiger Lohlker, Paul Losensky, George Michell, Partha Mitter, Alfred Pfabigan, Adeela Qureshi, Markus Ritter, Sunil Sharma (for checking translations), Giles Tillotson, Stefanie Walker, and Benjamin Zucker.

For hospitality I thank in London Dr Johannes Wimmer, Director of the Austrian Cultural Forum, and his assistant Melitta Essenko; and in New Delhi Ambassador Dr Herbert Traxl and Shovana Narayan, as well as Ambassador Dr Jutta-Stefan Bastl and Peter Stefan. Of the Embassy staff in Delhi Munish Bahl was particularly helpful. I am also grateful to Dr Heinz Rampitsch, Dr Sepp Dabringer and Monika Sharma of the Austrian Trade Commission for practical assistance.

For support of my project of the documentation and analysis of the Taj Mahal I wish to thank the Jubiläumsfonds der Oesterreichischen Nationalbank, the Bundesministerium für Unterricht und kulturelle Angelegenheiten, Austria, and Franz Zöchbauer of Austrian Airlines. I am also indebted to Mr Ebrahim Alkazi for his generous support.

At Thames & Hudson I appreciate Colin Ridler's interest in the book. Emily Lane's special connection to India made her an extraordinarily involved editor and the book has much profited from her dedication, attention and sharp eye. I also value Geoff Penna's sensitive design. Susanna Friedman saw the book through the press with care and feeling.

And last but not least, I would like to thank my husband Benno, who after his retirement became my right hand in getting the book ready for publication.

Ebba Koch
Vienna, May 2006